Helck

5

Story and Art by
Nanaki Nanao

Contents

Chapter 42: Helck's Past VII

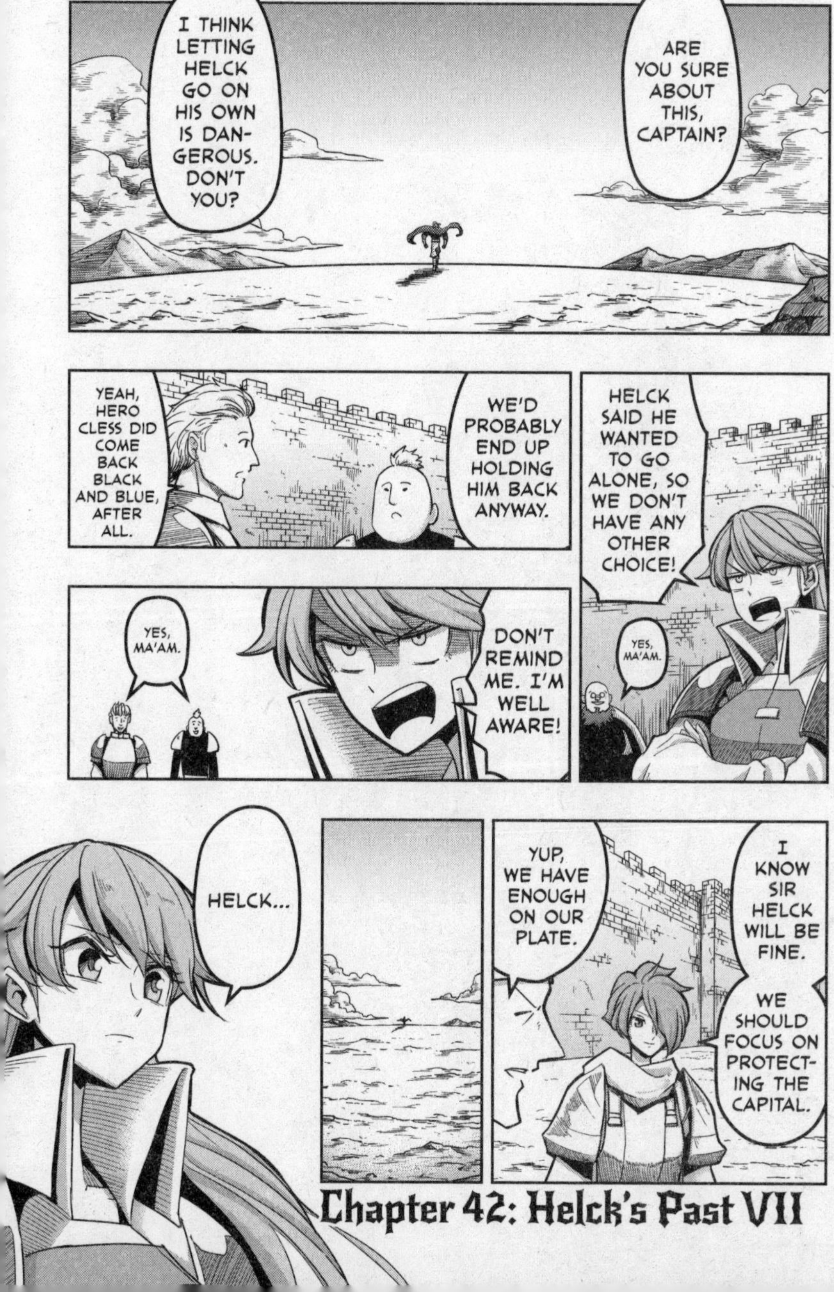

ARE YOU SURE ABOUT THIS, CAPTAIN?
I THINK LETTING HELCK GO ON HIS OWN IS DANGEROUS. DON'T YOU?
HELCK SAID HE WANTED TO GO ALONE, SO WE DON'T HAVE ANY OTHER CHOICE!
YES, MA'AM.
WE'D PROBABLY END UP HOLDING HIM BACK ANYWAY.
YEAH, HERO CLESS DID COME BACK BLACK AND BLUE, AFTER ALL.
DON'T REMIND ME. I'M WELL AWARE!
YES, MA'AM.
I KNOW SIR HELCK WILL BE FINE.
WE SHOULD FOCUS ON PROTECTING THE CAPITAL.
YUP, WE HAVE ENOUGH ON OUR PLATE.
HELCK...

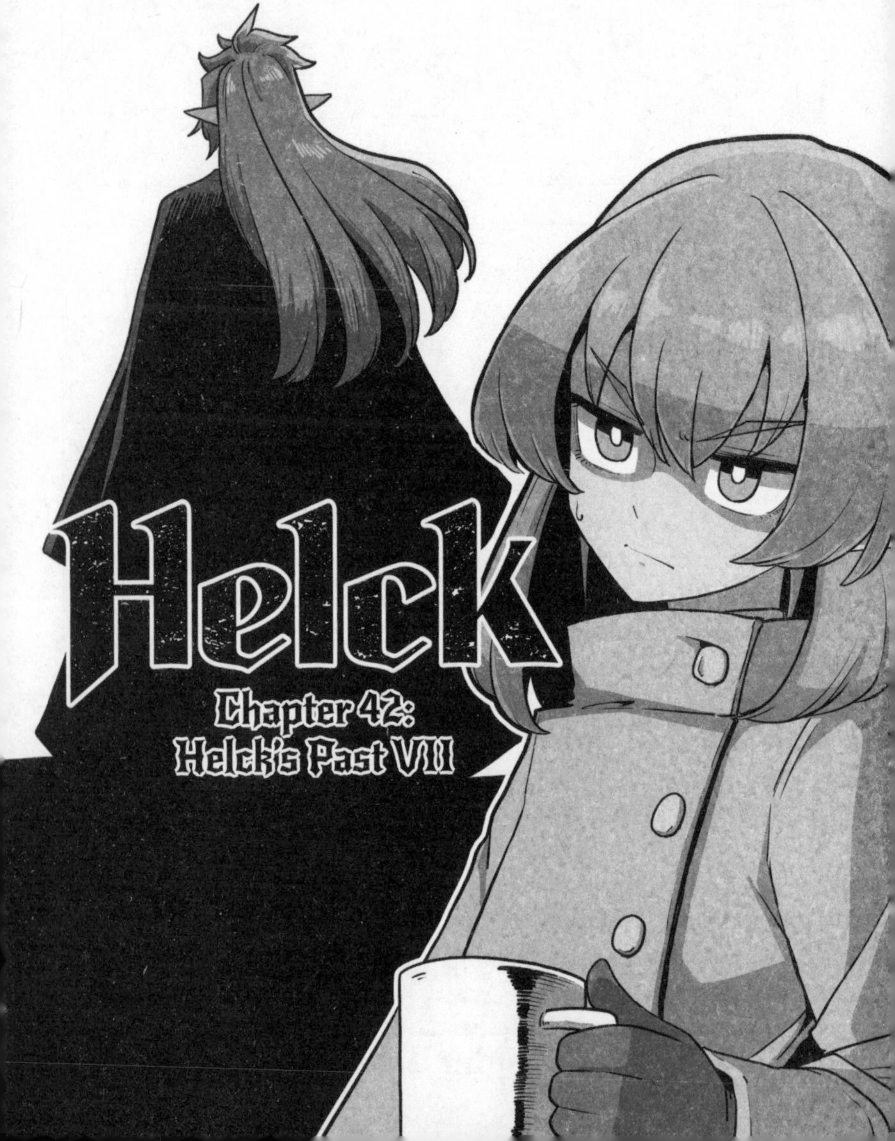
Helck
Chapter 42:
Helck's Past VII

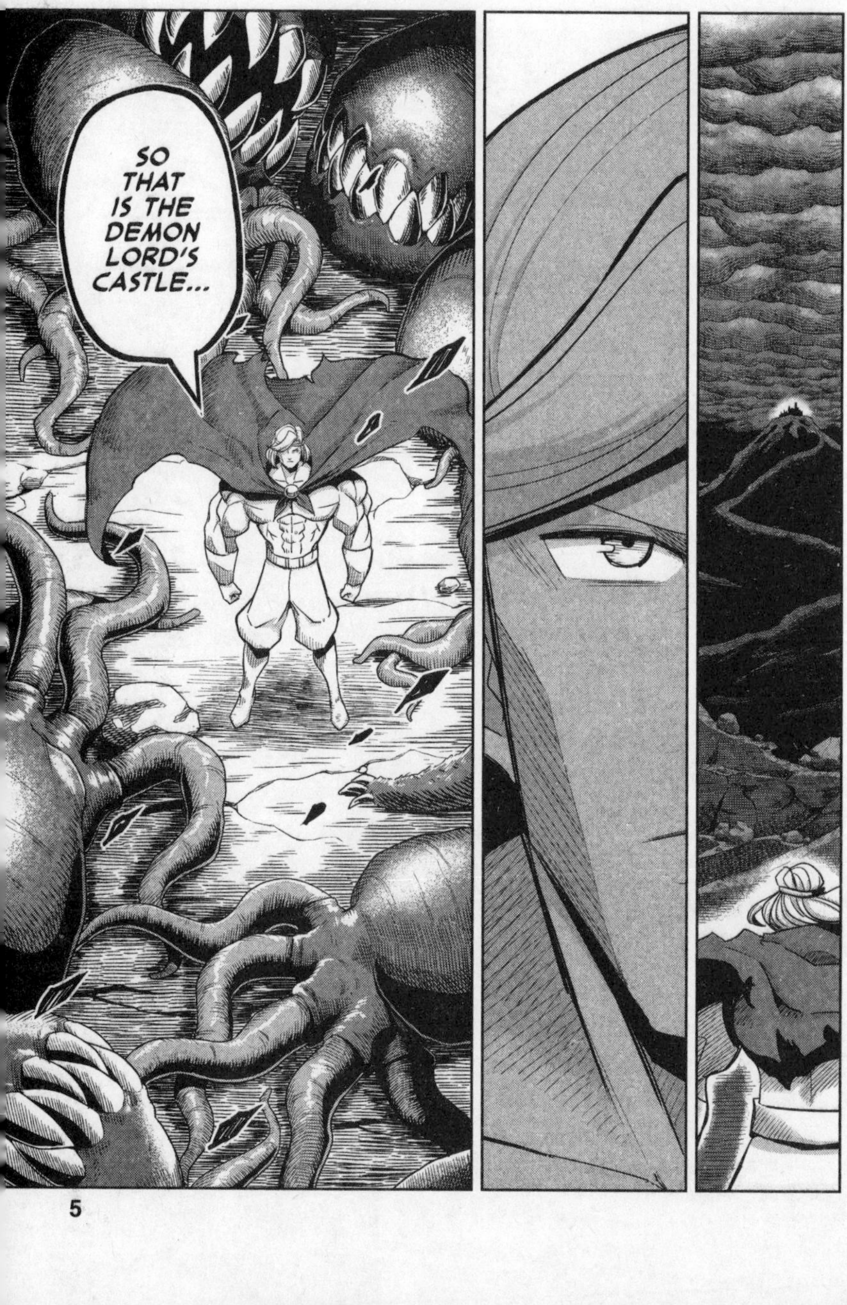
SO THAT IS THE DEMON LORD'S CASTLE...

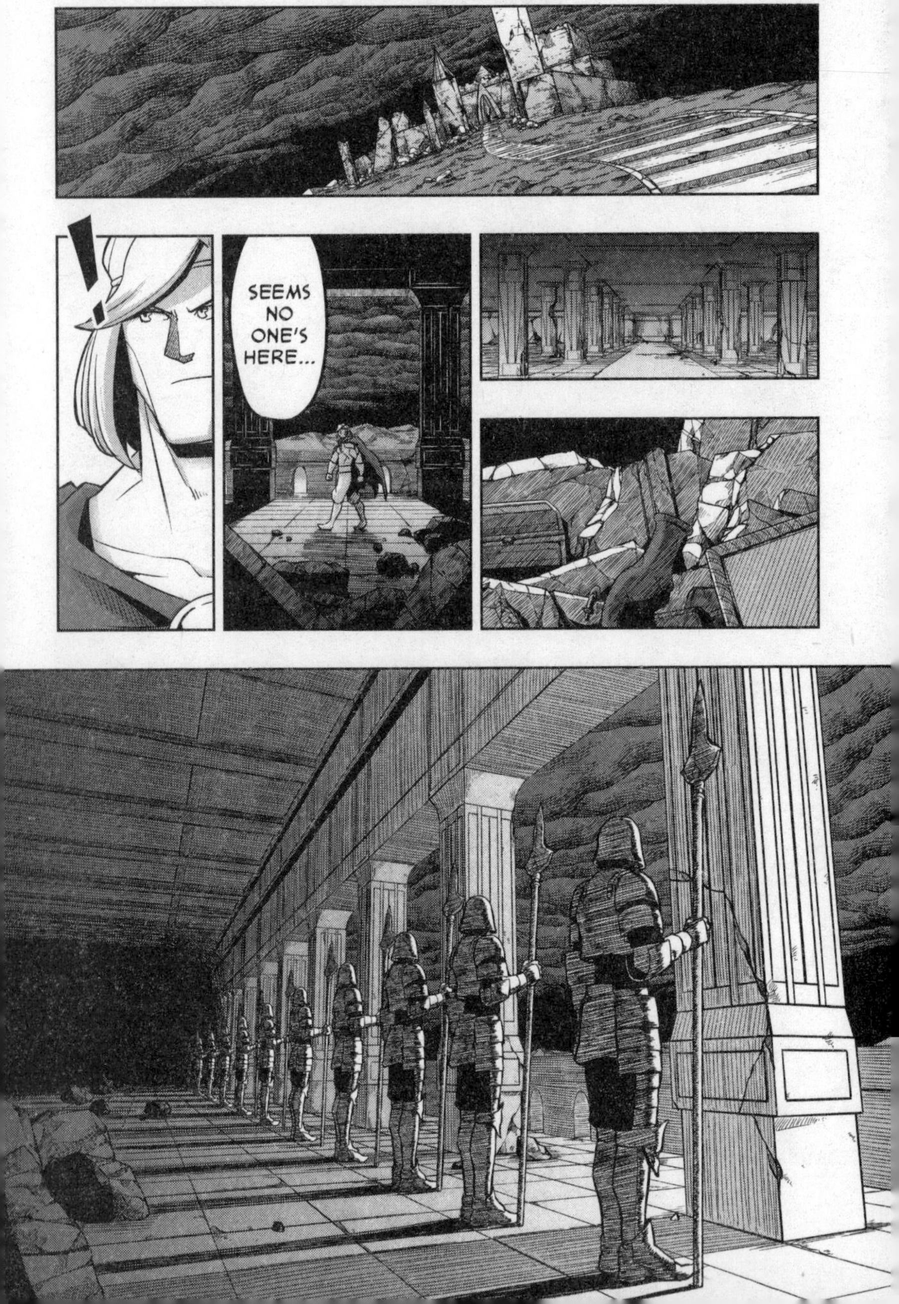
SEEMS NO ONE'S HERE...
!

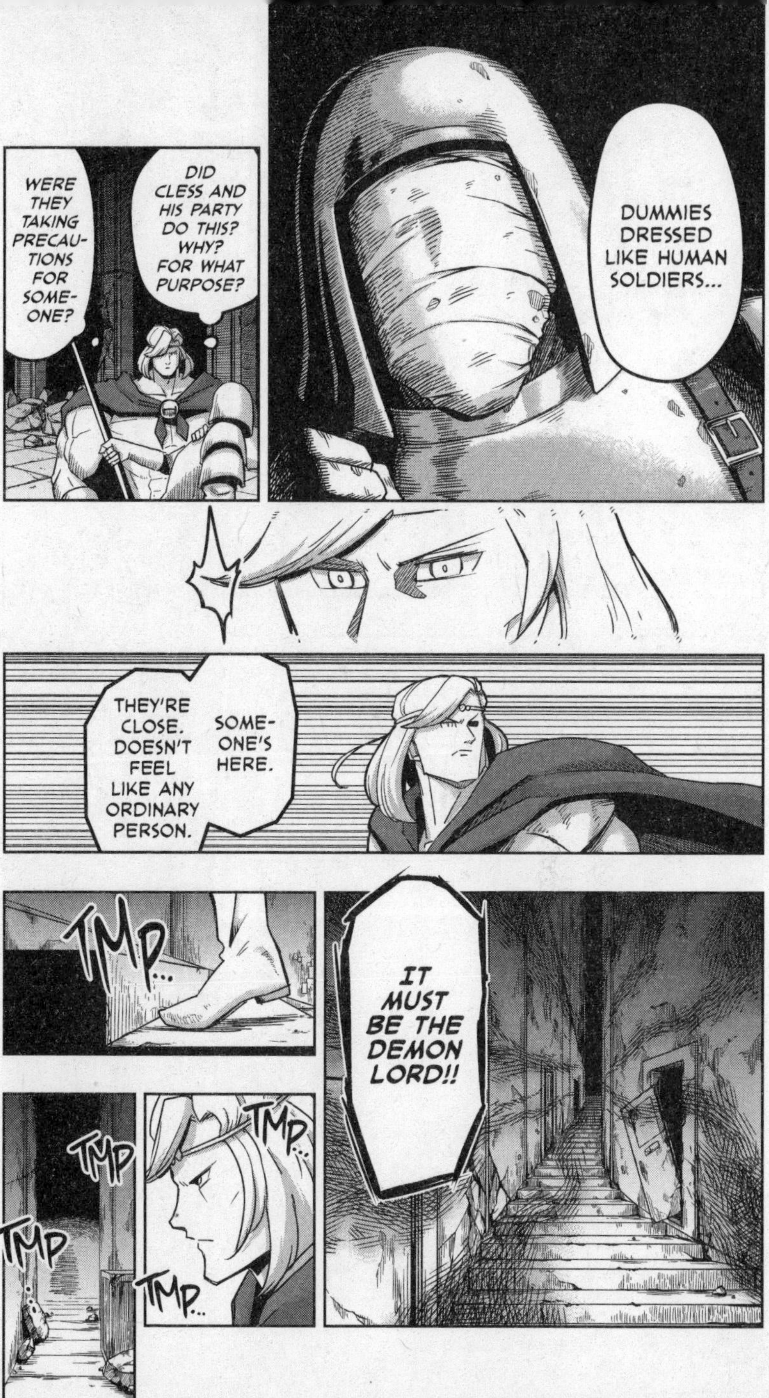
DUMMIES DRESSED LIKE HUMAN SOLDIERS...
DID CLESS AND HIS PARTY DO THIS? WHY? FOR WHAT PURPOSE?
WERE THEY TAKING PRECAU-TIONS FOR SOME-ONE?
SOME-ONE'S HERE.
THEY'RE CLOSE. DOESN'T FEEL LIKE ANY ORDINARY PERSON.
IT MUST BE THE DEMON LORD!!
TMP...
TMP...
TMP...
TMP
TMP

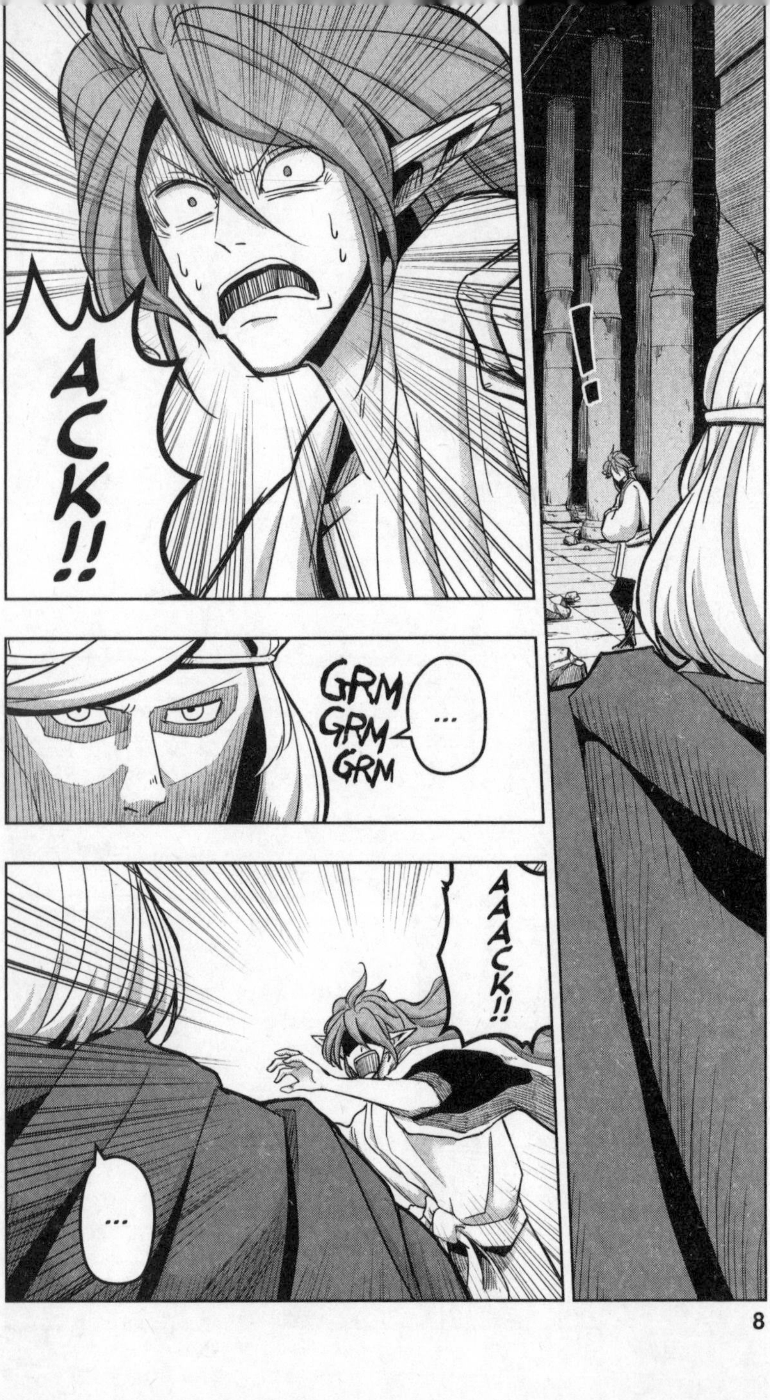
!!
ACK!!
GRM GRM GRM
...
AAACK!!
...

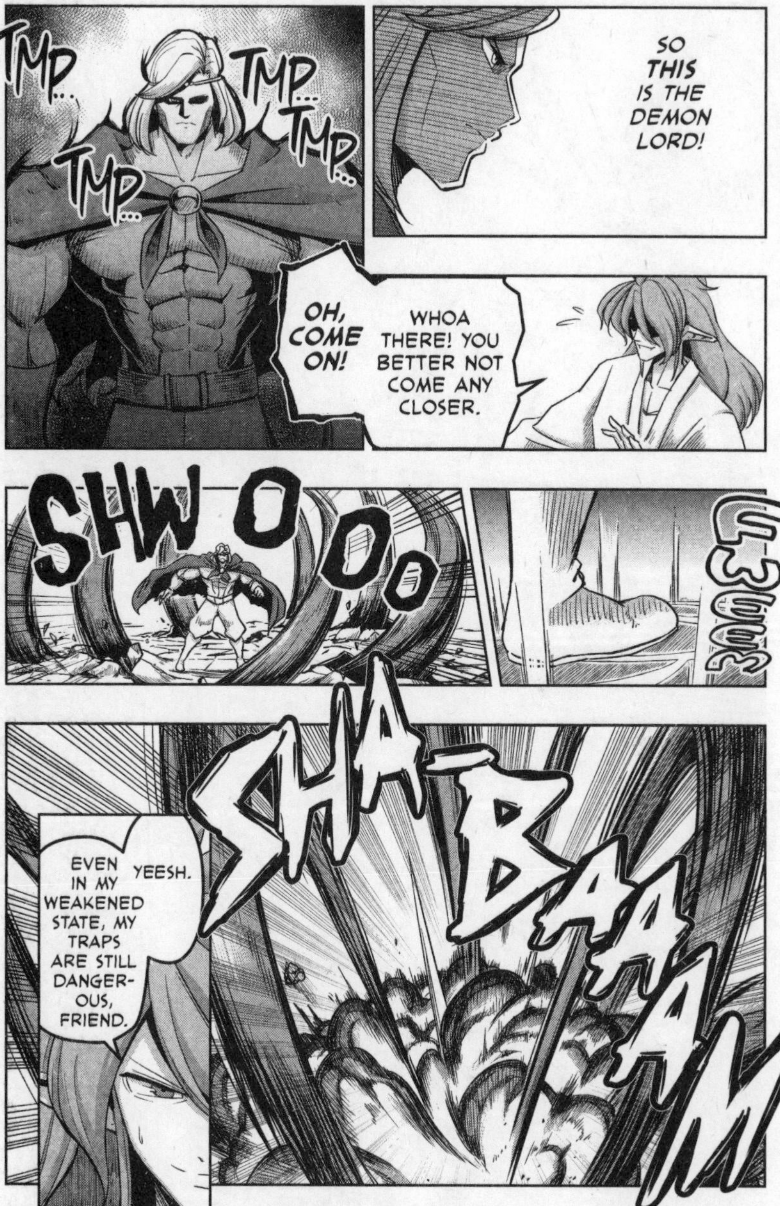
SO THIS IS THE DEMON LORD!
WHOA THERE! YOU BETTER NOT COME ANY CLOSER.
OH, COME ON!
TMP... TMP... TMP... TMP...
SHWOOOO
SHA-BAAAM
YEESH.
EVEN IN MY WEAKENED STATE, MY TRAPS ARE STILL DANGEROUS, FRIEND.

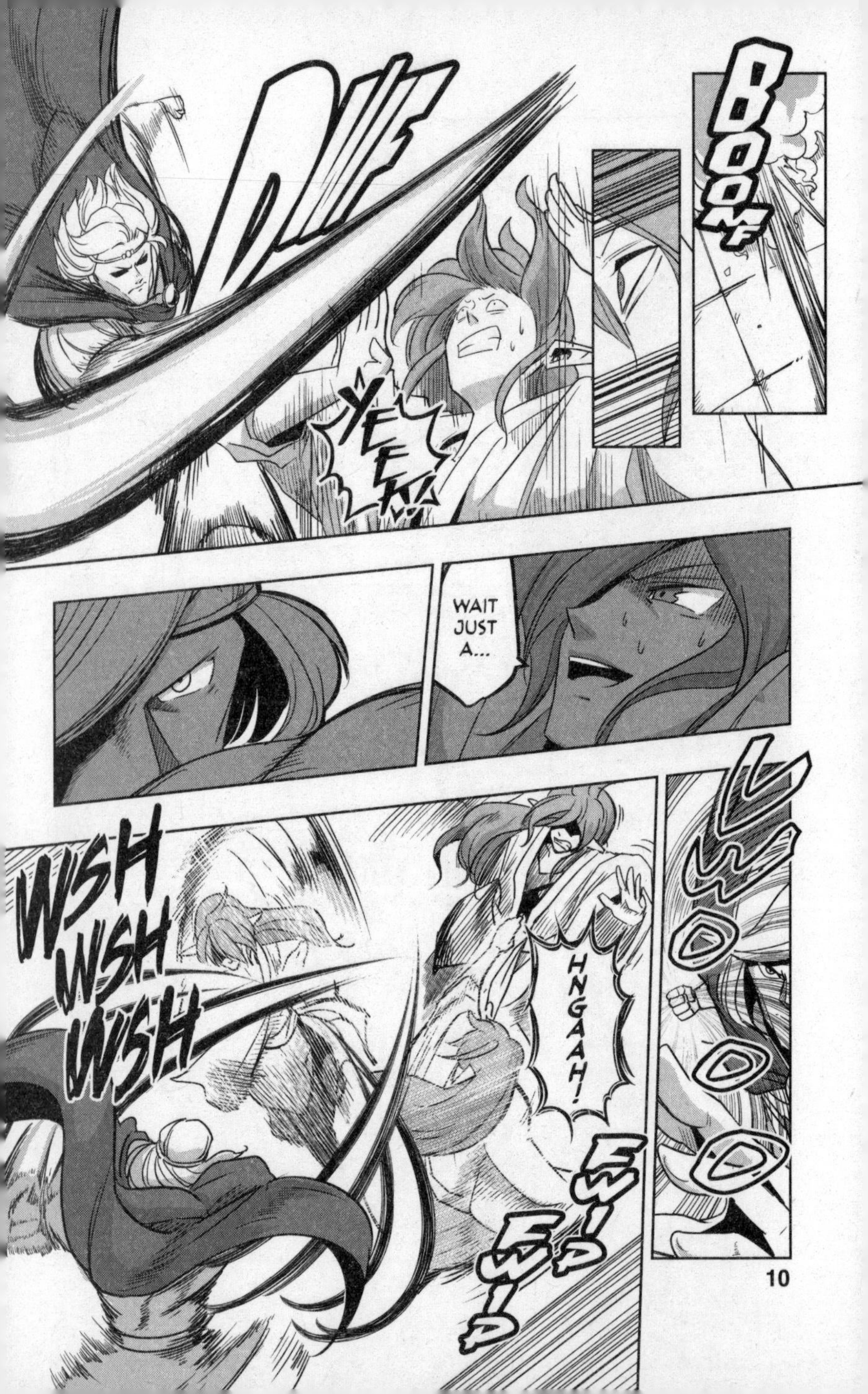
BOOMF
YEEK!!
WAIT JUST A...
HNGAAH!
EWIP
EWIP
WSH
WSH
WSH

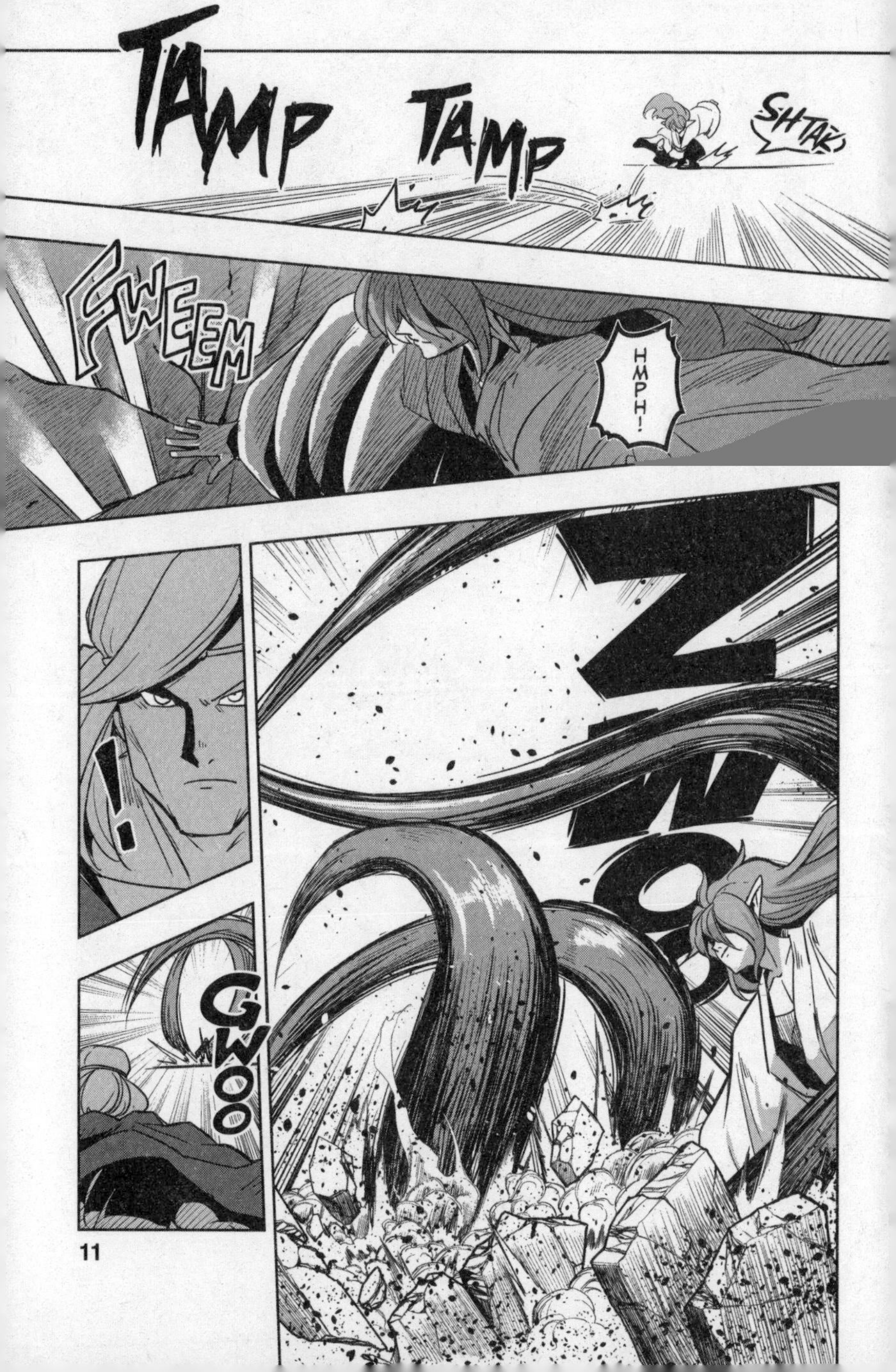
SHTAK
TAMP
TAMP
HMPH!
FWEEM
ZWOO
!
GWOO

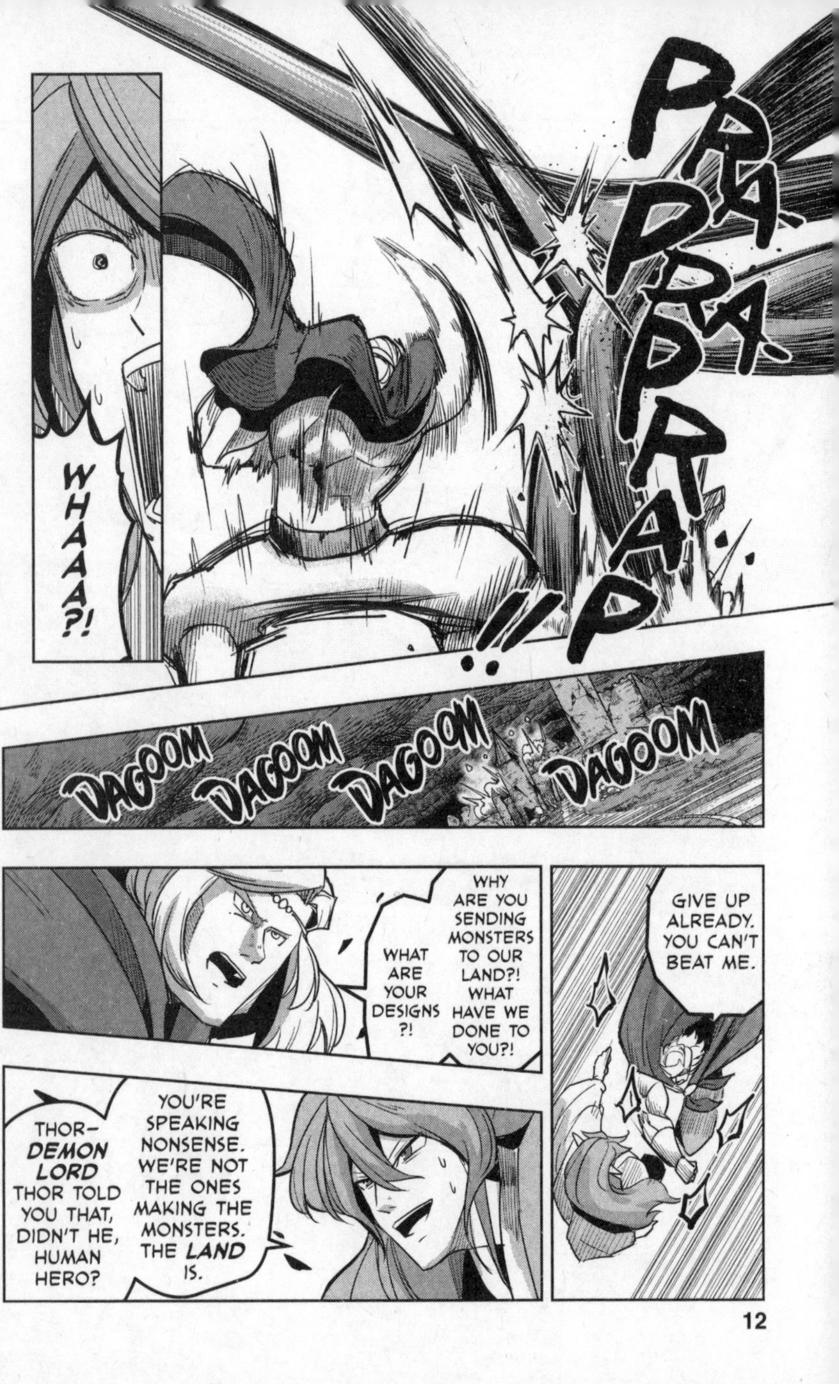
PRAPRAPRAP!!
WHAAAA?!
DAGOOM DAGOOM DAGOOM DAGOOM
GIVE UP ALREADY. YOU CAN'T BEAT ME.
WHY ARE YOU SENDING MONSTERS TO OUR LAND?! WHAT HAVE WE DONE TO YOU?!
WHAT ARE YOUR DESIGNS?!
YOU'RE SPEAKING NONSENSE. WE'RE NOT THE ONES MAKING THE MONSTERS. THE *LAND* IS.
THOR—*DEMON LORD* THOR TOLD YOU THAT, DIDN'T HE, HUMAN HERO?

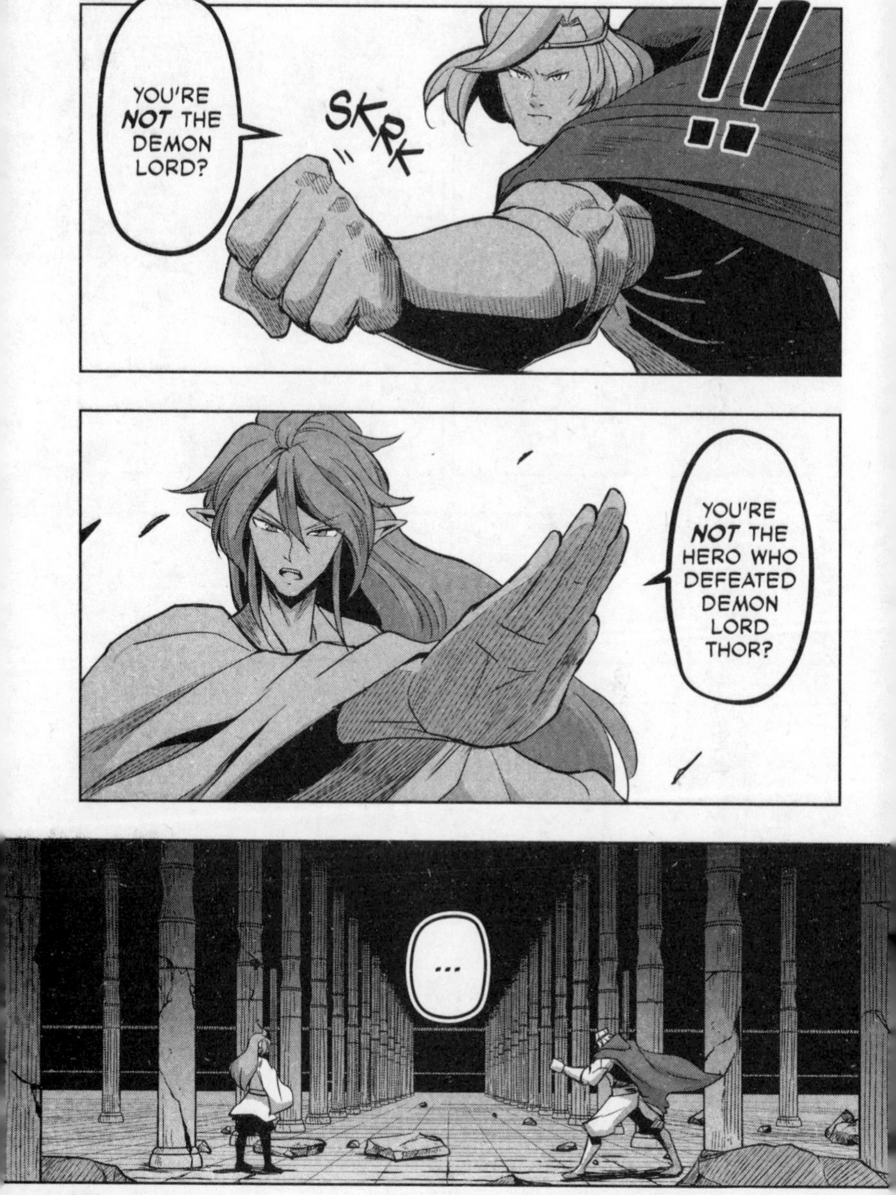
!!
SKRK
YOU'RE *NOT* THE DEMON LORD?
YOU'RE *NOT* THE HERO WHO DEFEATED DEMON LORD THOR?
...

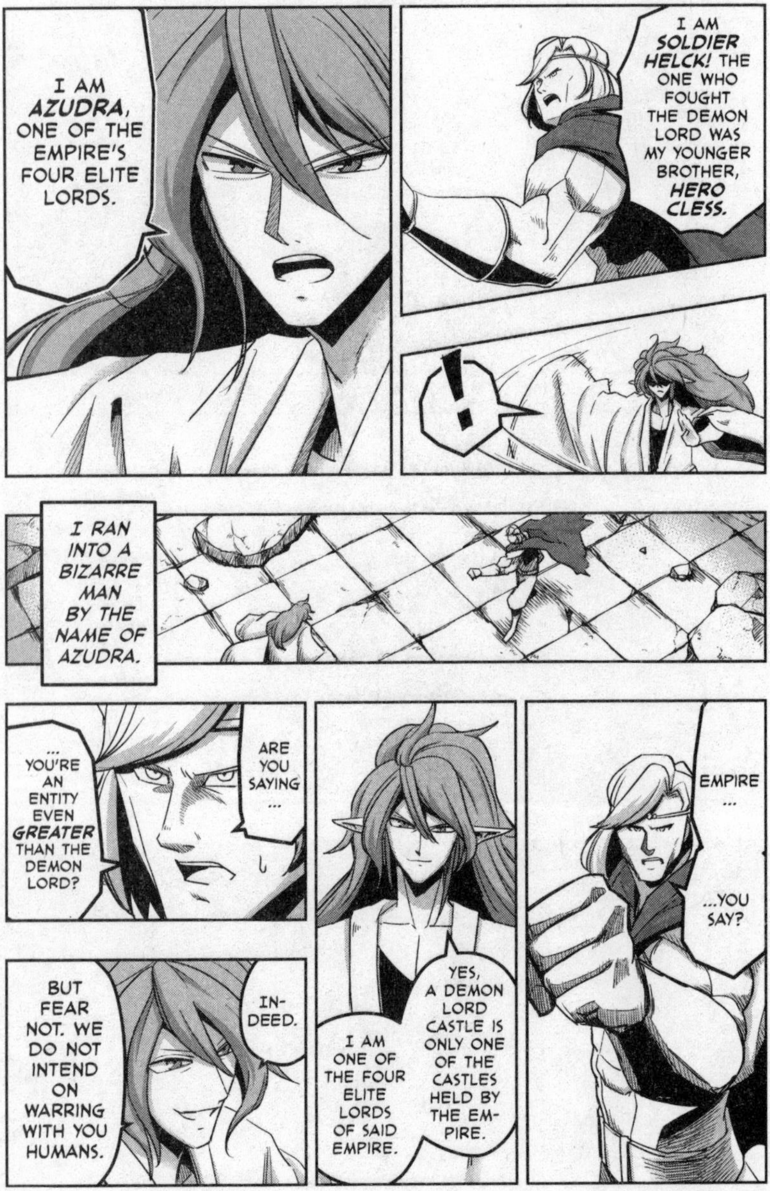

I AM SOLDIER HELCK! THE ONE WHO FOUGHT THE DEMON LORD WAS MY YOUNGER BROTHER, HERO CLESS.
!
I AM AZUDRA, ONE OF THE EMPIRE'S FOUR ELITE LORDS.
I RAN INTO A BIZARRE MAN BY THE NAME OF AZUDRA.
EMPIRE ...
...YOU SAY?
YES, A DEMON LORD CASTLE IS ONLY ONE OF THE CASTLES HELD BY THE EM-PIRE.
I AM ONE OF THE FOUR ELITE LORDS OF SAID EMPIRE.
ARE YOU SAYING ...
... YOU'RE AN ENTITY EVEN GREATER THAN THE DEMON LORD?
IN-DEED.
BUT FEAR NOT. WE DO NOT INTEND ON WARRING WITH YOU HUMANS.

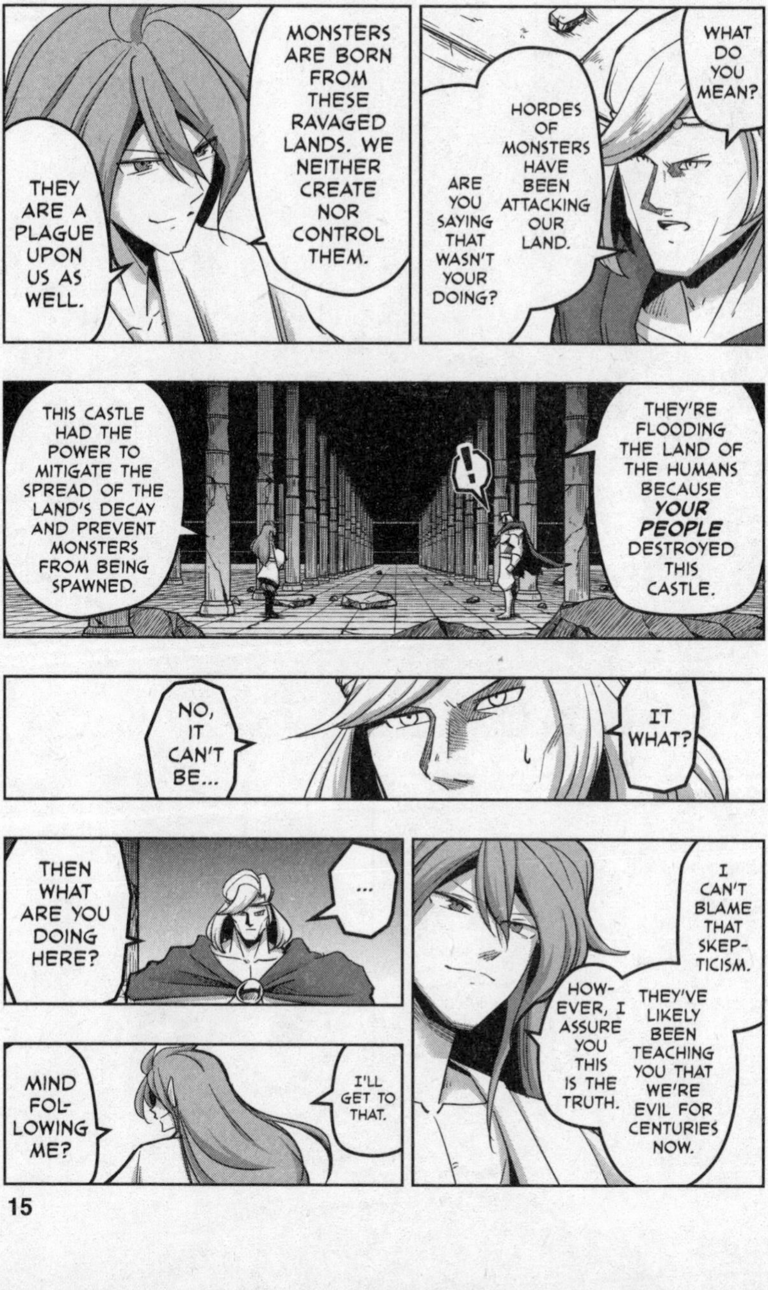
WHAT DO YOU MEAN?
HORDES OF MONSTERS HAVE BEEN ATTACKING OUR LAND.
ARE YOU SAYING THAT WASN'T YOUR DOING?
MONSTERS ARE BORN FROM THESE RAVAGED LANDS. WE NEITHER CREATE NOR CONTROL THEM.
THEY ARE A PLAGUE UPON US AS WELL.
THEY'RE FLOODING THE LAND OF THE HUMANS BECAUSE ***YOUR PEOPLE*** DESTROYED THIS CASTLE.
!
THIS CASTLE HAD THE POWER TO MITIGATE THE SPREAD OF THE LAND'S DECAY AND PREVENT MONSTERS FROM BEING SPAWNED.
IT WHAT?
NO, IT CAN'T BE...
I CAN'T BLAME THAT SKEPTICISM.
THEY'VE LIKELY BEEN TEACHING YOU THAT WE'RE EVIL FOR CENTURIES NOW.
HOWEVER, I ASSURE YOU THIS IS THE TRUTH.
...
THEN WHAT ARE YOU DOING HERE?
I'LL GET TO THAT.
MIND FOLLOWING ME?

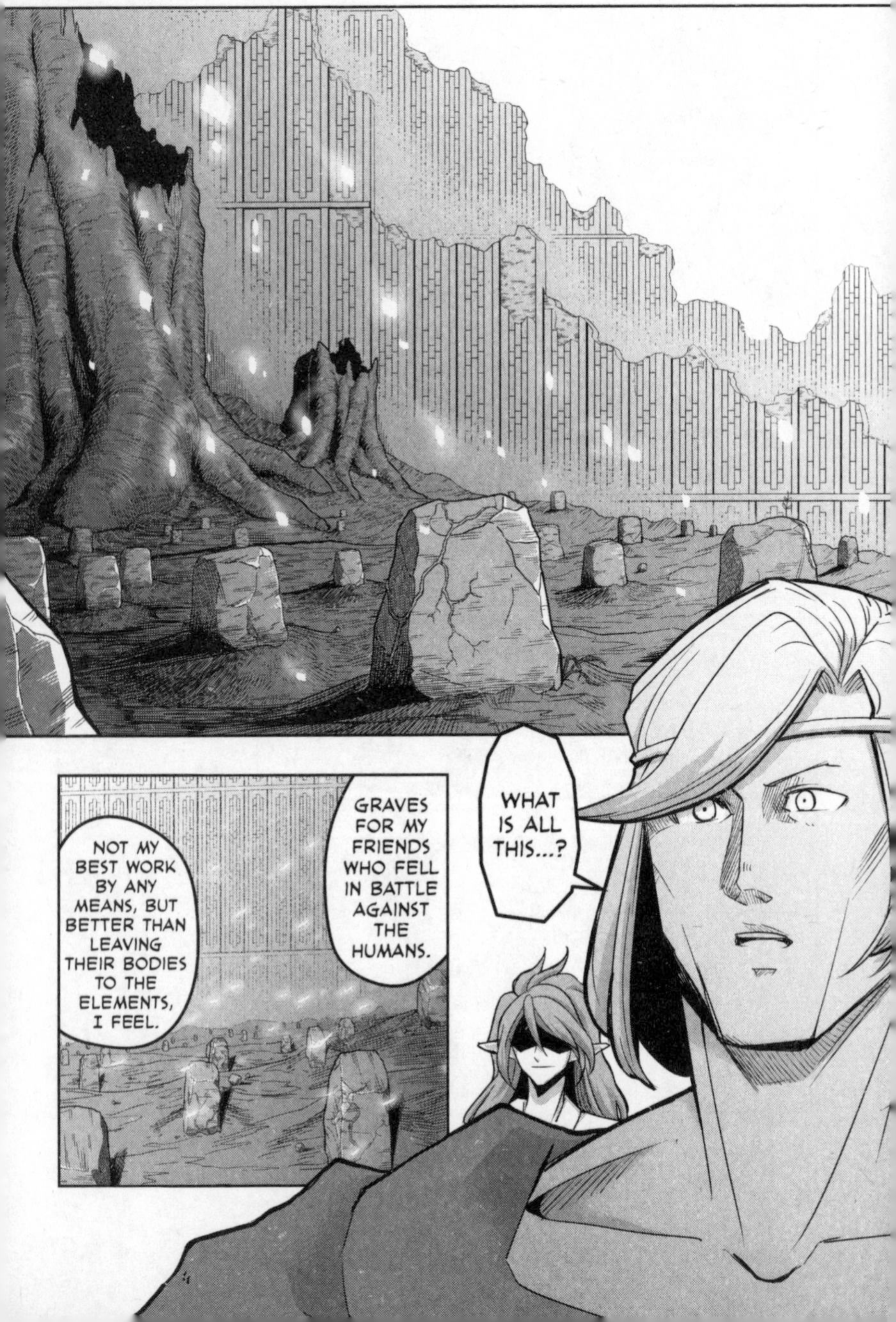
WHAT IS ALL THIS...?
GRAVES FOR MY FRIENDS WHO FELL IN BATTLE AGAINST THE HUMANS.
NOT MY BEST WORK BY ANY MEANS, BUT BETTER THAN LEAVING THEIR BODIES TO THE ELEMENTS, I FEEL.

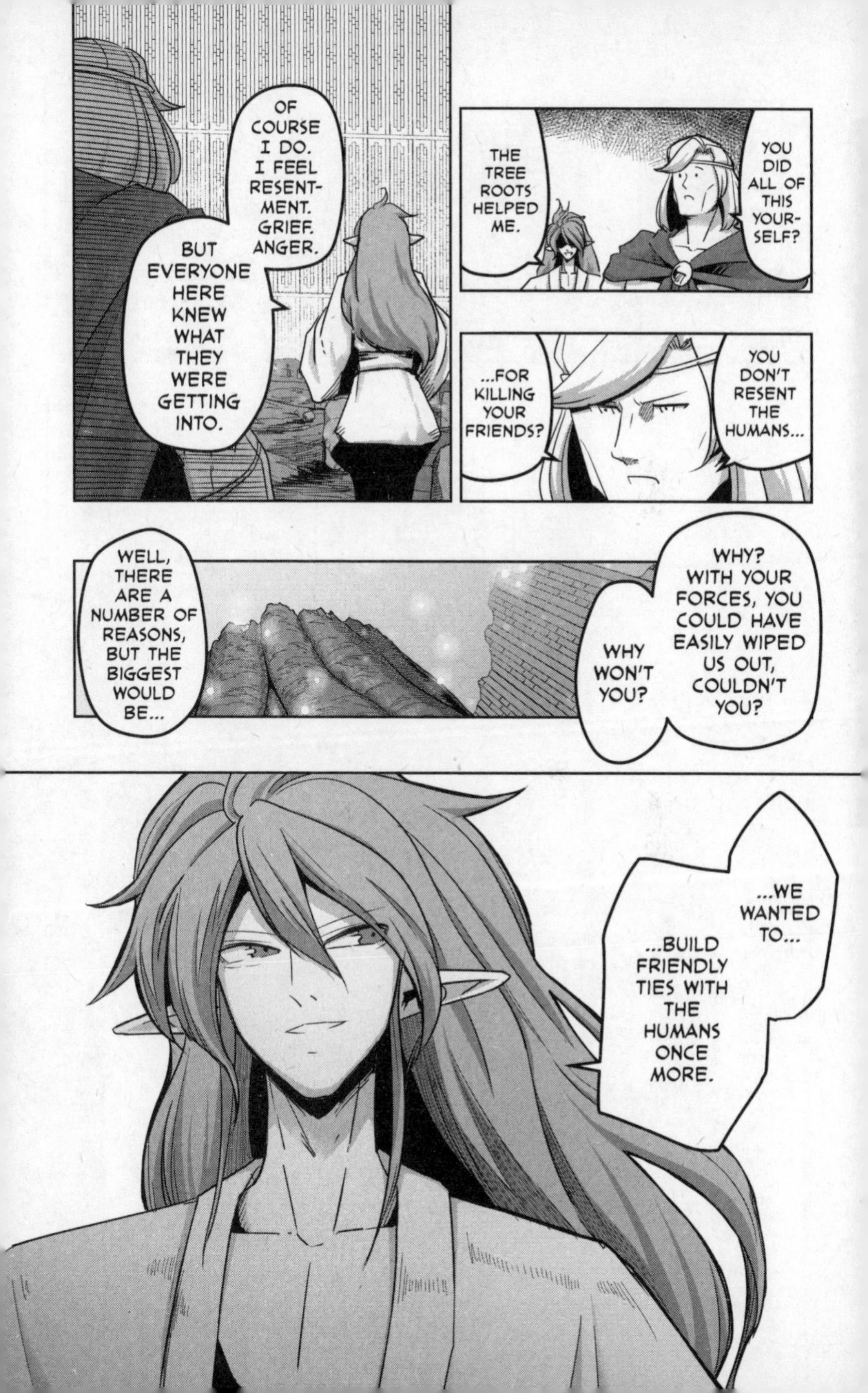
YOU DID ALL OF THIS YOURSELF?
THE TREE ROOTS HELPED ME.
YOU DON'T RESENT THE HUMANS...
...FOR KILLING YOUR FRIENDS?
OF COURSE I DO. I FEEL RESENTMENT. GRIEF. ANGER.
BUT EVERYONE HERE KNEW WHAT THEY WERE GETTING INTO.
WHY? WITH YOUR FORCES, YOU COULD HAVE EASILY WIPED US OUT, COULDN'T YOU?
WHY WON'T YOU?
WELL, THERE ARE A NUMBER OF REASONS, BUT THE BIGGEST WOULD BE...
...WE WANTED TO...
...BUILD FRIENDLY TIES WITH THE HUMANS ONCE MORE.

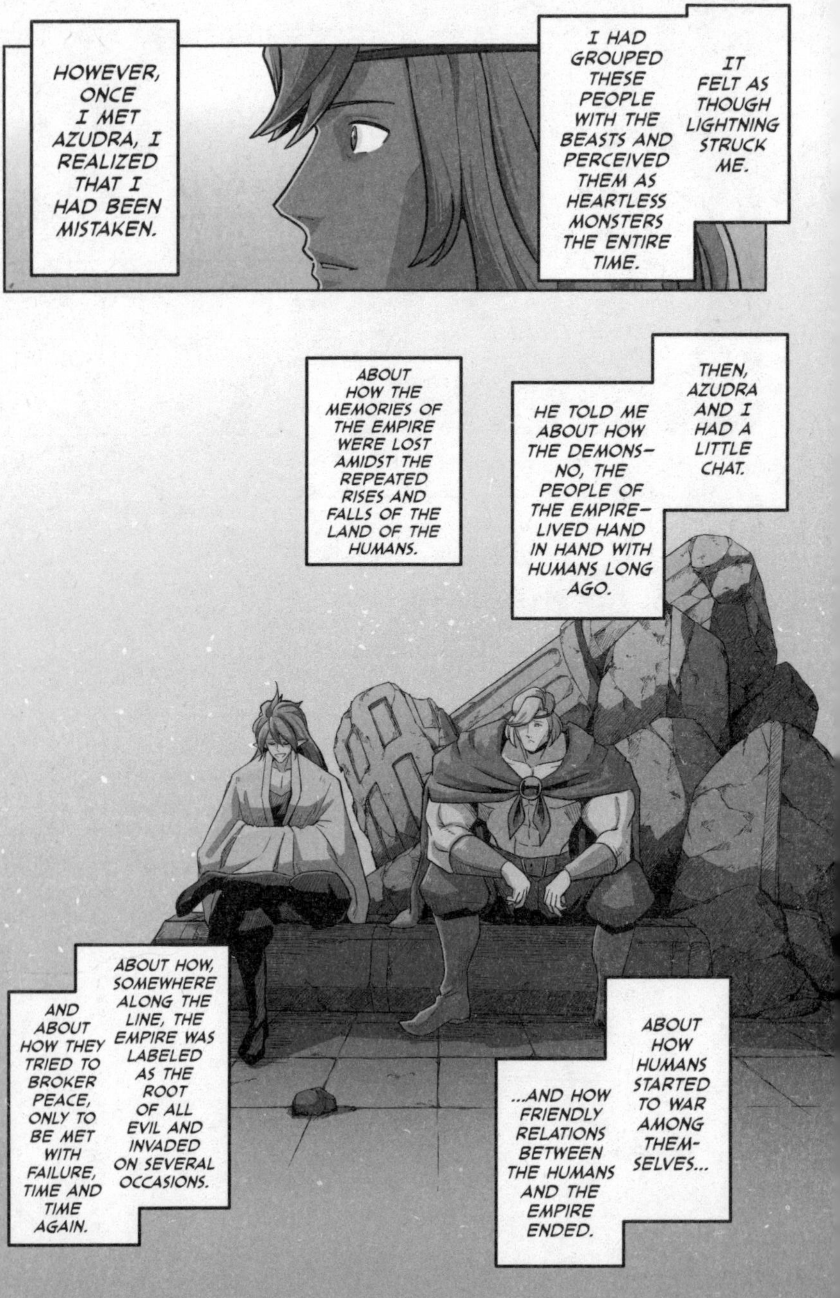
IT FELT AS THOUGH LIGHTNING STRUCK ME.
I HAD GROUPED THESE PEOPLE WITH THE BEASTS AND PERCEIVED THEM AS HEARTLESS MONSTERS THE ENTIRE TIME.
HOWEVER, ONCE I MET AZUDRA, I REALIZED THAT I HAD BEEN MISTAKEN.
THEN, AZUDRA AND I HAD A LITTLE CHAT.
HE TOLD ME ABOUT HOW THE DEMONS—NO, THE PEOPLE OF THE EMPIRE—LIVED HAND IN HAND WITH HUMANS LONG AGO.
ABOUT HOW THE MEMORIES OF THE EMPIRE WERE LOST AMIDST THE REPEATED RISES AND FALLS OF THE LAND OF THE HUMANS.
ABOUT HOW HUMANS STARTED TO WAR AMONG THEM-SELVES...
...AND HOW FRIENDLY RELATIONS BETWEEN THE HUMANS AND THE EMPIRE ENDED.
ABOUT HOW, SOMEWHERE ALONG THE LINE, THE EMPIRE WAS LABELED AS THE ROOT OF ALL EVIL AND INVADED ON SEVERAL OCCASIONS.
AND ABOUT HOW THEY TRIED TO BROKER PEACE, ONLY TO BE MET WITH FAILURE, TIME AND TIME AGAIN.

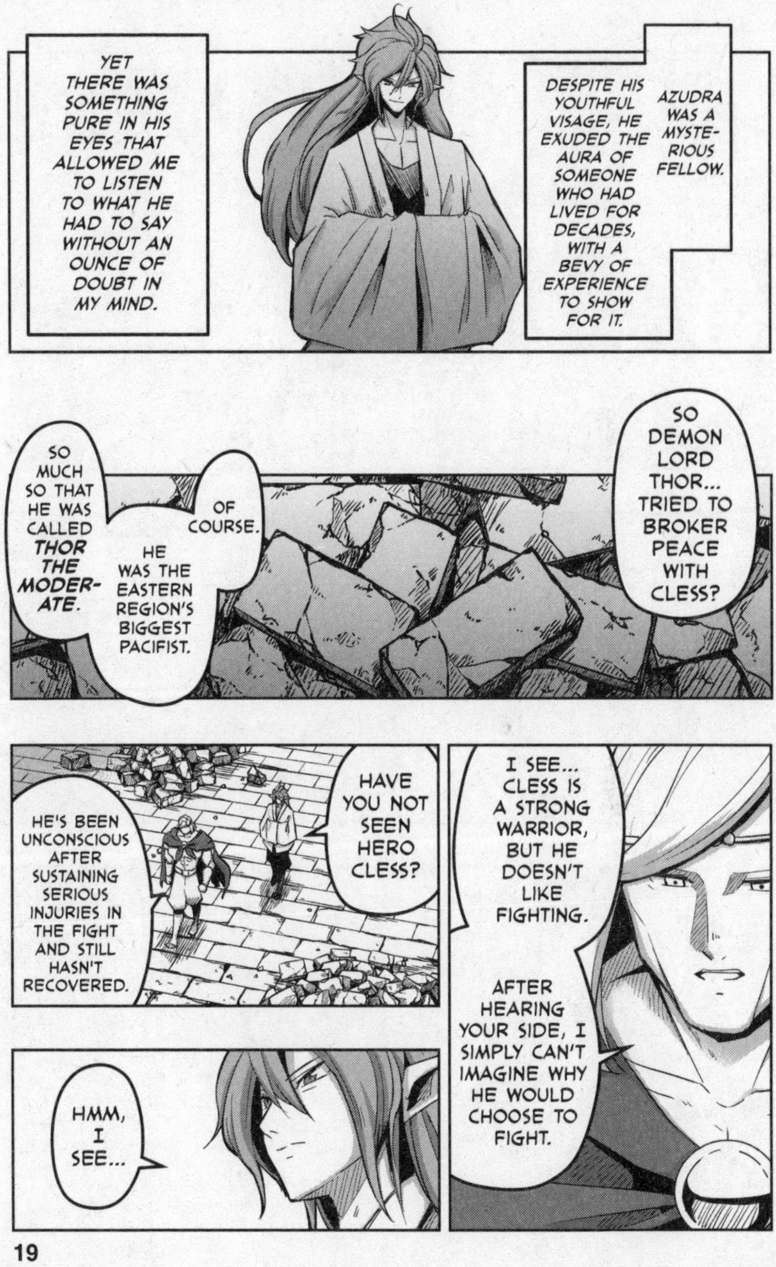
AZUDRA WAS A MYSTERIOUS FELLOW.
DESPITE HIS YOUTHFUL VISAGE, HE EXUDED THE AURA OF SOMEONE WHO HAD LIVED FOR DECADES, WITH A BEVY OF EXPERIENCE TO SHOW FOR IT.
YET THERE WAS SOMETHING PURE IN HIS EYES THAT ALLOWED ME TO LISTEN TO WHAT HE HAD TO SAY WITHOUT AN OUNCE OF DOUBT IN MY MIND.
SO DEMON LORD THOR... TRIED TO BROKER PEACE WITH CLESS?
OF COURSE.
HE WAS THE EASTERN REGION'S BIGGEST PACIFIST.
SO MUCH SO THAT HE WAS CALLED *THOR THE MODERATE*.
I SEE... CLESS IS A STRONG WARRIOR, BUT HE DOESN'T LIKE FIGHTING.
AFTER HEARING YOUR SIDE, I SIMPLY CAN'T IMAGINE WHY HE WOULD CHOOSE TO FIGHT.
HAVE YOU NOT SEEN HERO CLESS?
HE'S BEEN UNCONSCIOUS AFTER SUSTAINING SERIOUS INJURIES IN THE FIGHT AND STILL HASN'T RECOVERED.
HMM, I SEE...

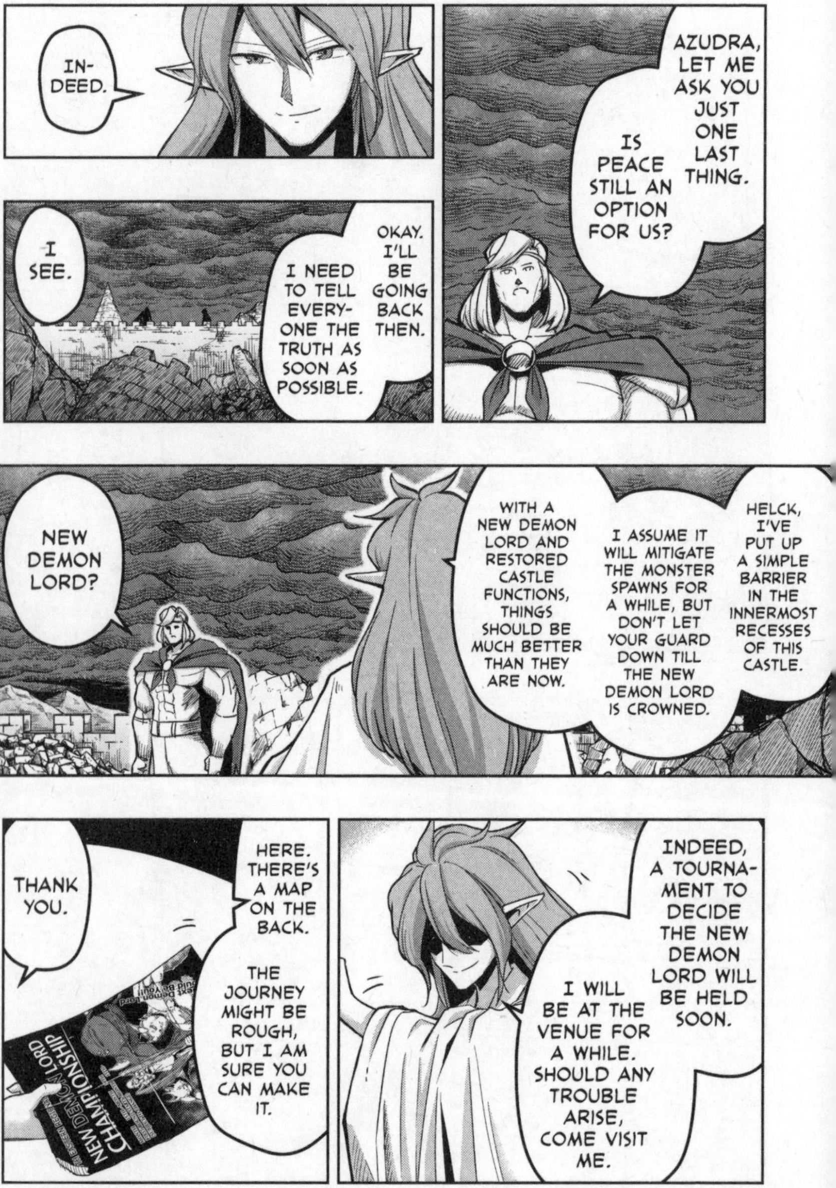
AZUDRA, LET ME ASK YOU JUST ONE LAST THING.
IS PEACE STILL AN OPTION FOR US?
IN-DEED.
OKAY. I'LL BE GOING BACK THEN.
I NEED TO TELL EVERY-ONE THE TRUTH AS SOON AS POSSIBLE.
I SEE.
HELCK, I'VE PUT UP A SIMPLE BARRIER IN THE INNERMOST RECESSES OF THIS CASTLE.
I ASSUME IT WILL MITIGATE THE MONSTER SPAWNS FOR A WHILE, BUT DON'T LET YOUR GUARD DOWN TILL THE NEW DEMON LORD IS CROWNED.
WITH A NEW DEMON LORD AND RESTORED CASTLE FUNCTIONS, THINGS SHOULD BE MUCH BETTER THAN THEY ARE NOW.
NEW DEMON LORD?
INDEED, A TOURNA-MENT TO DECIDE THE NEW DEMON LORD WILL BE HELD SOON.
I WILL BE AT THE VENUE FOR A WHILE. SHOULD ANY TROUBLE ARISE, COME VISIT ME.
HERE. THERE'S A MAP ON THE BACK.
THE JOURNEY MIGHT BE ROUGH, BUT I AM SURE YOU CAN MAKE IT.
THANK YOU.
NEW DEMON LORD CHAMPIONSHIP

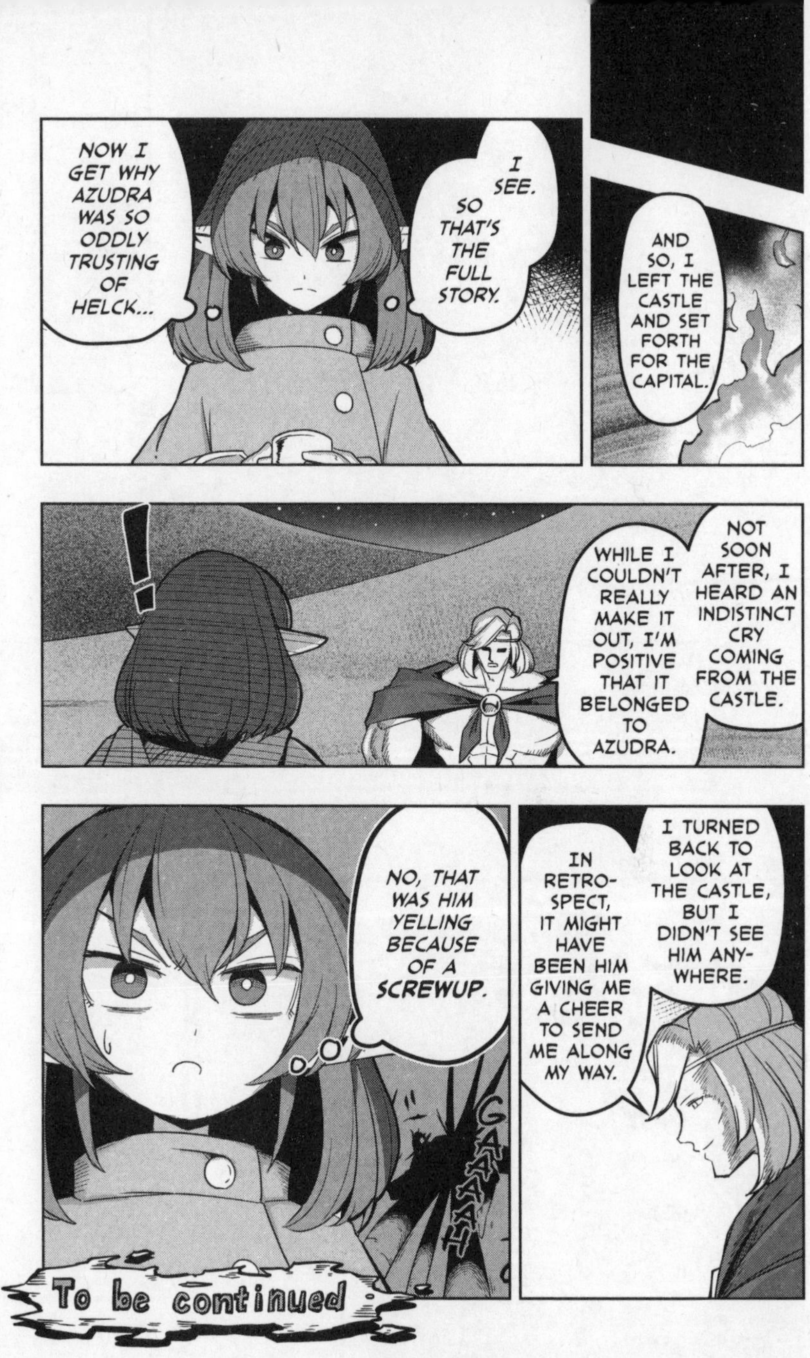
AND SO, I LEFT THE CASTLE AND SET FORTH FOR THE CAPITAL.
I SEE. SO THAT'S THE FULL STORY.
NOW I GET WHY AZUDRA WAS SO ODDLY TRUSTING OF HELCK...
NOT SOON AFTER, I HEARD AN INDISTINCT CRY COMING FROM THE CASTLE.
WHILE I COULDN'T REALLY MAKE IT OUT, I'M POSITIVE THAT IT BELONGED TO AZUDRA.
!
I TURNED BACK TO LOOK AT THE CASTLE, BUT I DIDN'T SEE HIM ANY-WHERE.
IN RETRO-SPECT, IT MIGHT HAVE BEEN HIM GIVING ME A CHEER TO SEND ME ALONG MY WAY.
NO, THAT WAS HIM YELLING BECAUSE OF A SCREWUP.
GAAAAH
To be continued

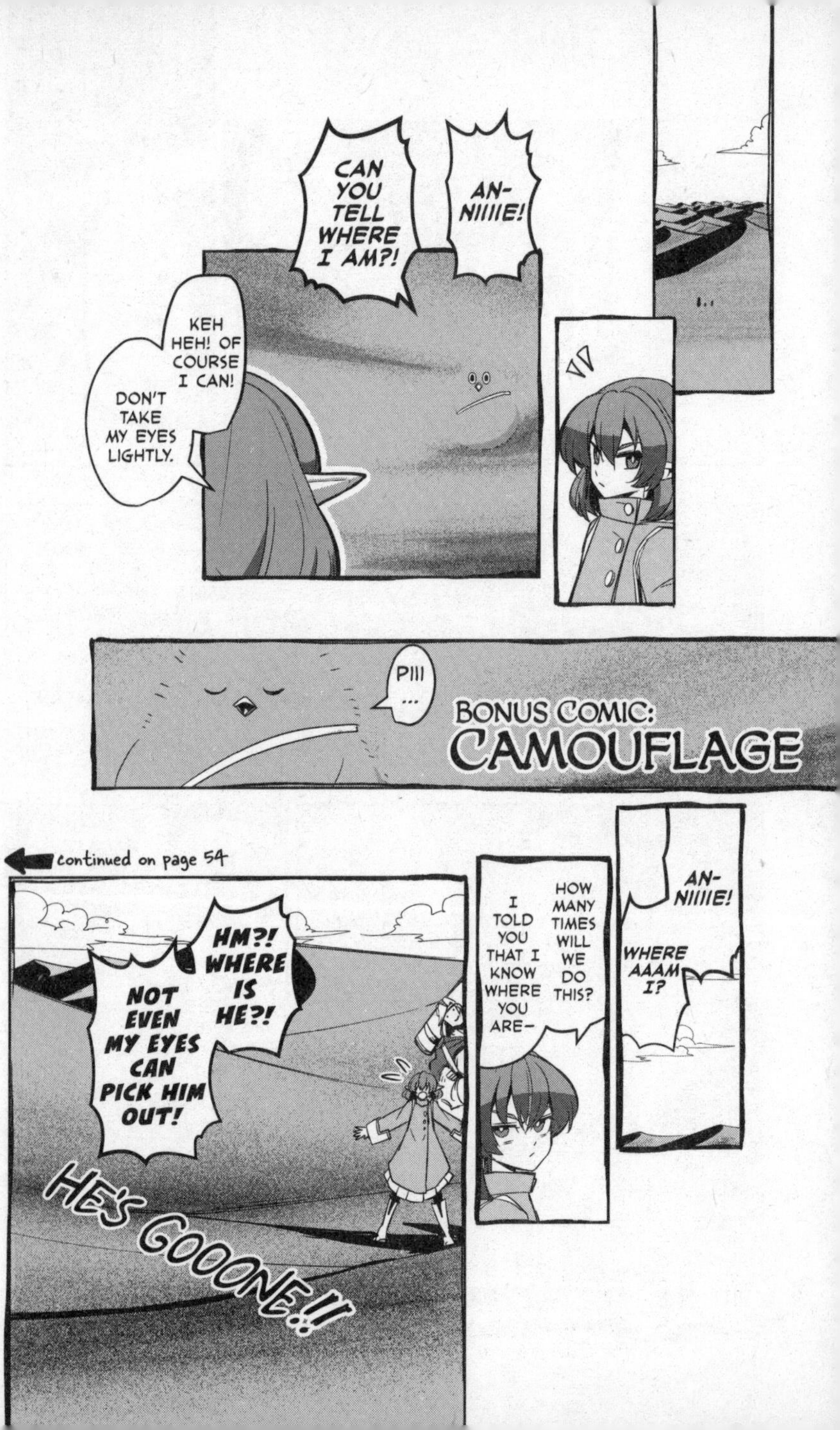
AN-NIIIIE!
CAN YOU TELL WHERE I AM?!
KEH HEH! OF COURSE I CAN! DON'T TAKE MY EYES LIGHTLY.
PIII ...
BONUS COMIC: CAMOUFLAGE
AN-NIIIIE!
WHERE AAAM I?
HOW MANY TIMES WILL WE DO THIS?
I TOLD YOU THAT I KNOW WHERE YOU ARE—
HM?! WHERE IS HE?!
NOT EVEN MY EYES CAN PICK HIM OUT!
HE'S GOOONE!!
continued on page 54

Chapter 43: Helck's Past VIII

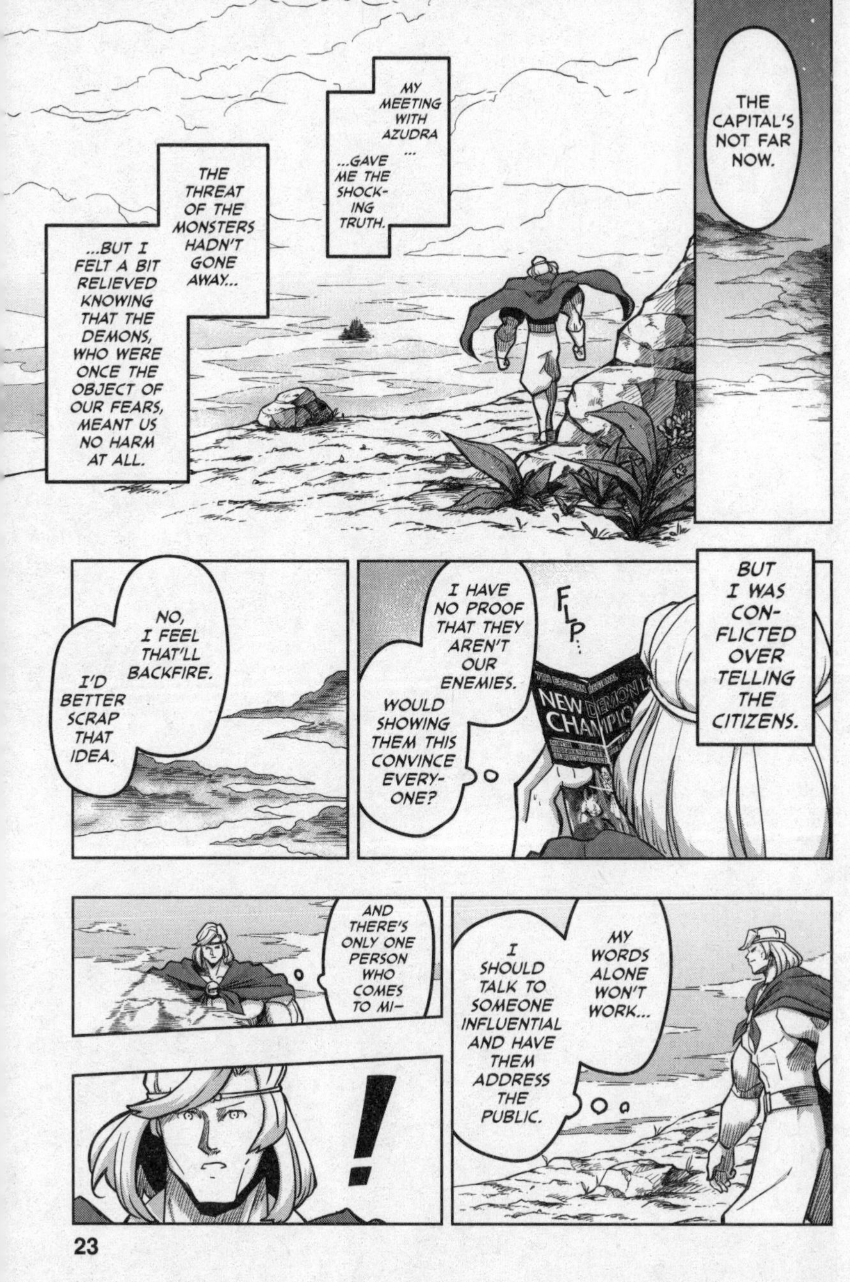
THE CAPITAL'S NOT FAR NOW.
MY MEETING WITH AZUDRA ... ...GAVE ME THE SHOCKING TRUTH.
THE THREAT OF THE MONSTERS HADN'T GONE AWAY...
...BUT I FELT A BIT RELIEVED KNOWING THAT THE DEMONS, WHO WERE ONCE THE OBJECT OF OUR FEARS, MEANT US NO HARM AT ALL.
BUT I WAS CONFLICTED OVER TELLING THE CITIZENS.
I HAVE NO PROOF THAT THEY AREN'T OUR ENEMIES.
FLP...
WOULD SHOWING THEM THIS CONVINCE EVERYONE?
NO, I FEEL THAT'LL BACKFIRE.
I'D BETTER SCRAP THAT IDEA.
MY WORDS ALONE WON'T WORK...
I SHOULD TALK TO SOMEONE INFLUENTIAL AND HAVE THEM ADDRESS THE PUBLIC.
AND THERE'S ONLY ONE PERSON WHO COMES TO MI—
!

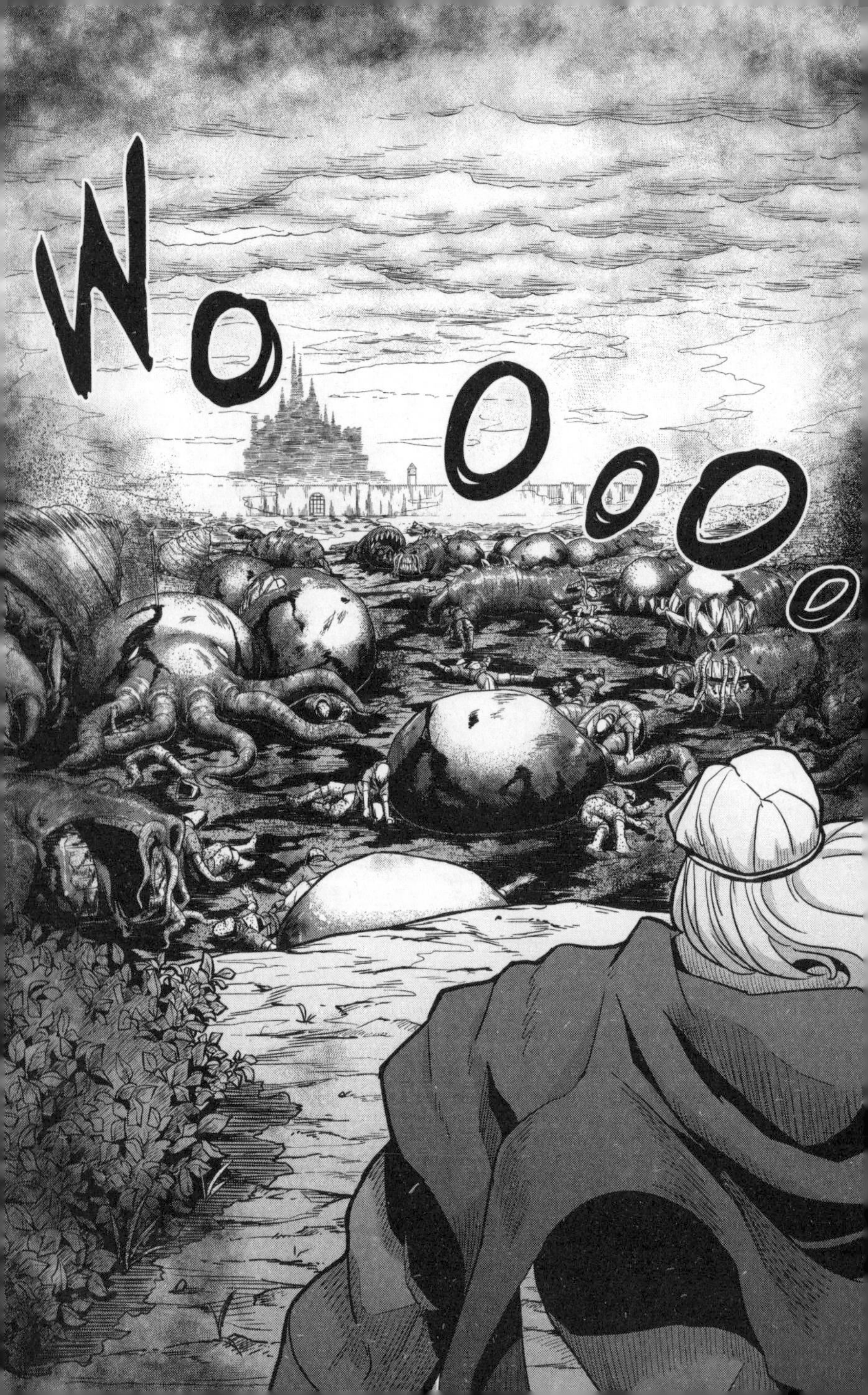
WOOOOOO

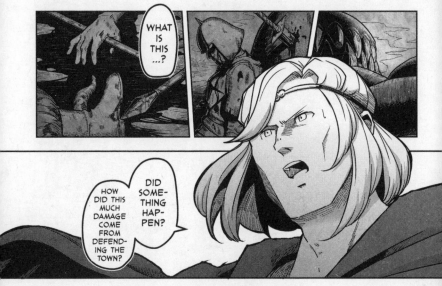

WHAT IS THIS ...?
DID SOMETHING HAPPEN?
HOW DID THIS MUCH DAMAGE COME FROM DEFENDING THE TOWN?
SHUDDR
FOR A SPLIT SECOND ...
...A HORRIBLE FEELING THAT I'VE NEVER FELT BEFORE CAME OVER ME.
WHAT WAS THAT JUST NOW ...?
AT THE TIME, I FIGURED THAT IT WAS FROM SEEING THE GHASTLY SIGHT BEFORE ME.
NO TIME TO STAND AROUND CONFUSED.
I NEED TO SEE IF EVERYONE IS SAFE.
OPEN UP, PLEASE!!
HM? A SURVIVOR?
HOLD ON!

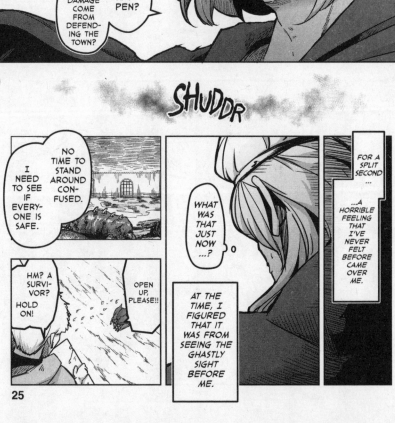

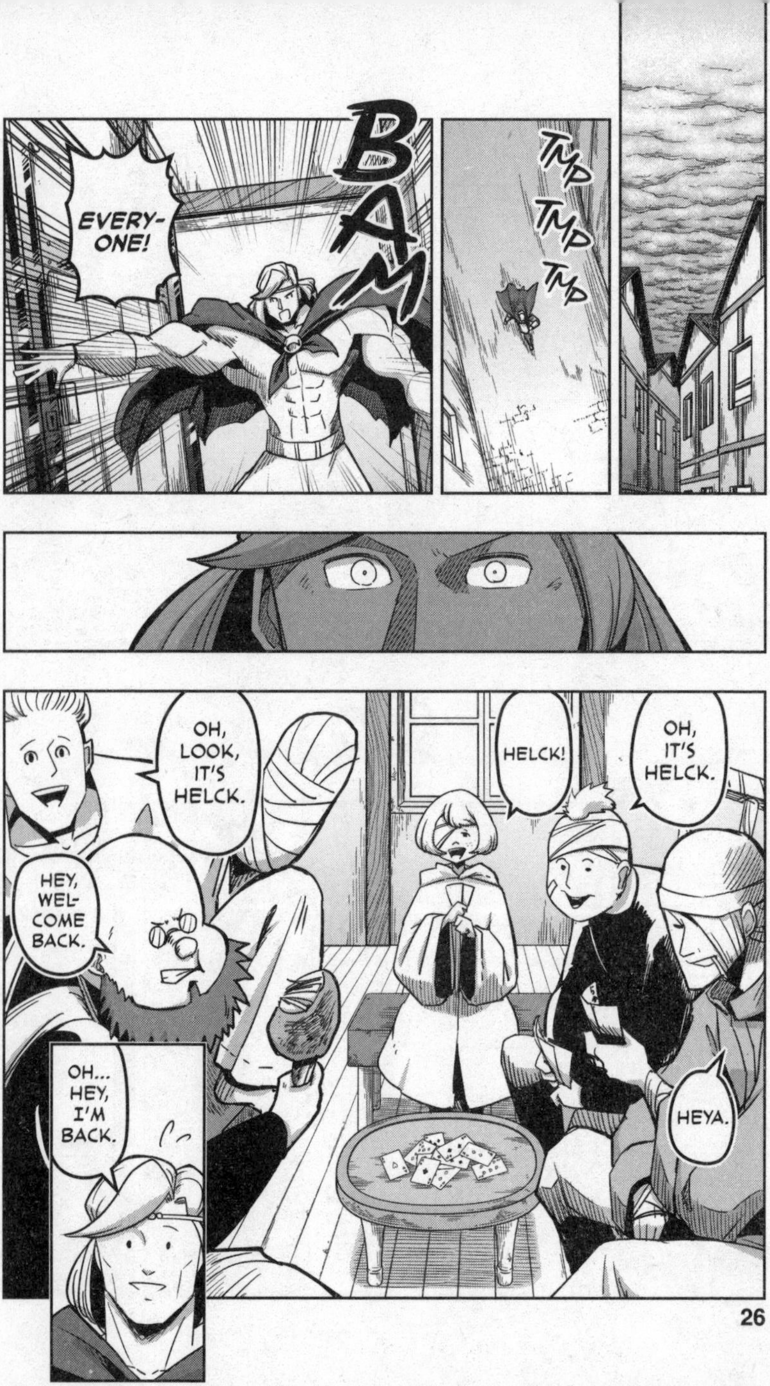
TMP TMP TMP TMP
BAM
EVERY-ONE!
OH, IT'S HELCK.
HELCK!
OH, LOOK, IT'S HELCK.
HEY, WEL-COME BACK.
HEYA.
OH... HEY, I'M BACK.

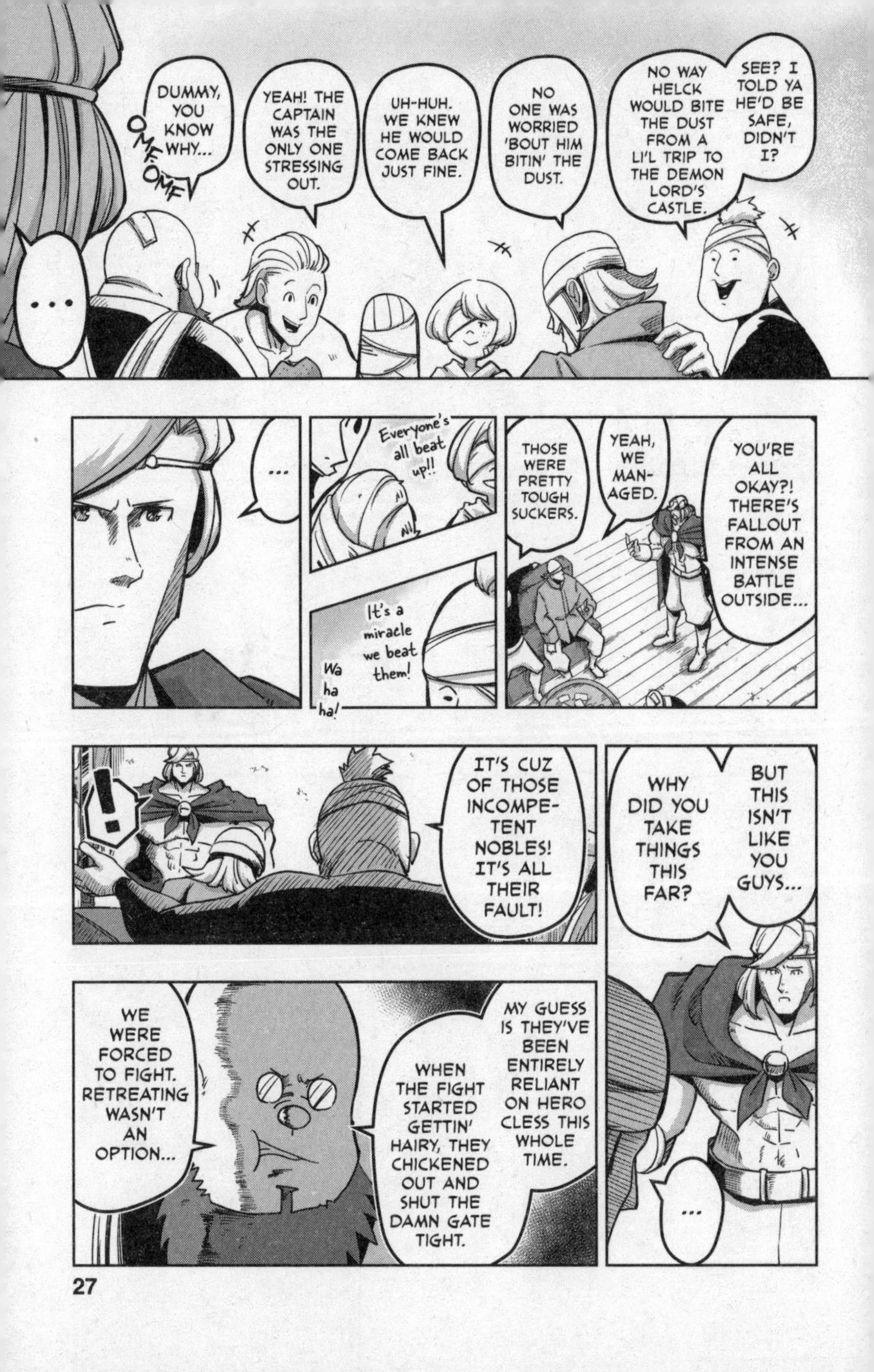
SEE? I TOLD YA HE'D BE SAFE, DIDN'T I?
NO WAY HELCK WOULD BITE THE DUST FROM A LI'L TRIP TO THE DEMON LORD'S CASTLE.
NO ONE WAS WORRIED 'BOUT HIM BITIN' THE DUST.
UH-HUH. WE KNEW HE WOULD COME BACK JUST FINE.
YEAH! THE CAPTAIN WAS THE ONLY ONE STRESSING OUT.
DUMMY, YOU KNOW WHY...
OMF OMF
...
YOU'RE ALL OKAY?! THERE'S FALLOUT FROM AN INTENSE BATTLE OUTSIDE...
YEAH, WE MAN-AGED.
THOSE WERE PRETTY TOUGH SUCKERS.
Everyone's all beat up!!
It's a miracle we beat them!
Wa ha ha!
...
BUT THIS ISN'T LIKE YOU GUYS...
WHY DID YOU TAKE THINGS THIS FAR?
...
IT'S CUZ OF THOSE INCOMPE-TENT NOBLES! IT'S ALL THEIR FAULT!
!
MY GUESS IS THEY'VE BEEN ENTIRELY RELIANT ON HERO CLESS THIS WHOLE TIME.
WHEN THE FIGHT STARTED GETTIN' HAIRY, THEY CHICKENED OUT AND SHUT THE DAMN GATE TIGHT.
WE WERE FORCED TO FIGHT. RETREATING WASN'T AN OPTION...

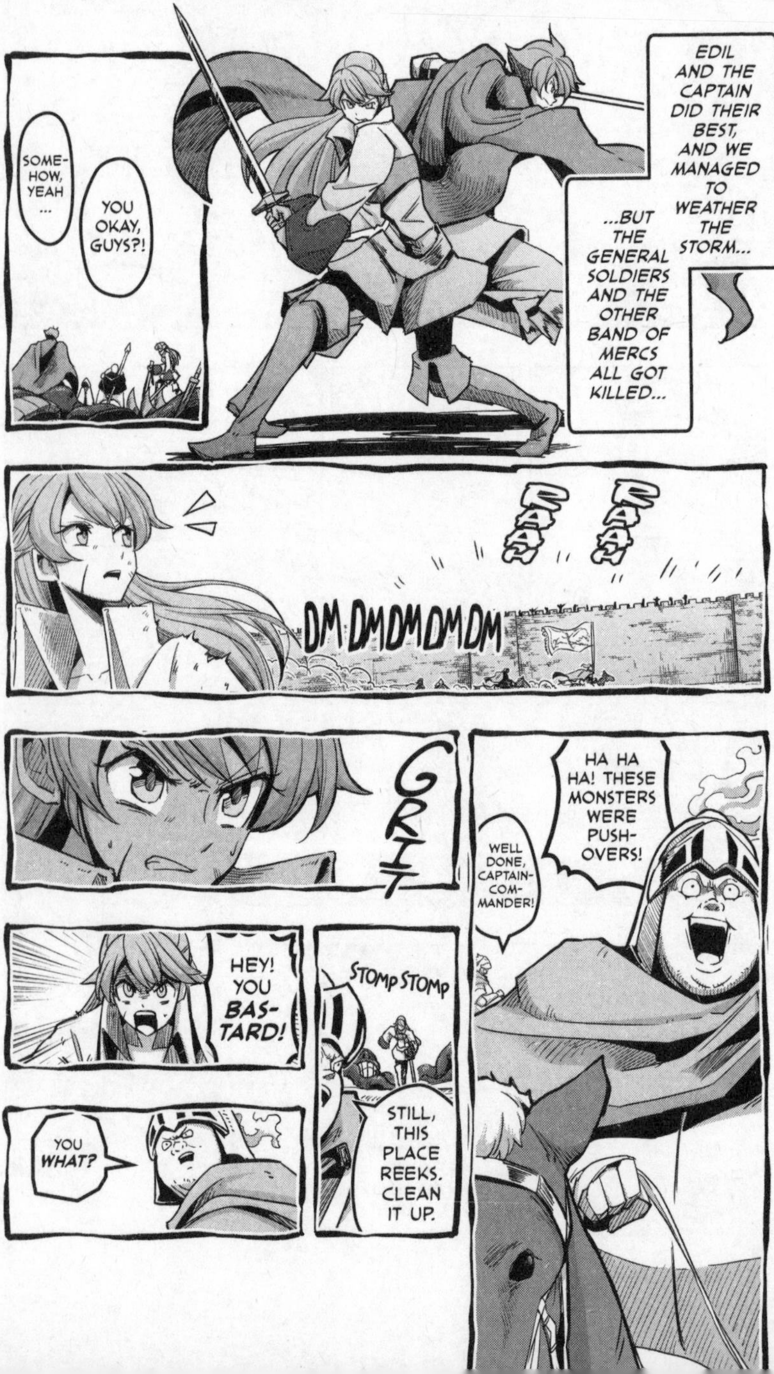
EDIL AND THE CAPTAIN DID THEIR BEST, AND WE MANAGED TO WEATHER THE STORM...
...BUT THE GENERAL SOLDIERS AND THE OTHER BAND OF MERCS ALL GOT KILLED...
YOU OKAY, GUYS?!
SOME-HOW, YEAH ...
RAAAH
RAAAH
DMDMDMDMDM
HA HA HA! THESE MONSTERS WERE PUSH-OVERS!
WELL DONE, CAPTAIN-COMMANDER!
GRIT
STOMP STOMP
STILL, THIS PLACE REEKS. CLEAN IT UP.
HEY! YOU BAS-TARD!
YOU WHAT?

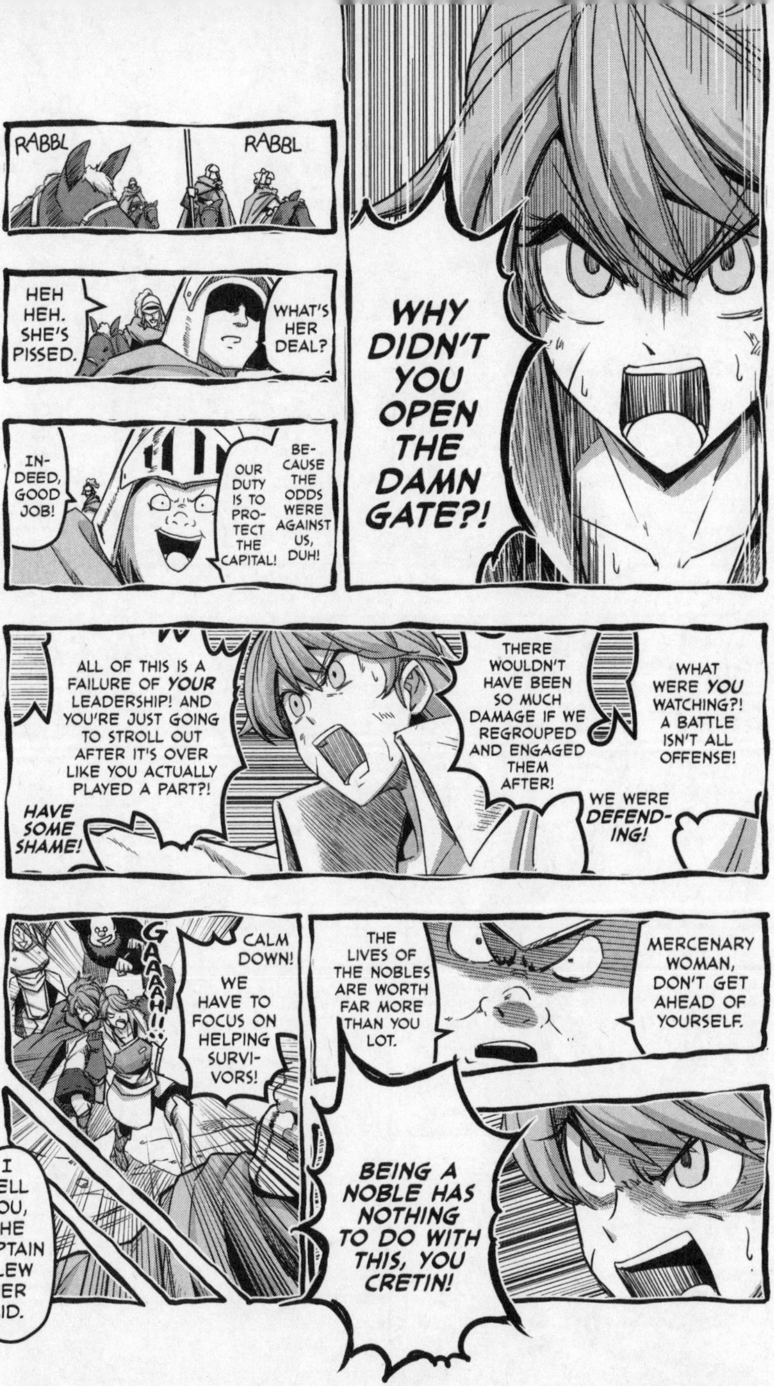
WHY DIDN'T YOU OPEN THE DAMN GATE?!
RABBL
RABBL
WHAT'S HER DEAL?
HEH HEH. SHE'S PISSED.
BECAUSE THE ODDS WERE AGAINST US, DUH!
OUR DUTY IS TO PROTECT THE CAPITAL!
INDEED, GOOD JOB!
WHAT WERE YOU WATCHING?! A BATTLE ISN'T ALL OFFENSE!
WE WERE DEFENDING!
THERE WOULDN'T HAVE BEEN SO MUCH DAMAGE IF WE REGROUPED AND ENGAGED THEM AFTER!
ALL OF THIS IS A FAILURE OF YOUR LEADERSHIP! AND YOU'RE JUST GOING TO STROLL OUT AFTER IT'S OVER LIKE YOU ACTUALLY PLAYED A PART?!
HAVE SOME SHAME!
MERCENARY WOMAN, DON'T GET AHEAD OF YOURSELF.
THE LIVES OF THE NOBLES ARE WORTH FAR MORE THAN YOU LOT.
BEING A NOBLE HAS NOTHING TO DO WITH THIS, YOU CRETIN!
GAAAAH!!
CALM DOWN!
WE HAVE TO FOCUS ON HELPING SURVIVORS!
I TELL YOU, THE CAPTAIN BLEW HER LID.

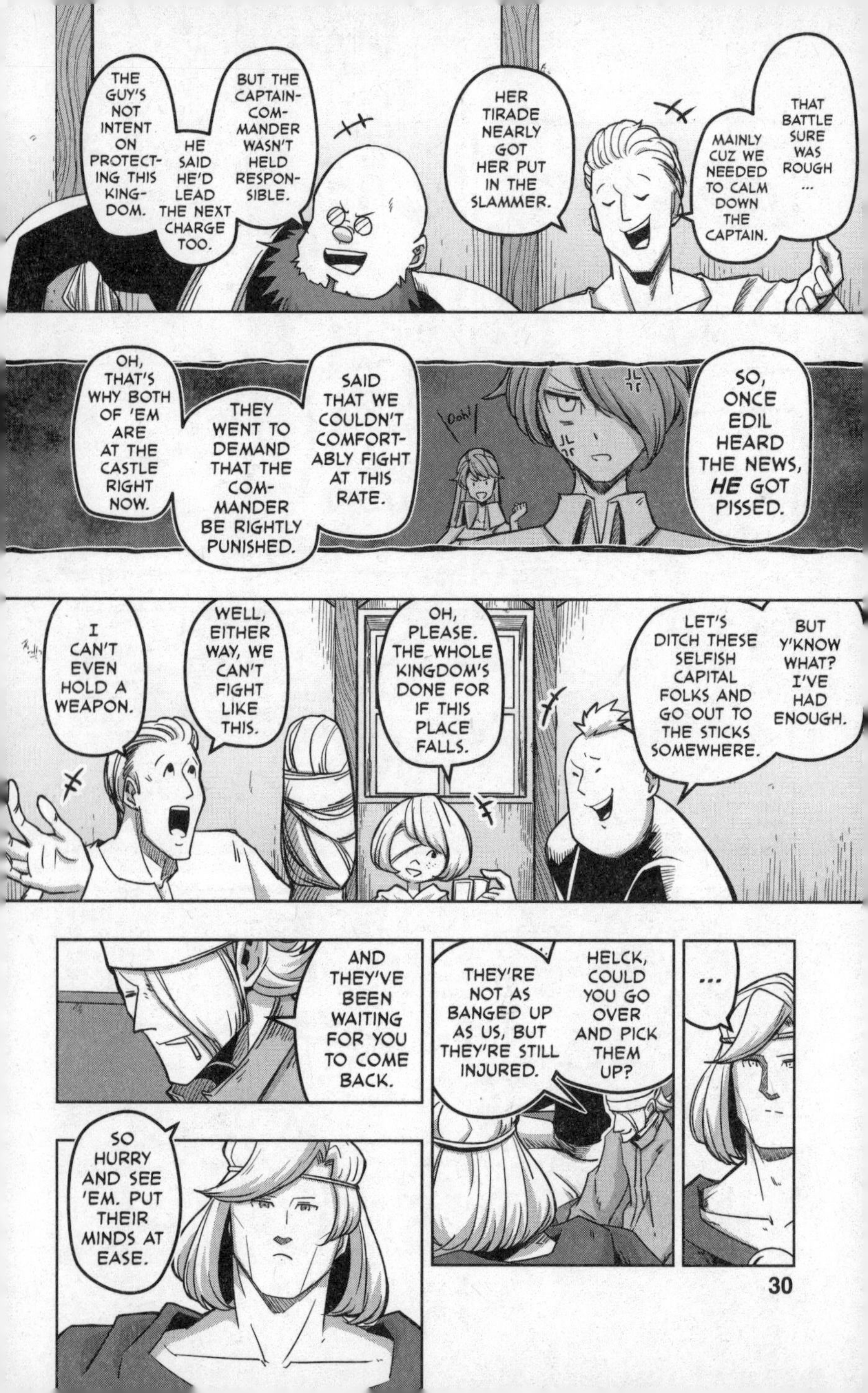
THAT BATTLE SURE WAS ROUGH ...
MAINLY CUZ WE NEEDED TO CALM DOWN THE CAPTAIN.
HER TIRADE NEARLY GOT HER PUT IN THE SLAMMER.
BUT THE CAPTAIN-COMMANDER WASN'T HELD RESPONSIBLE.
HE SAID HE'D LEAD THE NEXT CHARGE TOO.
THE GUY'S NOT INTENT ON PROTECTING THIS KINGDOM.
SO, ONCE EDIL HEARD THE NEWS, *HE* GOT PISSED.
SAID THAT WE COULDN'T COMFORTABLY FIGHT AT THIS RATE.
THEY WENT TO DEMAND THAT THE COMMANDER BE RIGHTLY PUNISHED.
OH, THAT'S WHY BOTH OF 'EM ARE AT THE CASTLE RIGHT NOW.
BUT Y'KNOW WHAT? I'VE HAD ENOUGH.
LET'S DITCH THESE SELFISH CAPITAL FOLKS AND GO OUT TO THE STICKS SOMEWHERE.
OH, PLEASE. THE WHOLE KINGDOM'S DONE FOR IF THIS PLACE FALLS.
WELL, EITHER WAY, WE CAN'T FIGHT LIKE THIS.
I CAN'T EVEN HOLD A WEAPON.
...
HELCK, COULD YOU GO OVER AND PICK THEM UP?
THEY'RE NOT AS BANGED UP AS US, BUT THEY'RE STILL INJURED.
AND THEY'VE BEEN WAITING FOR YOU TO COME BACK.
SO HURRY AND SEE 'EM. PUT THEIR MINDS AT EASE.

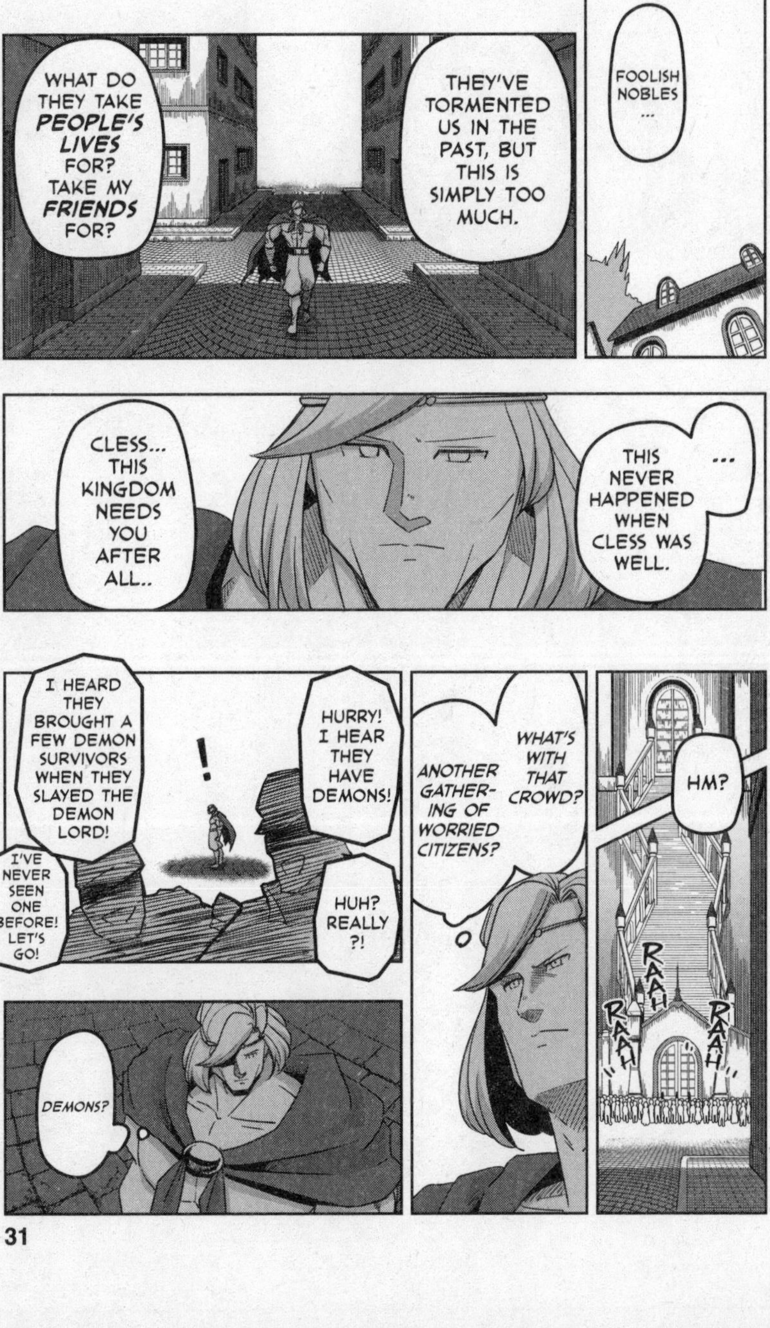
FOOLISH NOBLES ...
THEY'VE TORMENTED US IN THE PAST, BUT THIS IS SIMPLY TOO MUCH.
WHAT DO THEY TAKE *PEOPLE'S LIVES* FOR? TAKE MY *FRIENDS* FOR?
...
THIS NEVER HAPPENED WHEN CLESS WAS WELL.
CLESS... THIS KINGDOM NEEDS YOU AFTER ALL..
HM?
RAAH
RAAH
RAAH
WHAT'S WITH THAT CROWD?
ANOTHER GATHERING OF WORRIED CITIZENS?
HURRY! I HEAR THEY HAVE DEMONS!
I HEARD THEY BROUGHT A FEW DEMON SURVIVORS WHEN THEY SLAYED THE DEMON LORD!
!
HUH? REALLY ?!
I'VE NEVER SEEN ONE BEFORE! LET'S GO!
DEMONS?

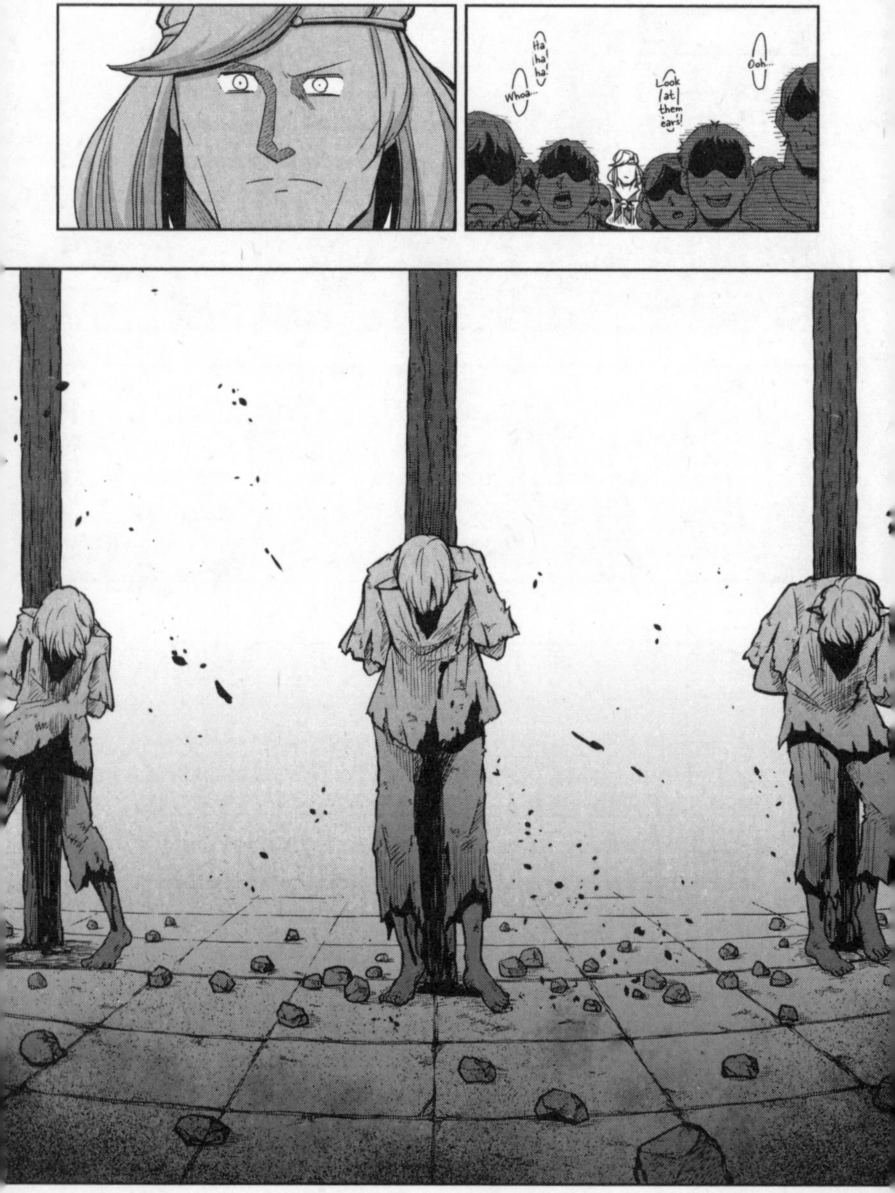
Ooh...
Look at them ears!
Ha ha ha!
Whoa...

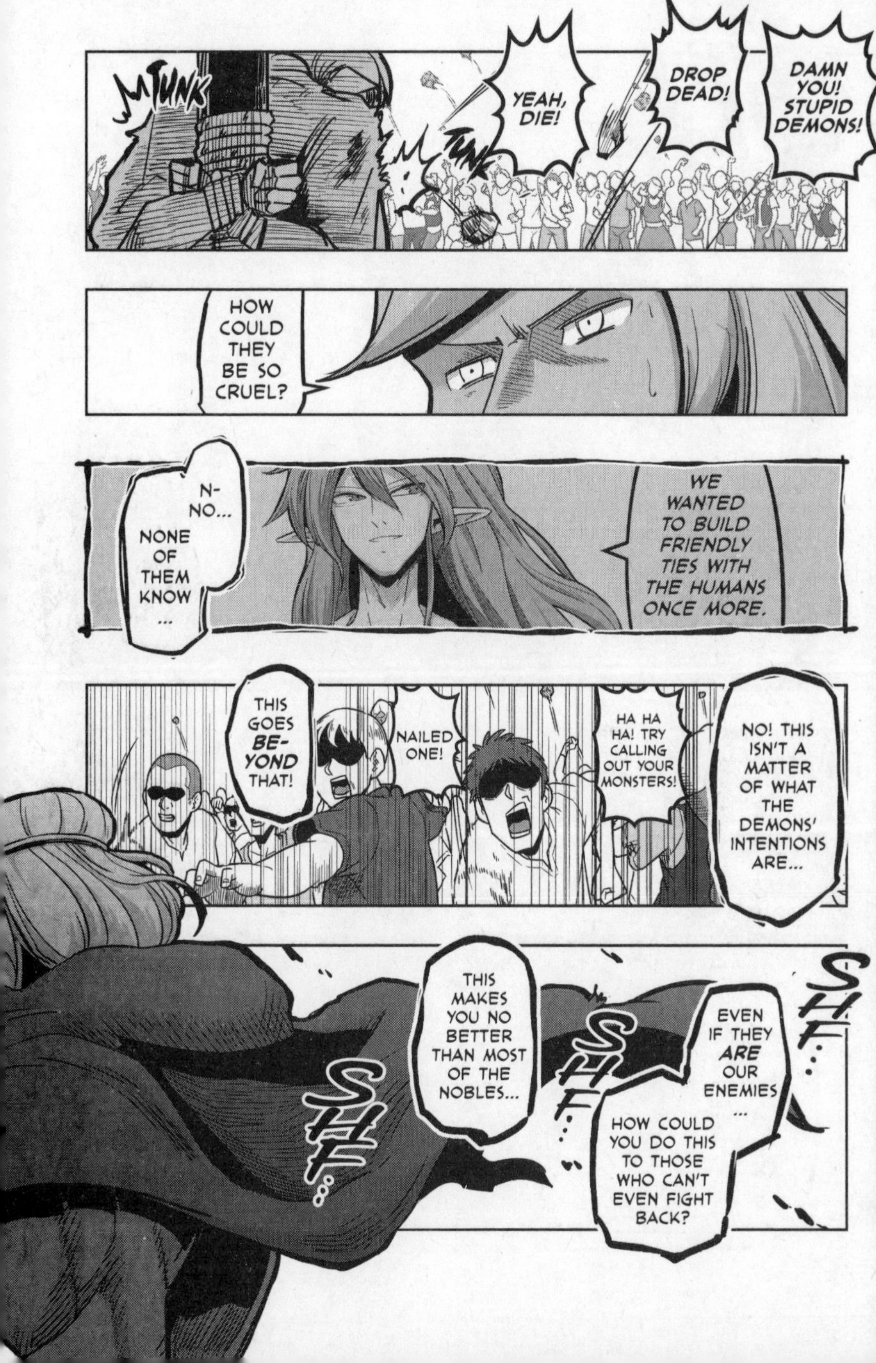
DAMN YOU! STUPID DEMONS!
DROP DEAD!
YEAH, DIE!
TUNK
TUNK
HOW COULD THEY BE SO CRUEL?
WE WANTED TO BUILD FRIENDLY TIES WITH THE HUMANS ONCE MORE.
N-NO... NONE OF THEM KNOW...
NO! THIS ISN'T A MATTER OF WHAT THE DEMONS' INTENTIONS ARE...
HA HA HA! TRY CALLING OUT YOUR MONSTERS!
NAILED ONE!
THIS GOES *BE-YOND* THAT!
SHF...
EVEN IF THEY *ARE* OUR ENEMIES...
HOW COULD YOU DO THIS TO THOSE WHO CAN'T EVEN FIGHT BACK?
SHF...
THIS MAKES YOU NO BETTER THAN MOST OF THE NOBLES...
SHF...

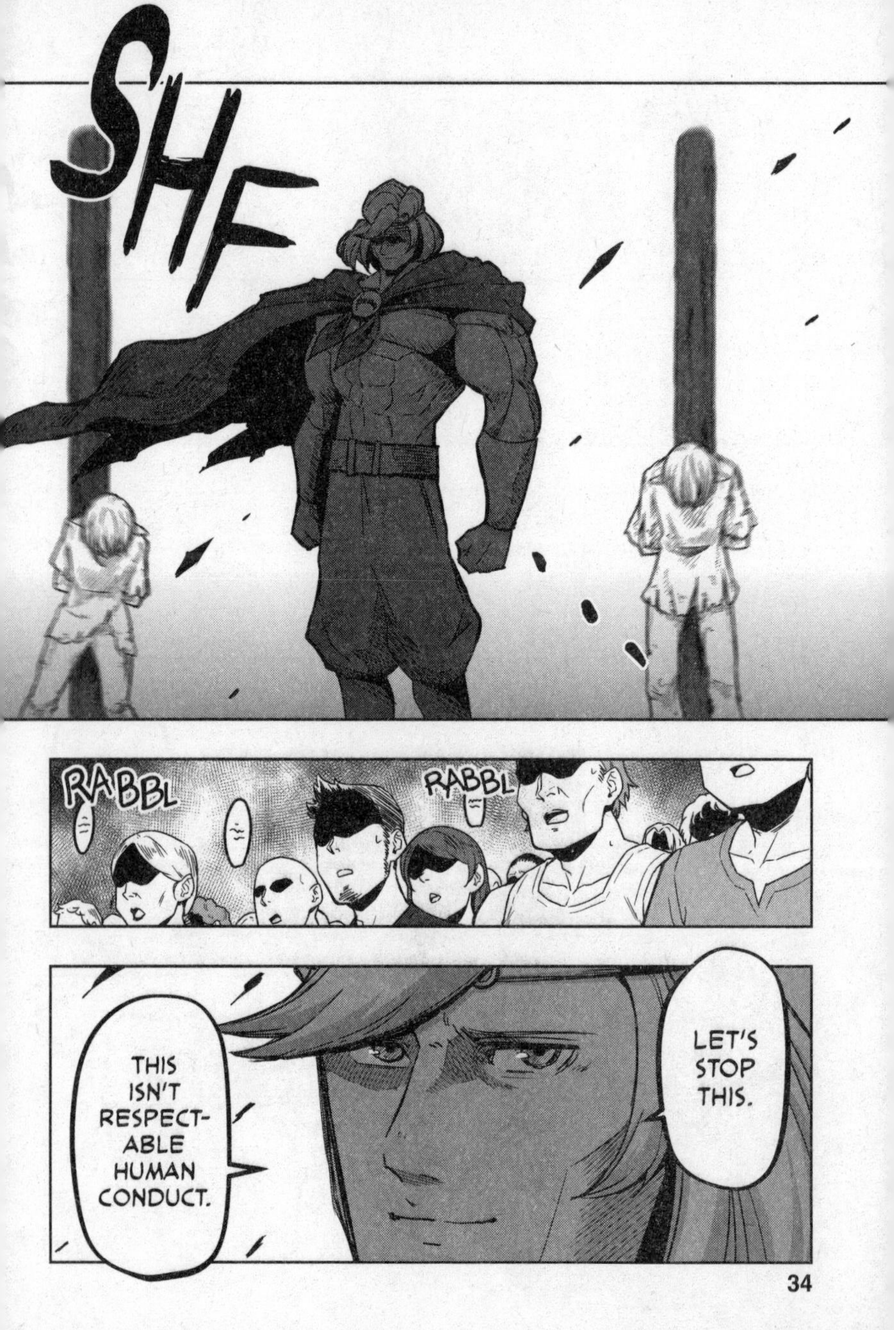
SHF
RABBL
RABBL
LET'S STOP THIS.
THIS ISN'T RESPECT-ABLE HUMAN CONDUCT.

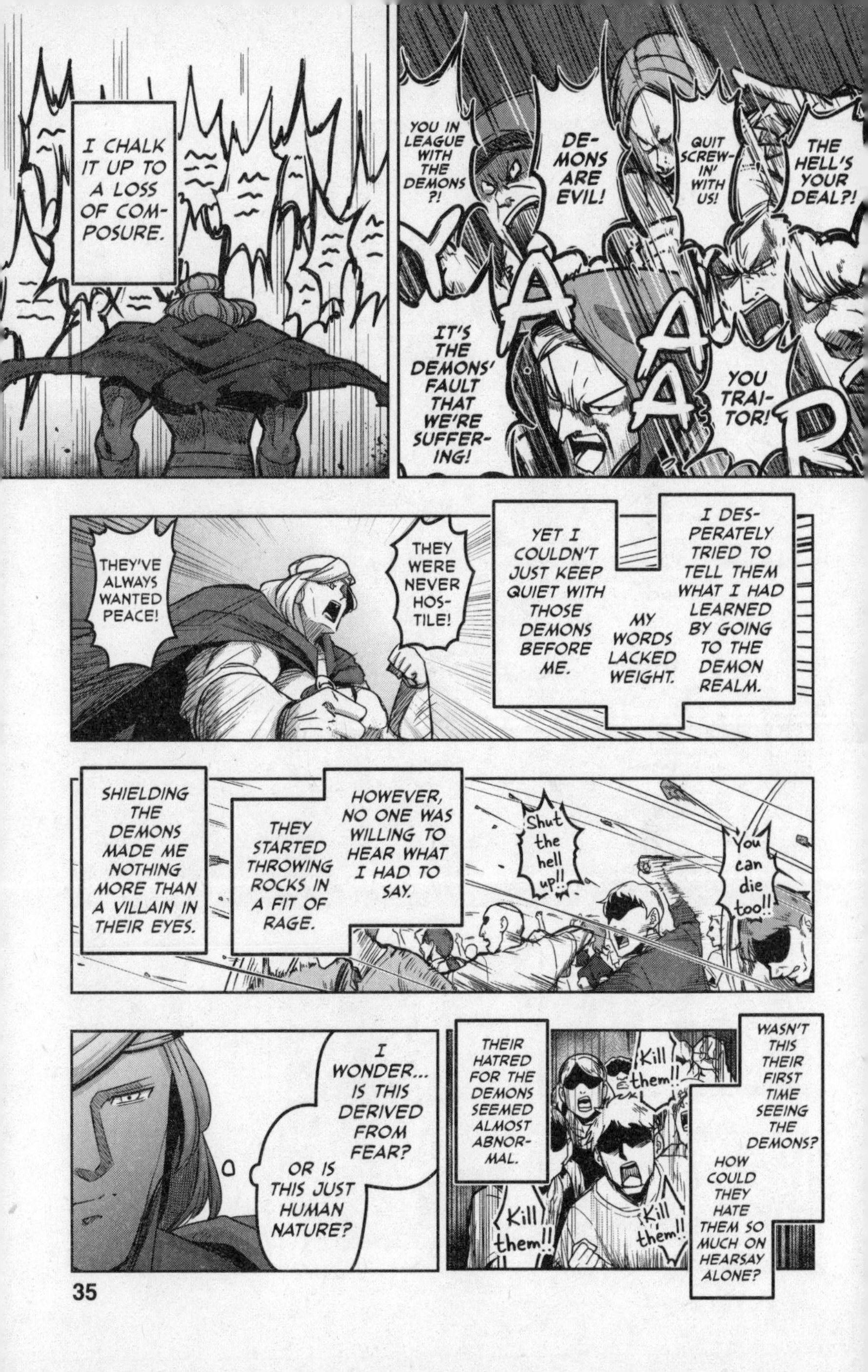
THE HELL'S YOUR DEAL?!
QUIT SCREWIN' WITH US!
DEMONS ARE EVIL!
YOU IN LEAGUE WITH THE DEMONS?!
YAAAR
YOU TRAITOR!
IT'S THE DEMONS' FAULT THAT WE'RE SUFFERING!
I CHALK IT UP TO A LOSS OF COMPOSURE.
I DESPERATELY TRIED TO TELL THEM WHAT I HAD LEARNED BY GOING TO THE DEMON REALM.
MY WORDS LACKED WEIGHT.
YET I COULDN'T JUST KEEP QUIET WITH THOSE DEMONS BEFORE ME.
THEY WERE NEVER HOSTILE!
THEY'VE ALWAYS WANTED PEACE!
You can die too!!
Shut the hell up!!
HOWEVER, NO ONE WAS WILLING TO HEAR WHAT I HAD TO SAY.
THEY STARTED THROWING ROCKS IN A FIT OF RAGE.
SHIELDING THE DEMONS MADE ME NOTHING MORE THAN A VILLAIN IN THEIR EYES.
WASN'T THIS THEIR FIRST TIME SEEING THE DEMONS?
Kill them!!
THEIR HATRED FOR THE DEMONS SEEMED ALMOST ABNORMAL.
HOW COULD THEY HATE THEM SO MUCH ON HEARSAY ALONE?
Kill them!!
Kill them!!
I WONDER... IS THIS DERIVED FROM FEAR?
OR IS THIS JUST HUMAN NATURE?

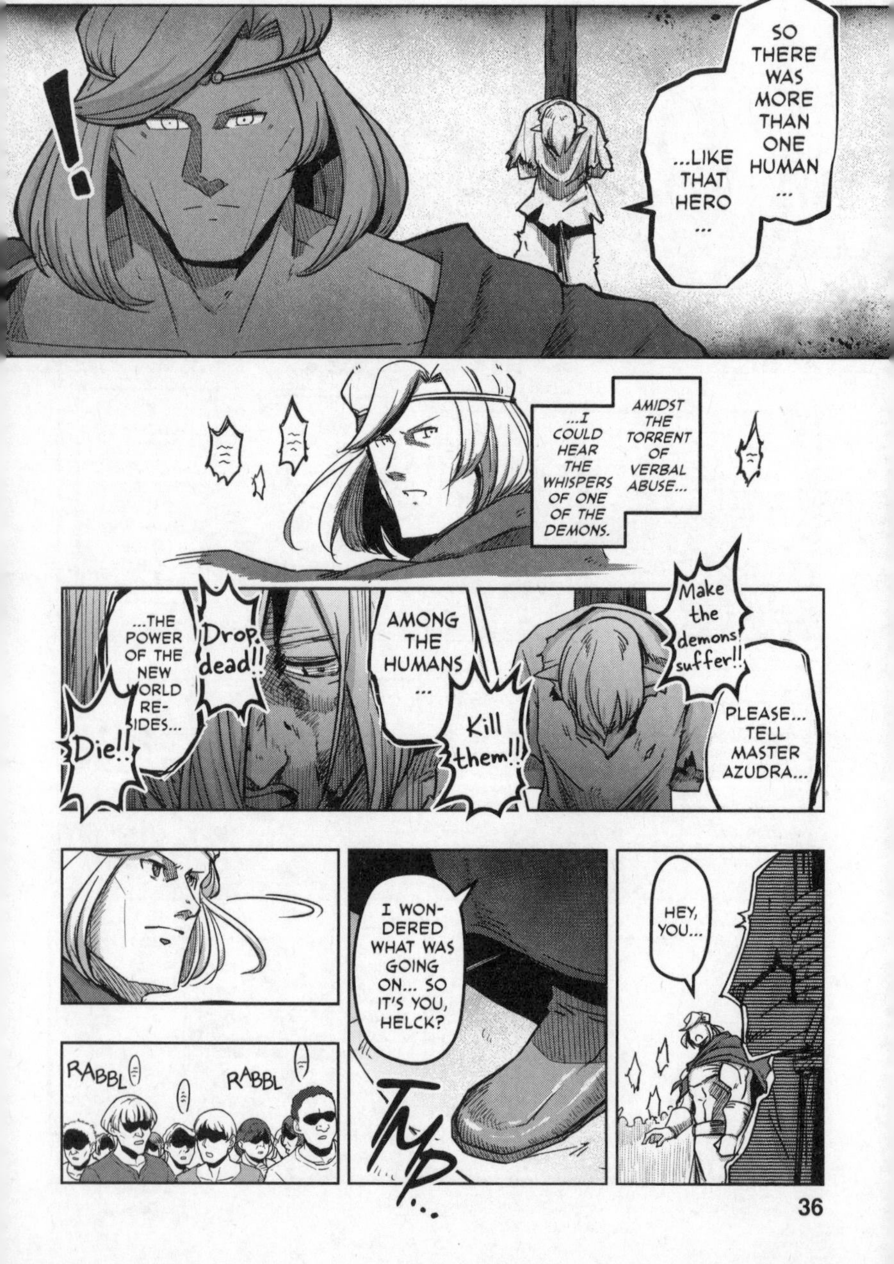
SO THERE WAS MORE THAN ONE HUMAN ...
...LIKE THAT HERO ...
!
AMIDST THE TORRENT OF VERBAL ABUSE...
...I COULD HEAR THE WHISPERS OF ONE OF THE DEMONS.
Make the demons suffer!!
PLEASE... TELL MASTER AZUDRA...
Kill them!!
AMONG THE HUMANS ...
Drop dead!!
...THE POWER OF THE NEW WORLD RESIDES...
Die!!
HEY, YOU...
I WONDERED WHAT WAS GOING ON... SO IT'S YOU, HELCK?
TMP...
RABBL
RABBL

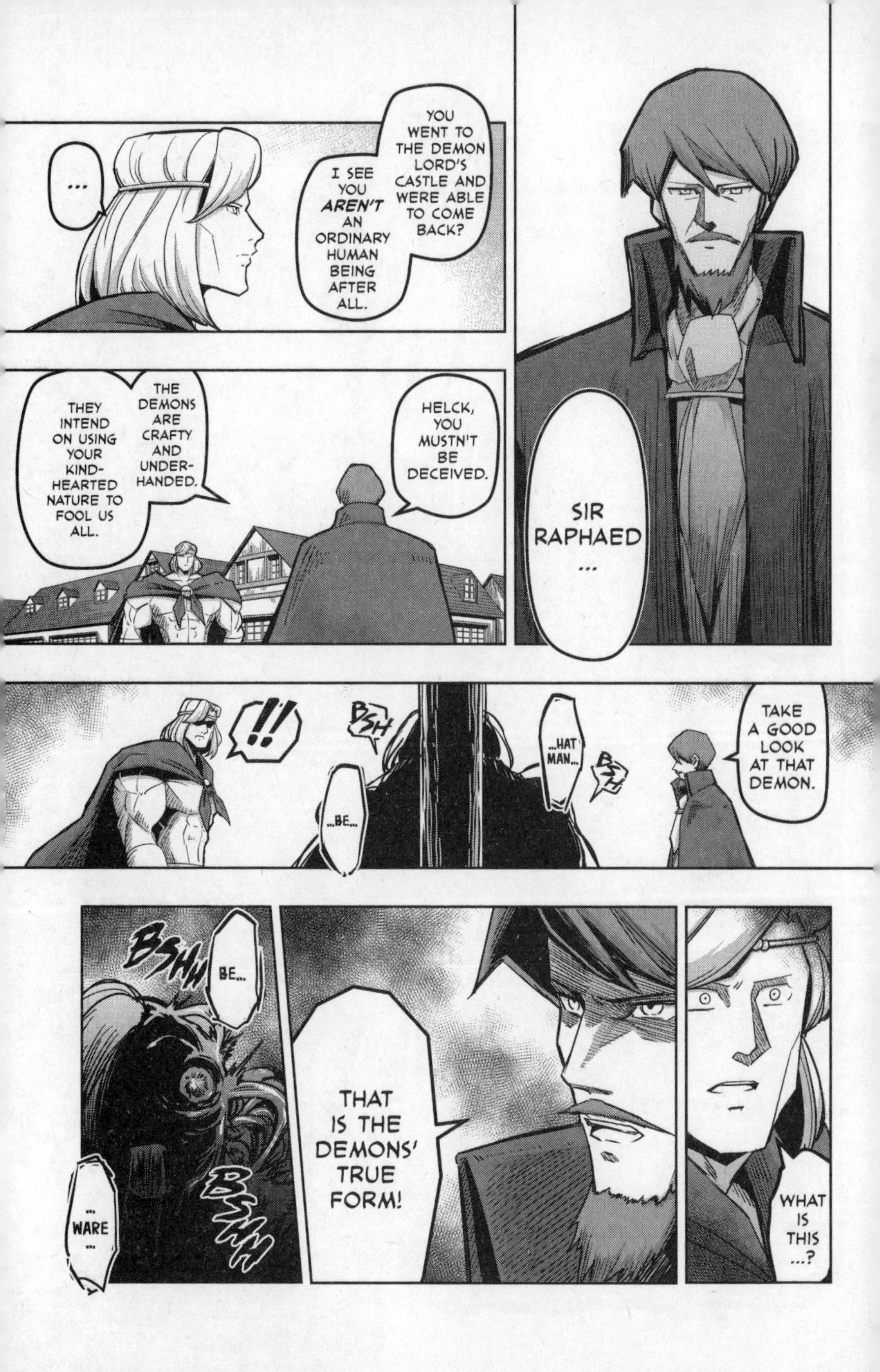
SIR RAPHAED ...
YOU WENT TO THE DEMON LORD'S CASTLE AND WERE ABLE TO COME BACK?
I SEE YOU *AREN'T* AN ORDINARY HUMAN BEING AFTER ALL.
...
HELCK, YOU MUSTN'T BE DECEIVED.
THE DEMONS ARE CRAFTY AND UNDER-HANDED.
THEY INTEND ON USING YOUR KIND-HEARTED NATURE TO FOOL US ALL.
TAKE A GOOD LOOK AT THAT DEMON.
BSH
...HAT MAN...
BSH
...BE...
!!
WHAT IS THIS ...?
THAT IS THE DEMONS' TRUE FORM!
BSHH
BE...
BSHH
... WARE ...

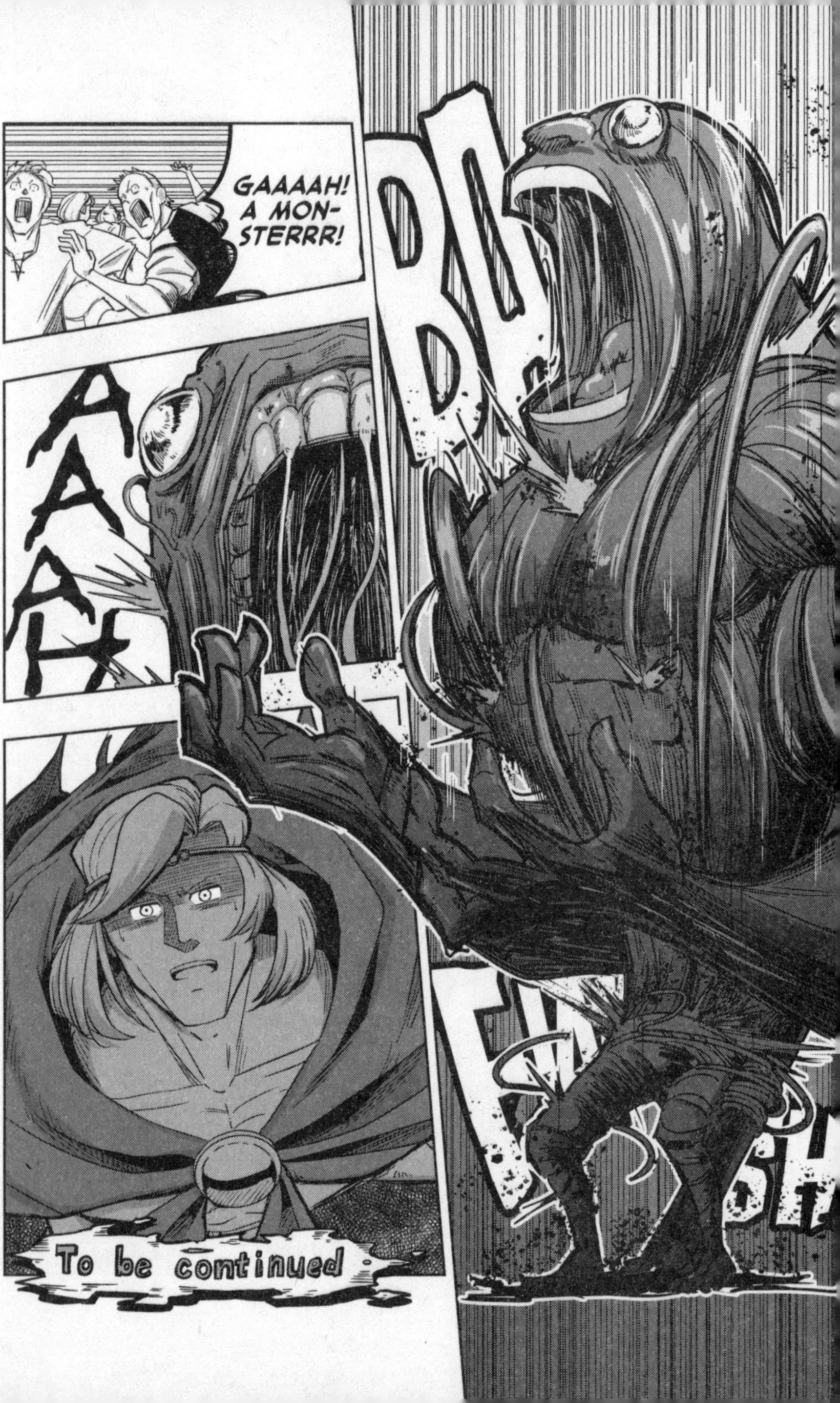
GAAAAH! A MONSTERRR!
AAAH
To be continued

BWSH
BWSH!
Chapter 44: Helck's Past IX
Eeeeek!
Aaah!!
WHAT IS THIS ...?
!!
AAAH!!
BWSH
BWSH
AGAAAH!!

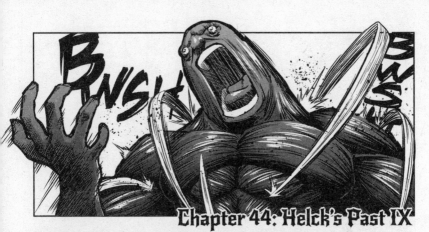

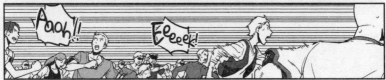

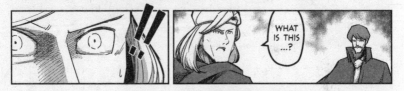

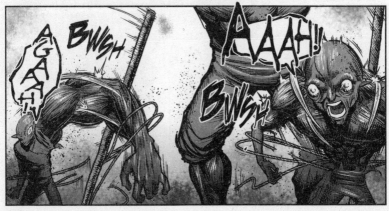

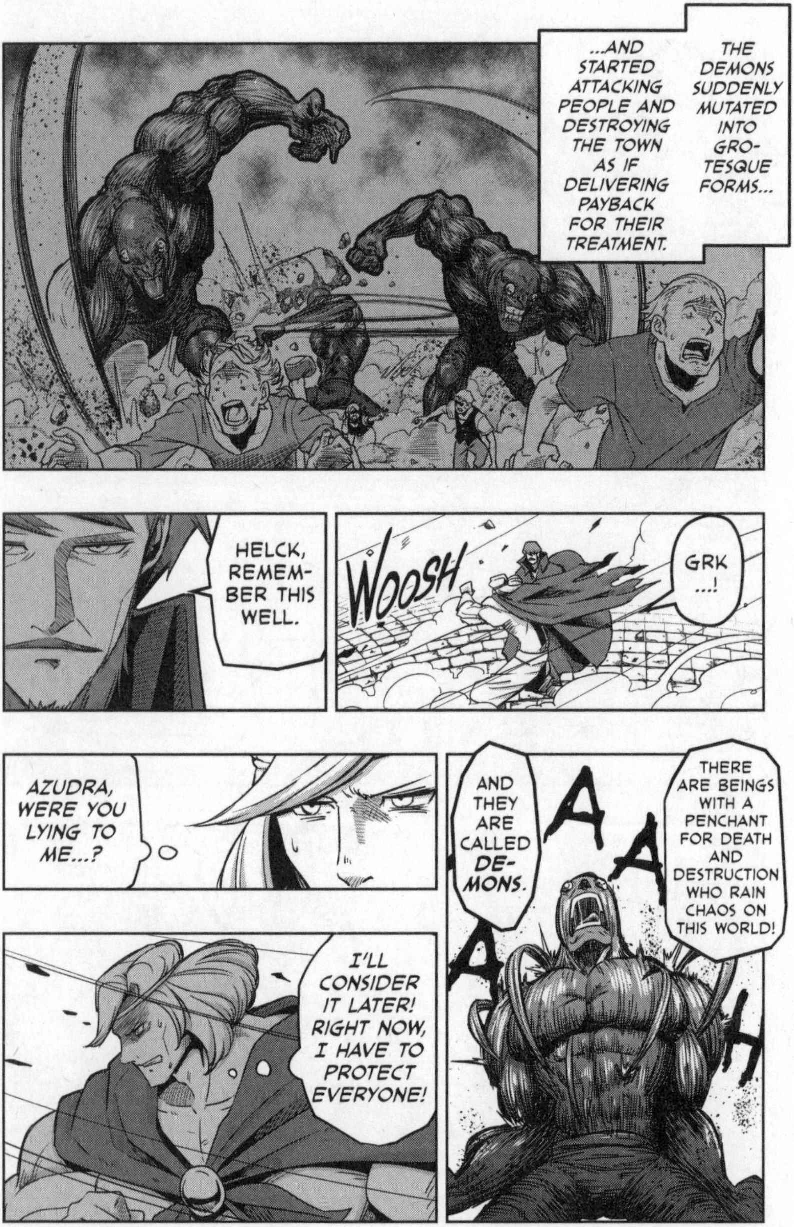
THE DEMONS SUDDENLY MUTATED INTO GRO-TESQUE FORMS...
...AND STARTED ATTACKING PEOPLE AND DESTROYING THE TOWN AS IF DELIVERING PAYBACK FOR THEIR TREATMENT.
WOOSH
GRK ...!
HELCK, REMEM-BER THIS WELL.
THERE ARE BEINGS WITH A PENCHANT FOR DEATH AND DESTRUCTION WHO RAIN CHAOS ON THIS WORLD!
AND THEY ARE CALLED *DE-MONS.*
AAAAH
AZUDRA, WERE YOU LYING TO ME...?
I'LL CONSIDER IT LATER! RIGHT NOW, I HAVE TO PROTECT EVERYONE!

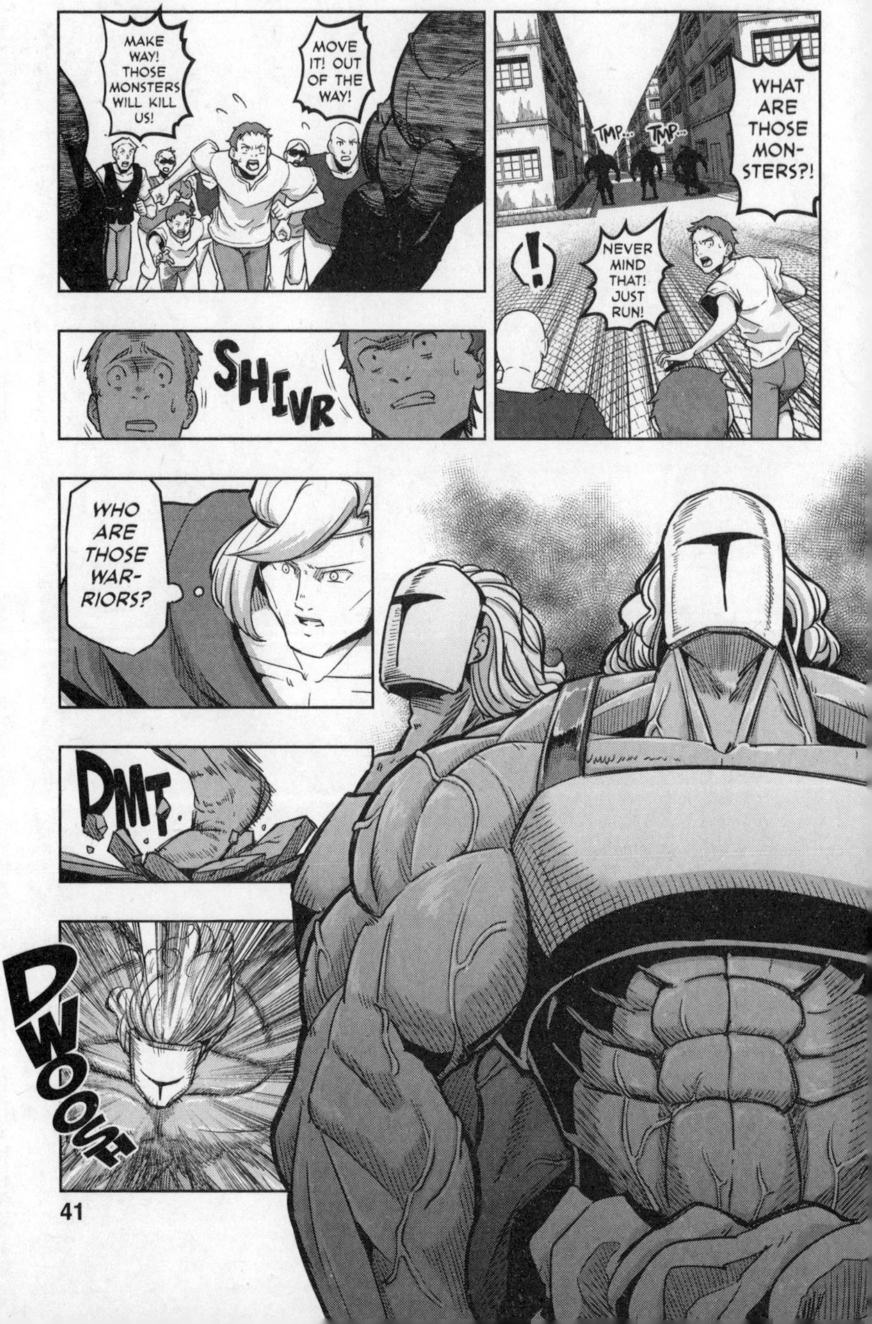
WHAT ARE THOSE MONSTERS?!
TMP... TMP...
!
NEVER MIND THAT! JUST RUN!
MOVE IT! OUT OF THE WAY!
MAKE WAY! THOSE MONSTERS WILL KILL US!
SHIVR
WHO ARE THOSE WARRIORS?
DMT
DWOOMF

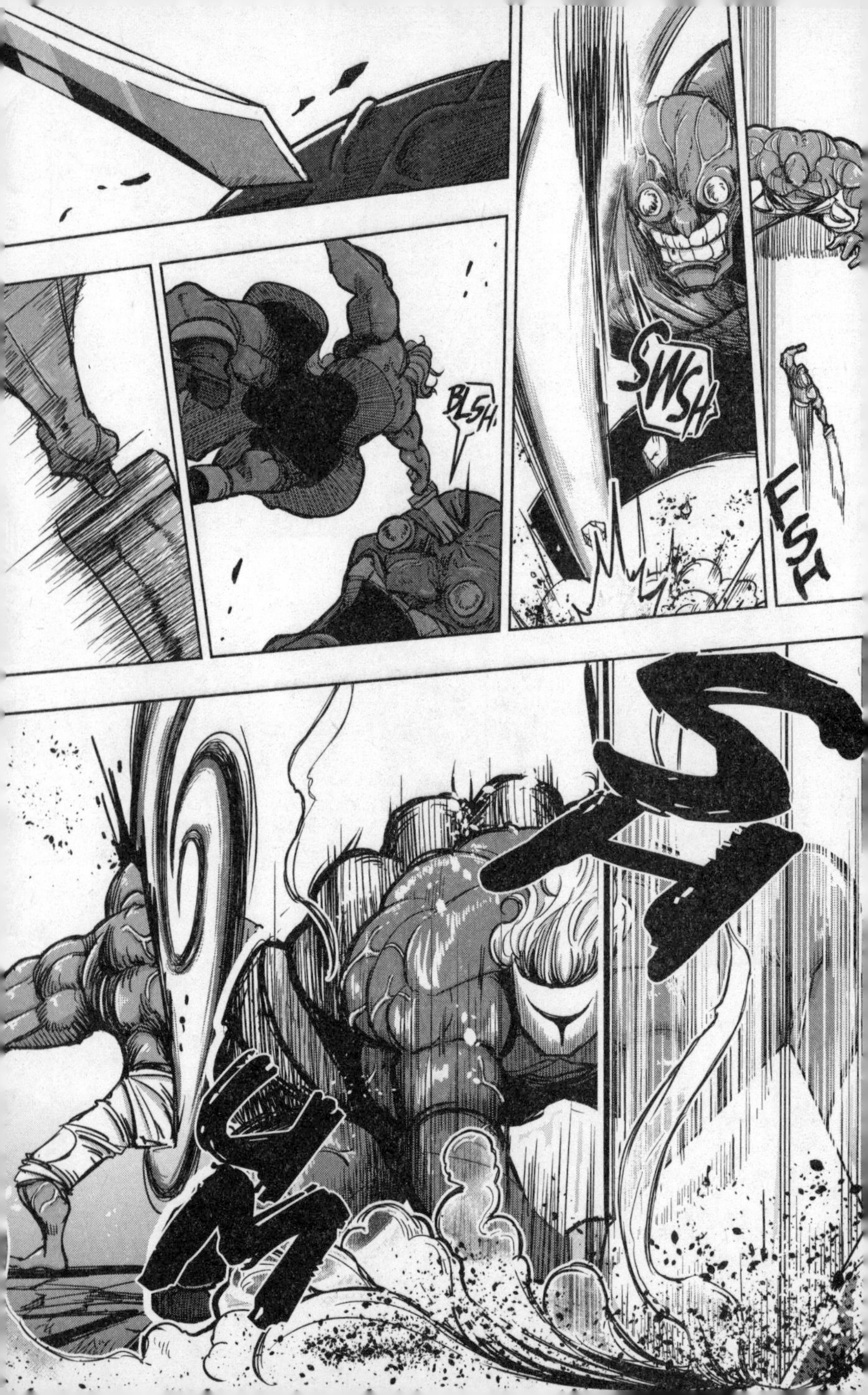
ESH
SWSH
BLSH.

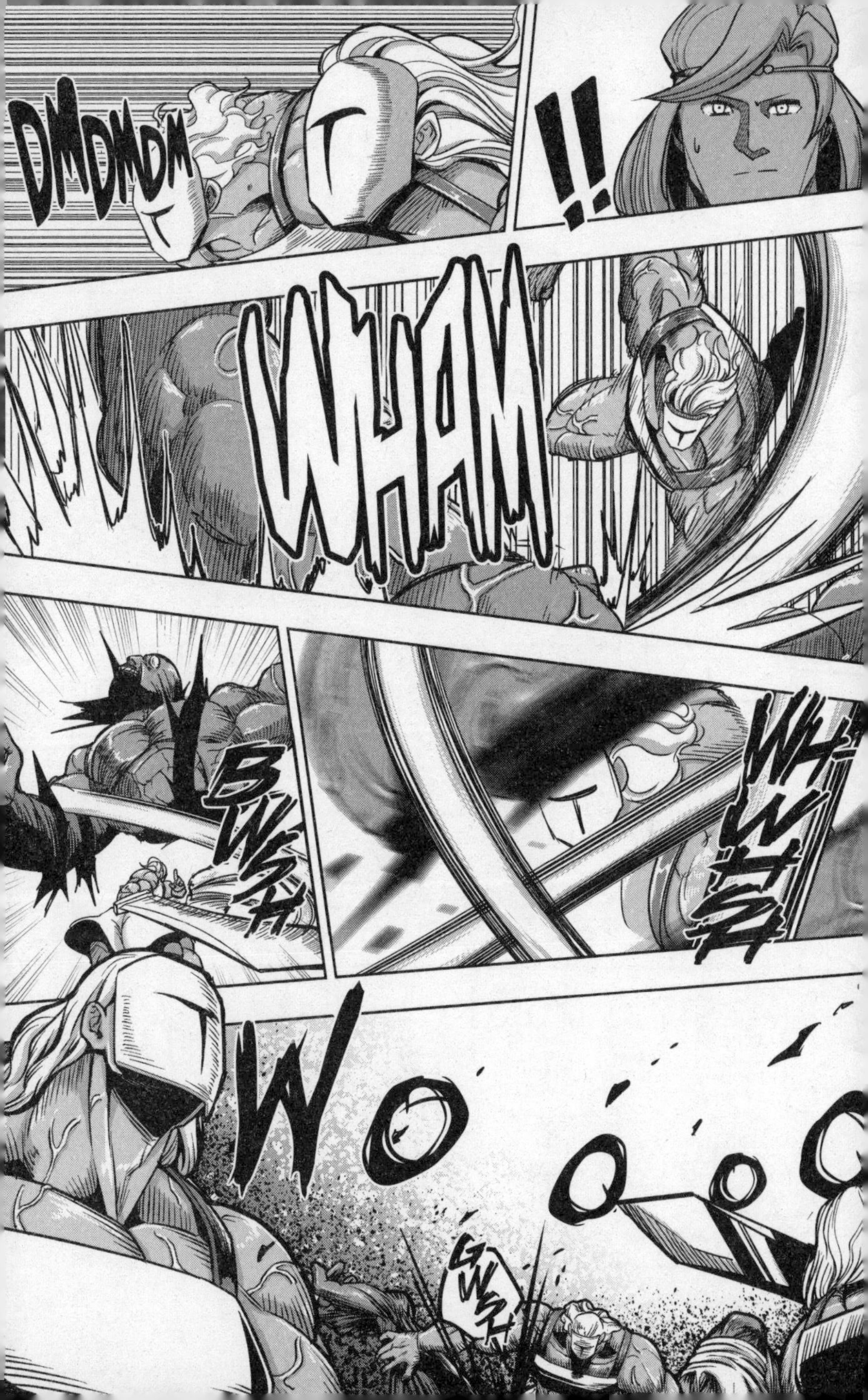
!!
DMDMDM
WHAM
WHWHSH
BWSH
WOOOOO
GWSH

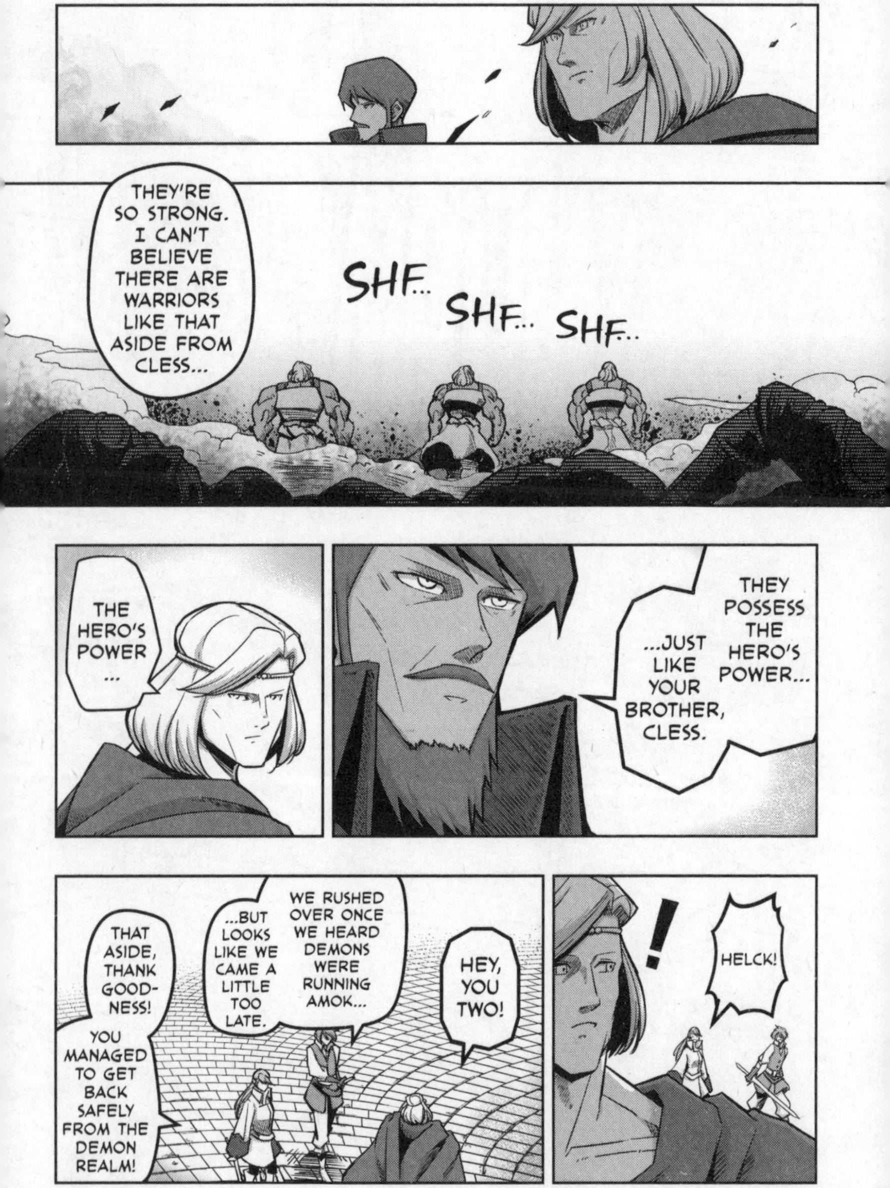
THEY'RE SO STRONG. I CAN'T BELIEVE THERE ARE WARRIORS LIKE THAT ASIDE FROM CLESS...
SHF...
SHF...
SHF...
THEY POSSESS THE HERO'S POWER...
...JUST LIKE YOUR BROTHER, CLESS.
THE HERO'S POWER ...
!
HELCK!
HEY, YOU TWO!
WE RUSHED OVER ONCE WE HEARD DEMONS WERE RUNNING AMOK...
...BUT LOOKS LIKE WE CAME A LITTLE TOO LATE.
THAT ASIDE, THANK GOOD-NESS!
YOU MANAGED TO GET BACK SAFELY FROM THE DEMON REALM!

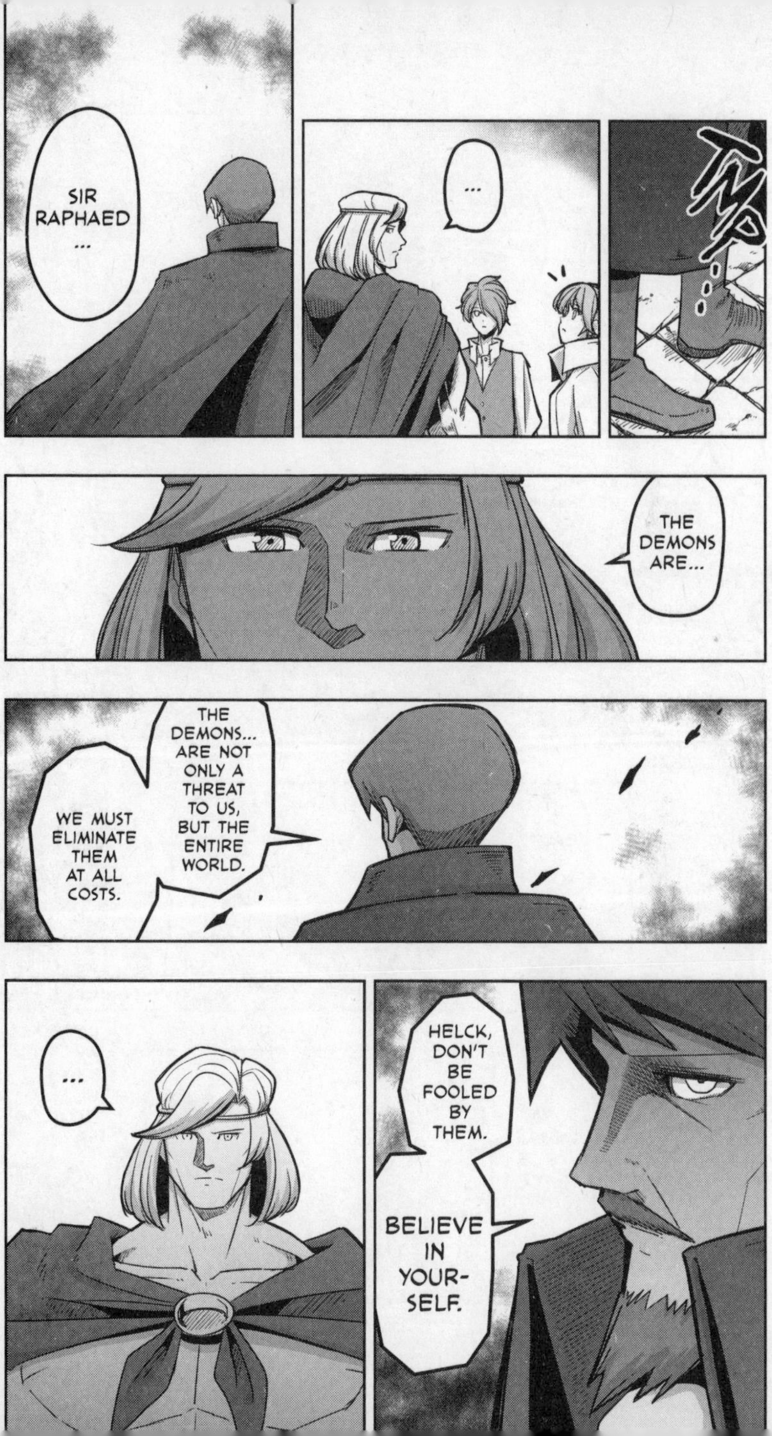
TMP...
...
SIR RAPHAED ...
THE DEMONS ARE...
THE DEMONS... ARE NOT ONLY A THREAT TO US, BUT THE ENTIRE WORLD.
WE MUST ELIMINATE THEM AT ALL COSTS.
HELCK, DON'T BE FOOLED BY THEM.
BELIEVE IN YOUR-SELF.
...

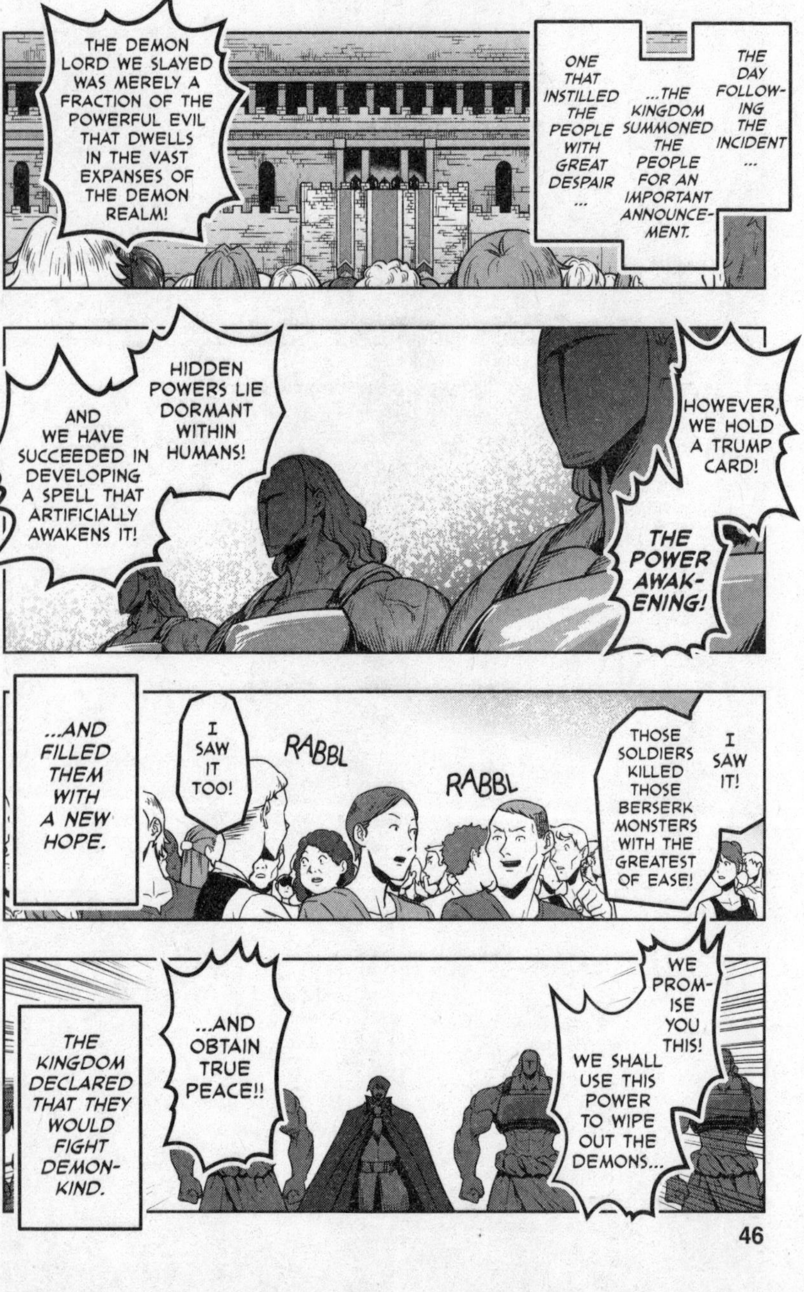

THE DAY FOLLOWING THE INCIDENT...
...THE KINGDOM SUMMONED THE PEOPLE FOR AN IMPORTANT ANNOUNCEMENT.
ONE THAT INSTILLED THE PEOPLE WITH GREAT DESPAIR...
THE DEMON LORD WE SLAYED WAS MERELY A FRACTION OF THE POWERFUL EVIL THAT DWELLS IN THE VAST EXPANSES OF THE DEMON REALM!
HOWEVER, WE HOLD A TRUMP CARD!
THE POWER AWAKENING!
HIDDEN POWERS LIE DORMANT WITHIN HUMANS!
AND WE HAVE SUCCEEDED IN DEVELOPING A SPELL THAT ARTIFICIALLY AWAKENS IT!
I SAW IT!
THOSE SOLDIERS KILLED THOSE BERSERK MONSTERS WITH THE GREATEST OF EASE!
RABBL
RABBL
I SAW IT TOO!
...AND FILLED THEM WITH A NEW HOPE.
WE PROMISE YOU THIS!
WE SHALL USE THIS POWER TO WIPE OUT THE DEMONS...
...AND OBTAIN TRUE PEACE!!
THE KINGDOM DECLARED THAT THEY WOULD FIGHT DEMONKIND.

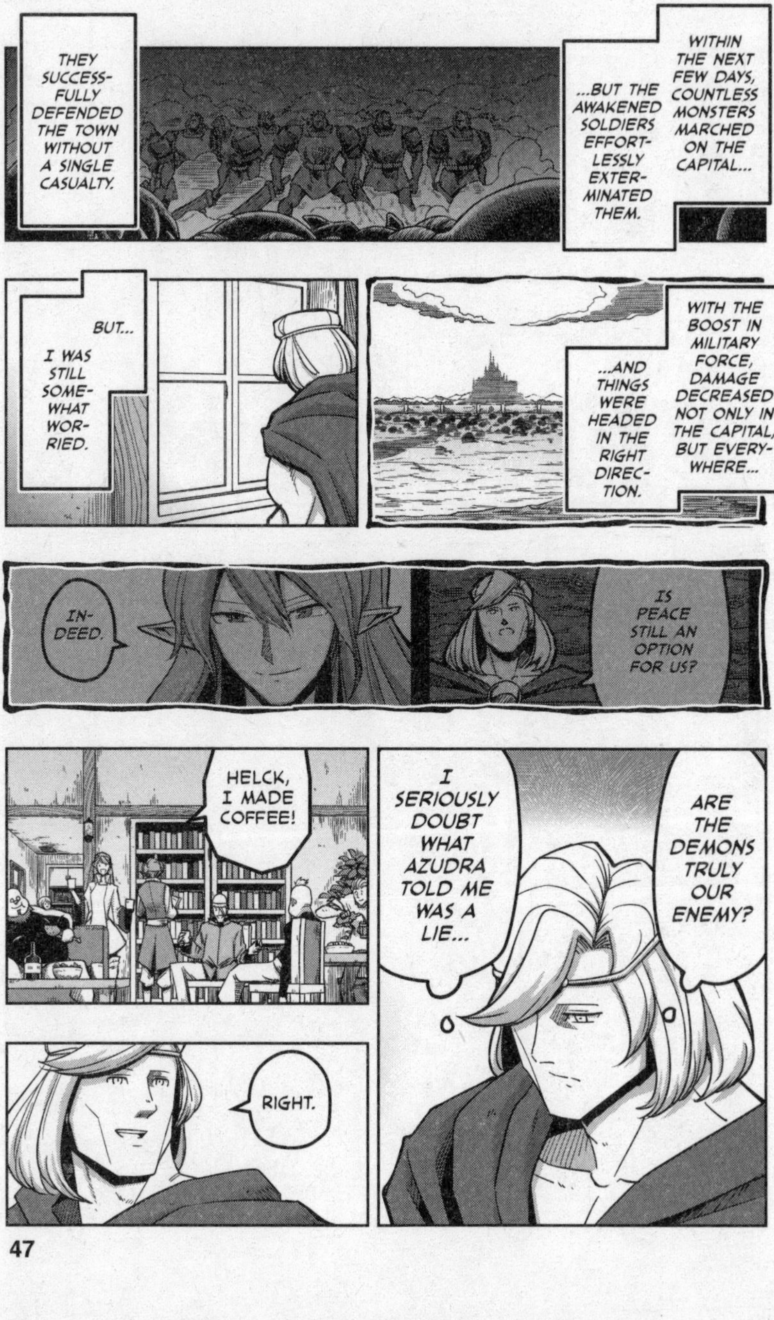
WITHIN THE NEXT FEW DAYS, COUNTLESS MONSTERS MARCHED ON THE CAPITAL...
...BUT THE AWAKENED SOLDIERS EFFORTLESSLY EXTERMINATED THEM.
THEY SUCCESSFULLY DEFENDED THE TOWN WITHOUT A SINGLE CASUALTY.
WITH THE BOOST IN MILITARY FORCE, DAMAGE DECREASED NOT ONLY IN THE CAPITAL, BUT EVERYWHERE...
...AND THINGS WERE HEADED IN THE RIGHT DIRECTION.
BUT...
I WAS STILL SOMEWHAT WORRIED.
IS PEACE STILL AN OPTION FOR US?
INDEED.
ARE THE DEMONS TRULY OUR ENEMY?
I SERIOUSLY DOUBT WHAT AZUDRA TOLD ME WAS A LIE...
HELCK, I MADE COFFEE!
RIGHT.

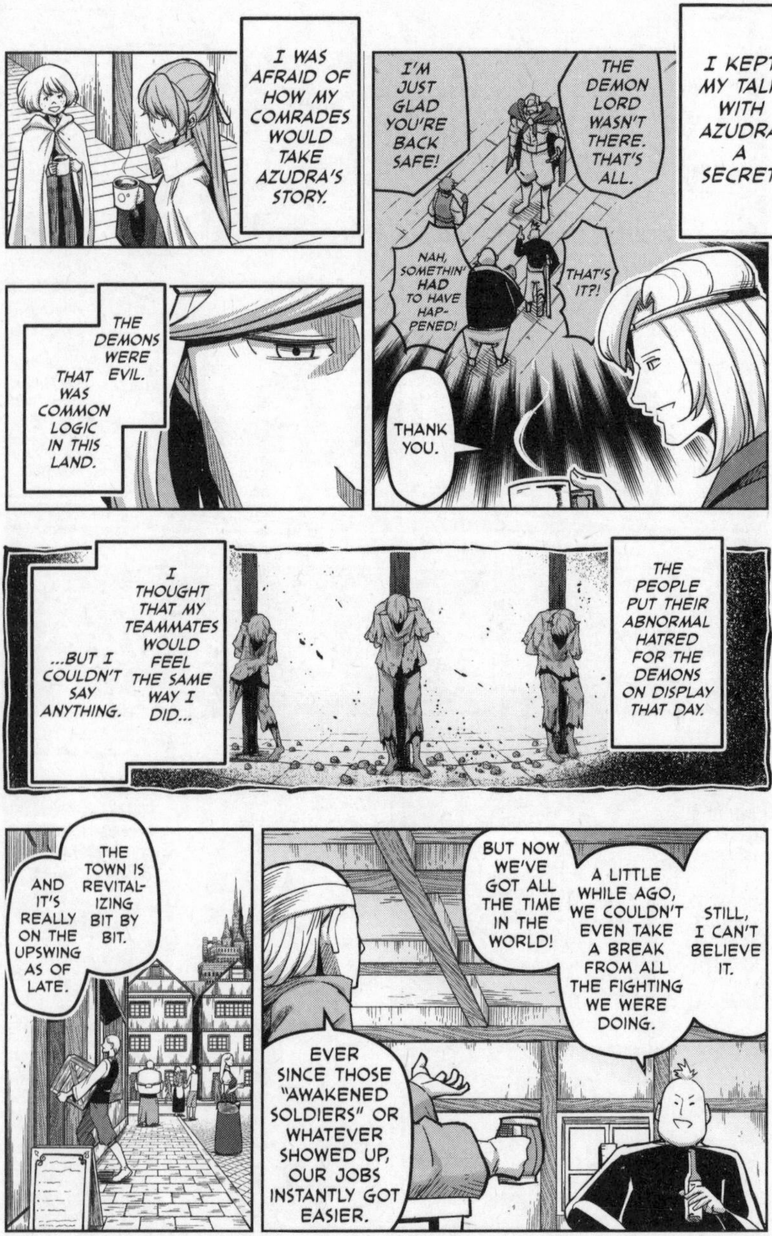
I KEPT MY TALK WITH AZUDRA A SECRET.
THE DEMON LORD WASN'T THERE. THAT'S ALL.
I'M JUST GLAD YOU'RE BACK SAFE!
THAT'S IT?!
NAH, SOMETHIN' HAD TO HAVE HAP-PENED!
THANK YOU.
I WAS AFRAID OF HOW MY COMRADES WOULD TAKE AZUDRA'S STORY.
THE DEMONS WERE EVIL.
THAT WAS COMMON LOGIC IN THIS LAND.
THE PEOPLE PUT THEIR ABNORMAL HATRED FOR THE DEMONS ON DISPLAY THAT DAY.
I THOUGHT THAT MY TEAMMATES WOULD FEEL THE SAME WAY I DID...
...BUT I COULDN'T SAY ANYTHING.
STILL, I CAN'T BELIEVE IT.
A LITTLE WHILE AGO, WE COULDN'T EVEN TAKE A BREAK FROM ALL THE FIGHTING WE WERE DOING.
BUT NOW WE'VE GOT ALL THE TIME IN THE WORLD!
EVER SINCE THOSE "AWAKENED SOLDIERS" OR WHATEVER SHOWED UP, OUR JOBS INSTANTLY GOT EASIER.
THE TOWN IS REVITAL-IZING BIT BY BIT.
AND IT'S REALLY ON THE UPSWING AS OF LATE.

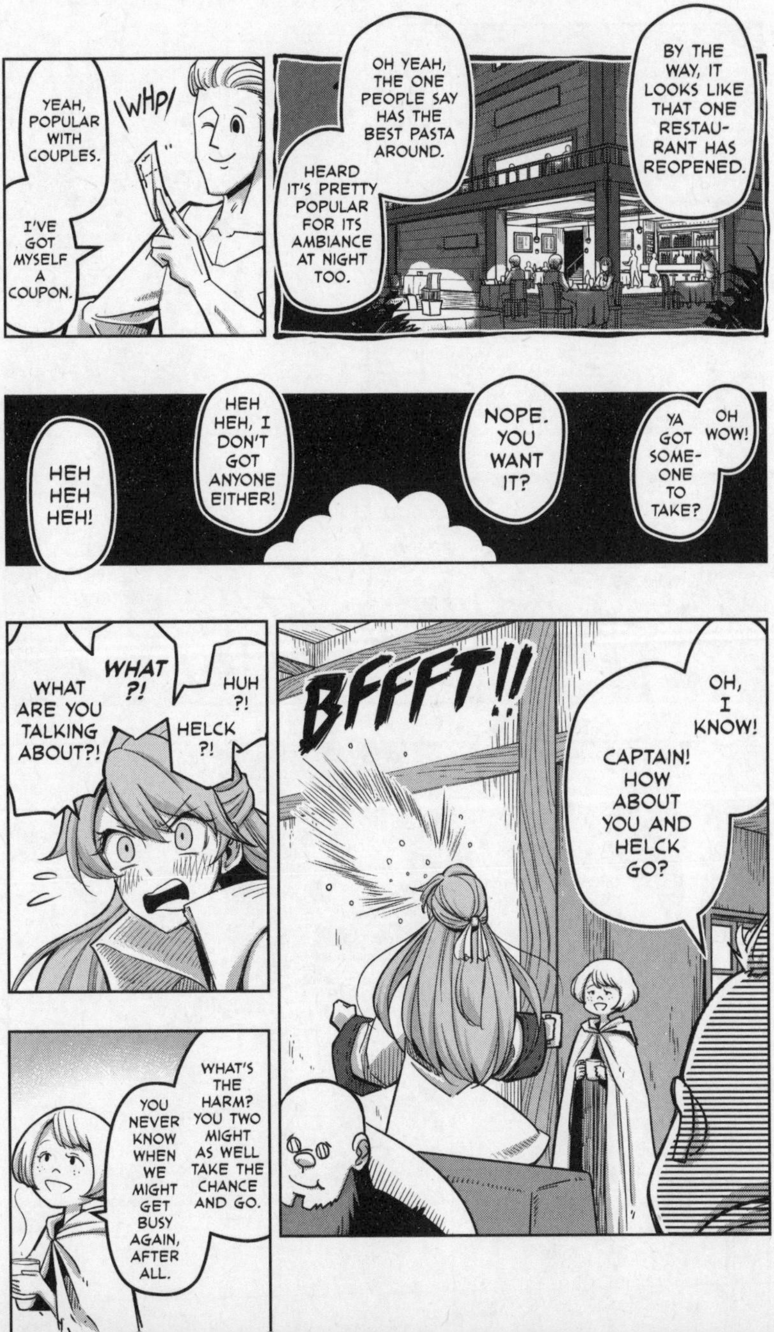
BY THE WAY, IT LOOKS LIKE THAT ONE RESTAU-RANT HAS REOPENED.
OH YEAH, THE ONE PEOPLE SAY HAS THE BEST PASTA AROUND.
HEARD IT'S PRETTY POPULAR FOR ITS AMBIANCE AT NIGHT TOO.
YEAH, POPULAR WITH COUPLES.
WHP
I'VE GOT MYSELF A COUPON.
OH WOW!
YA GOT SOME-ONE TO TAKE?
NOPE. YOU WANT IT?
HEH HEH, I DON'T GOT ANYONE EITHER!
HEH HEH HEH!
OH, I KNOW!
CAPTAIN! HOW ABOUT YOU AND HELCK GO?
BFFFT!!
HUH?!
HELCK?!
WHAT?!
WHAT ARE YOU TALKING ABOUT?!
WHAT'S THE HARM? YOU TWO MIGHT AS WELL TAKE THE CHANCE AND GO.
YOU NEVER KNOW WHEN WE MIGHT GET BUSY AGAIN, AFTER ALL.

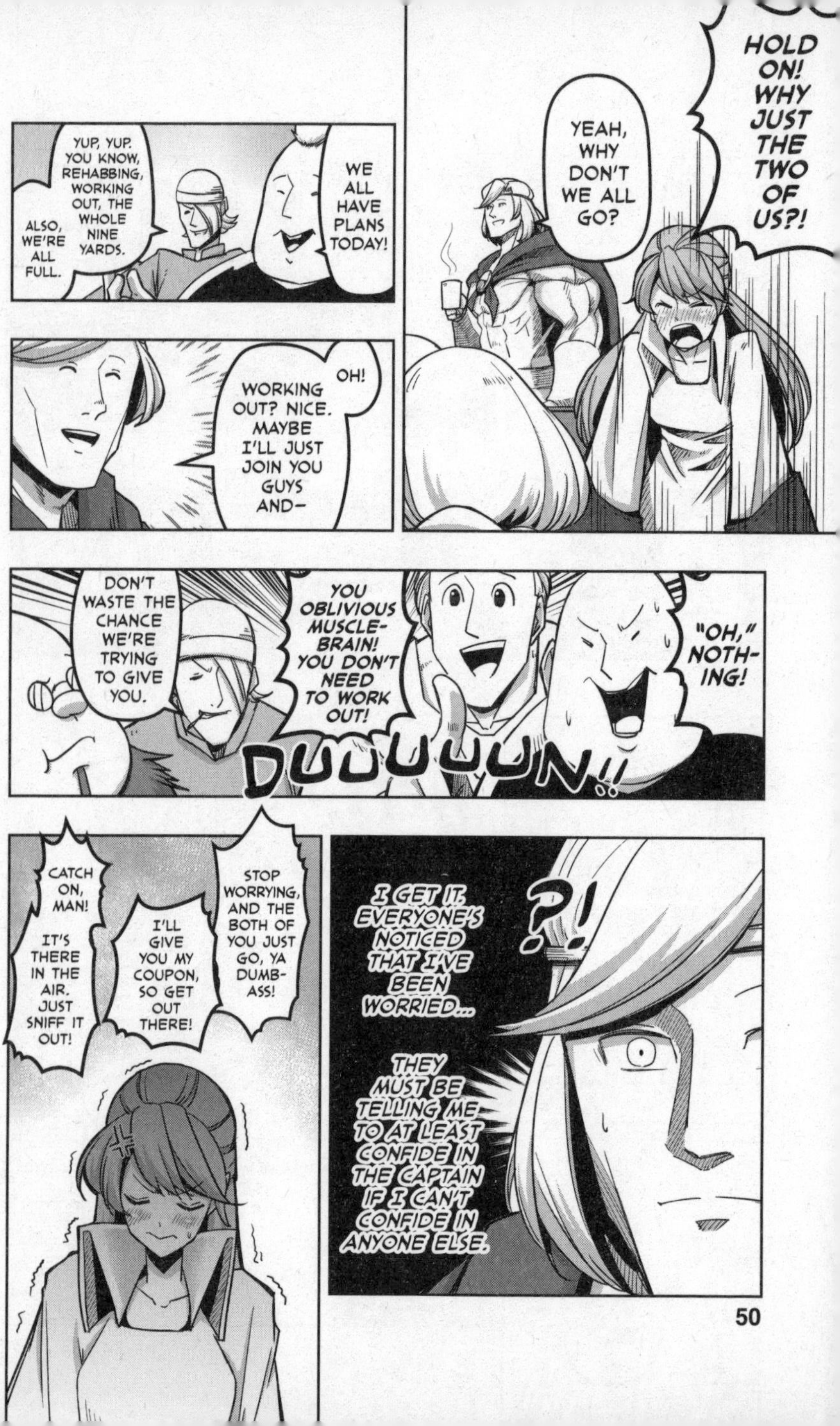
HOLD ON! WHY JUST THE TWO OF US?!
YEAH, WHY DON'T WE ALL GO?
WE ALL HAVE PLANS TODAY!
YUP, YUP. YOU KNOW, REHABBING, WORKING OUT, THE WHOLE NINE YARDS.
ALSO, WE'RE ALL FULL.
OH!
WORKING OUT? NICE. MAYBE I'LL JUST JOIN YOU GUYS AND–
"OH," NOTHING!
YOU OBLIVIOUS MUSCLE-BRAIN! YOU DON'T NEED TO WORK OUT!
DON'T WASTE THE CHANCE WE'RE TRYING TO GIVE YOU.
DUUUUUN!!
?!
I GET IT. EVERYONE'S NOTICED THAT I'VE BEEN WORRIED...
THEY MUST BE TELLING ME TO AT LEAST CONFIDE IN THE CAPTAIN IF I CAN'T CONFIDE IN ANYONE ELSE.
STOP WORRYING, AND THE BOTH OF YOU JUST GO, YA DUMB-ASS!
I'LL GIVE YOU MY COUPON, SO GET OUT THERE!
CATCH ON, MAN!
IT'S THERE IN THE AIR. JUST SNIFF IT OUT!

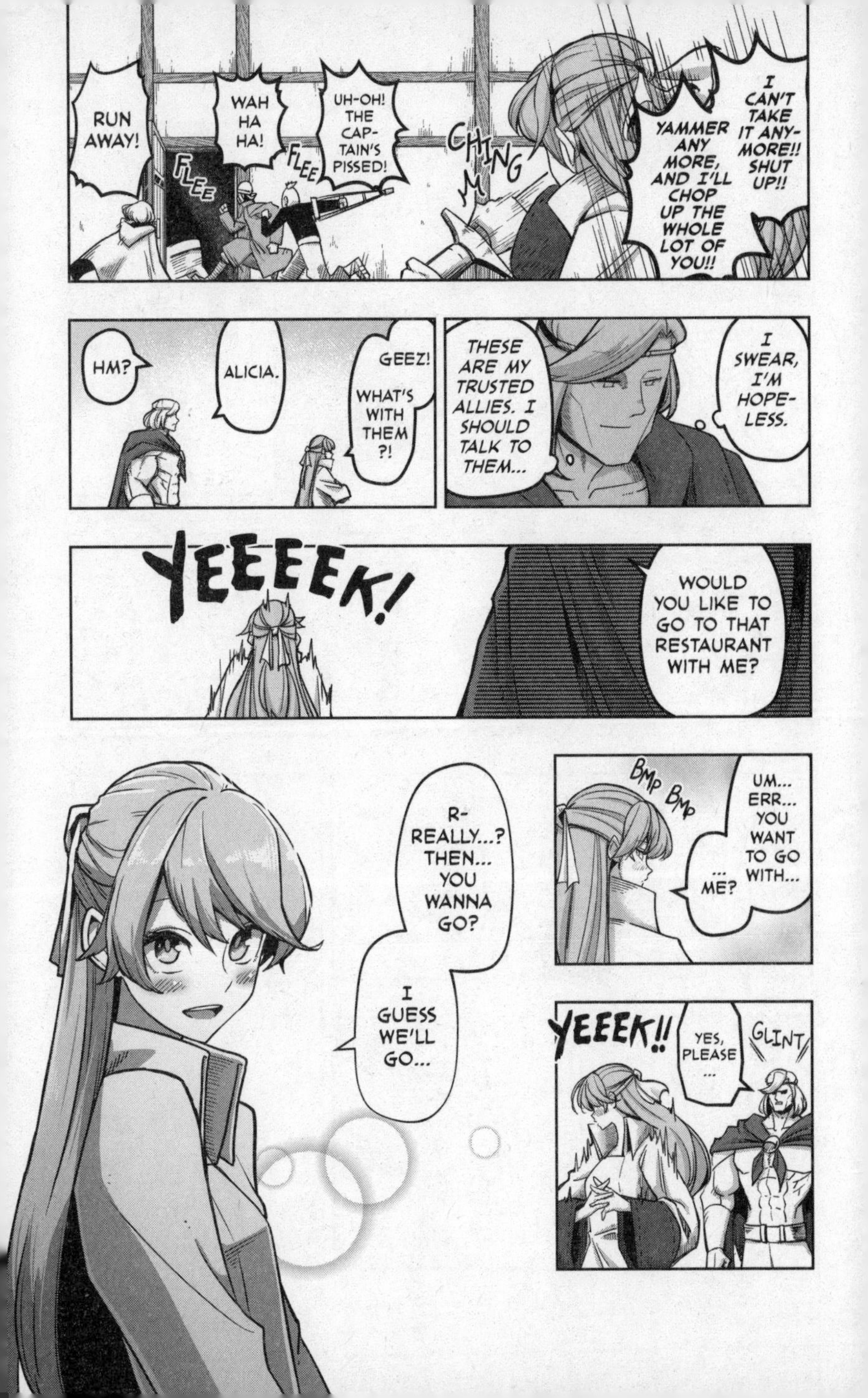
I CAN'T TAKE IT ANYMORE!! SHUT UP!!
YAMMER ANY MORE, AND I'LL CHOP UP THE WHOLE LOT OF YOU!!
CHING
UH-OH! THE CAP-TAIN'S PISSED!
FLEE
WAH HA HA!
FLEE
RUN AWAY!
I SWEAR, I'M HOPE-LESS.
THESE ARE MY TRUSTED ALLIES. I SHOULD TALK TO THEM...
GEEZ! WHAT'S WITH THEM ?!
ALICIA.
HM?
WOULD YOU LIKE TO GO TO THAT RESTAURANT WITH ME?
YEEEEK!
UM... ERR... YOU WANT TO GO WITH...
... ME?
BMP BMP
GLINT
YES, PLEASE ...
YEEEK!!
R-REALLY...? THEN... YOU WANNA GO?
I GUESS WE'LL GO...

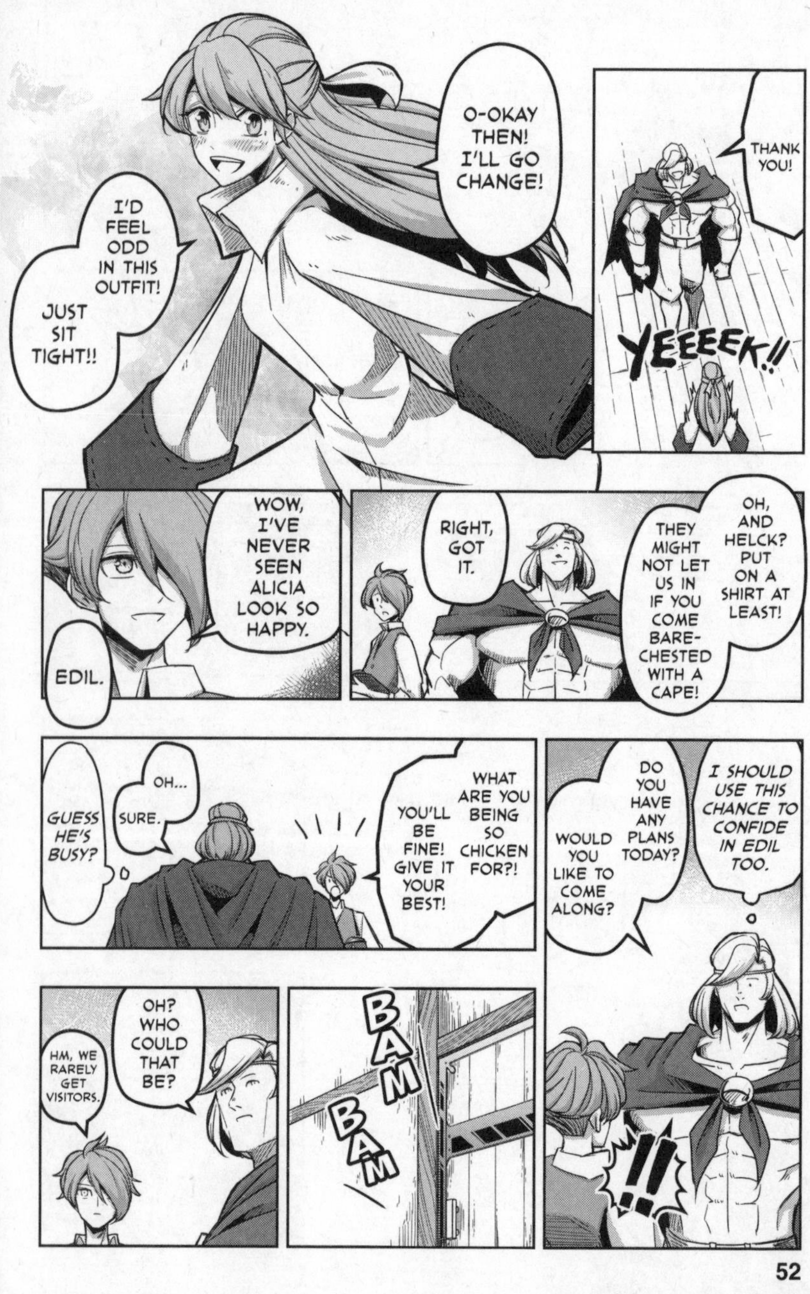
THANK YOU!
YEEEEK!!
O-OKAY THEN! I'LL GO CHANGE!
I'D FEEL ODD IN THIS OUTFIT!
JUST SIT TIGHT!!
OH, AND HELCK? PUT ON A SHIRT AT LEAST!
THEY MIGHT NOT LET US IN IF YOU COME BARE-CHESTED WITH A CAPE!
RIGHT, GOT IT.
WOW, I'VE NEVER SEEN ALICIA LOOK SO HAPPY.
EDIL.
I SHOULD USE THIS CHANCE TO CONFIDE IN EDIL TOO.
DO YOU HAVE ANY PLANS TODAY?
WOULD YOU LIKE TO COME ALONG?
!!
WHAT ARE YOU BEING SO CHICKEN FOR?!
YOU'LL BE FINE! GIVE IT YOUR BEST!
OH... SURE.
GUESS HE'S BUSY?
BAM
BAM
OH? WHO COULD THAT BE?
HM, WE RARELY GET VISITORS.

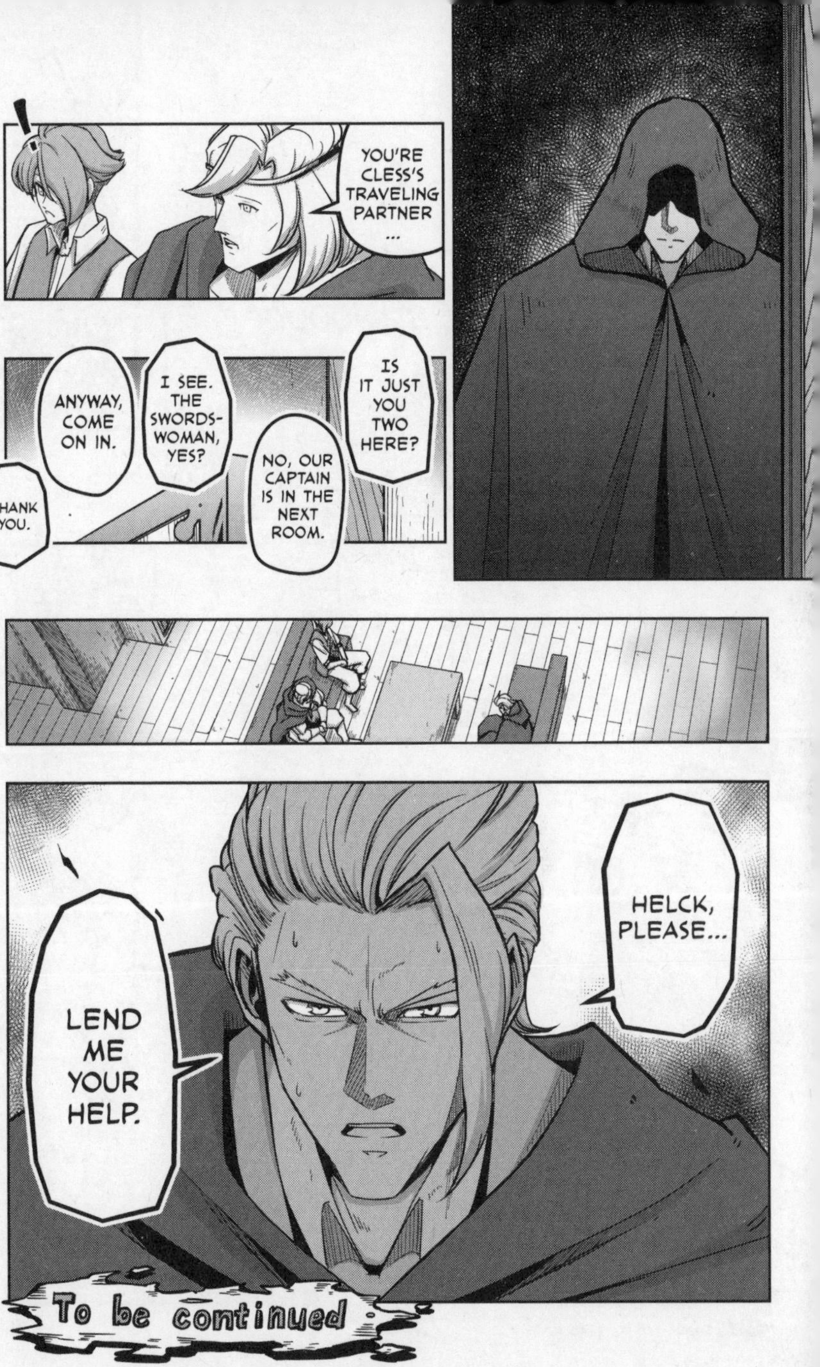
YOU'RE CLESS'S TRAVELING PARTNER ...
IS IT JUST YOU TWO HERE?
NO, OUR CAPTAIN IS IN THE NEXT ROOM.
I SEE. THE SWORDS-WOMAN, YES?
ANYWAY, COME ON IN.
THANK YOU.
HELCK, PLEASE...
LEND ME YOUR HELP.
To be continued

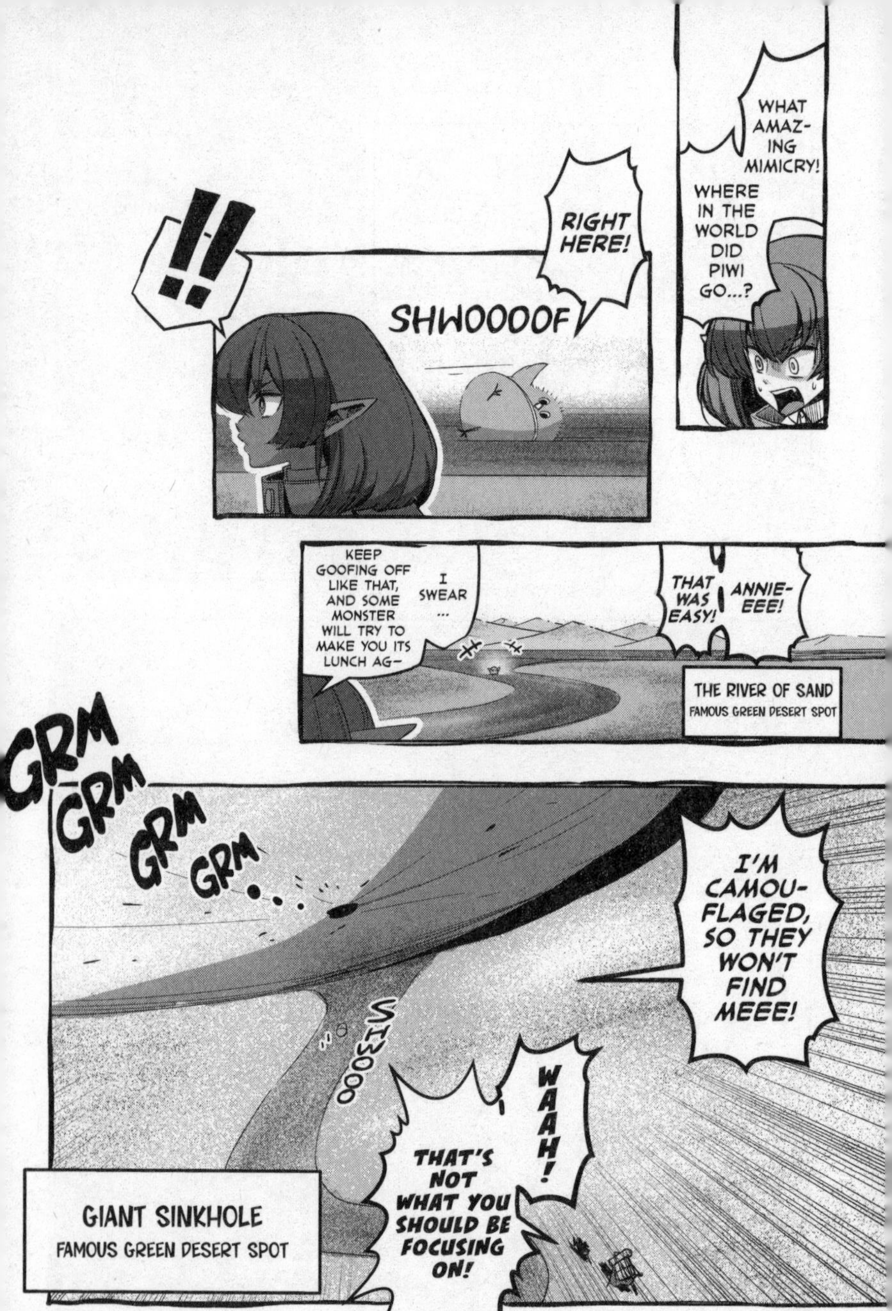

WHAT AMAZ-ING MIMICRY!
WHERE IN THE WORLD DID PIWI GO...?
RIGHT HERE!
!!
SHWOOOOF
ANNIE-EEE!
THAT WAS EASY!
THE RIVER OF SAND
FAMOUS GREEN DESERT SPOT
I SWEAR ...
KEEP GOOFING OFF LIKE THAT, AND SOME MONSTER WILL TRY TO MAKE YOU ITS LUNCH AG–
GRM GRM GRM GRM
I'M CAMOU-FLAGED, SO THEY WON'T FIND MEEE!
WAAH!
THAT'S NOT WHAT YOU SHOULD BE FOCUSING ON!
SHWOOOO
GIANT SINKHOLE
FAMOUS GREEN DESERT SPOT

continued on page 152

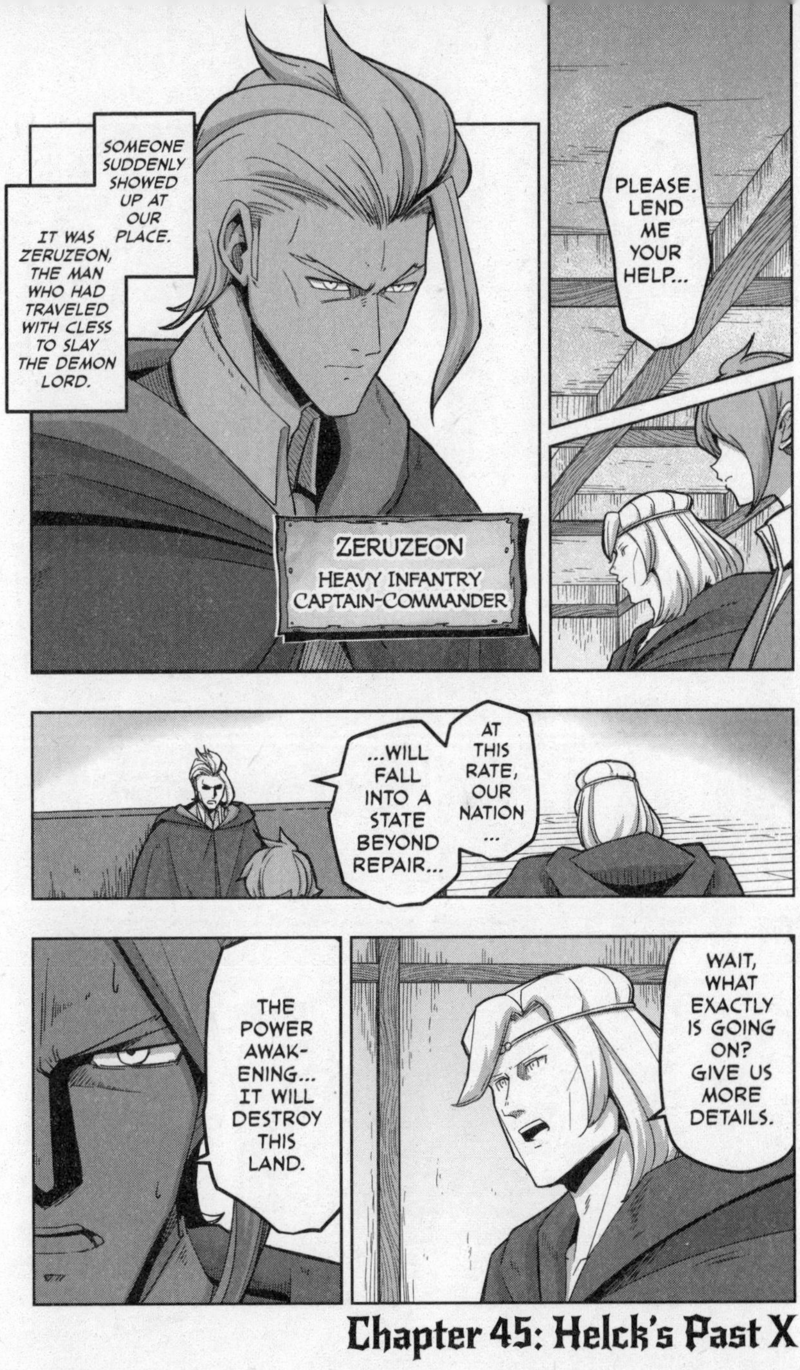
PLEASE. LEND ME YOUR HELP...
SOMEONE SUDDENLY SHOWED UP AT OUR PLACE.
IT WAS ZERUZEON, THE MAN WHO HAD TRAVELED WITH CLESS TO SLAY THE DEMON LORD.
ZERUZEON
HEAVY INFANTRY CAPTAIN-COMMANDER
AT THIS RATE, OUR NATION...
...WILL FALL INTO A STATE BEYOND REPAIR...
WAIT, WHAT EXACTLY IS GOING ON? GIVE US MORE DETAILS.
THE POWER AWAKENING... IT WILL DESTROY THIS LAND.

Chapter 45: Helck's Past X

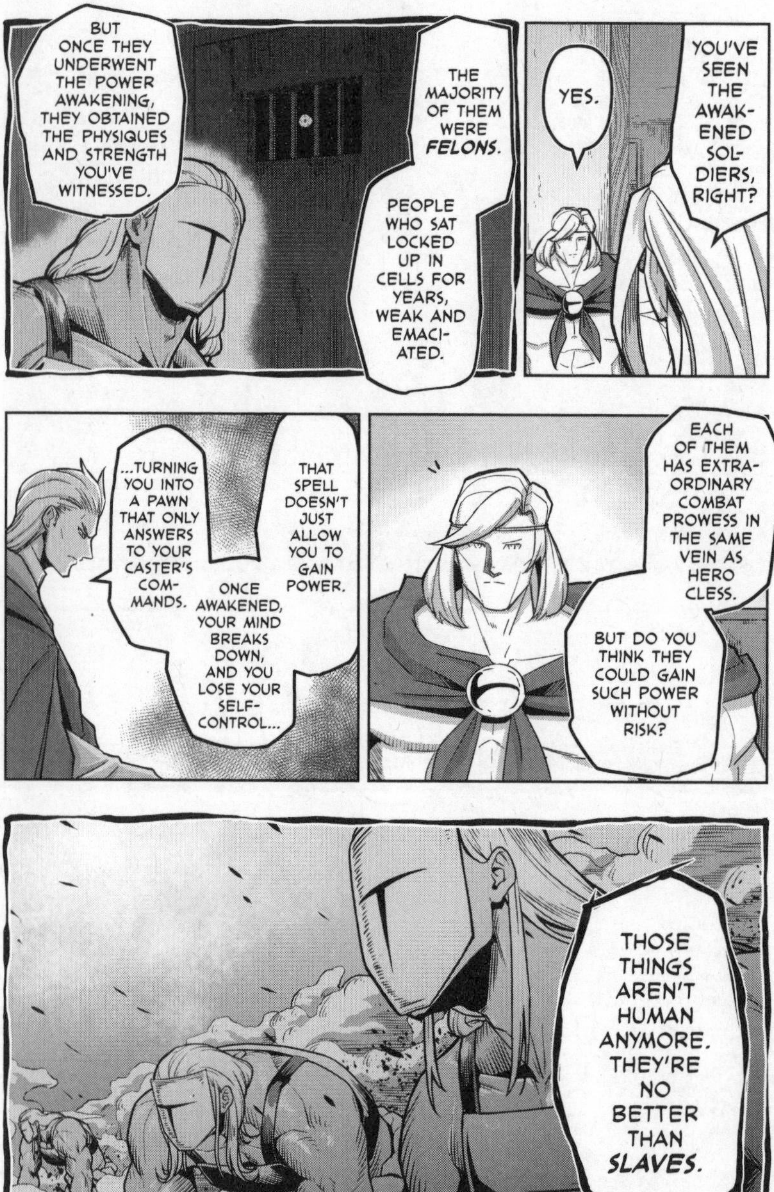
YOU'VE SEEN THE AWAKENED SOLDIERS, RIGHT?
YES.
THE MAJORITY OF THEM WERE *FELONS*.
PEOPLE WHO SAT LOCKED UP IN CELLS FOR YEARS, WEAK AND EMACIATED.
BUT ONCE THEY UNDERWENT THE POWER AWAKENING, THEY OBTAINED THE PHYSIQUES AND STRENGTH YOU'VE WITNESSED.
EACH OF THEM HAS EXTRAORDINARY COMBAT PROWESS IN THE SAME VEIN AS HERO CLESS.
BUT DO YOU THINK THEY COULD GAIN SUCH POWER WITHOUT RISK?
THAT SPELL DOESN'T JUST ALLOW YOU TO GAIN POWER.
ONCE AWAKENED, YOUR MIND BREAKS DOWN, AND YOU LOSE YOUR SELF-CONTROL...
...TURNING YOU INTO A PAWN THAT ONLY ANSWERS TO YOUR CASTER'S COMMANDS.
THOSE THINGS AREN'T HUMAN ANYMORE. THEY'RE NO BETTER THAN *SLAVES*.

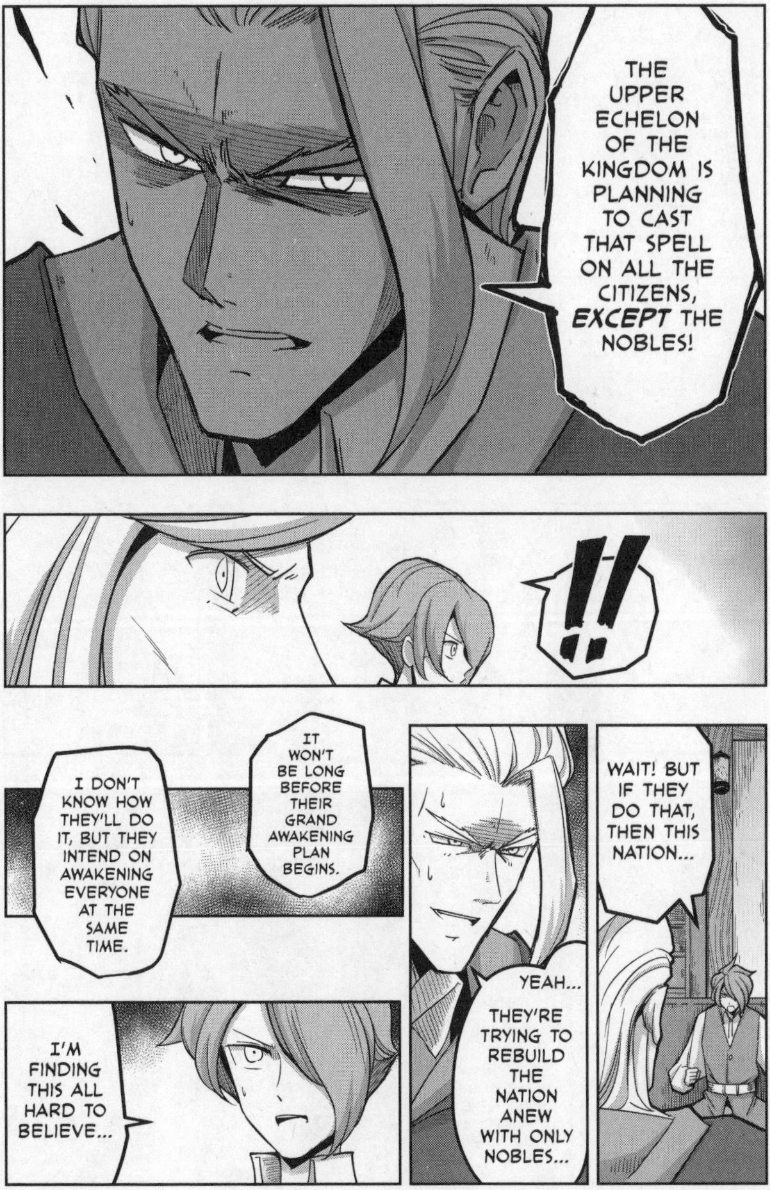

THE UPPER ECHELON OF THE KINGDOM IS PLANNING TO CAST THAT SPELL ON ALL THE CITIZENS, ***EXCEPT*** THE NOBLES!
!!
WAIT! BUT IF THEY DO THAT, THEN THIS NATION...
YEAH...
THEY'RE TRYING TO REBUILD THE NATION ANEW WITH ONLY NOBLES...
IT WON'T BE LONG BEFORE THEIR GRAND AWAKENING PLAN BEGINS.
I DON'T KNOW HOW THEY'LL DO IT, BUT THEY INTEND ON AWAKENING EVERYONE AT THE SAME TIME.
I'M FINDING THIS ALL HARD TO BELIEVE...

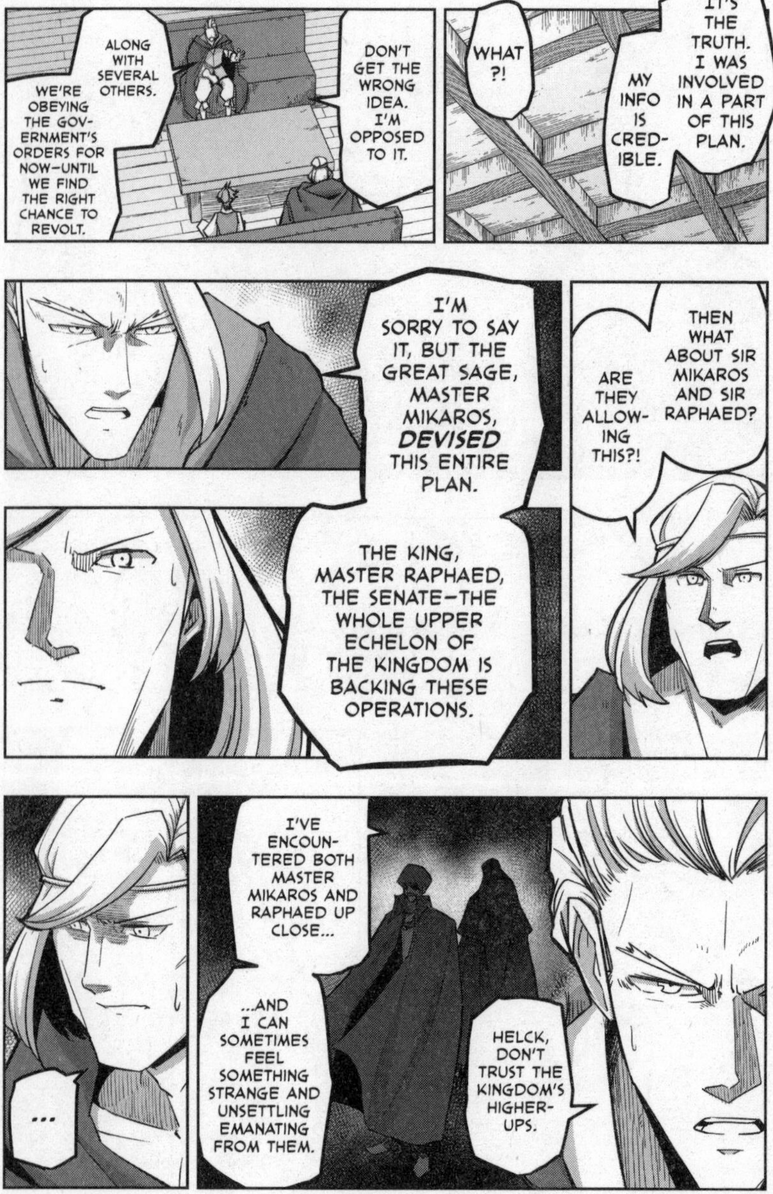

WHAT?!
IT'S THE TRUTH. I WAS INVOLVED IN A PART OF THIS PLAN.
MY INFO IS CREDIBLE.
DON'T GET THE WRONG IDEA. I'M OPPOSED TO IT.
WE'RE OBEYING THE GOVERNMENT'S ORDERS FOR NOW—UNTIL WE FIND THE RIGHT CHANCE TO REVOLT.
ALONG WITH SEVERAL OTHERS.
THEN WHAT ABOUT SIR MIKAROS AND SIR RAPHAED?
ARE THEY ALLOWING THIS?!
I'M SORRY TO SAY IT, BUT THE GREAT SAGE, MASTER MIKAROS, DEVISED THIS ENTIRE PLAN.
THE KING, MASTER RAPHAED, THE SENATE—THE WHOLE UPPER ECHELON OF THE KINGDOM IS BACKING THESE OPERATIONS.
HELCK, DON'T TRUST THE KINGDOM'S HIGHER-UPS.
I'VE ENCOUNTERED BOTH MASTER MIKAROS AND RAPHAED UP CLOSE...
...AND I CAN SOMETIMES FEEL SOMETHING STRANGE AND UNSETTLING EMANATING FROM THEM.
...

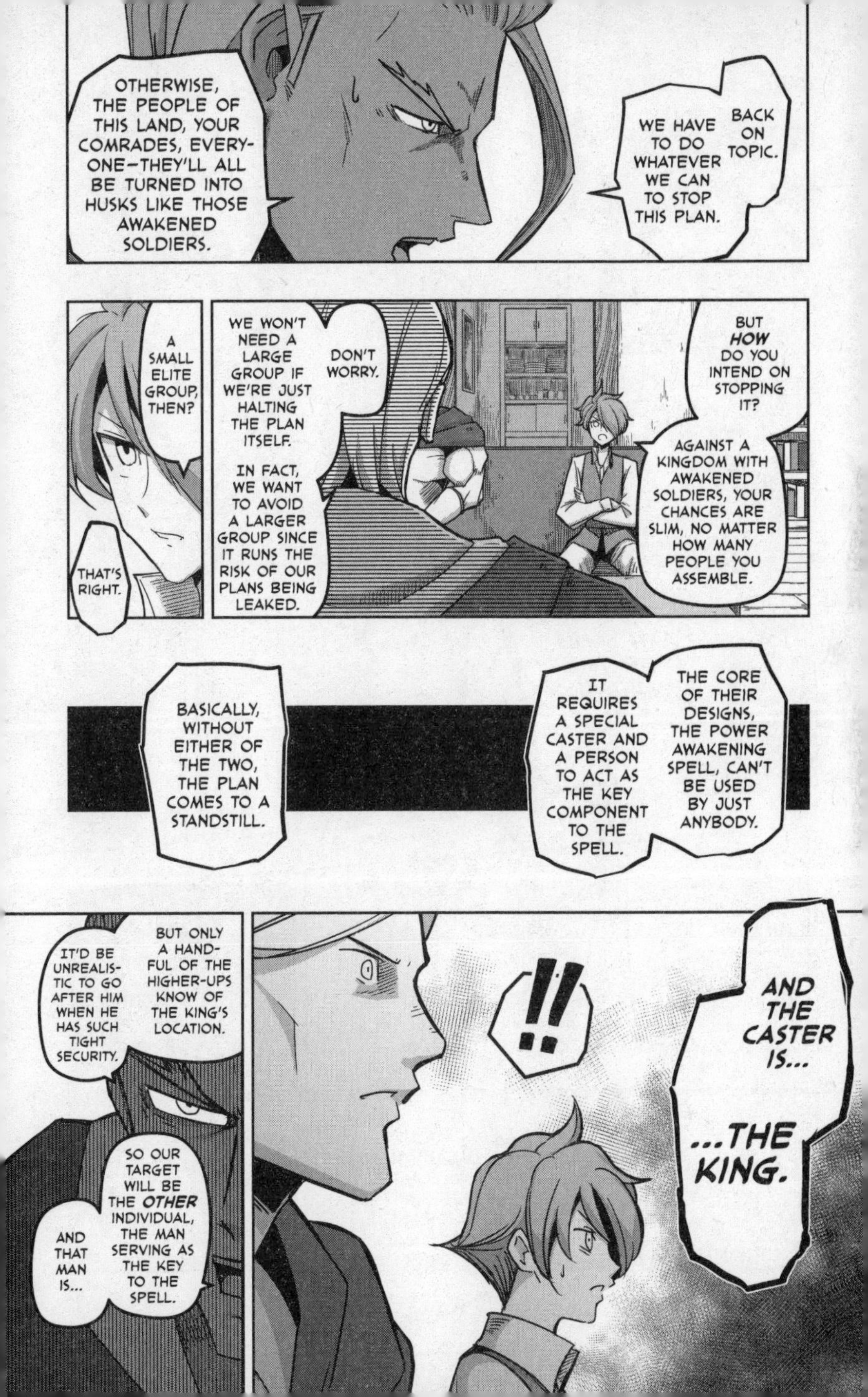
BACK ON TOPIC.
WE HAVE TO DO WHATEVER WE CAN TO STOP THIS PLAN.
OTHERWISE, THE PEOPLE OF THIS LAND, YOUR COMRADES, EVERY-ONE—THEY'LL ALL BE TURNED INTO HUSKS LIKE THOSE AWAKENED SOLDIERS.
BUT *HOW* DO YOU INTEND ON STOPPING IT?
AGAINST A KINGDOM WITH AWAKENED SOLDIERS, YOUR CHANCES ARE SLIM, NO MATTER HOW MANY PEOPLE YOU ASSEMBLE.
DON'T WORRY.
WE WON'T NEED A LARGE GROUP IF WE'RE JUST HALTING THE PLAN ITSELF.
IN FACT, WE WANT TO AVOID A LARGER GROUP SINCE IT RUNS THE RISK OF OUR PLANS BEING LEAKED.
A SMALL ELITE GROUP, THEN?
THAT'S RIGHT.
THE CORE OF THEIR DESIGNS, THE POWER AWAKENING SPELL, CAN'T BE USED BY JUST ANYBODY.
IT REQUIRES A SPECIAL CASTER AND A PERSON TO ACT AS THE KEY COMPONENT TO THE SPELL.
BASICALLY, WITHOUT EITHER OF THE TWO, THE PLAN COMES TO A STANDSTILL.
AND THE CASTER IS...
...THE KING.
!!
BUT ONLY A HAND-FUL OF THE HIGHER-UPS KNOW OF THE KING'S LOCATION.
IT'D BE UNREALIS-TIC TO GO AFTER HIM WHEN HE HAS SUCH TIGHT SECURITY.
SO OUR TARGET WILL BE THE *OTHER* INDIVIDUAL, THE MAN SERVING AS THE KEY TO THE SPELL.
AND THAT MAN IS...

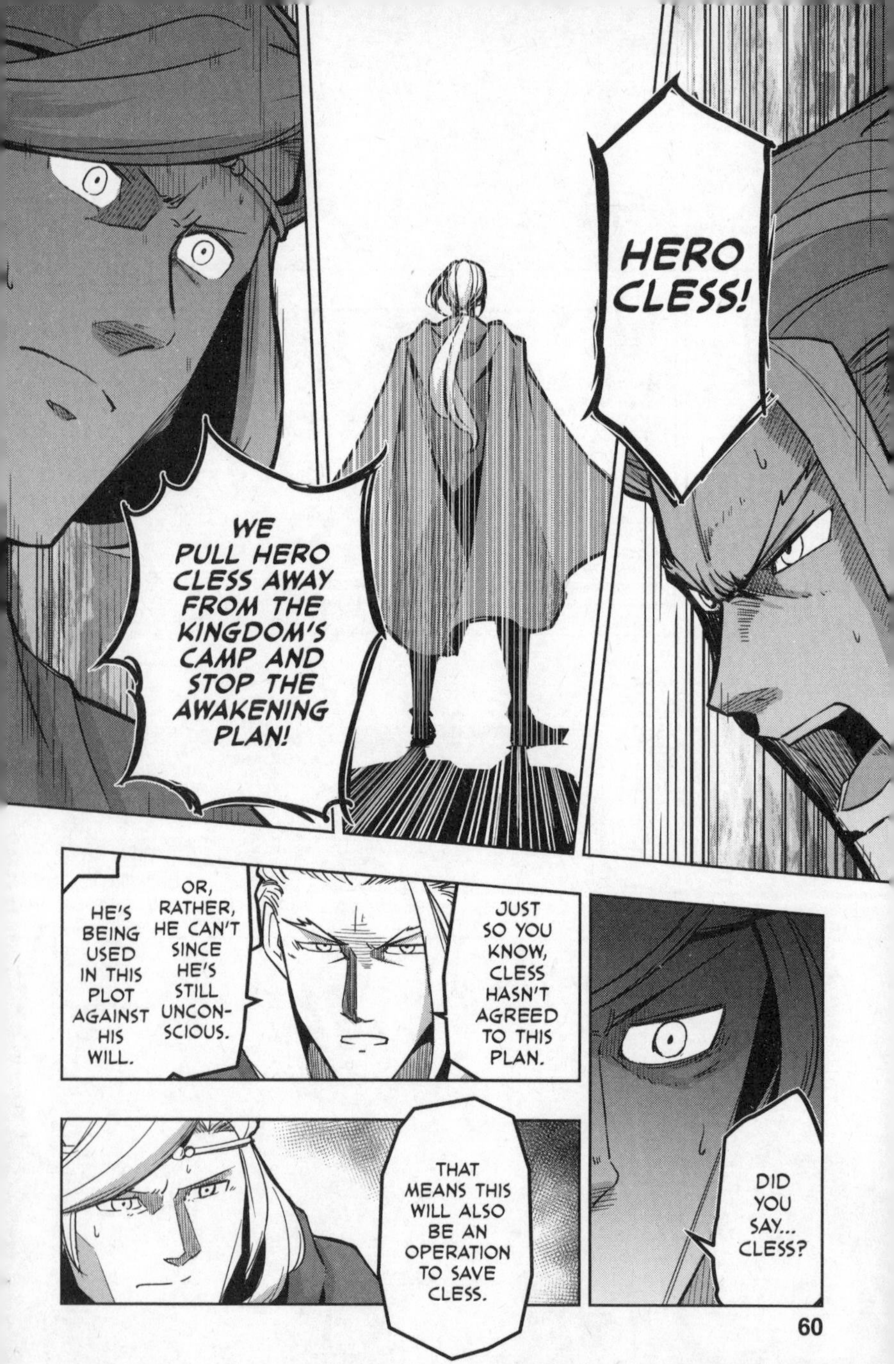

HERO CLESS!
WE PULL HERO CLESS AWAY FROM THE KINGDOM'S CAMP AND STOP THE AWAKENING PLAN!
DID YOU SAY... CLESS?
JUST SO YOU KNOW, CLESS HASN'T AGREED TO THIS PLAN.
OR, RATHER, HE CAN'T SINCE HE'S STILL UNCON-SCIOUS.
HE'S BEING USED IN THIS PLOT AGAINST HIS WILL.
THAT MEANS THIS WILL ALSO BE AN OPERATION TO SAVE CLESS.

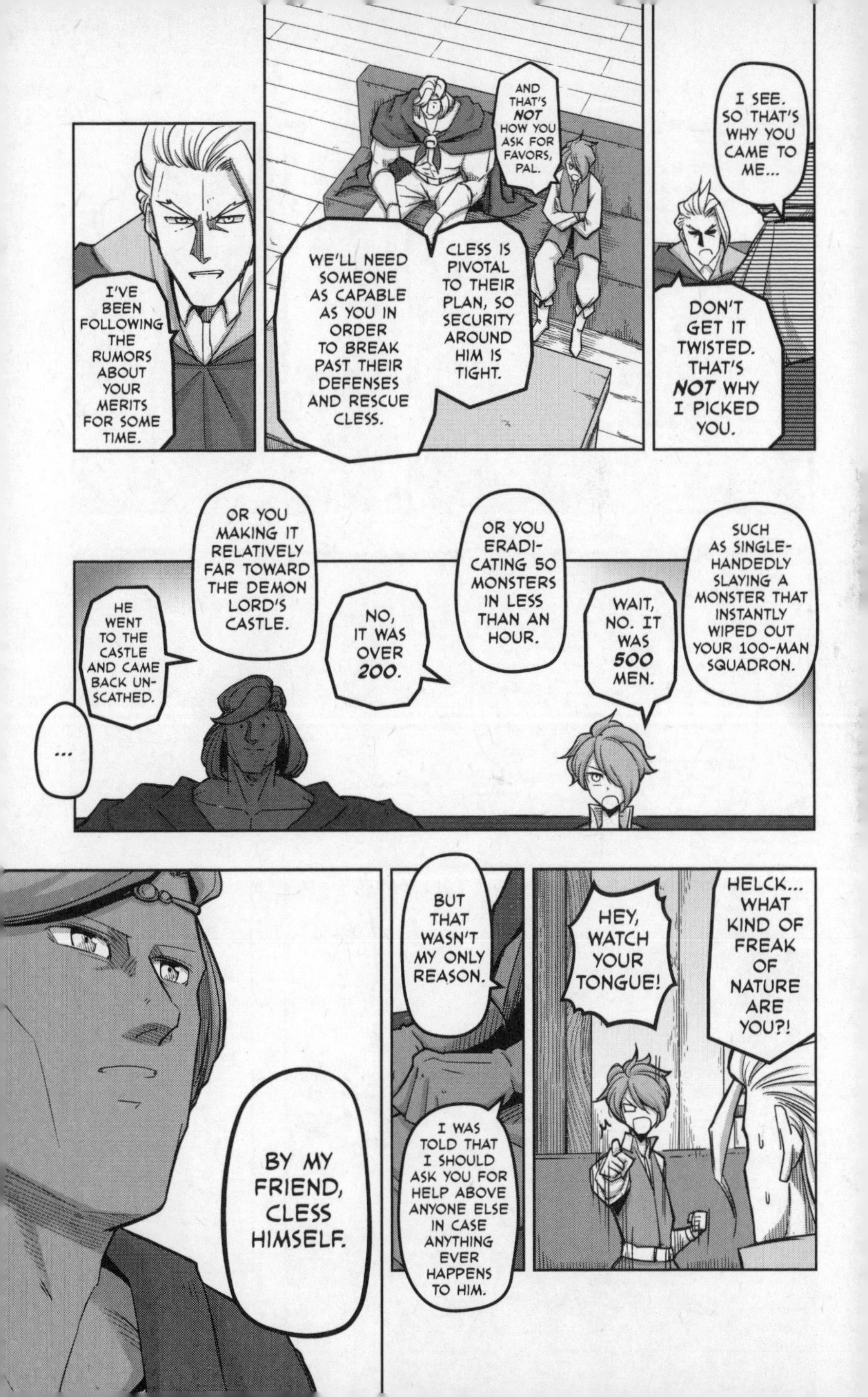
I SEE. SO THAT'S WHY YOU CAME TO ME...
DON'T GET IT TWISTED. THAT'S NOT WHY I PICKED YOU.
AND THAT'S NOT HOW YOU ASK FOR FAVORS, PAL.
CLESS IS PIVOTAL TO THEIR PLAN, SO SECURITY AROUND HIM IS TIGHT.
WE'LL NEED SOMEONE AS CAPABLE AS YOU IN ORDER TO BREAK PAST THEIR DEFENSES AND RESCUE CLESS.
I'VE BEEN FOLLOWING THE RUMORS ABOUT YOUR MERITS FOR SOME TIME.
SUCH AS SINGLE-HANDEDLY SLAYING A MONSTER THAT INSTANTLY WIPED OUT YOUR 100-MAN SQUADRON.
WAIT, NO. IT WAS 500 MEN.
OR YOU ERADICATING 50 MONSTERS IN LESS THAN AN HOUR.
NO, IT WAS OVER 200.
OR YOU MAKING IT RELATIVELY FAR TOWARD THE DEMON LORD'S CASTLE.
HE WENT TO THE CASTLE AND CAME BACK UNSCATHED.
...
HELCK... WHAT KIND OF FREAK OF NATURE ARE YOU?!
HEY, WATCH YOUR TONGUE!
BUT THAT WASN'T MY ONLY REASON.
I WAS TOLD THAT I SHOULD ASK YOU FOR HELP ABOVE ANYONE ELSE IN CASE ANYTHING EVER HAPPENS TO HIM.
BY MY FRIEND, CLESS HIMSELF.

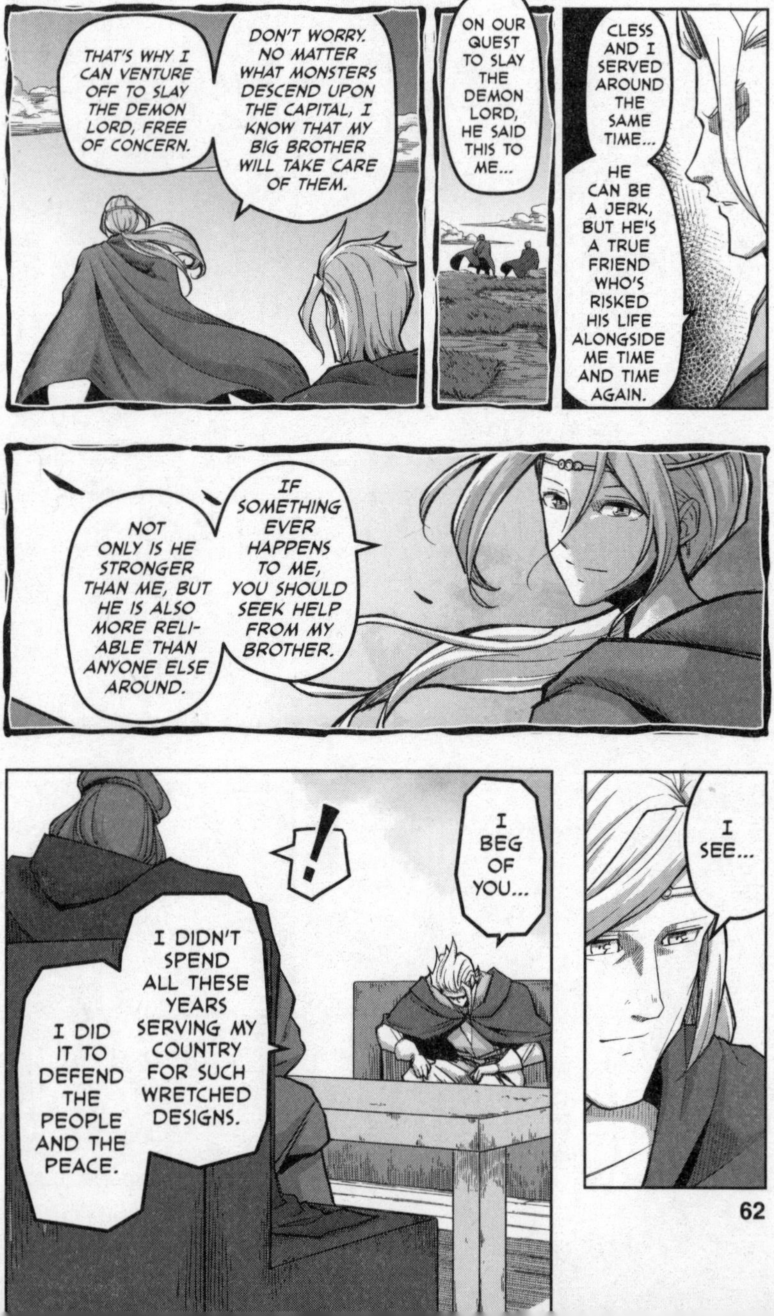
CLESS AND I SERVED AROUND THE SAME TIME...
HE CAN BE A JERK, BUT HE'S A TRUE FRIEND WHO'S RISKED HIS LIFE ALONGSIDE ME TIME AND TIME AGAIN.
ON OUR QUEST TO SLAY THE DEMON LORD, HE SAID THIS TO ME...
DON'T WORRY. NO MATTER WHAT MONSTERS DESCEND UPON THE CAPITAL, I KNOW THAT MY BIG BROTHER WILL TAKE CARE OF THEM.
THAT'S WHY I CAN VENTURE OFF TO SLAY THE DEMON LORD, FREE OF CONCERN.
IF SOMETHING EVER HAPPENS TO ME, YOU SHOULD SEEK HELP FROM MY BROTHER.
NOT ONLY IS HE STRONGER THAN ME, BUT HE IS ALSO MORE RELI-ABLE THAN ANYONE ELSE AROUND.
I SEE...
I BEG OF YOU...
!
I DIDN'T SPEND ALL THESE YEARS SERVING MY COUNTRY FOR SUCH WRETCHED DESIGNS.
I DID IT TO DEFEND THE PEOPLE AND THE PEACE.

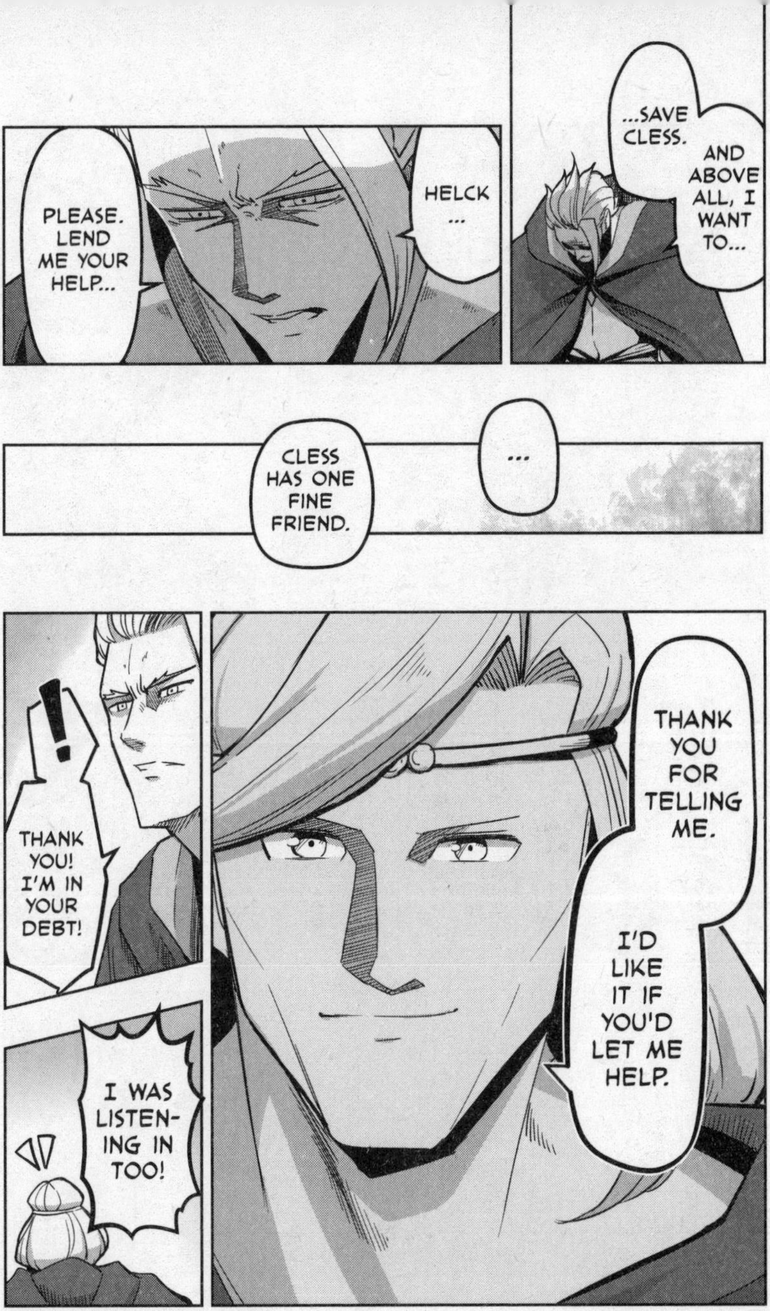
AND ABOVE ALL, I WANT TO...
...SAVE CLESS.
HELCK ...
PLEASE. LEND ME YOUR HELP...
...
CLESS HAS ONE FINE FRIEND.
THANK YOU FOR TELLING ME.
I'D LIKE IT IF YOU'D LET ME HELP.
!
THANK YOU! I'M IN YOUR DEBT!
I WAS LISTENING-ING IN TOO!

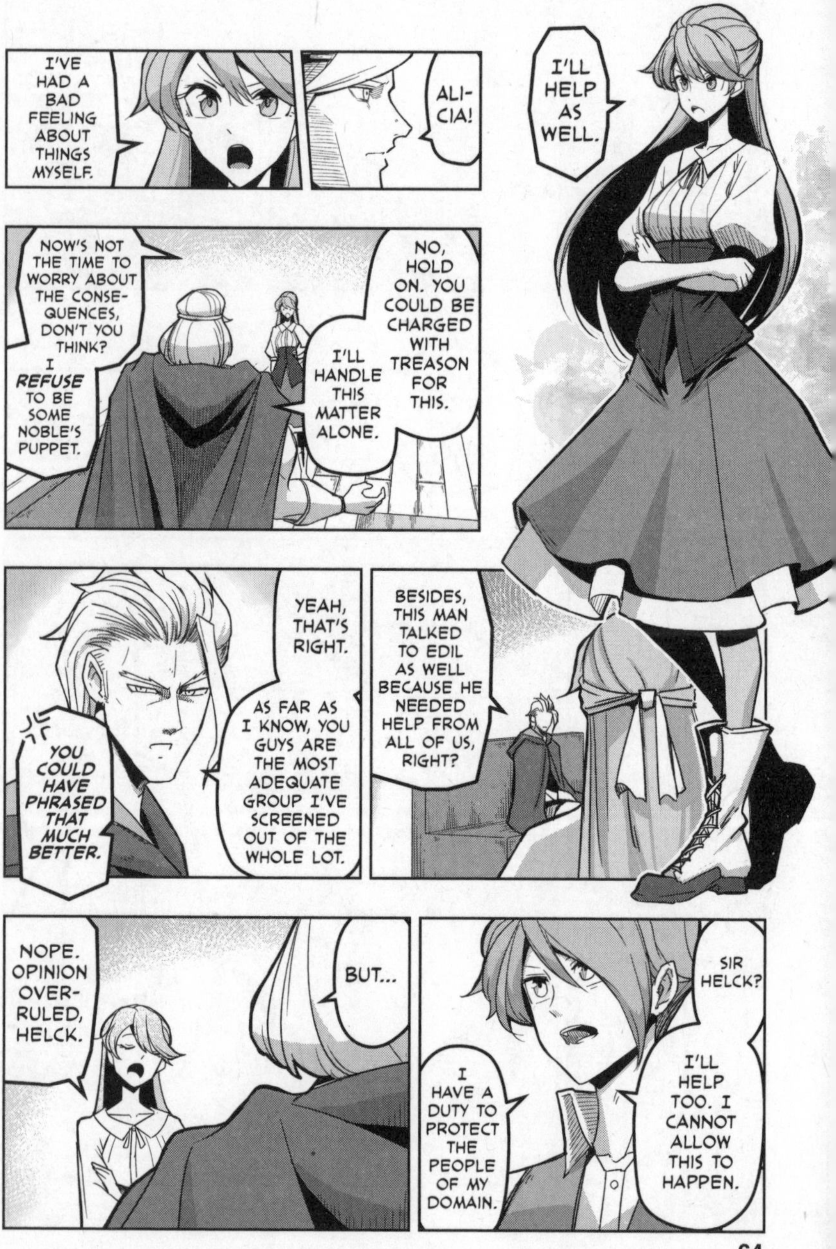
I'LL HELP AS WELL.
ALI-CIA!
I'VE HAD A BAD FEELING ABOUT THINGS MYSELF.
NO, HOLD ON. YOU COULD BE CHARGED WITH TREASON FOR THIS.
I'LL HANDLE THIS MATTER ALONE.
NOW'S NOT THE TIME TO WORRY ABOUT THE CONSE-QUENCES, DON'T YOU THINK? I *REFUSE* TO BE SOME NOBLE'S PUPPET.
BESIDES, THIS MAN TALKED TO EDIL AS WELL BECAUSE HE NEEDED HELP FROM ALL OF US, RIGHT?
YEAH, THAT'S RIGHT.
AS FAR AS I KNOW, YOU GUYS ARE THE MOST ADEQUATE GROUP I'VE SCREENED OUT OF THE WHOLE LOT.
YOU COULD HAVE PHRASED THAT MUCH BETTER.
SIR HELCK?
I'LL HELP TOO. I CANNOT ALLOW THIS TO HAPPEN.
I HAVE A DUTY TO PROTECT THE PEOPLE OF MY DOMAIN.
BUT...
NOPE. OPINION OVER-RULED, HELCK.

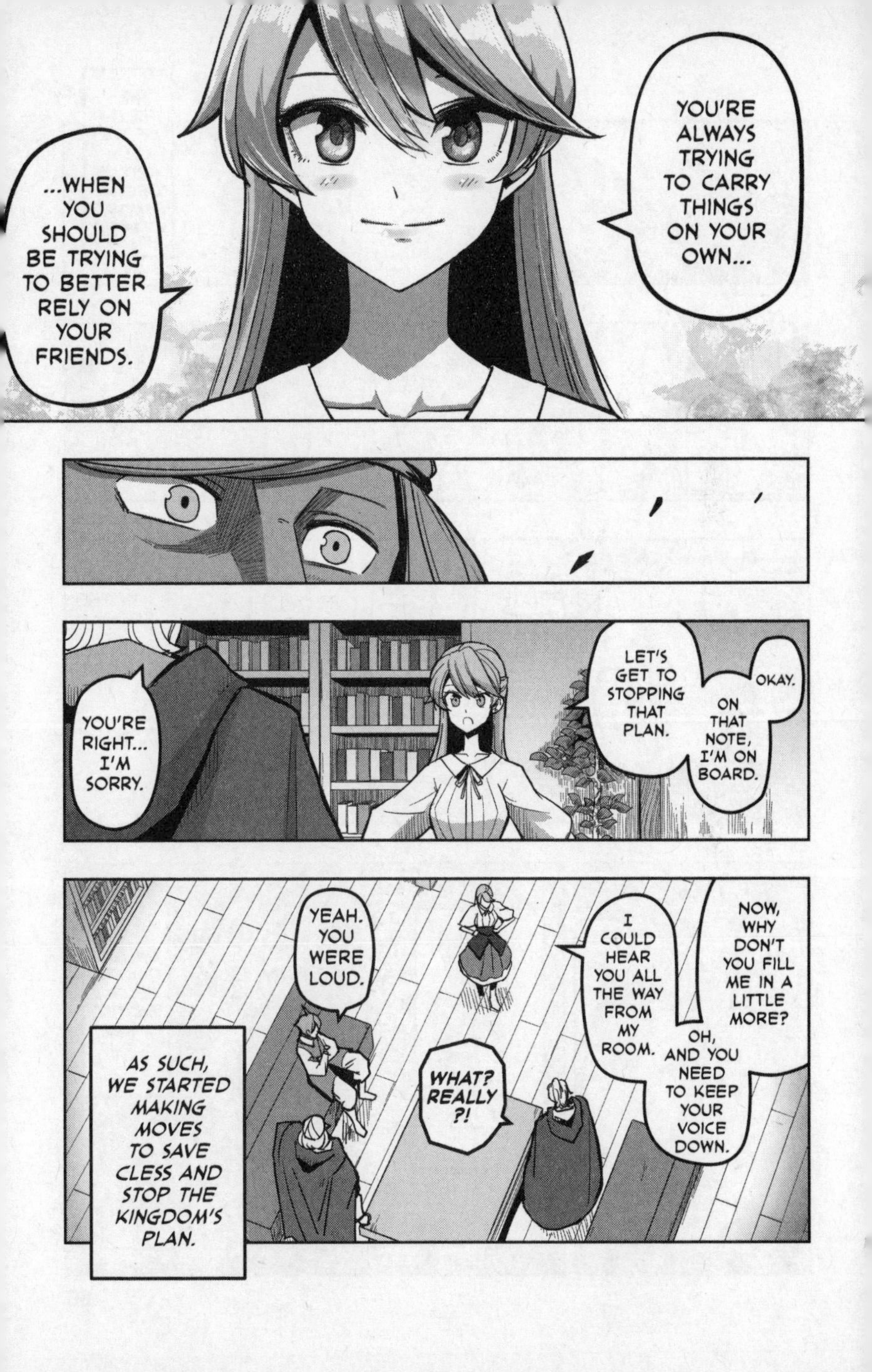
YOU'RE ALWAYS TRYING TO CARRY THINGS ON YOUR OWN...
...WHEN YOU SHOULD BE TRYING TO BETTER RELY ON YOUR FRIENDS.
OKAY. ON THAT NOTE, I'M ON BOARD.
LET'S GET TO STOPPING THAT PLAN.
YOU'RE RIGHT... I'M SORRY.
NOW, WHY DON'T YOU FILL ME IN A LITTLE MORE?
OH, AND YOU NEED TO KEEP YOUR VOICE DOWN.
I COULD HEAR YOU ALL THE WAY FROM MY ROOM.
WHAT? REALLY?!
YEAH. YOU WERE LOUD.
AS SUCH, WE STARTED MAKING MOVES TO SAVE CLESS AND STOP THE KINGDOM'S PLAN.

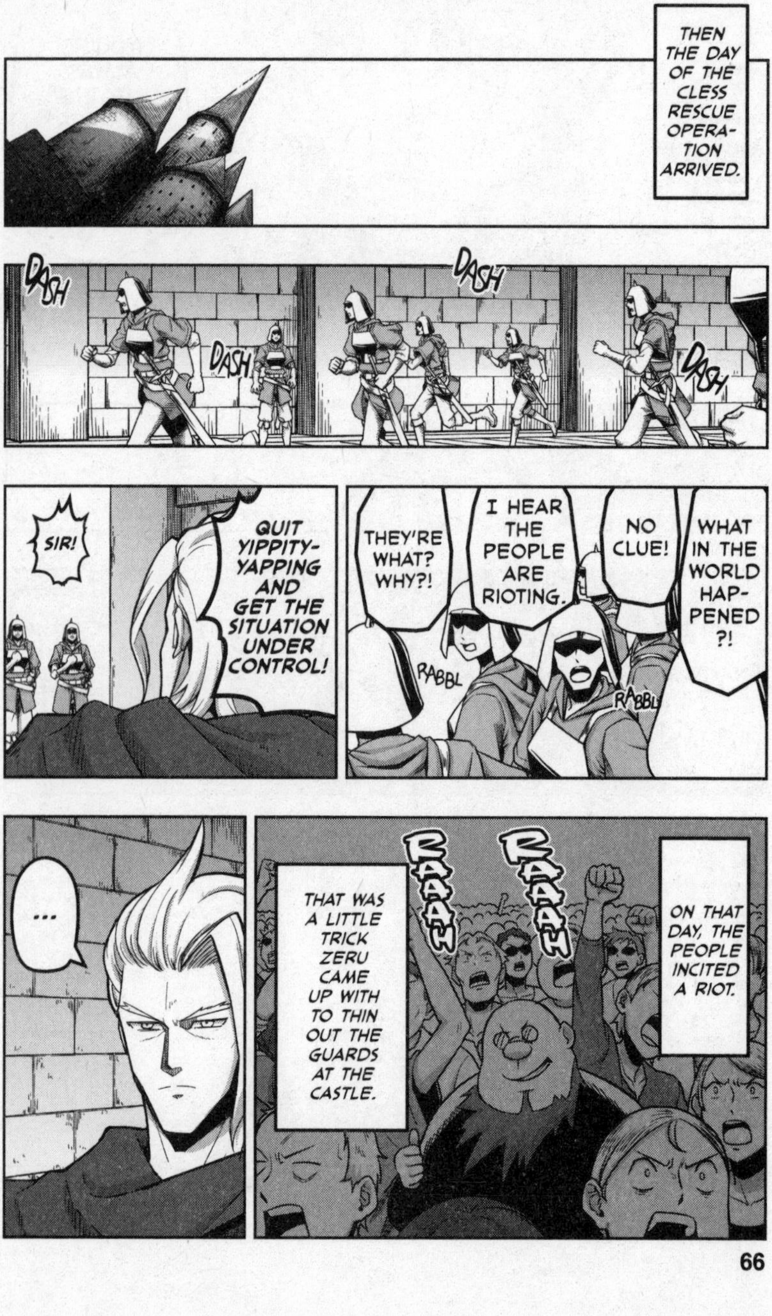

THEN THE DAY OF THE CLESS RESCUE OPERATION ARRIVED.
DASH
DASH
DASH
DASH
WHAT IN THE WORLD HAPPENED?!
NO CLUE!
I HEAR THE PEOPLE ARE RIOTING.
THEY'RE WHAT? WHY?!
RABBL
RABBL
QUIT YIPPITY-YAPPING AND GET THE SITUATION UNDER CONTROL!
SIR!
ON THAT DAY, THE PEOPLE INCITED A RIOT.
RAAAAH
RAAAAH
THAT WAS A LITTLE TRICK ZERU CAME UP WITH TO THIN OUT THE GUARDS AT THE CASTLE.
...

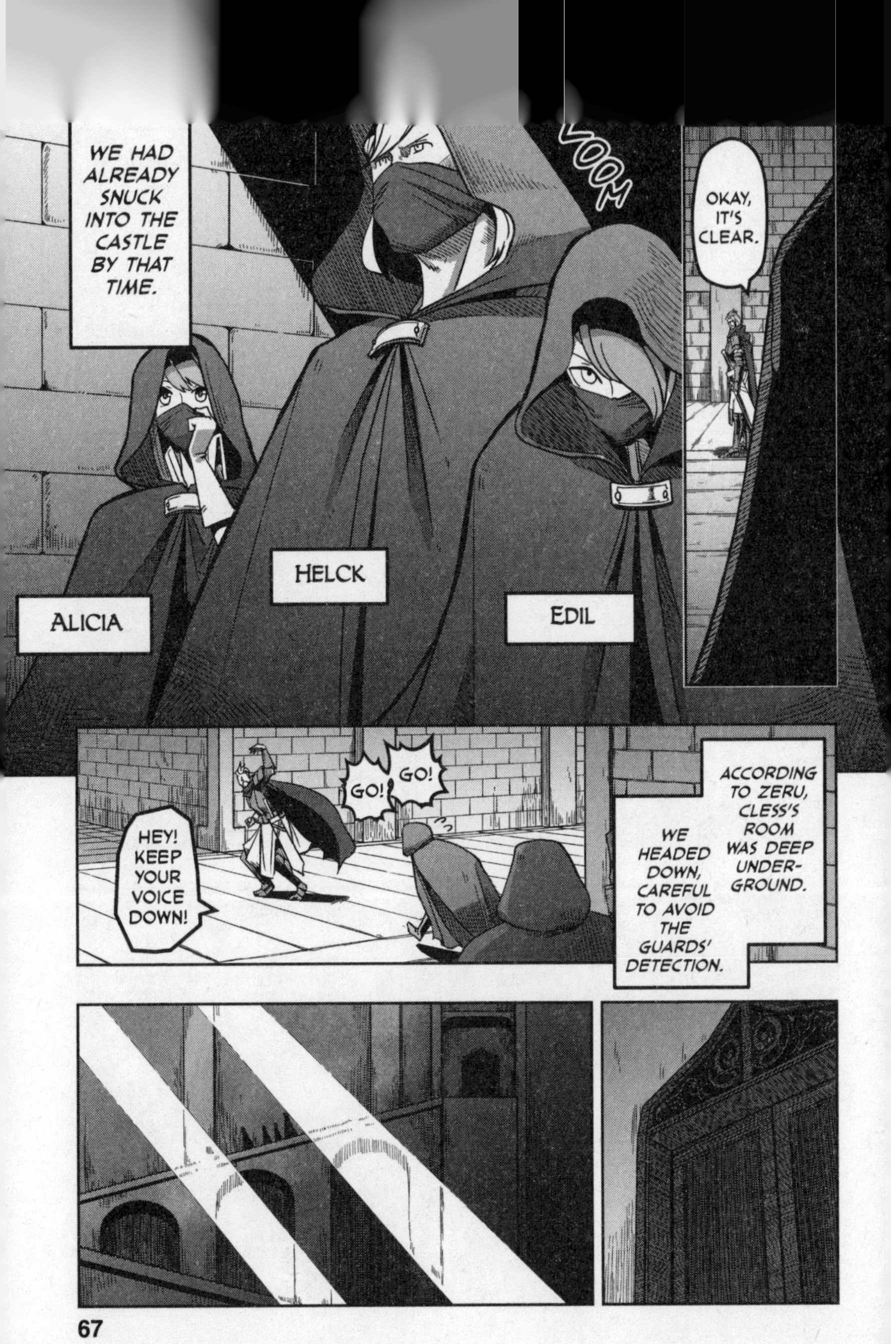
OKAY, IT'S CLEAR.
VOOM
WE HAD ALREADY SNUCK INTO THE CASTLE BY THAT TIME.
EDIL
HELCK
ALICIA
ACCORDING TO ZERU, CLESS'S ROOM WAS DEEP UNDER-GROUND.
WE HEADED DOWN, CAREFUL TO AVOID THE GUARDS' DETECTION.
GO!
GO!
HEY! KEEP YOUR VOICE DOWN!

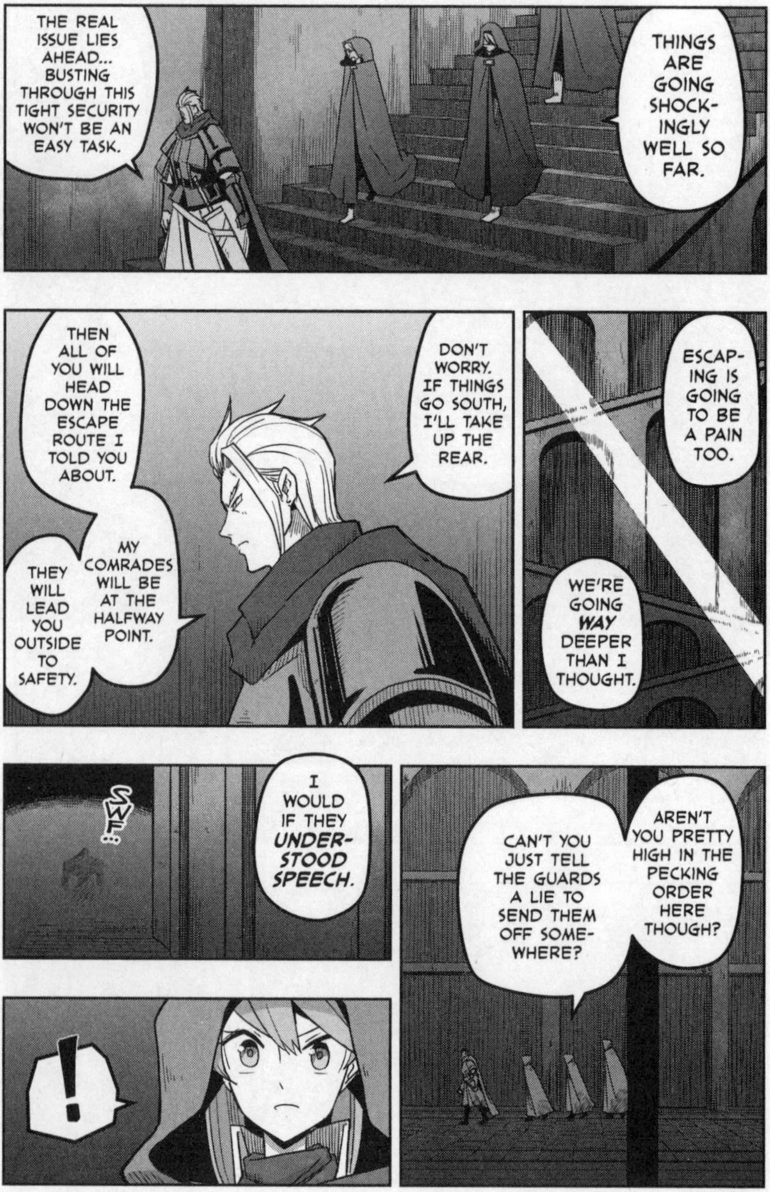
THINGS ARE GOING SHOCKINGLY WELL SO FAR.
THE REAL ISSUE LIES AHEAD... BUSTING THROUGH THIS TIGHT SECURITY WON'T BE AN EASY TASK.
ESCAPING IS GOING TO BE A PAIN TOO.
WE'RE GOING *WAY* DEEPER THAN I THOUGHT.
DON'T WORRY. IF THINGS GO SOUTH, I'LL TAKE UP THE REAR.
THEN ALL OF YOU WILL HEAD DOWN THE ESCAPE ROUTE I TOLD YOU ABOUT.
MY COMRADES WILL BE AT THE HALFWAY POINT.
THEY WILL LEAD YOU OUTSIDE TO SAFETY.
AREN'T YOU PRETTY HIGH IN THE PECKING ORDER HERE THOUGH?
CAN'T YOU JUST TELL THE GUARDS A LIE TO SEND THEM OFF SOMEWHERE?
I WOULD IF THEY *UNDERSTOOD SPEECH*.
SWF..
!

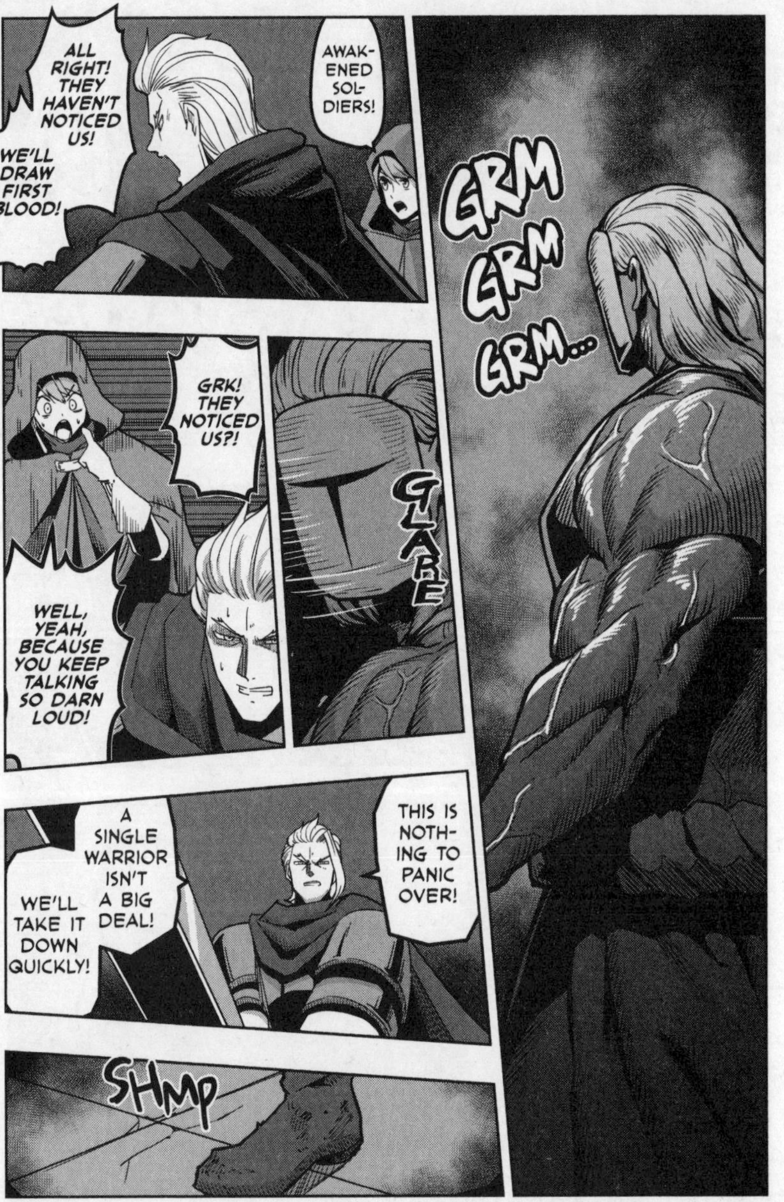
GRM GRM GRM...
AWAKENED SOLDIERS!
ALL RIGHT! THEY HAVEN'T NOTICED US!
WE'LL DRAW FIRST BLOOD!
GLARE
GRK! THEY NOTICED US?!
WELL, YEAH, BECAUSE YOU KEEP TALKING SO DARN LOUD!
THIS IS NOTHING TO PANIC OVER!
A SINGLE WARRIOR ISN'T A BIG DEAL!
WE'LL TAKE IT DOWN QUICKLY!
SHMP

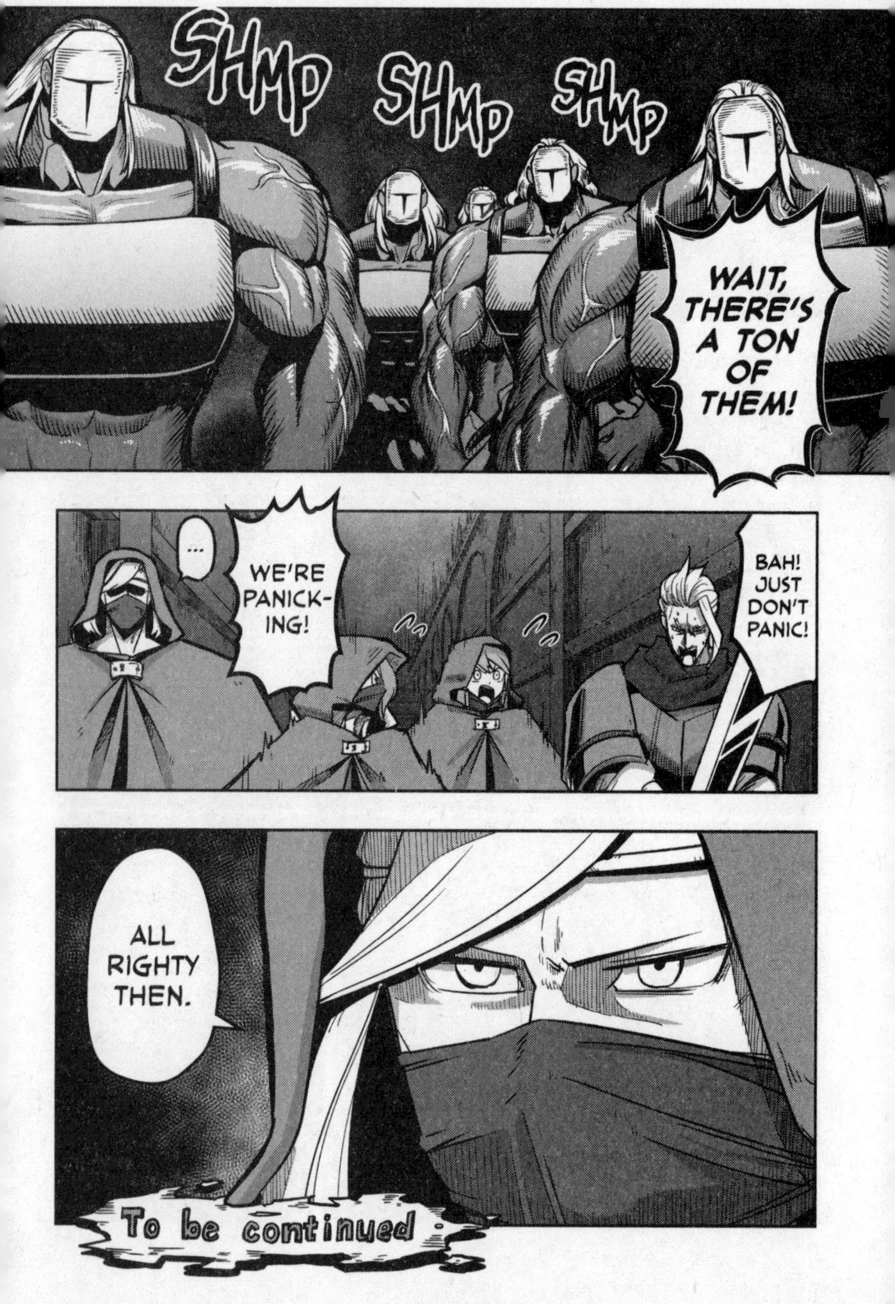
SHMP
SHMP
SHMP
WAIT, THERE'S A TON OF THEM!
BAH! JUST DON'T PANIC!
WE'RE PANICK-ING!
...
ALL RIGHTY THEN.
To be continued

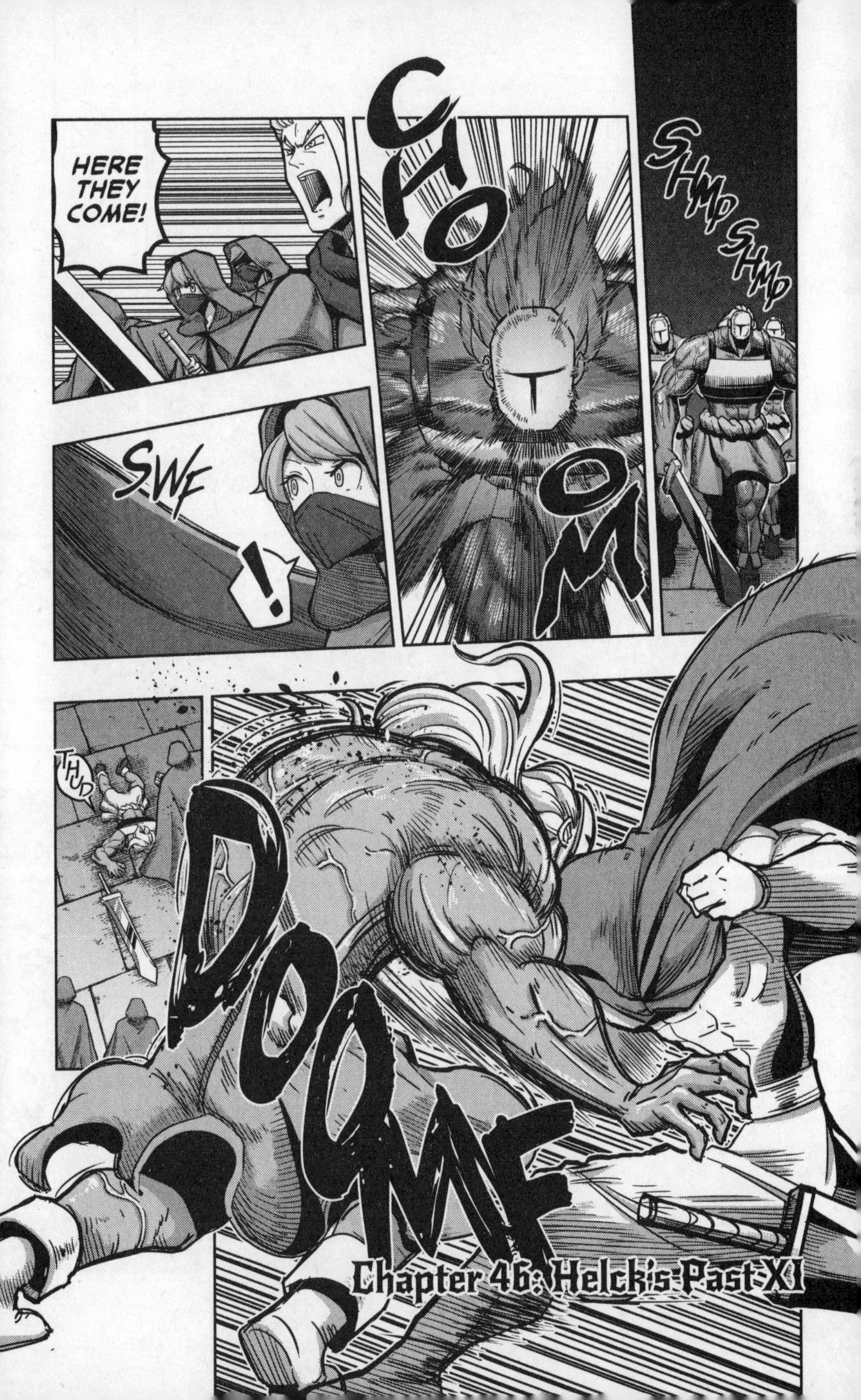
SHMP SHMP SHMP
CHOOM
HERE THEY COME!
SWF
!
DOOMF
Chapter 46: Helck's Past XI
THUD

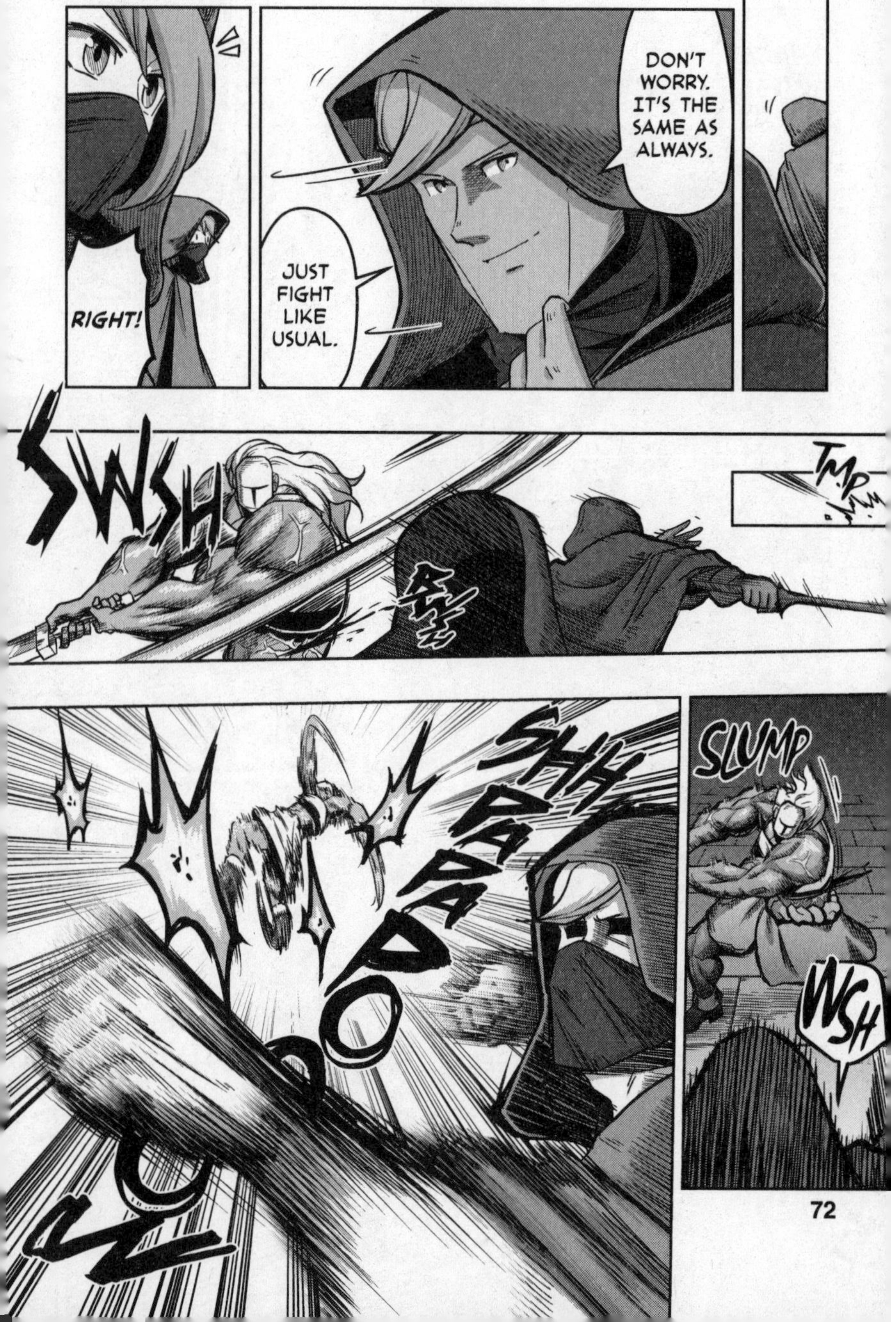
DON'T WORRY. IT'S THE SAME AS ALWAYS.
JUST FIGHT LIKE USUAL.
RIGHT!
TMP
SWSH
SLUMP
VVSH

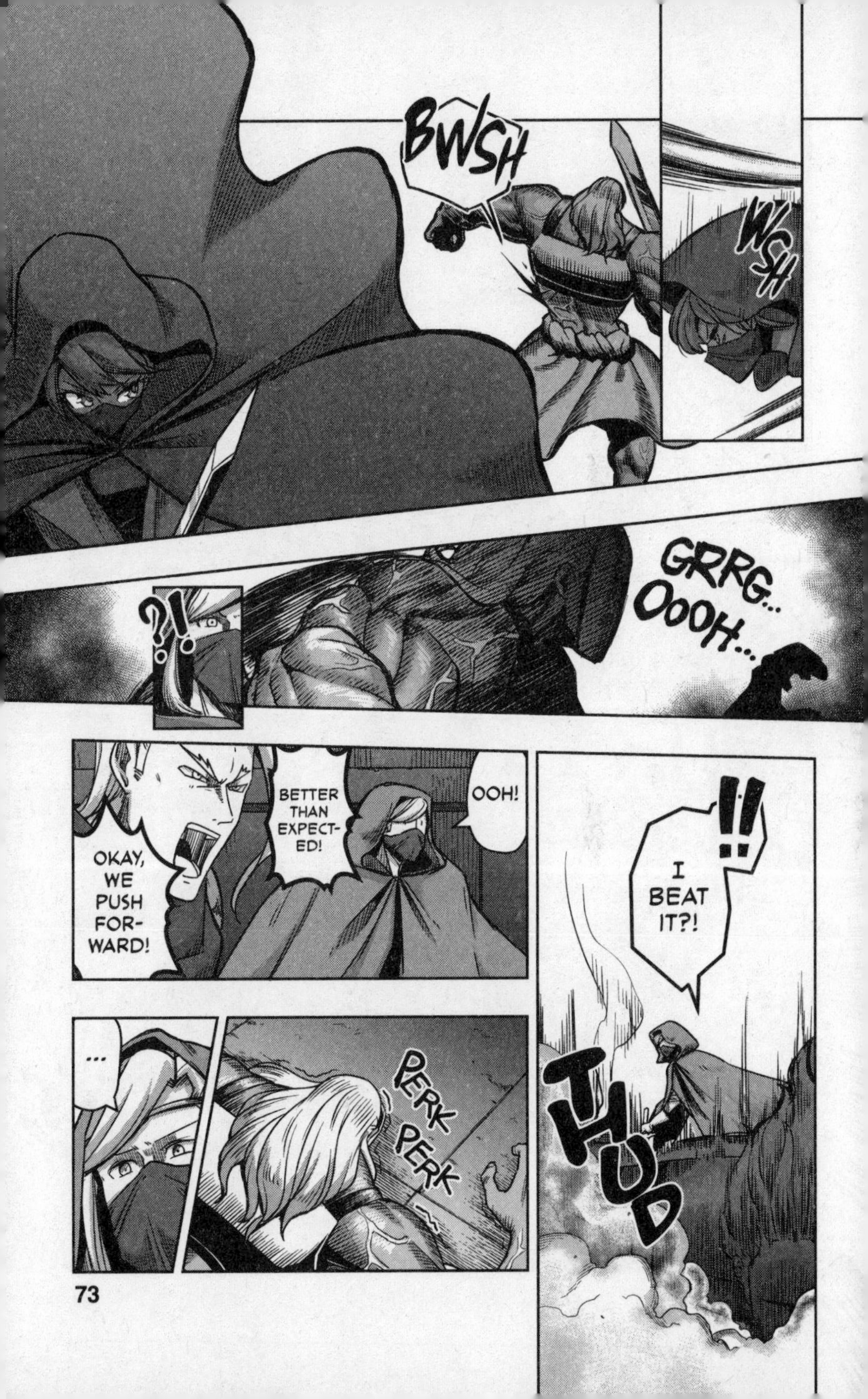
WSH
BWSH
GRRG... OOOH...
?!
!!
I BEAT IT?!
THUD
OOH!
BETTER THAN EXPECTED!
OKAY, WE PUSH FORWARD!
PERK PERK
...

TMP TMP TMP..

WH-
WH-
WHP

PERK
PERK

HWSH

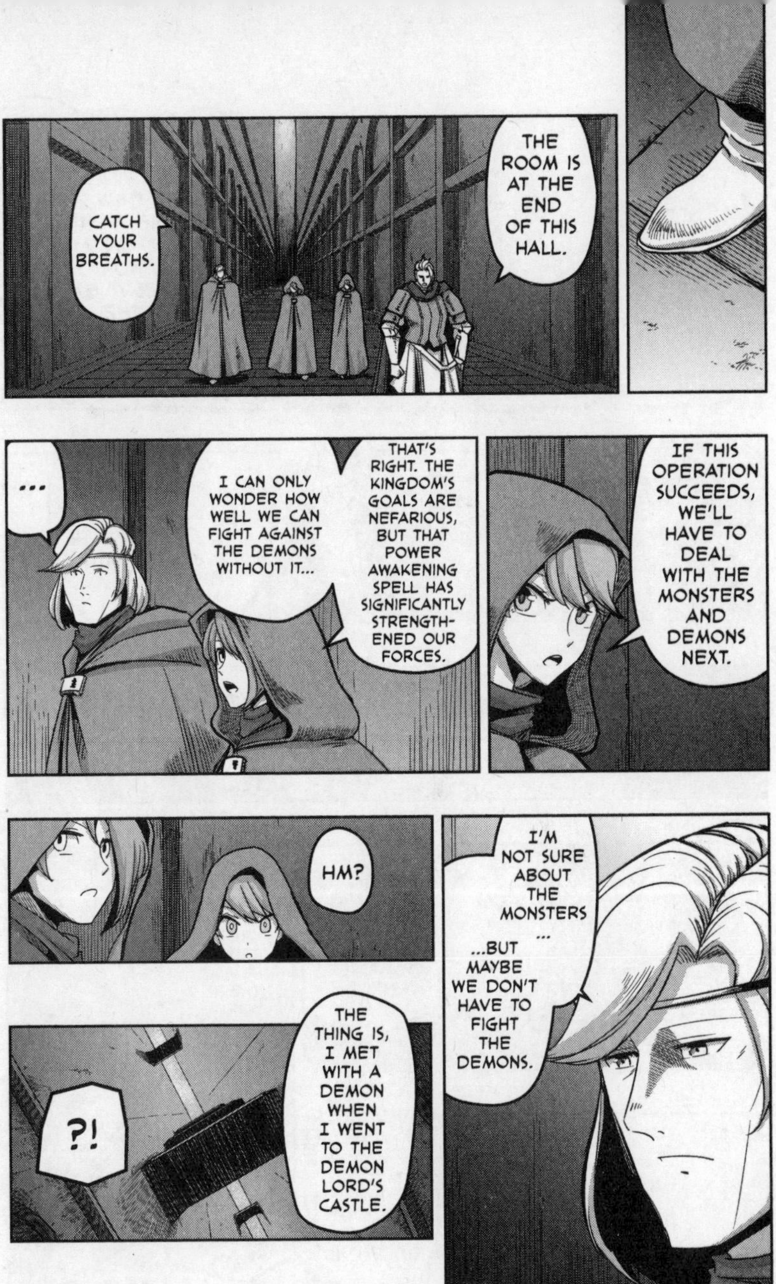
THE ROOM IS AT THE END OF THIS HALL.
CATCH YOUR BREATHS.
IF THIS OPERATION SUCCEEDS, WE'LL HAVE TO DEAL WITH THE MONSTERS AND DEMONS NEXT.
THAT'S RIGHT. THE KINGDOM'S GOALS ARE NEFARIOUS, BUT THAT POWER AWAKENING SPELL HAS SIGNIFICANTLY STRENGTH-ENED OUR FORCES.
I CAN ONLY WONDER HOW WELL WE CAN FIGHT AGAINST THE DEMONS WITHOUT IT...
...
I'M NOT SURE ABOUT THE MONSTERS...
...BUT MAYBE WE DON'T HAVE TO FIGHT THE DEMONS.
HM?
THE THING IS, I MET WITH A DEMON WHEN I WENT TO THE DEMON LORD'S CASTLE.
?!

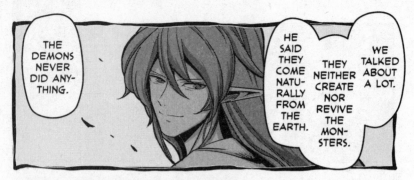

WE TALKED ABOUT A LOT.
THEY NEITHER CREATE NOR REVIVE THE MONSTERS.
HE SAID THEY COME NATURALLY FROM THE EARTH.
THE DEMONS NEVER DID ANYTHING.
AND LASTLY, HE SAID HE WANTED ...
... PEACE.
...
STA
ARE
HUH ?!
THAT'S SO LIKE YOU, SIR HELCK.
HOWEVER, YOU CAN'T JUST TRUST THEM AT THEIR WORD.
NOT ONLY ARE DEMONS CRUEL AND UNDERHANDED, BUT OUR RECORDS SHOW THAT THEY'VE BETRAYED AND NEARLY DESTROYED MANKIND TIME AND TIME AGAIN.
I'M GUESSING HE REALIZED HOW STRONG YOU WERE AND TOLD YOU WHATEVER CAME TO HIS HEAD.
FOR WHAT IT'S WORTH, EVERY DEMON I'VE EVER MET WAS A SAVAGE WHO COULDN'T EVEN SPEAK PROPERLY.
THEY'RE LESS TRUSTWORTHY THAN THE KINGDOM'S UPPER ECHELON.
I-I SEE...

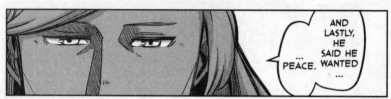

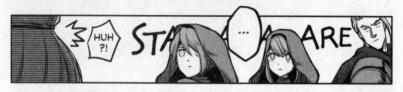

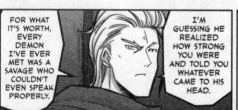

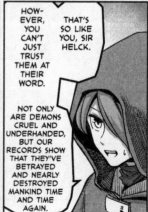

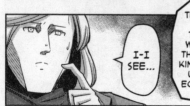

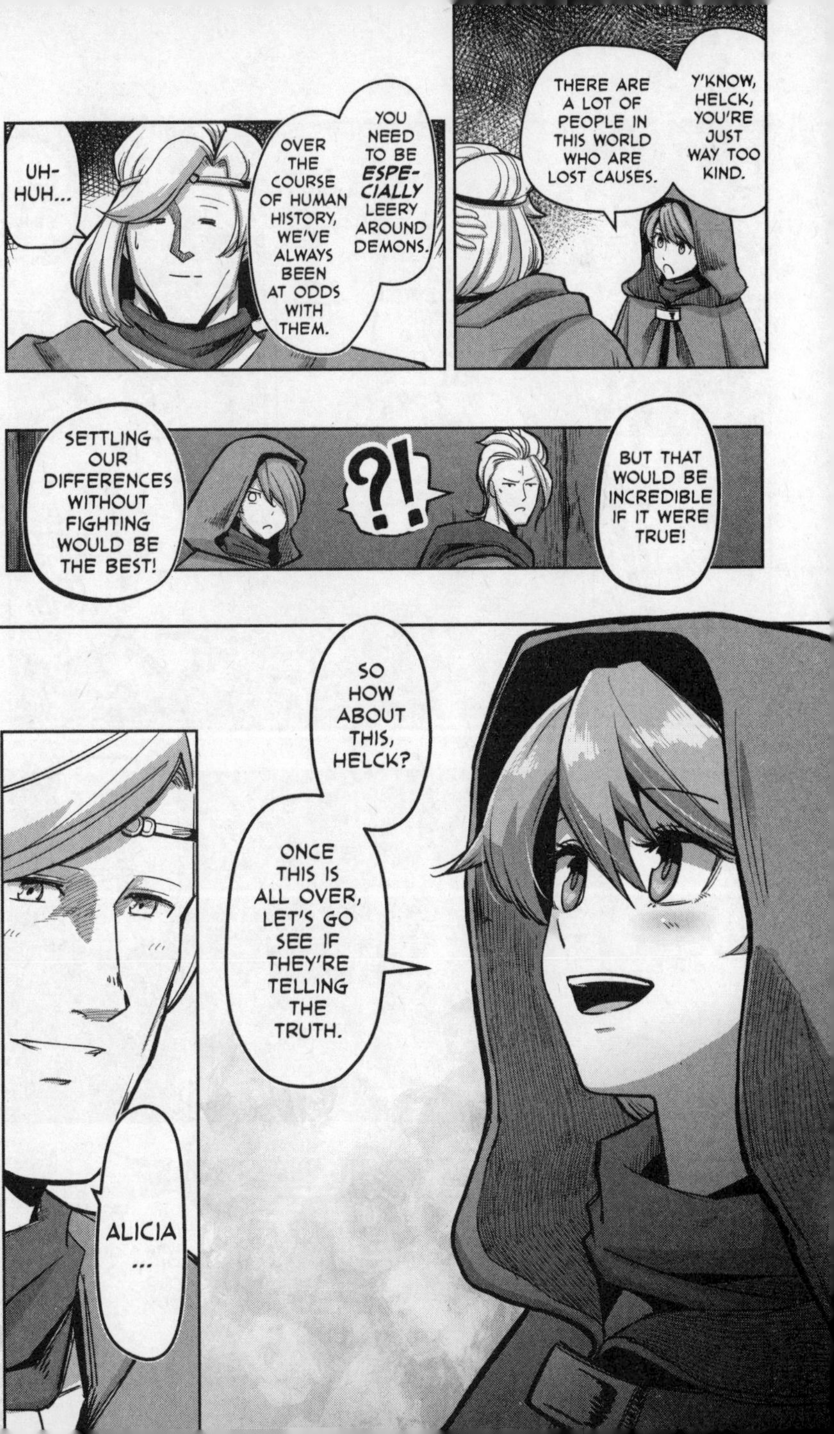
Y'KNOW, HELCK, YOU'RE JUST WAY TOO KIND.
THERE ARE A LOT OF PEOPLE IN THIS WORLD WHO ARE LOST CAUSES.
YOU NEED TO BE *ESPECIALLY* LEERY AROUND DEMONS.
OVER THE COURSE OF HUMAN HISTORY, WE'VE ALWAYS BEEN AT ODDS WITH THEM.
UH-HUH...
BUT THAT WOULD BE INCREDIBLE IF IT WERE TRUE!
?!
SETTLING OUR DIFFERENCES WITHOUT FIGHTING WOULD BE THE BEST!
SO HOW ABOUT THIS, HELCK?
ONCE THIS IS ALL OVER, LET'S GO SEE IF THEY'RE TELLING THE TRUTH.
ALICIA...

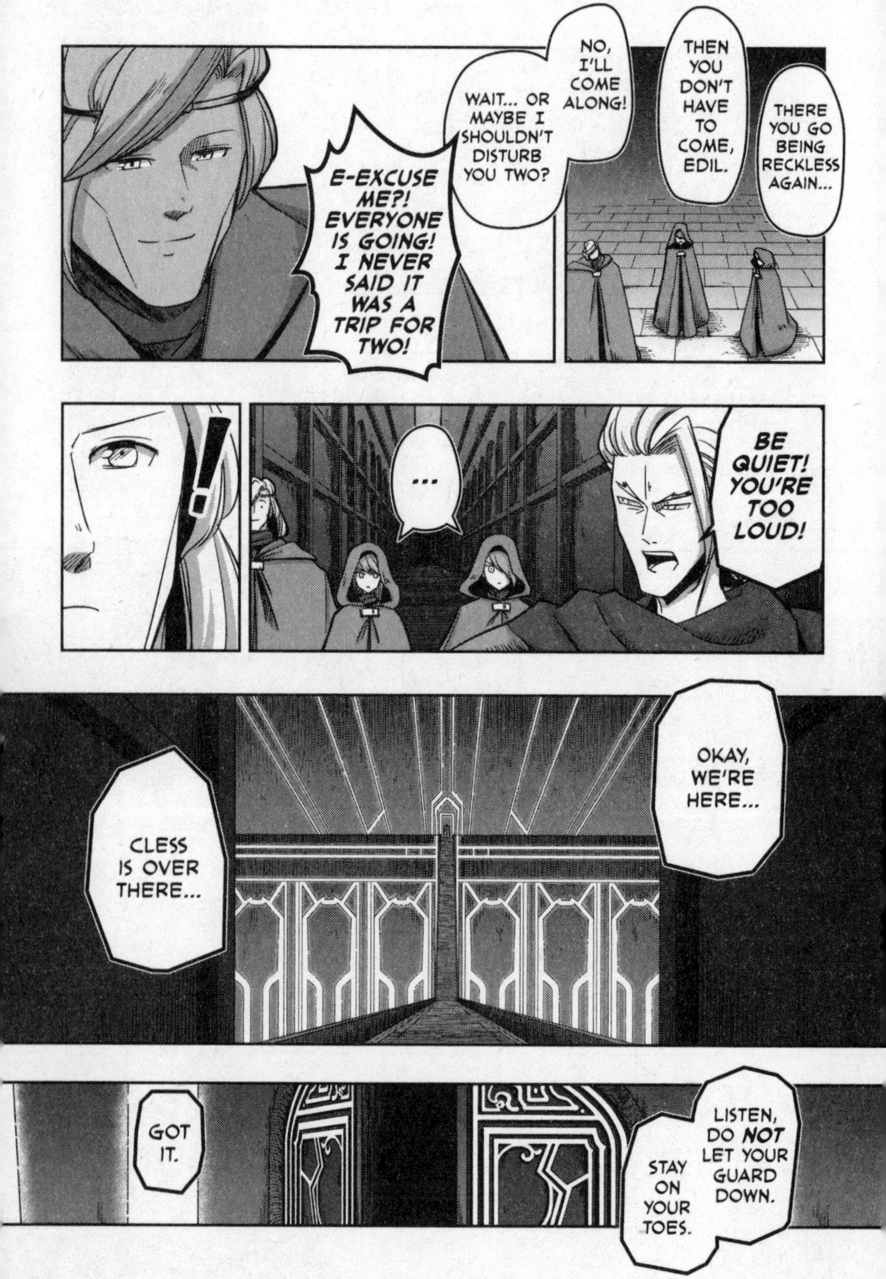
THERE YOU GO BEING RECKLESS AGAIN...
THEN YOU DON'T HAVE TO COME, EDIL.
NO, I'LL COME ALONG!
WAIT... OR MAYBE I SHOULDN'T DISTURB YOU TWO?
E-EXCUSE ME?! EVERYONE IS GOING! I NEVER SAID IT WAS A TRIP FOR TWO!
BE QUIET! YOU'RE TOO LOUD!
...
OKAY, WE'RE HERE...
CLESS IS OVER THERE...
LISTEN, DO **NOT** LET YOUR GUARD DOWN.
STAY ON YOUR TOES.
GOT IT.

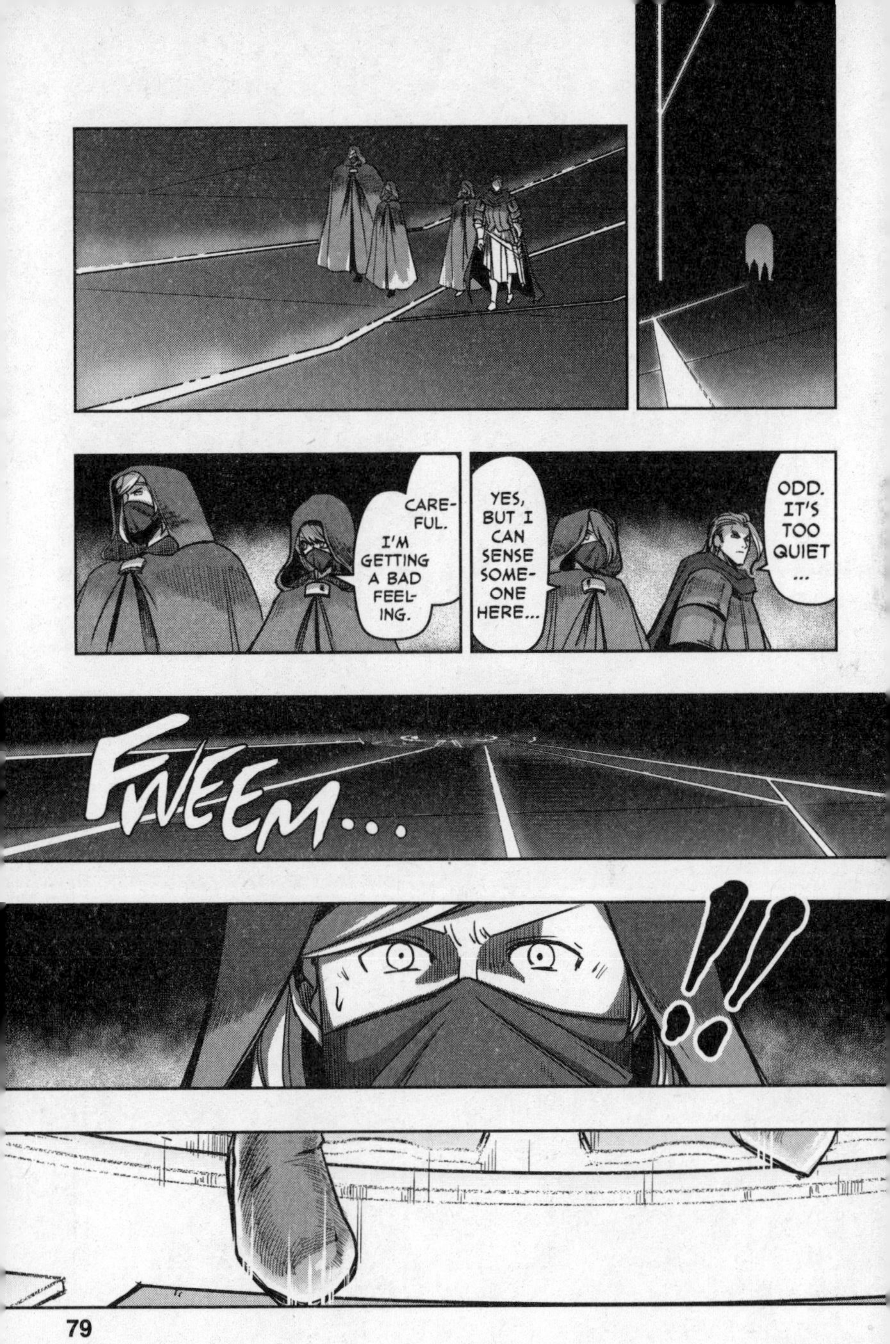
ODD. IT'S TOO QUIET ...
YES, BUT I CAN SENSE SOME-ONE HERE...
CARE-FUL. I'M GETTING A BAD FEEL-ING.
FWEEM...
!!

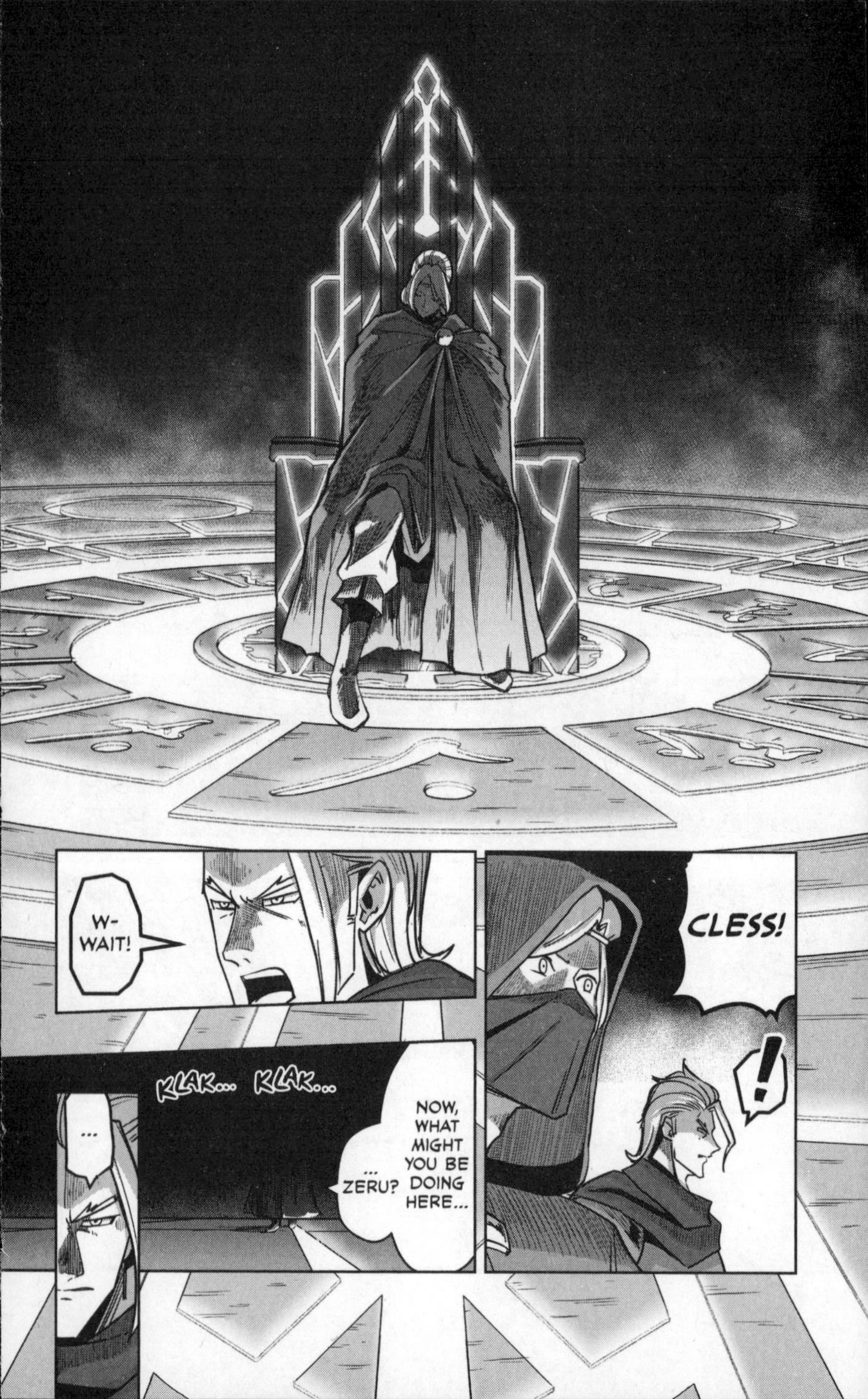
CLESS!
!
W-WAIT!
KLAK... KLAK...
NOW, WHAT MIGHT YOU BE DOING HERE...
... ZERU?
...

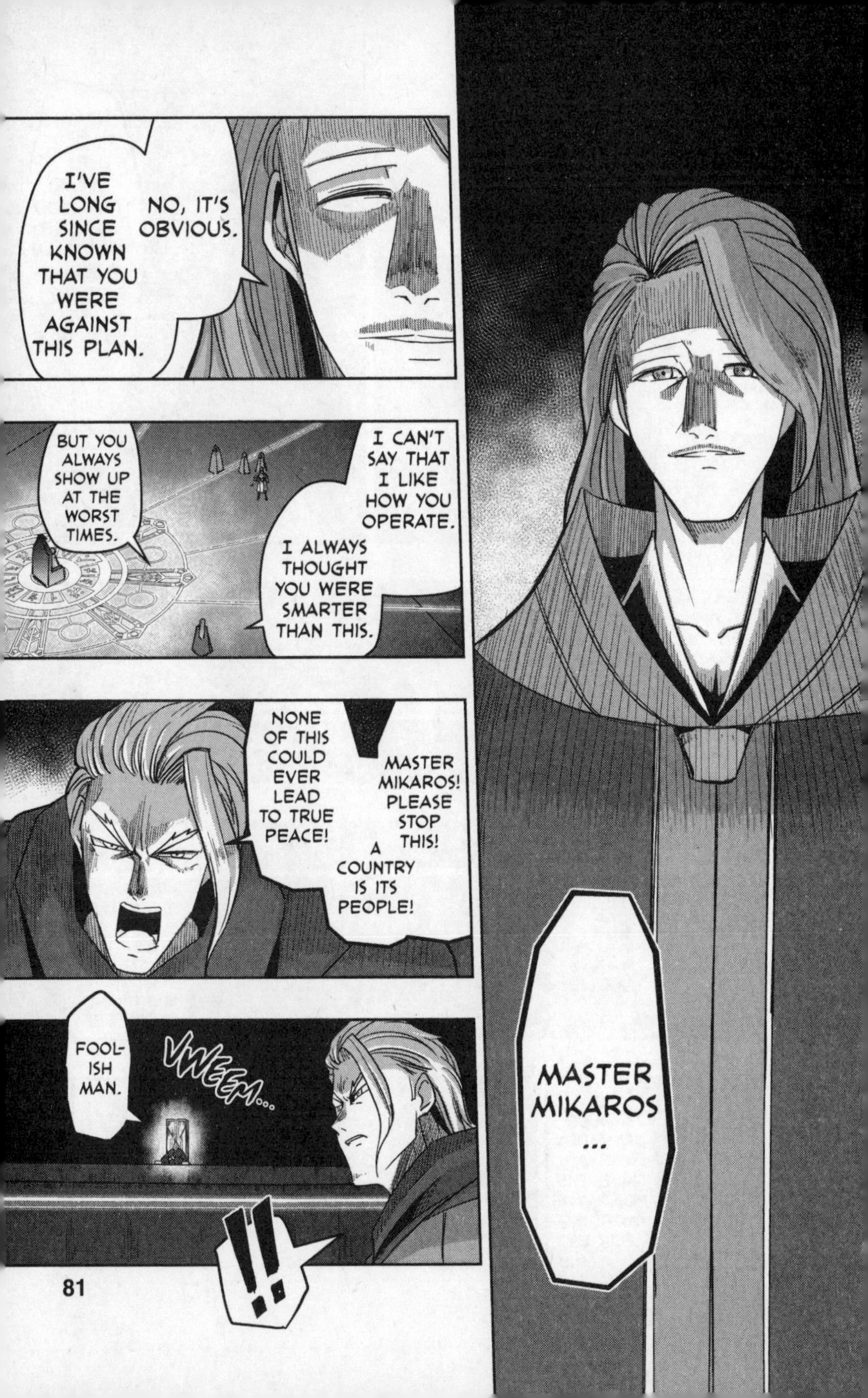
MASTER MIKAROS ...
NO, IT'S OBVIOUS.
I'VE LONG SINCE KNOWN THAT YOU WERE AGAINST THIS PLAN.
I CAN'T SAY THAT I LIKE HOW YOU OPERATE.
I ALWAYS THOUGHT YOU WERE SMARTER THAN THIS.
BUT YOU ALWAYS SHOW UP AT THE WORST TIMES.
MASTER MIKAROS! PLEASE STOP THIS!
NONE OF THIS COULD EVER LEAD TO TRUE PEACE!
A COUNTRY IS ITS PEOPLE!
FOOL-ISH MAN.
VWEEM...
!!

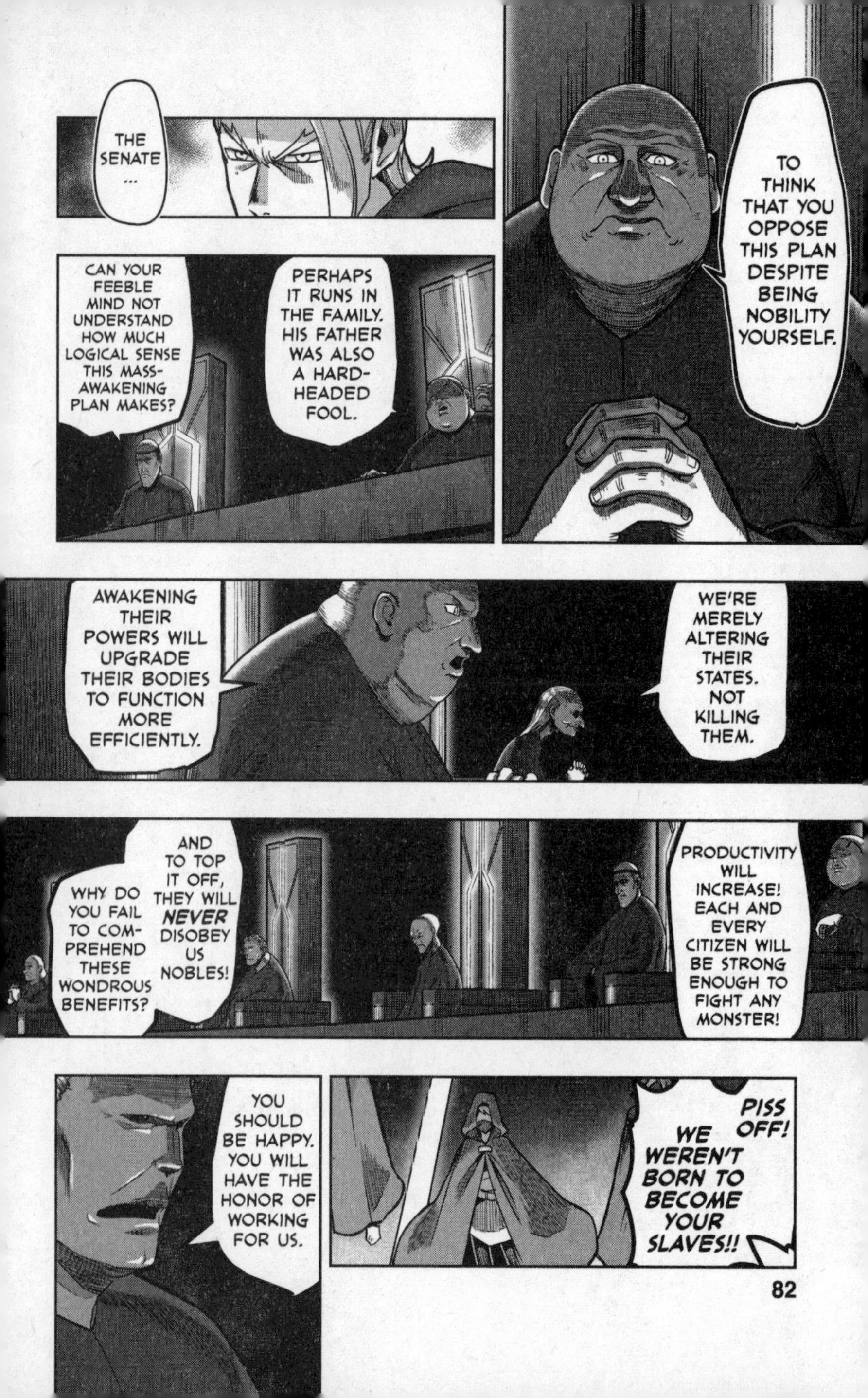
THE SENATE ...
CAN YOUR FEEBLE MIND NOT UNDERSTAND HOW MUCH LOGICAL SENSE THIS MASS-AWAKENING PLAN MAKES?
PERHAPS IT RUNS IN THE FAMILY. HIS FATHER WAS ALSO A HARD-HEADED FOOL.
TO THINK THAT YOU OPPOSE THIS PLAN DESPITE BEING NOBILITY YOURSELF.
AWAKENING THEIR POWERS WILL UPGRADE THEIR BODIES TO FUNCTION MORE EFFICIENTLY.
WE'RE MERELY ALTERING THEIR STATES. NOT KILLING THEM.
WHY DO YOU FAIL TO COMPREHEND THESE WONDROUS BENEFITS?
AND TO TOP IT OFF, THEY WILL *NEVER* DISOBEY US NOBLES!
PRODUCTIVITY WILL INCREASE! EACH AND EVERY CITIZEN WILL BE STRONG ENOUGH TO FIGHT ANY MONSTER!
YOU SHOULD BE HAPPY. YOU WILL HAVE THE HONOR OF WORKING FOR US.
PISS OFF!
WE WEREN'T BORN TO BECOME YOUR SLAVES!!

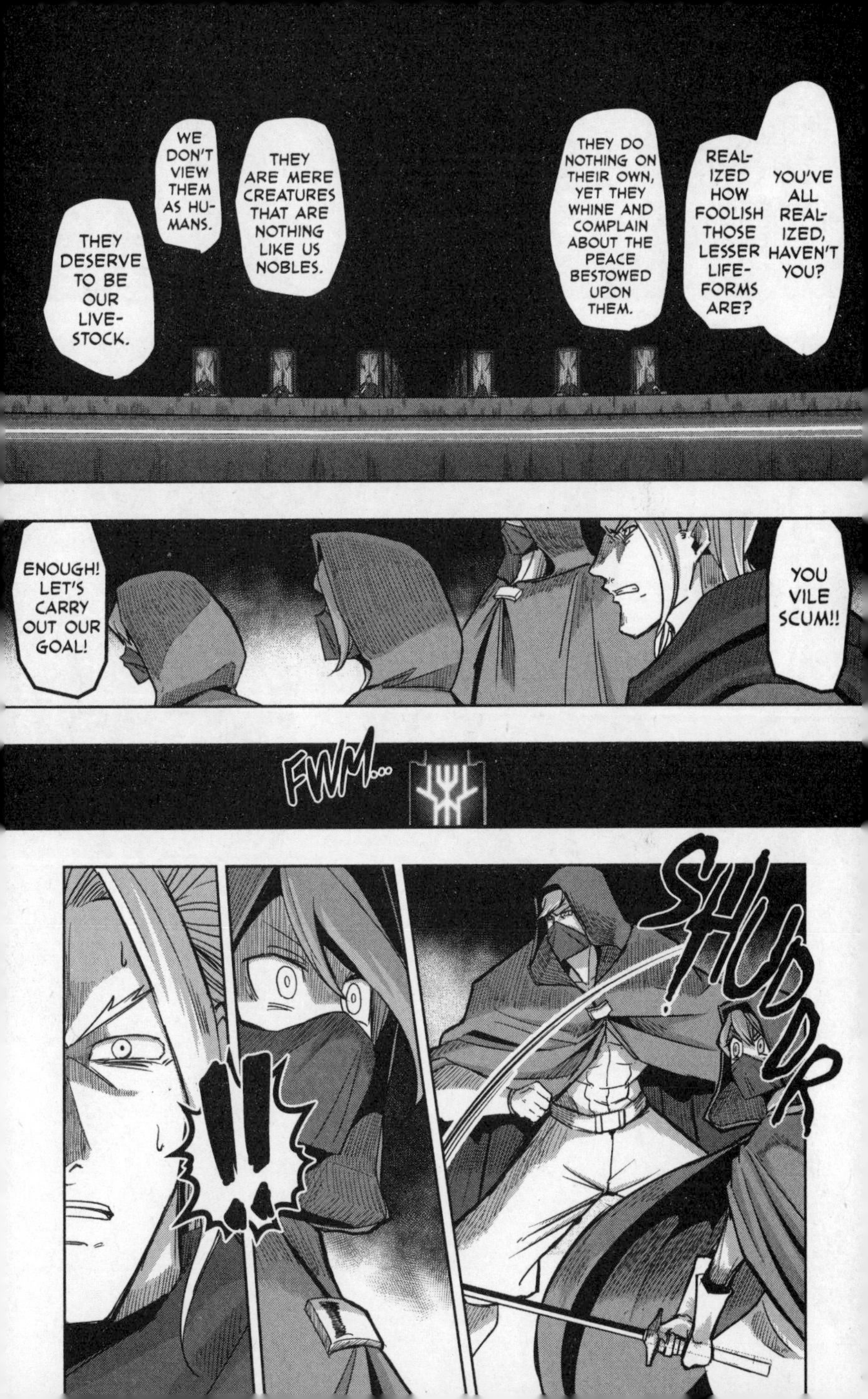
YOU'VE ALL REALIZED, HAVEN'T YOU?
REALIZED HOW FOOLISH THOSE LESSER LIFE-FORMS ARE?
THEY DO NOTHING ON THEIR OWN, YET THEY WHINE AND COMPLAIN ABOUT THE PEACE BESTOWED UPON THEM.
THEY ARE MERE CREATURES THAT ARE NOTHING LIKE US NOBLES.
WE DON'T VIEW THEM AS HUMANS.
THEY DESERVE TO BE OUR LIVESTOCK.
YOU VILE SCUM!!
ENOUGH! LET'S CARRY OUT OUR GOAL!
FWM...
SHUDDR
!!

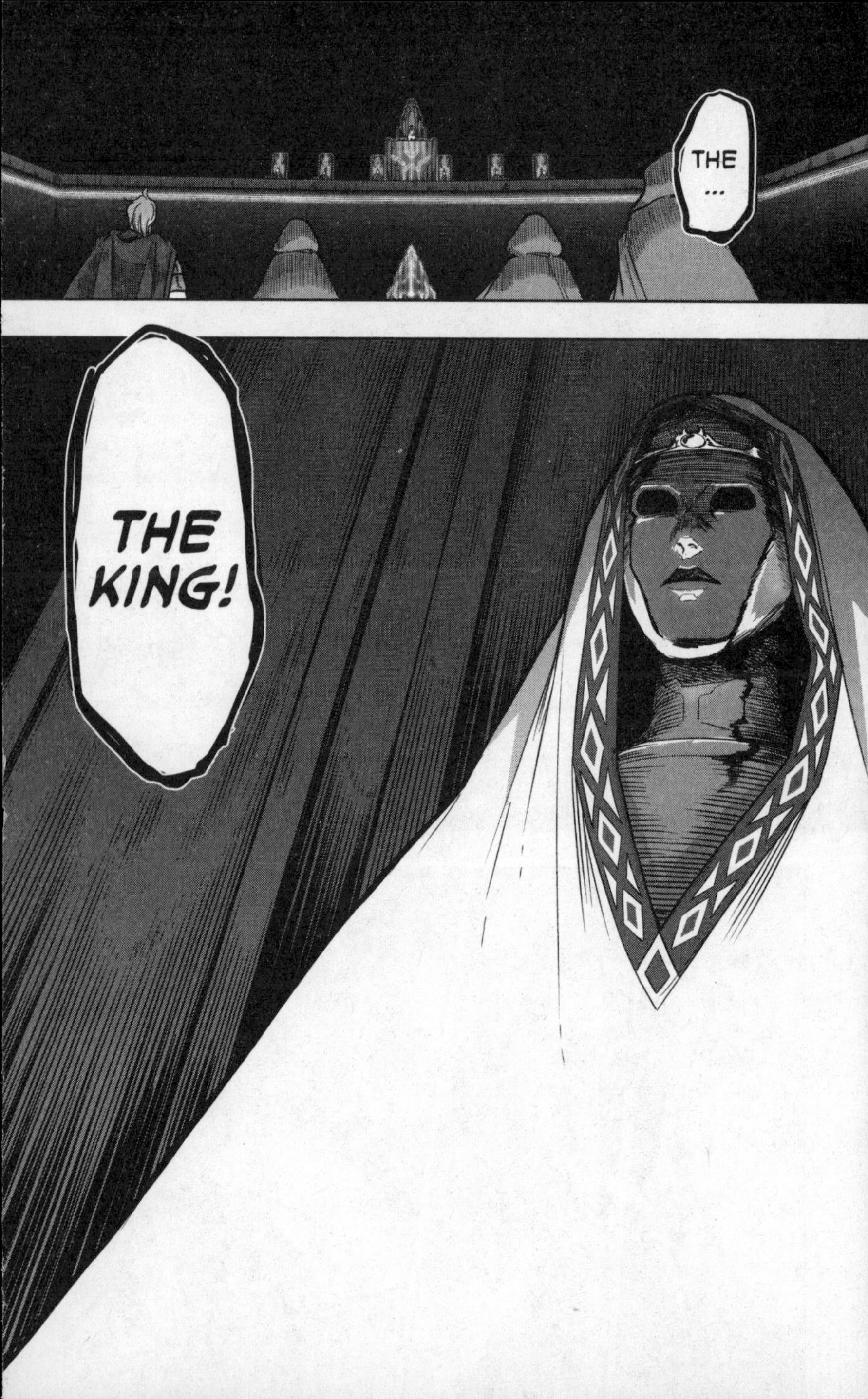
THE ...
THE KING!

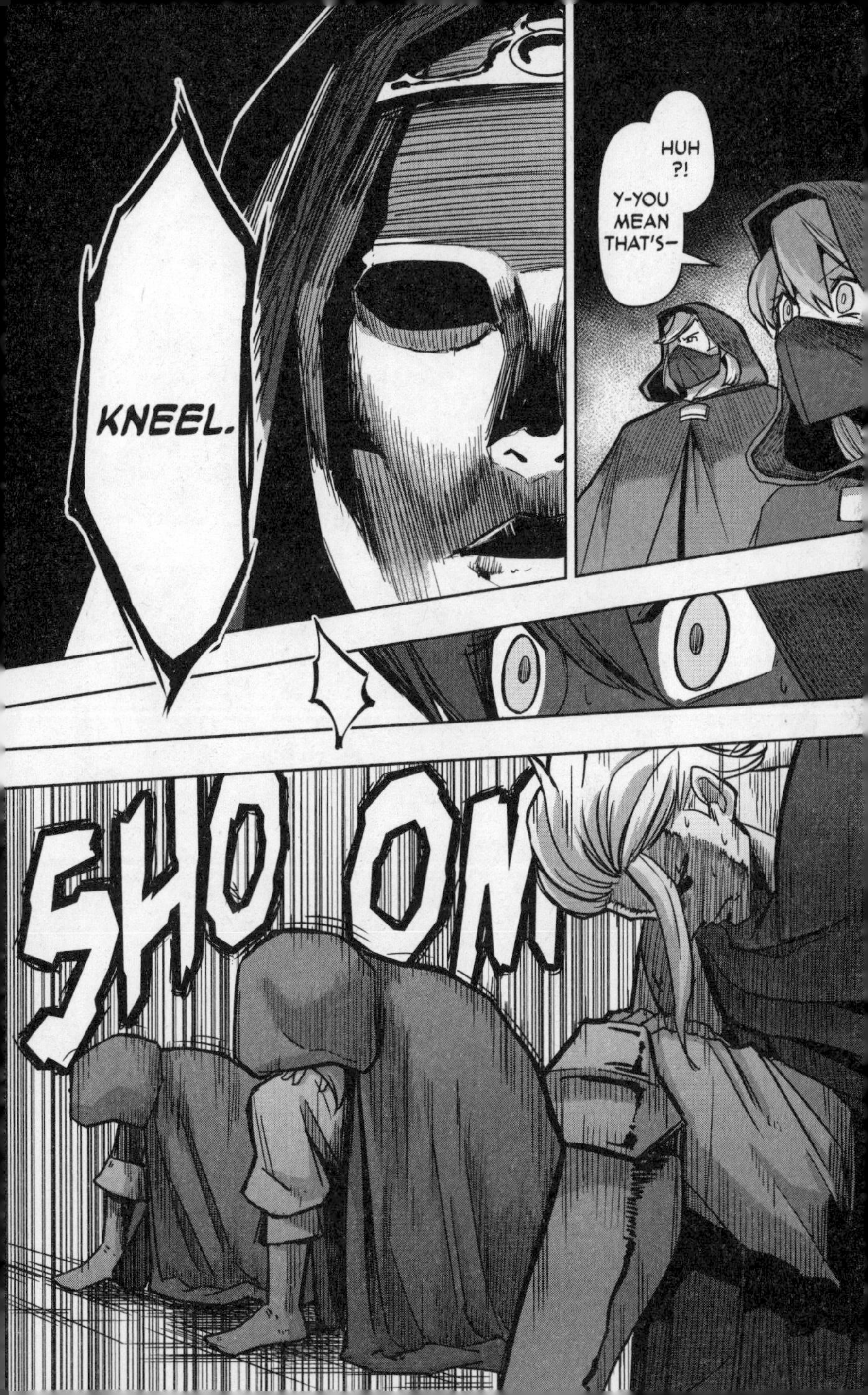
HUH ?! Y-YOU MEAN THAT'S—
KNEEL.
SHOOM

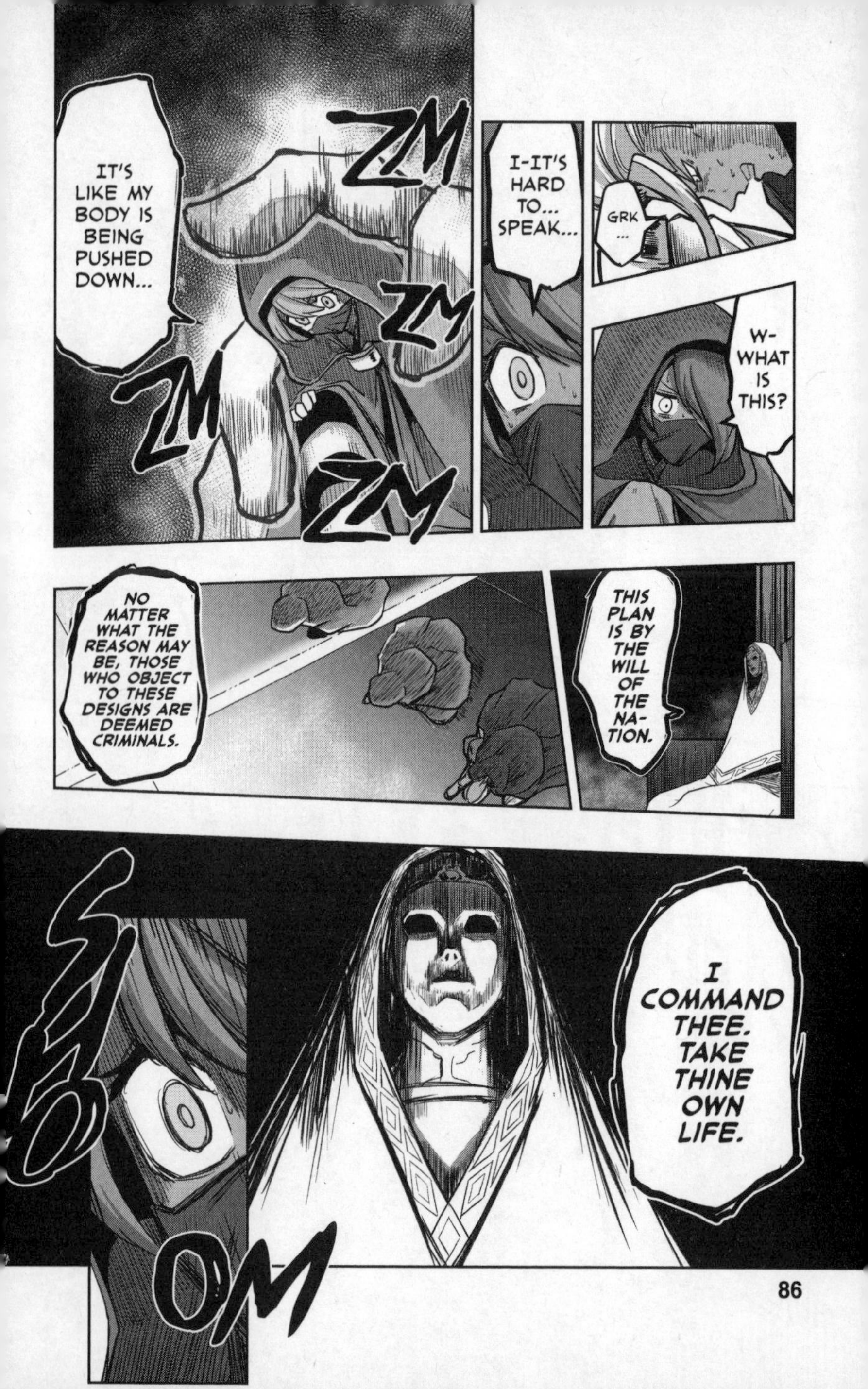
GRK ...
W-WHAT IS THIS?
I-IT'S HARD TO... SPEAK...
IT'S LIKE MY BODY IS BEING PUSHED DOWN...
ZM
ZM
ZM
ZM
THIS PLAN IS BY THE WILL OF THE NATION.
NO MATTER WHAT THE REASON MAY BE, THOSE WHO OBJECT TO THESE DESIGNS ARE DEEMED CRIMINALS.
I COMMAND THEE. TAKE THINE OWN LIFE.
SHOOM

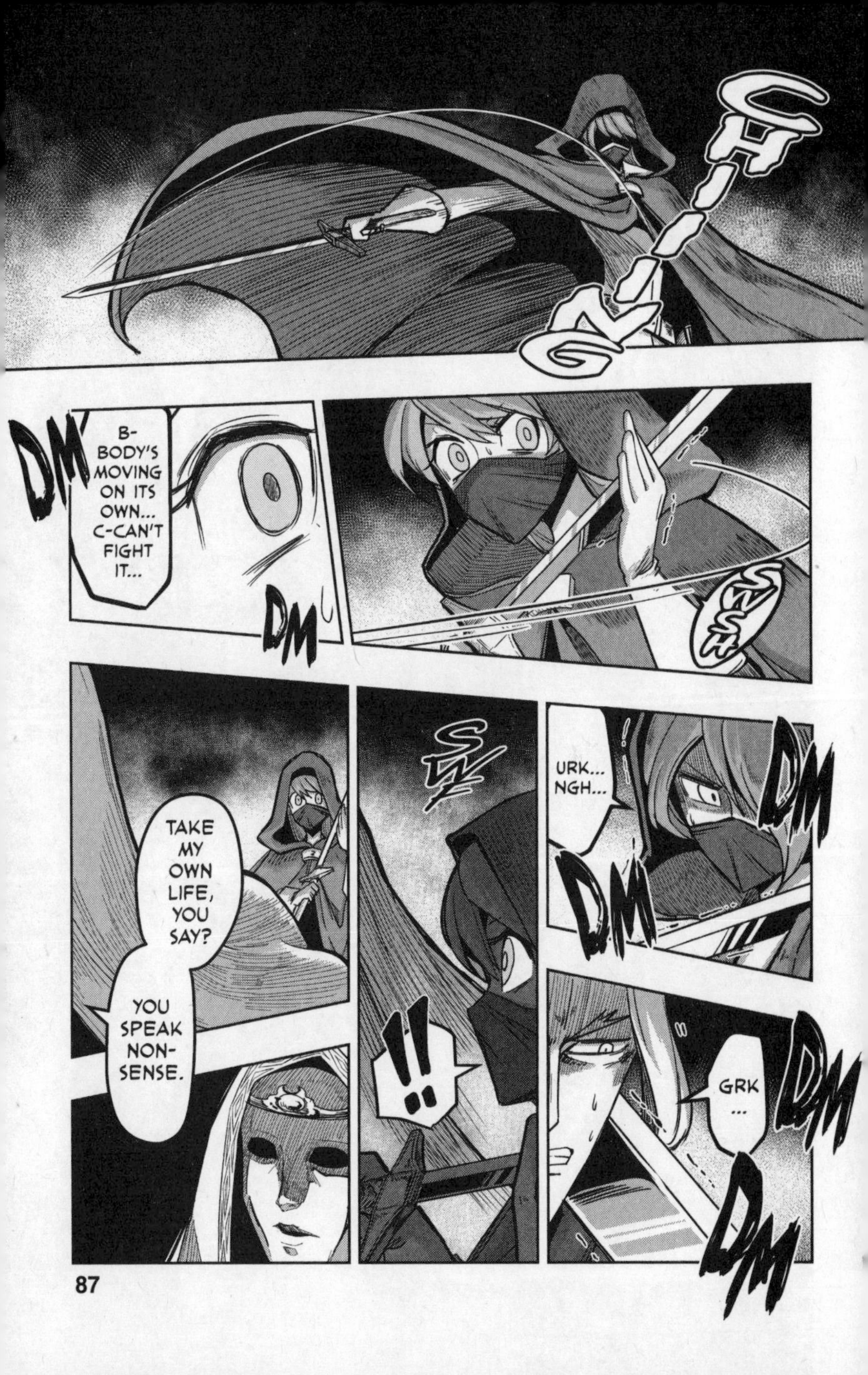
CHIIING
SWSH
DM
B-BODY'S MOVING ON ITS OWN... C-CAN'T FIGHT IT...
DM
URK... NGH...
DM
DM
DM
GRK ...
DM
DM
DM
DM
!!
TAKE MY OWN LIFE, YOU SAY?
YOU SPEAK NON-SENSE.

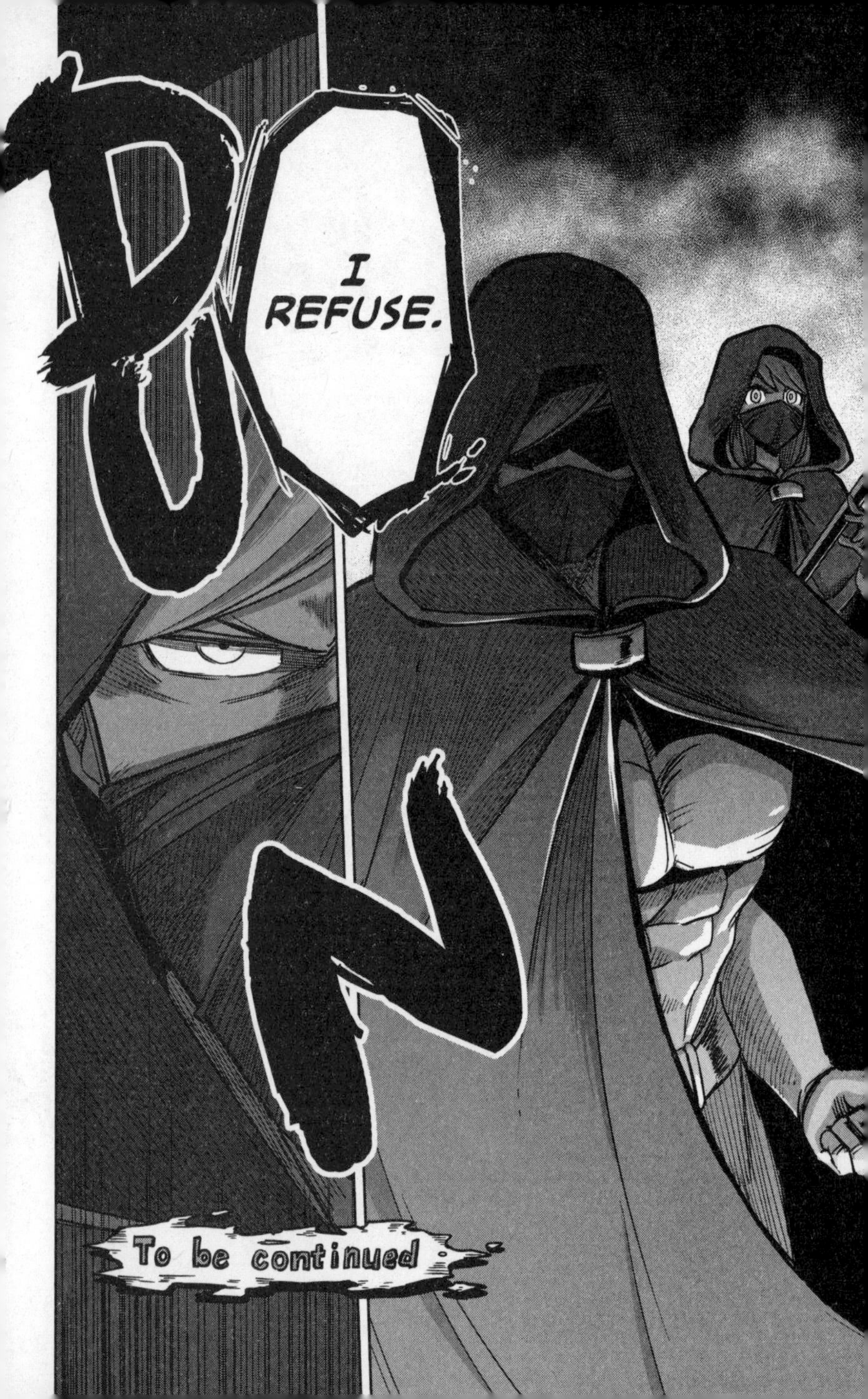
I REFUSE.
To be continued

Chapter 47: Helck's Past XII

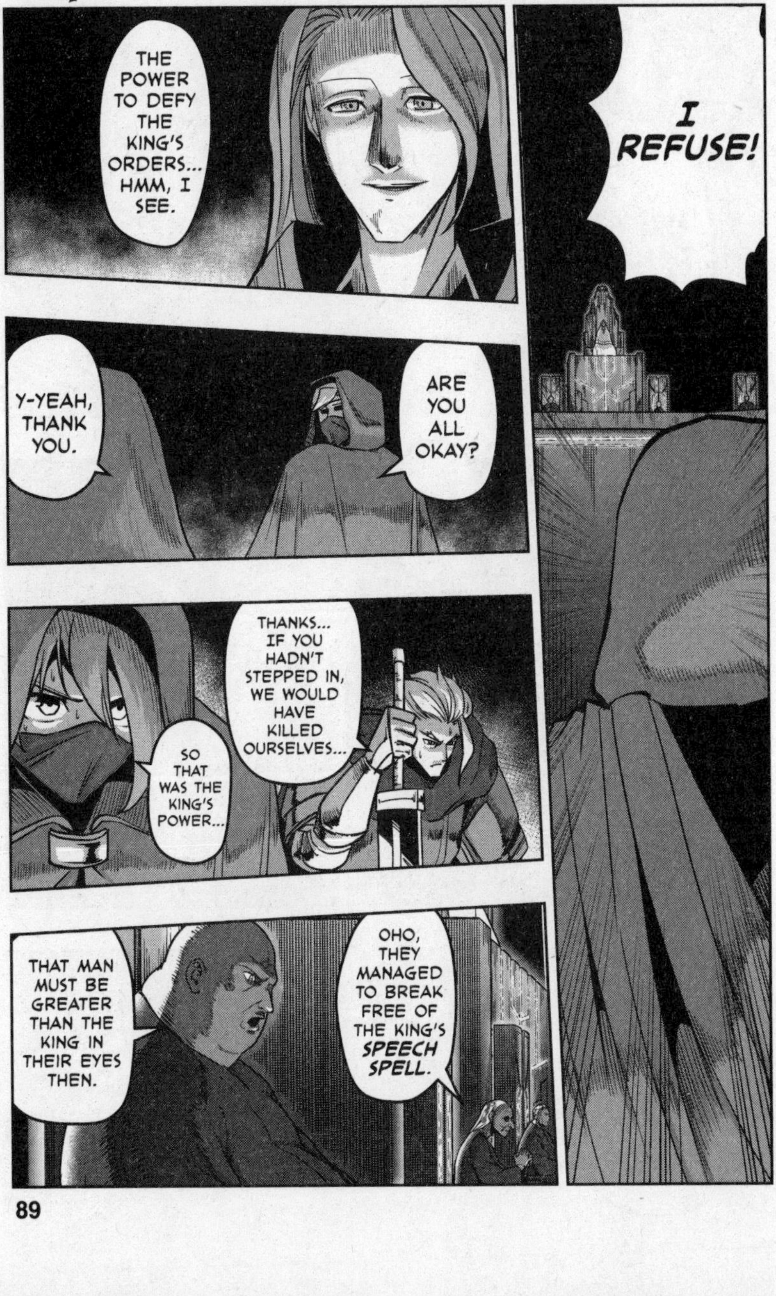
I REFUSE!
THE POWER TO DEFY THE KING'S ORDERS... HMM, I SEE.
ARE YOU ALL OKAY?
Y-YEAH, THANK YOU.
THANKS... IF YOU HADN'T STEPPED IN, WE WOULD HAVE KILLED OURSELVES...
SO THAT WAS THE KING'S POWER...
OHO, THEY MANAGED TO BREAK FREE OF THE KING'S *SPEECH SPELL*.
THAT MAN MUST BE GREATER THAN THE KING IN THEIR EYES THEN.

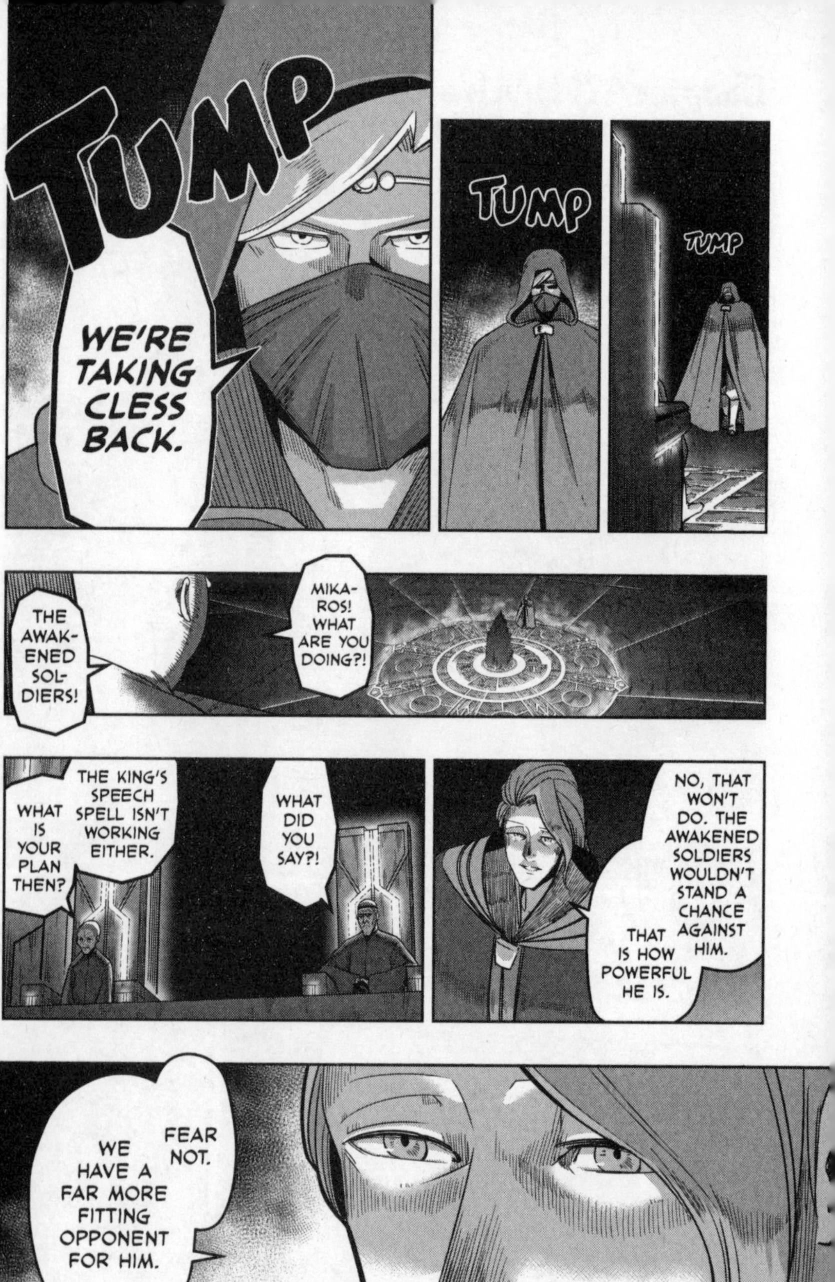
TUMP
TUMP
TUMP
WE'RE TAKING CLESS BACK.
MIKAROS! WHAT ARE YOU DOING?!
THE AWAKENED SOLDIERS!
NO, THAT WON'T DO. THE AWAKENED SOLDIERS WOULDN'T STAND A CHANCE AGAINST HIM.
THAT IS HOW POWERFUL HE IS.
WHAT DID YOU SAY?!
THE KING'S SPEECH SPELL ISN'T WORKING EITHER.
WHAT IS YOUR PLAN THEN?
FEAR NOT.
WE HAVE A FAR MORE FITTING OPPONENT FOR HIM.

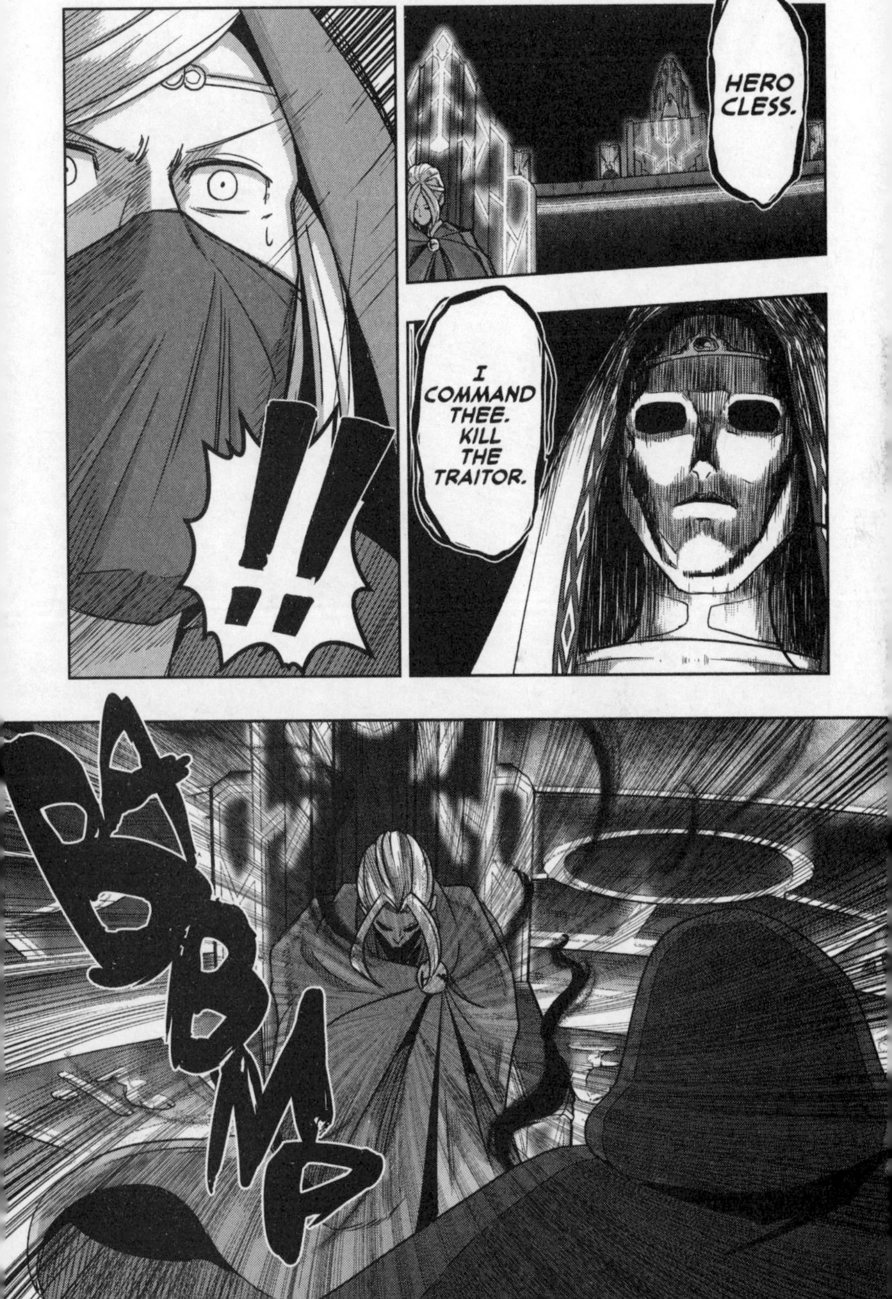
HERO CLESS.
I COMMAND THEE. KILL THE TRAITOR.
!!

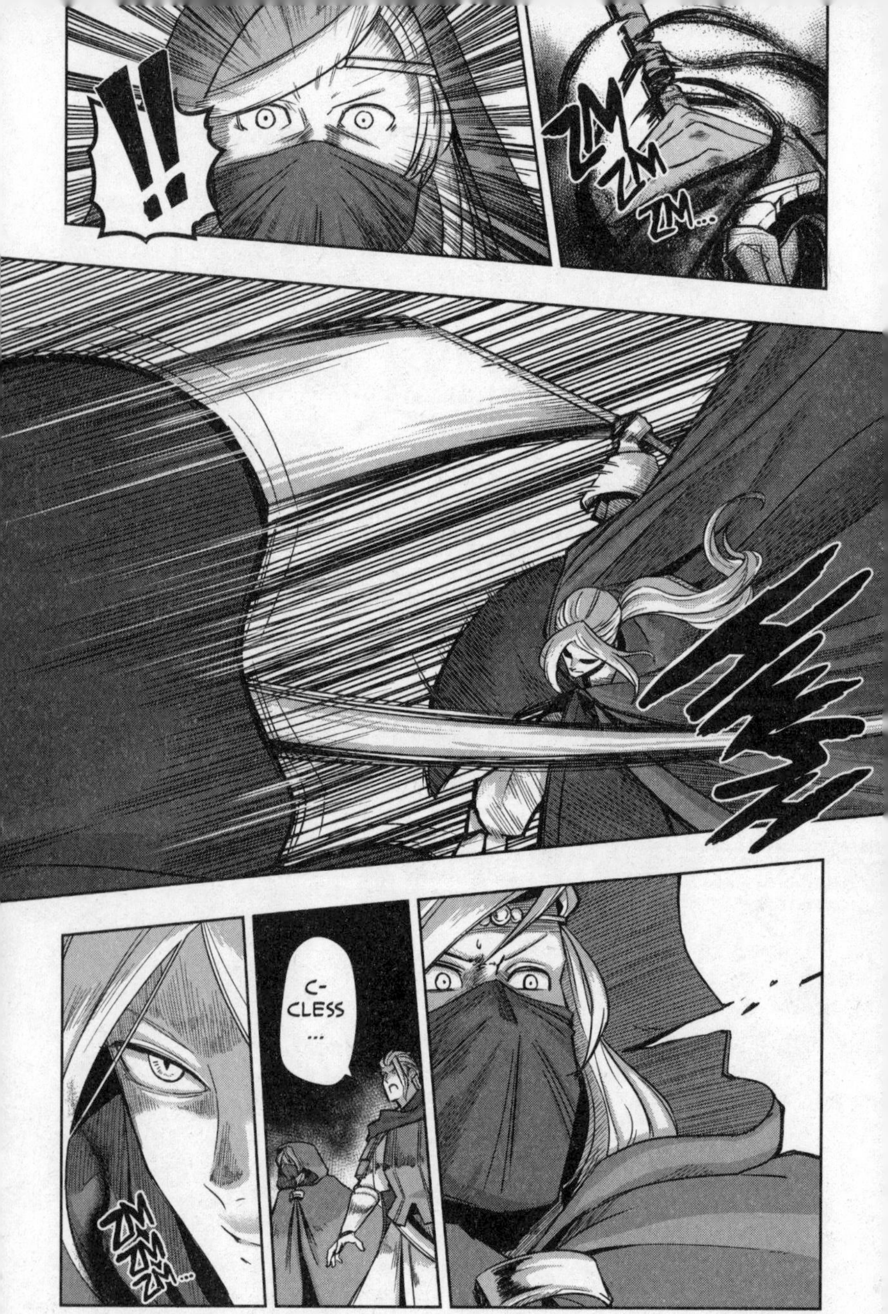

ZM ZM ZM...
!!
C-CLESS ...
ZM ZM ZM...

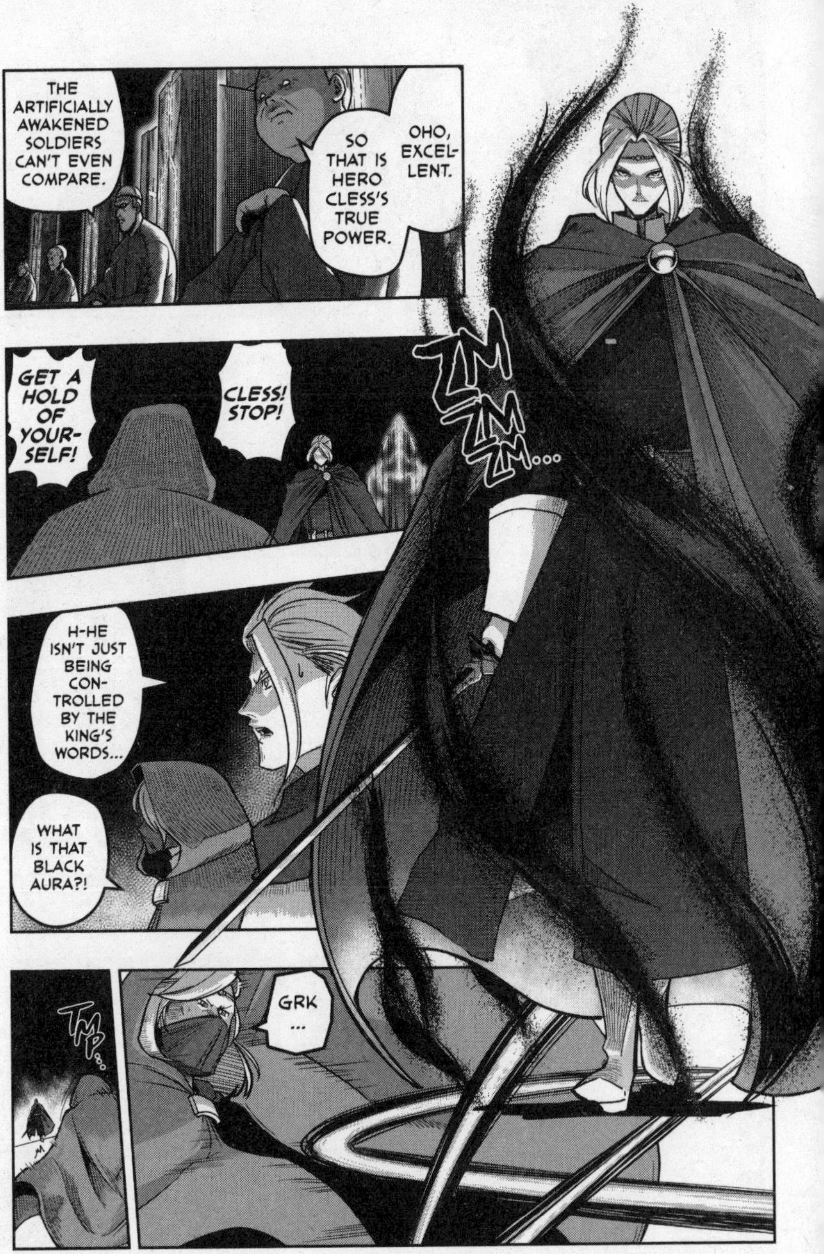
ZM ZM ZM...
OHO, EXCEL-LENT.
SO THAT IS HERO CLESS'S TRUE POWER.
THE ARTIFICIALLY AWAKENED SOLDIERS CAN'T EVEN COMPARE.
CLESS! STOP!
GET A HOLD OF YOUR-SELF!
H-HE ISN'T JUST BEING CON-TROLLED BY THE KING'S WORDS...
WHAT IS THAT BLACK AURA?!
GRK ...
TMP...

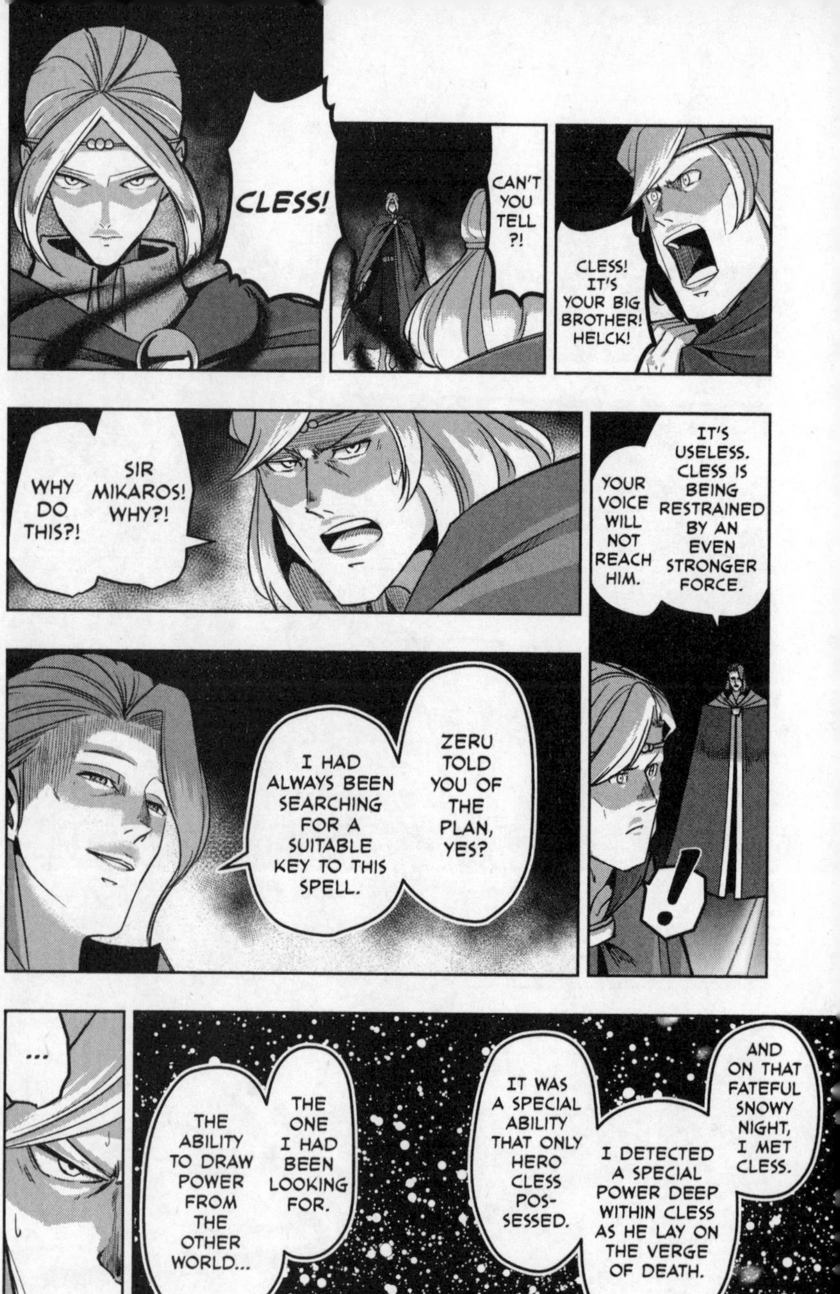
CLESS! IT'S YOUR BIG BROTHER! HELCK!
CAN'T YOU TELL ?!
CLESS!
IT'S USELESS. CLESS IS BEING RESTRAINED BY AN EVEN STRONGER FORCE.
YOUR VOICE WILL NOT REACH HIM.
SIR MIKAROS! WHY?!
WHY DO THIS?!
!
ZERU TOLD YOU OF THE PLAN, YES?
I HAD ALWAYS BEEN SEARCHING FOR A SUITABLE KEY TO THIS SPELL.
AND ON THAT FATEFUL SNOWY NIGHT, I MET CLESS.
I DETECTED A SPECIAL POWER DEEP WITHIN CLESS AS HE LAY ON THE VERGE OF DEATH.
IT WAS A SPECIAL ABILITY THAT ONLY HERO CLESS POS-SESSED.
THE ONE I HAD BEEN LOOKING FOR.
THE ABILITY TO DRAW POWER FROM THE OTHER WORLD...
...

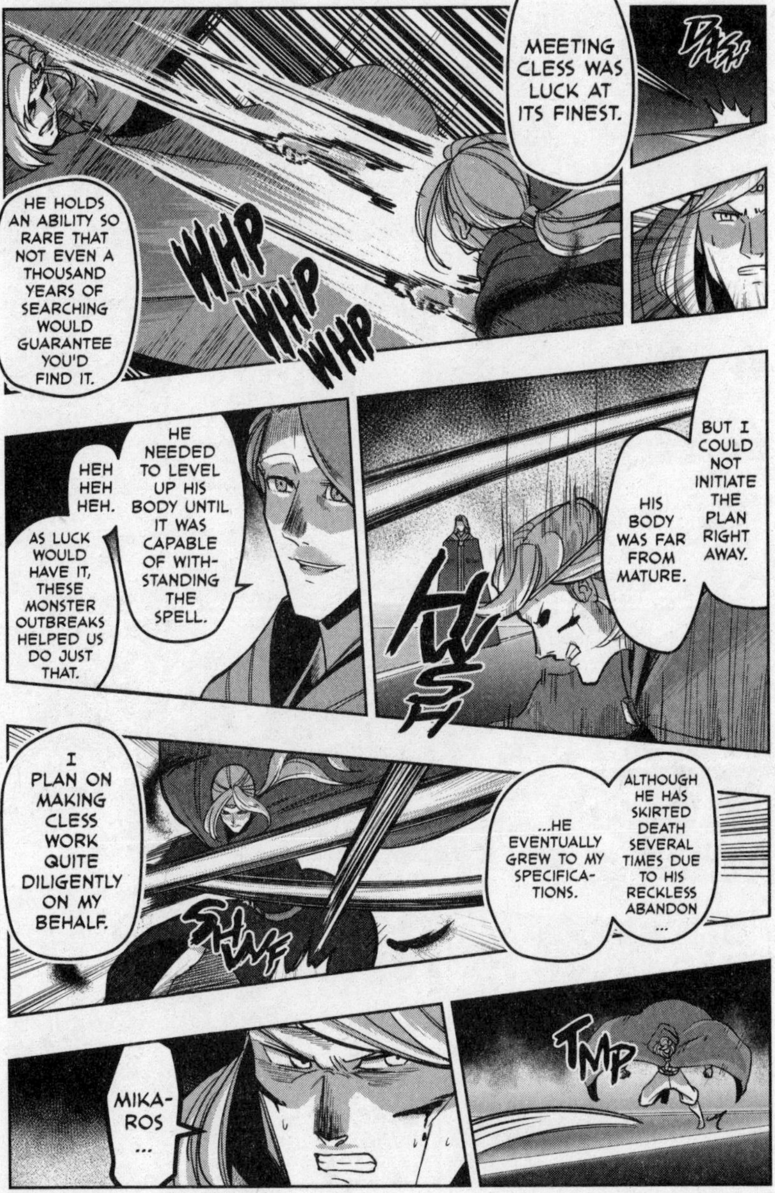

DASH
MEETING CLESS WAS LUCK AT ITS FINEST.
WHP WHP WHP
HE HOLDS AN ABILITY SO RARE THAT NOT EVEN A THOUSAND YEARS OF SEARCHING WOULD GUARANTEE YOU'D FIND IT.
BUT I COULD NOT INITIATE THE PLAN RIGHT AWAY.
HIS BODY WAS FAR FROM MATURE.
HWSH
HE NEEDED TO LEVEL UP HIS BODY UNTIL IT WAS CAPABLE OF WITH-STANDING THE SPELL.
HEH HEH HEH.
AS LUCK WOULD HAVE IT, THESE MONSTER OUTBREAKS HELPED US DO JUST THAT.
ALTHOUGH HE HAS SKIRTED DEATH SEVERAL TIMES DUE TO HIS RECKLESS ABANDON ...
...HE EVENTUALLY GREW TO MY SPECIFICA-TIONS.
SHWF
I PLAN ON MAKING CLESS WORK QUITE DILIGENTLY ON MY BEHALF.
TMP
MIKA-ROS ...

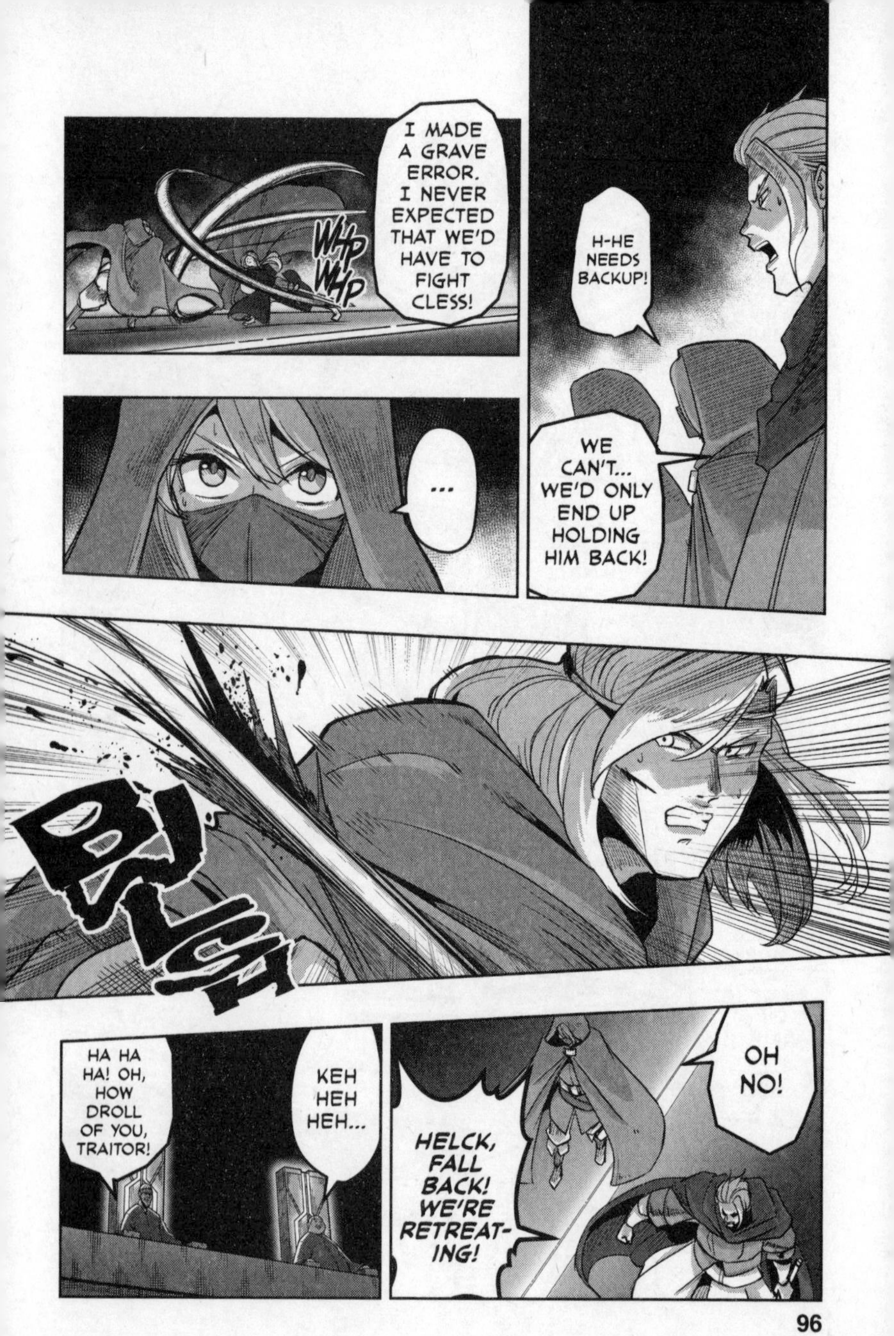
H-HE NEEDS BACKUP!
WE CAN'T... WE'D ONLY END UP HOLDING HIM BACK!
WHIP WHIP
I MADE A GRAVE ERROR. I NEVER EXPECTED THAT WE'D HAVE TO FIGHT CLESS!
...
BLISH
OH NO!
HELCK, FALL BACK! WE'RE RETREAT-ING!
KEH HEH HEH...
HA HA HA! OH, HOW DROLL OF YOU, TRAITOR!

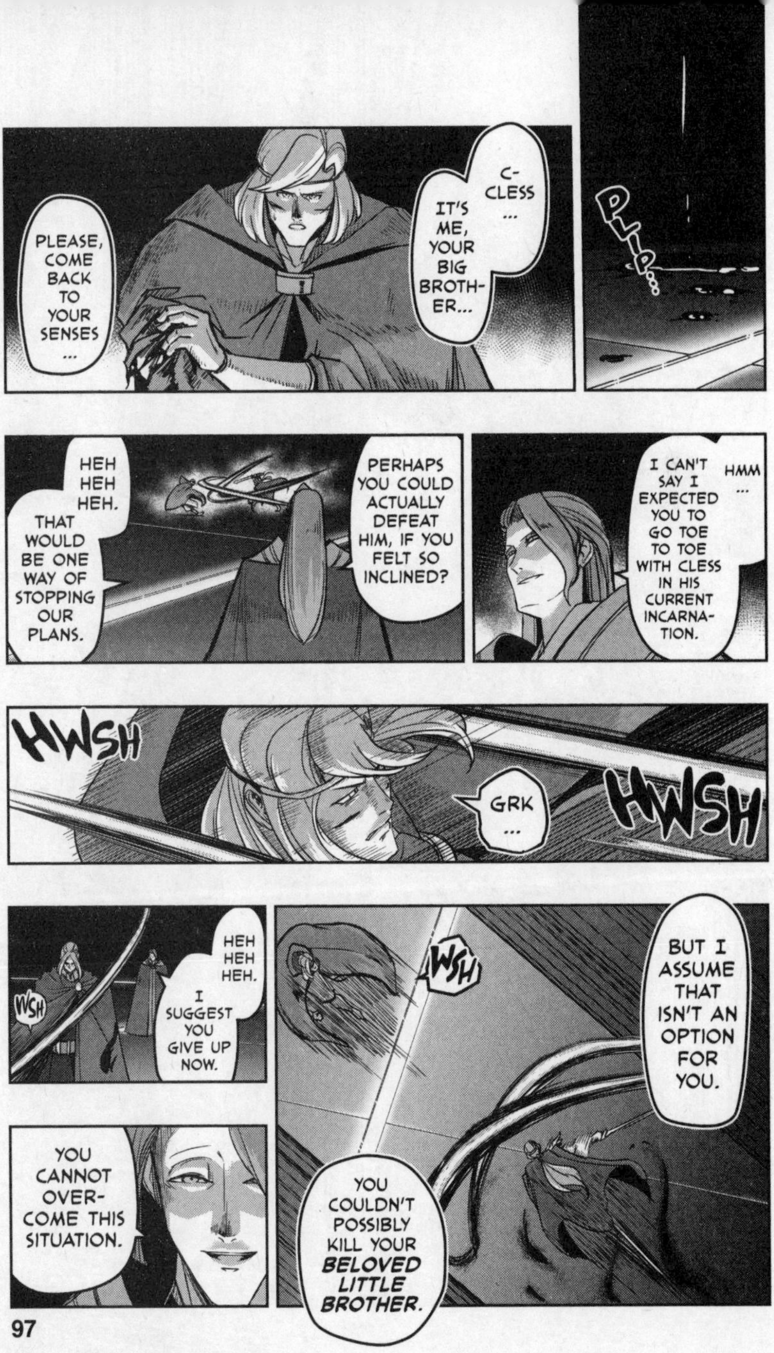
PLIP...
C-CLESS...
IT'S ME, YOUR BIG BROTHER...
PLEASE, COME BACK TO YOUR SENSES...
HMM...
I CAN'T SAY I EXPECTED YOU TO GO TOE TO TOE WITH CLESS IN HIS CURRENT INCARNATION.
PERHAPS YOU COULD ACTUALLY DEFEAT HIM, IF YOU FELT SO INCLINED?
HEH HEH HEH. THAT WOULD BE ONE WAY OF STOPPING OUR PLANS.
HWSH
GRK...
HWSH
WSH
BUT I ASSUME THAT ISN'T AN OPTION FOR YOU.
YOU COULDN'T POSSIBLY KILL YOUR *BELOVED LITTLE BROTHER.*
WSH
HEH HEH HEH. I SUGGEST YOU GIVE UP NOW.
YOU CANNOT OVERCOME THIS SITUATION.

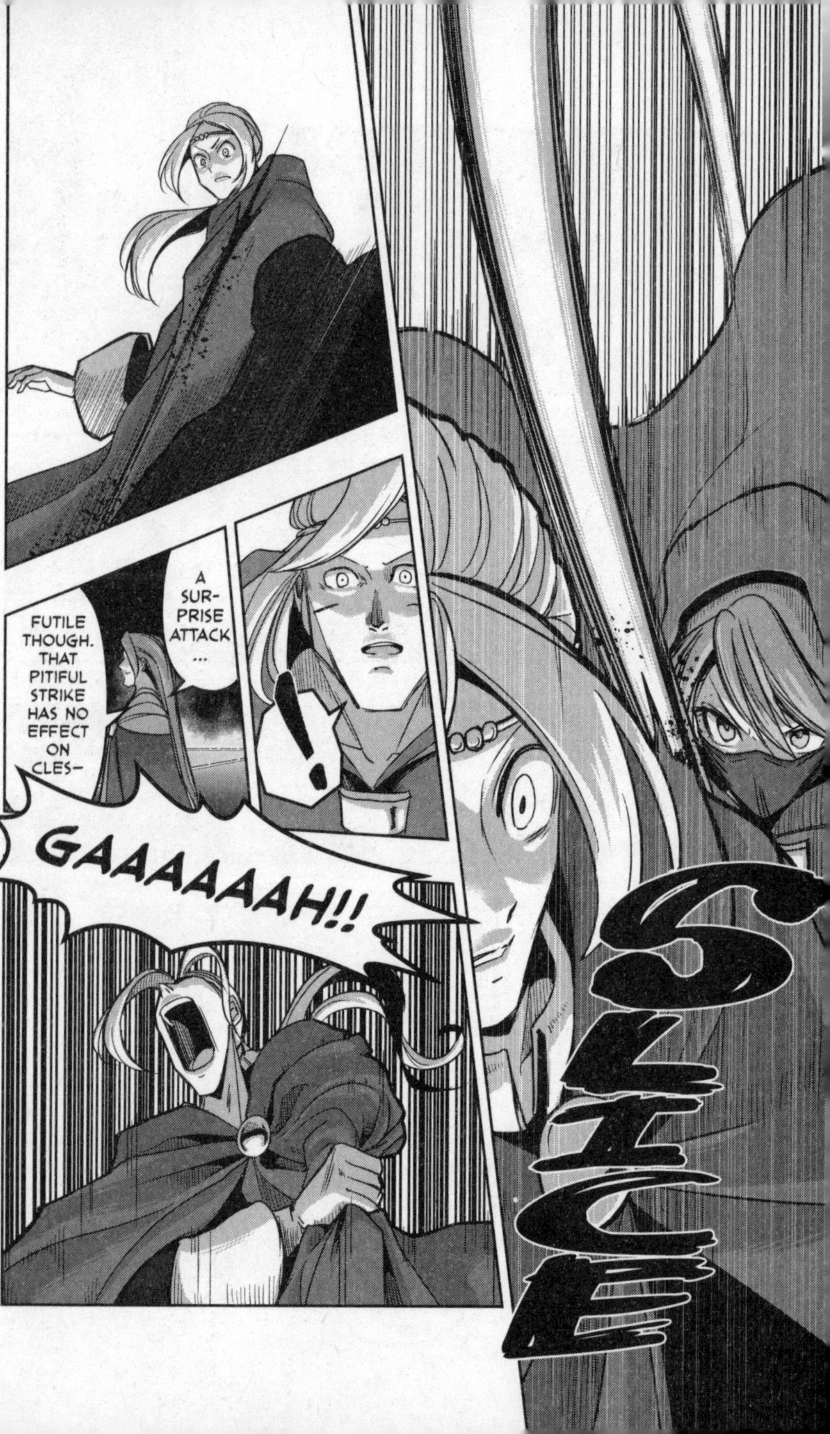
SLICE
A SURPRISE ATTACK...
FUTILE THOUGH. THAT PITIFUL STRIKE HAS NO EFFECT ON CLES—
GAAAAAAH!!

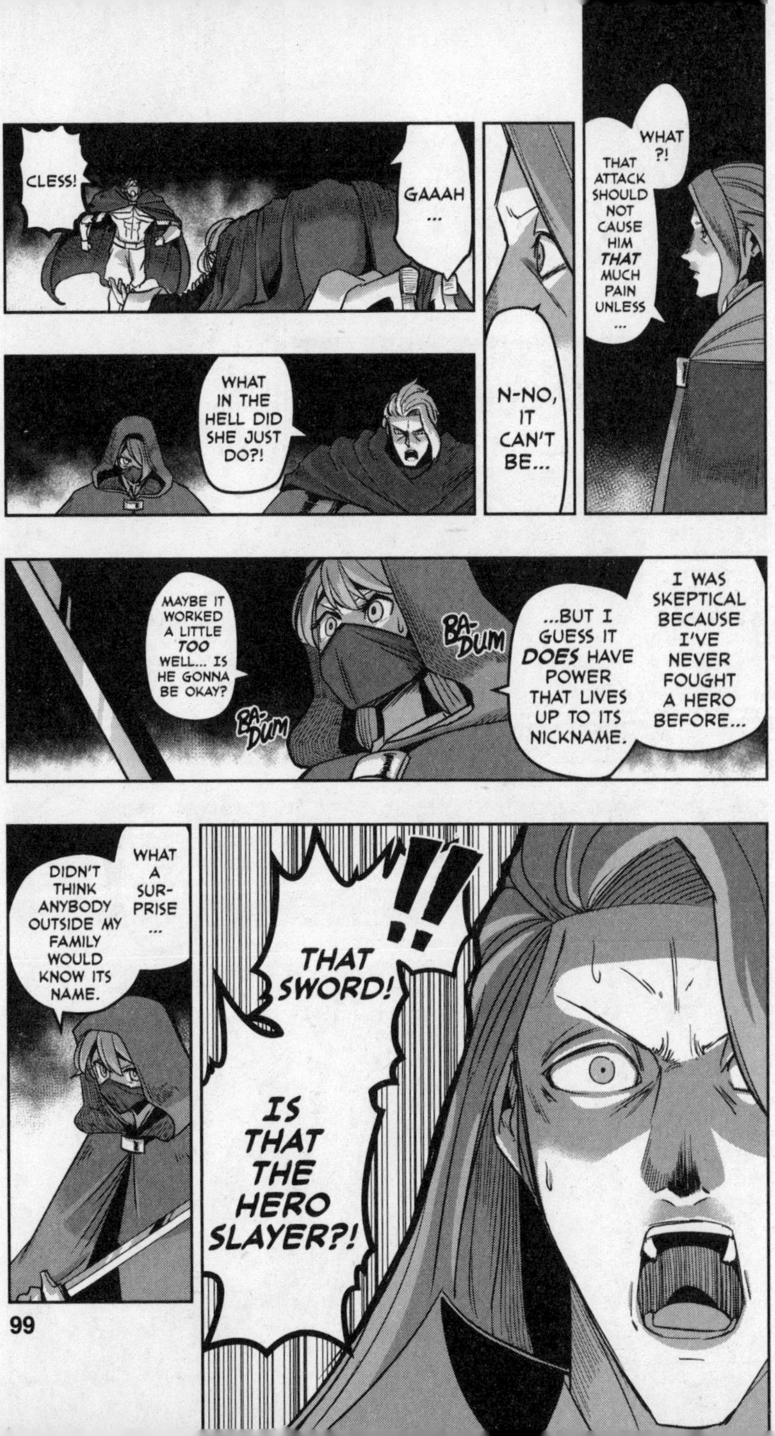

WHAT ?!
THAT ATTACK SHOULD NOT CAUSE HIM *THAT* MUCH PAIN UNLESS ...
N-NO, IT CAN'T BE...
GAAAH ...
CLESS!
WHAT IN THE HELL DID SHE JUST DO?!
I WAS SKEPTICAL BECAUSE I'VE NEVER FOUGHT A HERO BEFORE...
...BUT I GUESS IT *DOES* HAVE POWER THAT LIVES UP TO ITS NICKNAME.
BA-DUM
MAYBE IT WORKED A LITTLE *TOO* WELL... IS HE GONNA BE OKAY?
BA-DUM
!!
THAT SWORD!
IS THAT THE HERO SLAYER?!
WHAT A SUR-PRISE ...
DIDN'T THINK ANYBODY OUTSIDE MY FAMILY WOULD KNOW ITS NAME.

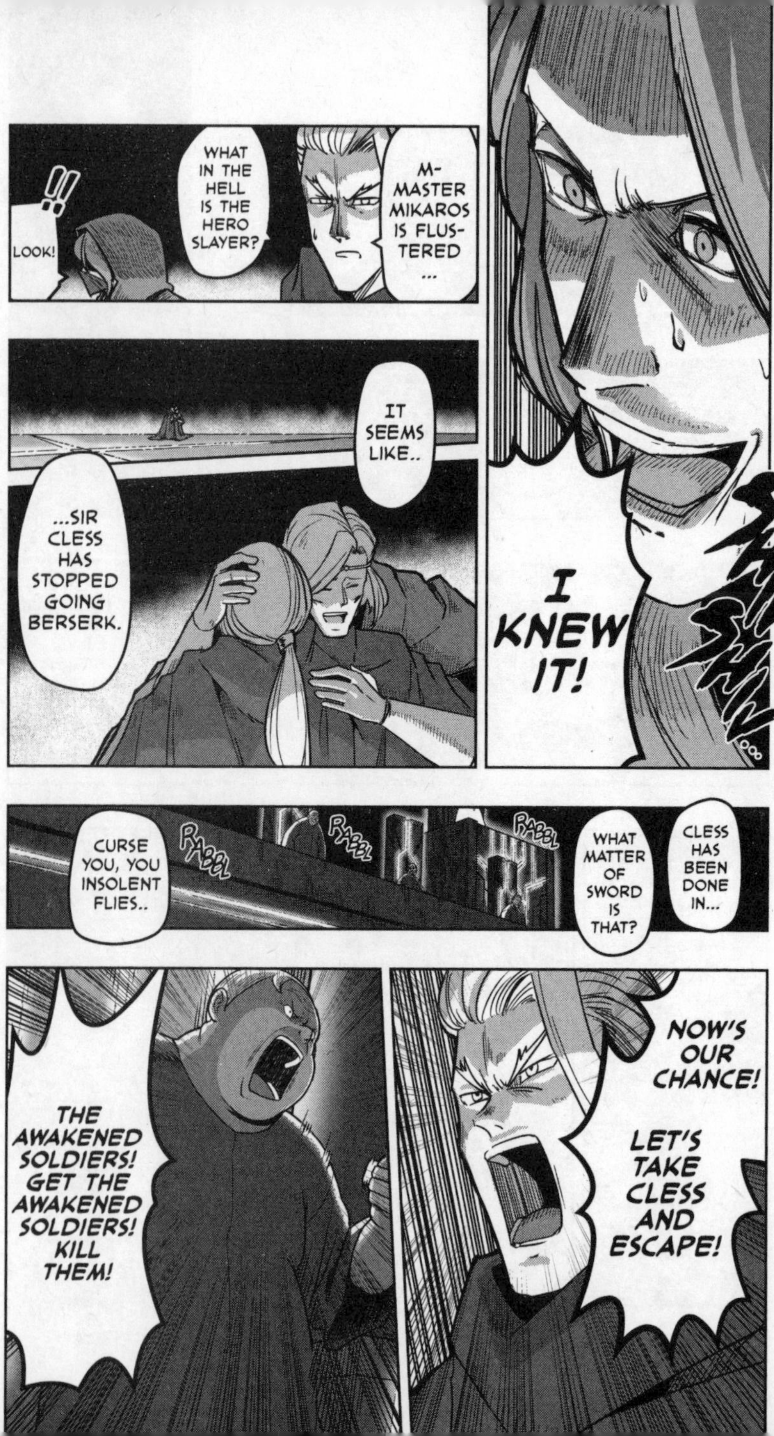
I KNEW IT!
M-MASTER MIKAROS IS FLUSTERED ...
WHAT IN THE HELL IS THE HERO SLAYER?
!!
LOOK!
IT SEEMS LIKE..
...SIR CLESS HAS STOPPED GOING BERSERK.
CLESS HAS BEEN DONE IN...
WHAT MATTER OF SWORD IS THAT?
RABBL
RABBL
RABBL
CURSE YOU, YOU INSOLENT FLIES..
NOW'S OUR CHANCE!
LET'S TAKE CLESS AND ESCAPE!
THE AWAKENED SOLDIERS! GET THE AWAKENED SOLDIERS! KILL THEM!

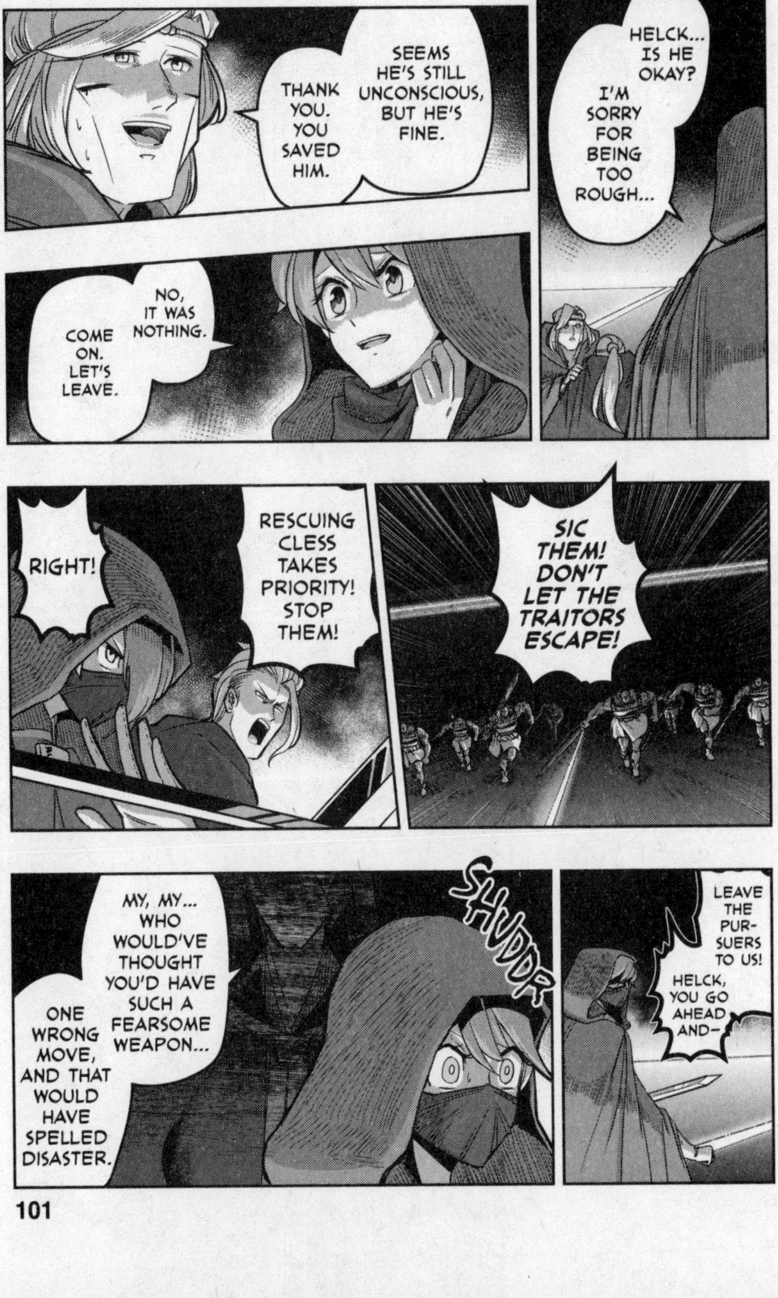
HELCK... IS HE OKAY?
I'M SORRY FOR BEING TOO ROUGH...
SEEMS HE'S STILL UNCONSCIOUS, BUT HE'S FINE.
THANK YOU. YOU SAVED HIM.
NO, IT WAS NOTHING.
COME ON. LET'S LEAVE.
SIC THEM! DON'T LET THE TRAITORS ESCAPE!
RESCUING CLESS TAKES PRIORITY! STOP THEM!
RIGHT!
LEAVE THE PUR-SUERS TO US!
HELCK, YOU GO AHEAD AND—
SHUDDR
MY, MY... WHO WOULD'VE THOUGHT YOU'D HAVE SUCH A FEARSOME WEAPON...
ONE WRONG MOVE, AND THAT WOULD HAVE SPELLED DISASTER.

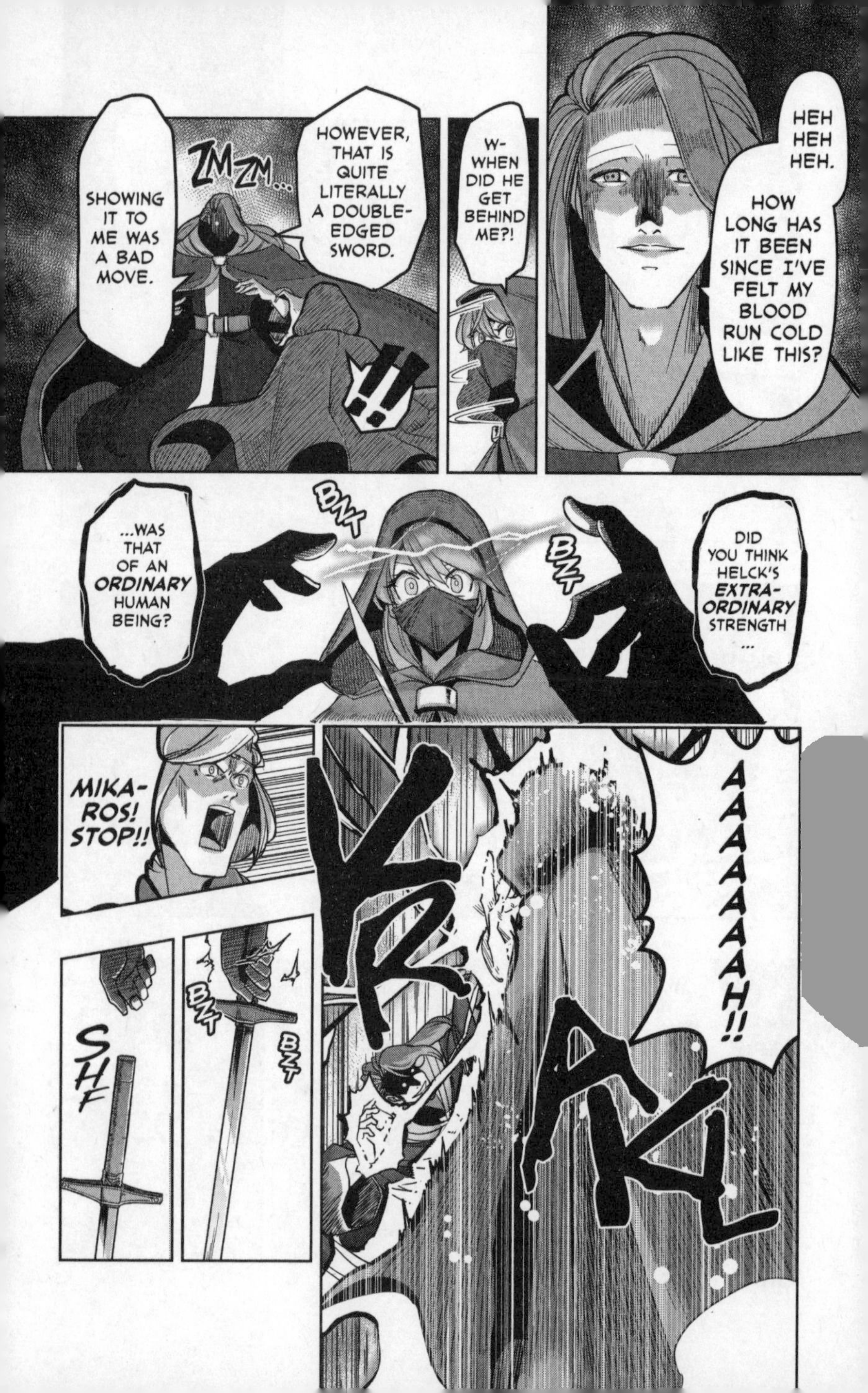
HEH HEH HEH.
HOW LONG HAS IT BEEN SINCE I'VE FELT MY BLOOD RUN COLD LIKE THIS?
W-WHEN DID HE GET BEHIND ME?!
HOWEVER, THAT IS QUITE LITERALLY A DOUBLE-EDGED SWORD.
ZMZM...
!!
SHOWING IT TO ME WAS A BAD MOVE.
DID YOU THINK HELCK'S EXTRAORDINARY STRENGTH...
BZT
BNK
...WAS THAT OF AN ORDINARY HUMAN BEING?
AAAAAAAH!!
KRAK
MIKAROS! STOP!!
BZT
BZT
SHF

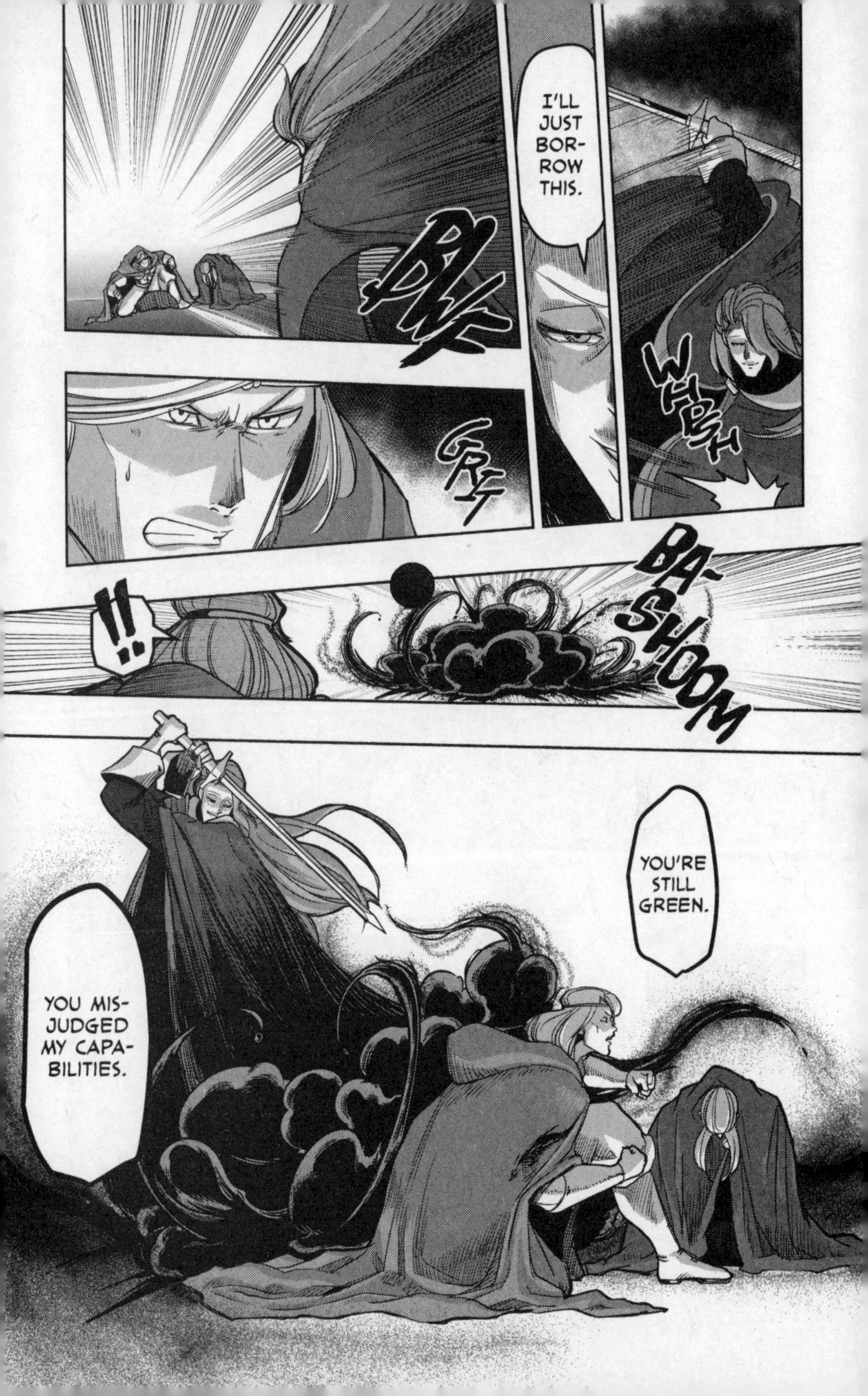
WHISK
I'LL JUST BORROW THIS.
BLINK
GRIT
BA-SHOOM
!!
YOU'RE STILL GREEN.
YOU MISJUDGED MY CAPABILITIES.

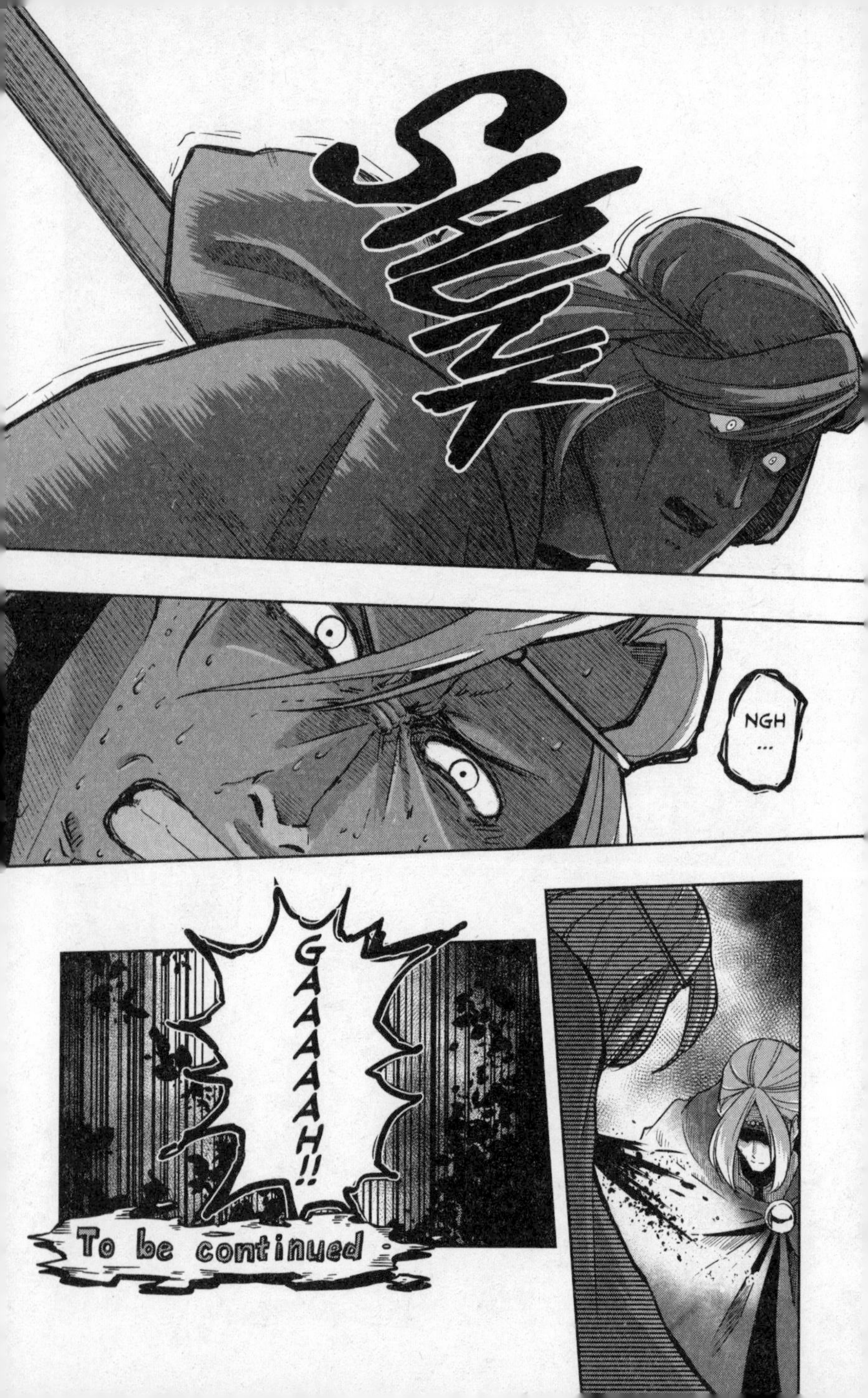
SHUNK
NGH ...
GAAAAAH!!
To be continued

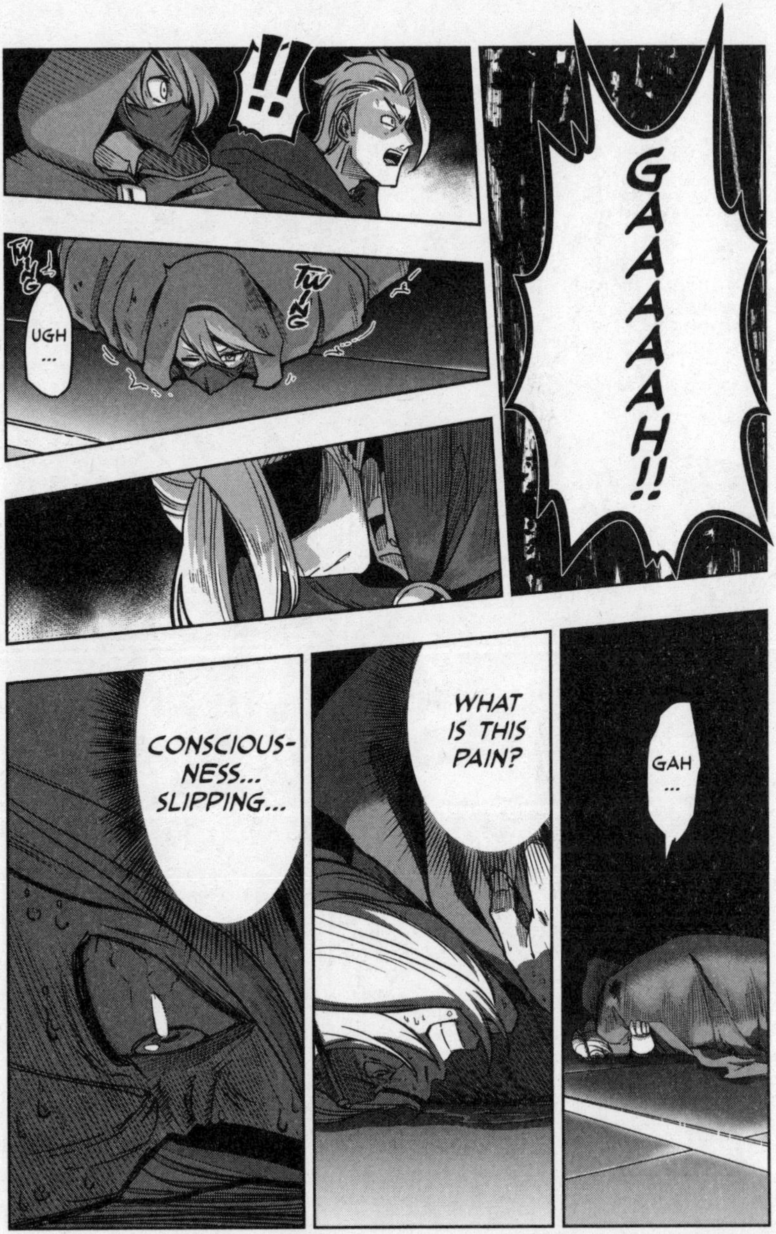
GAAAAAAH!!
!!
TWING
TWING
UGH...
GAH...
WHAT IS THIS PAIN?
CONSCIOUS-NESS... SLIPPING...

Chapter 48: Helck's Past XIII

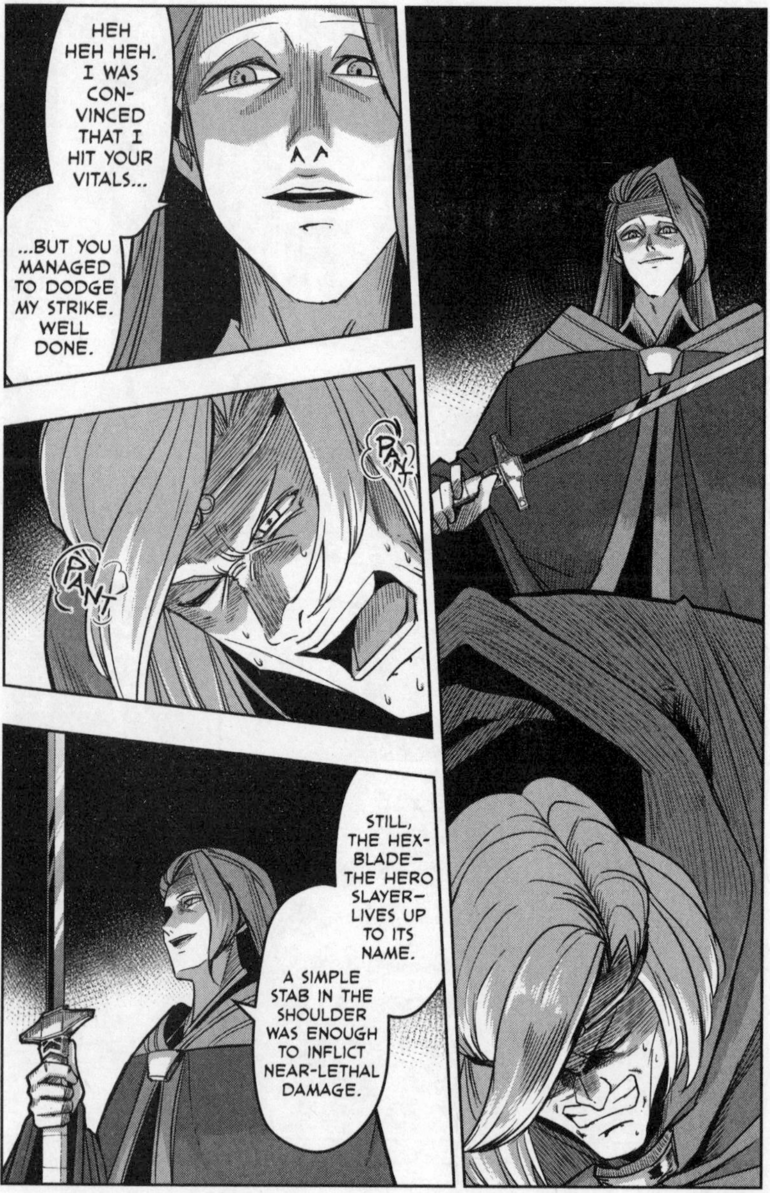
HEH HEH HEH. I WAS CON-VINCED THAT I HIT YOUR VITALS...
...BUT YOU MANAGED TO DODGE MY STRIKE. WELL DONE.
PANT
PANT
STILL, THE HEX-BLADE—THE HERO SLAYER—LIVES UP TO ITS NAME.
A SIMPLE STAB IN THE SHOULDER WAS ENOUGH TO INFLICT NEAR-LETHAL DAMAGE.

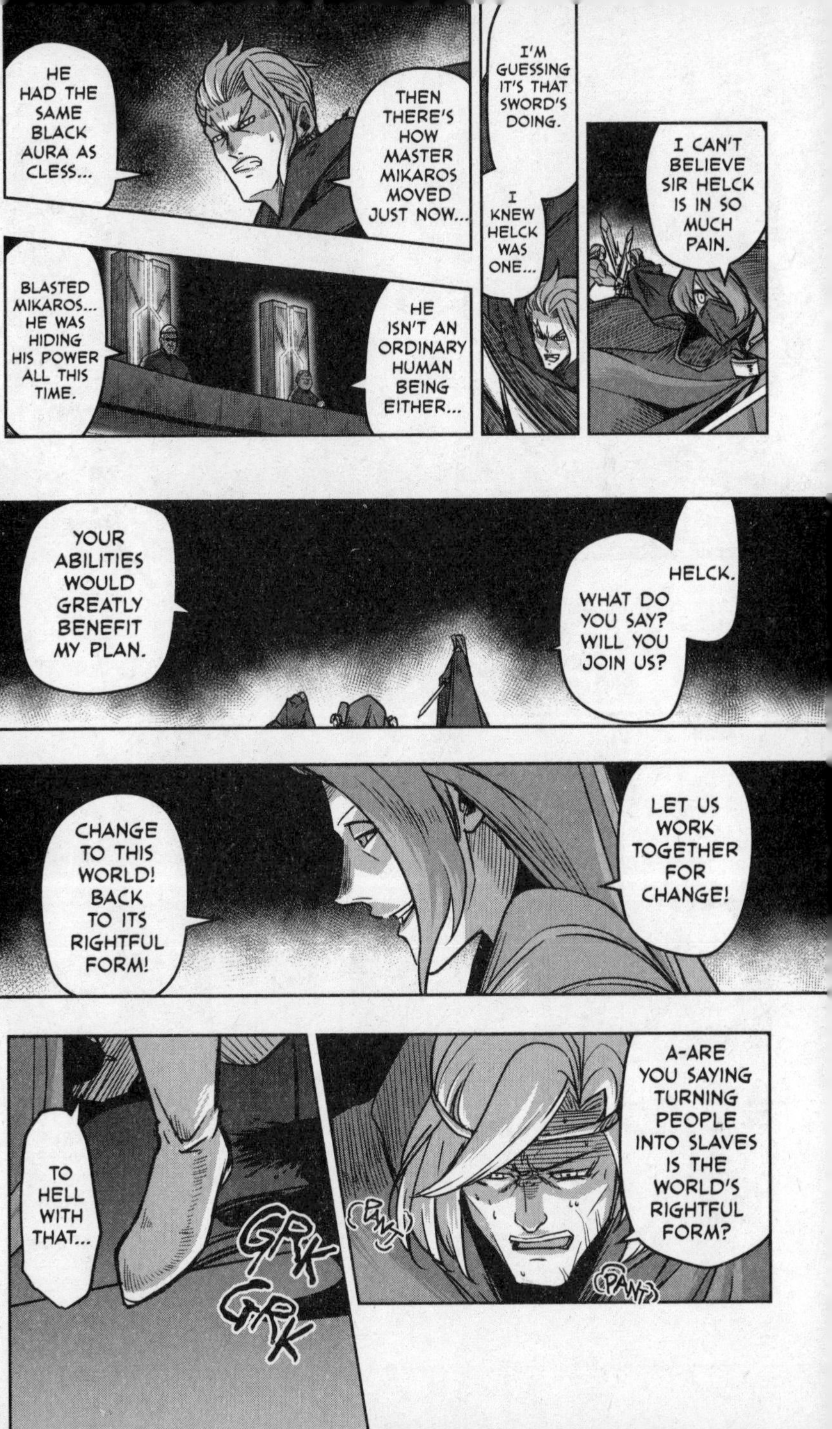
I CAN'T BELIEVE SIR HELCK IS IN SO MUCH PAIN.
I'M GUESSING IT'S THAT SWORD'S DOING.
I KNEW HELCK WAS ONE...
THEN THERE'S HOW MASTER MIKAROS MOVED JUST NOW...
HE HAD THE SAME BLACK AURA AS CLESS...
HE ISN'T AN ORDINARY HUMAN BEING EITHER...
BLASTED MIKAROS... HE WAS HIDING HIS POWER ALL THIS TIME.
HELCK. WHAT DO YOU SAY? WILL YOU JOIN US?
YOUR ABILITIES WOULD GREATLY BENEFIT MY PLAN.
LET US WORK TOGETHER FOR CHANGE!
CHANGE TO THIS WORLD! BACK TO ITS RIGHTFUL FORM!
A-ARE YOU SAYING TURNING PEOPLE INTO SLAVES IS THE WORLD'S RIGHTFUL FORM?
(PANT)
(PANT)
TO HELL WITH THAT...
GRK
GRK

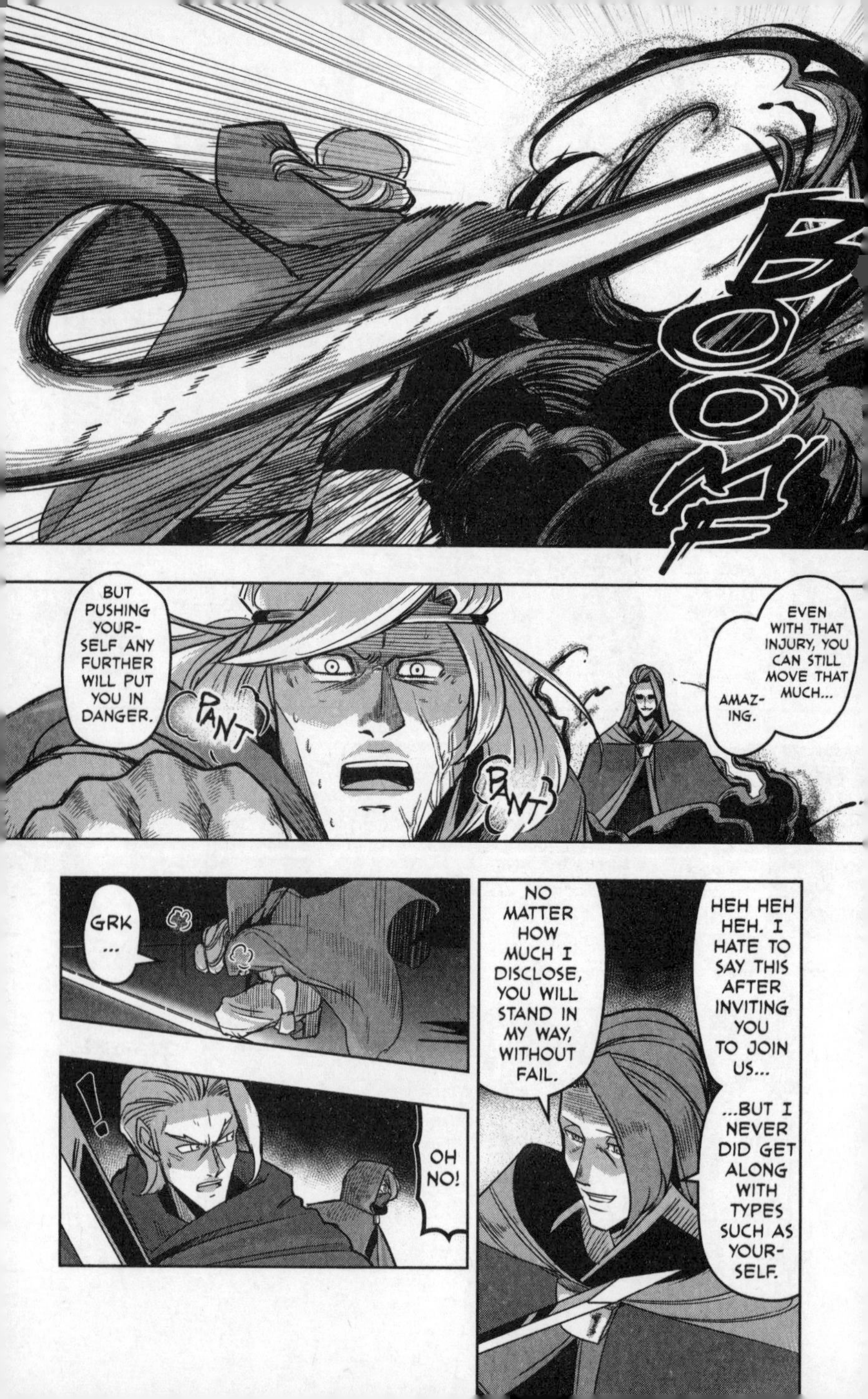
BOOM
EVEN WITH THAT INJURY, YOU CAN STILL MOVE THAT MUCH... AMAZ-ING.
BUT PUSHING YOUR-SELF ANY FURTHER WILL PUT YOU IN DANGER.
PANT
PANT
HEH HEH HEH. I HATE TO SAY THIS AFTER INVITING YOU TO JOIN US...
...BUT I NEVER DID GET ALONG WITH TYPES SUCH AS YOUR-SELF.
NO MATTER HOW MUCH I DISCLOSE, YOU WILL STAND IN MY WAY, WITHOUT FAIL.
GRK ...
!
OH NO!

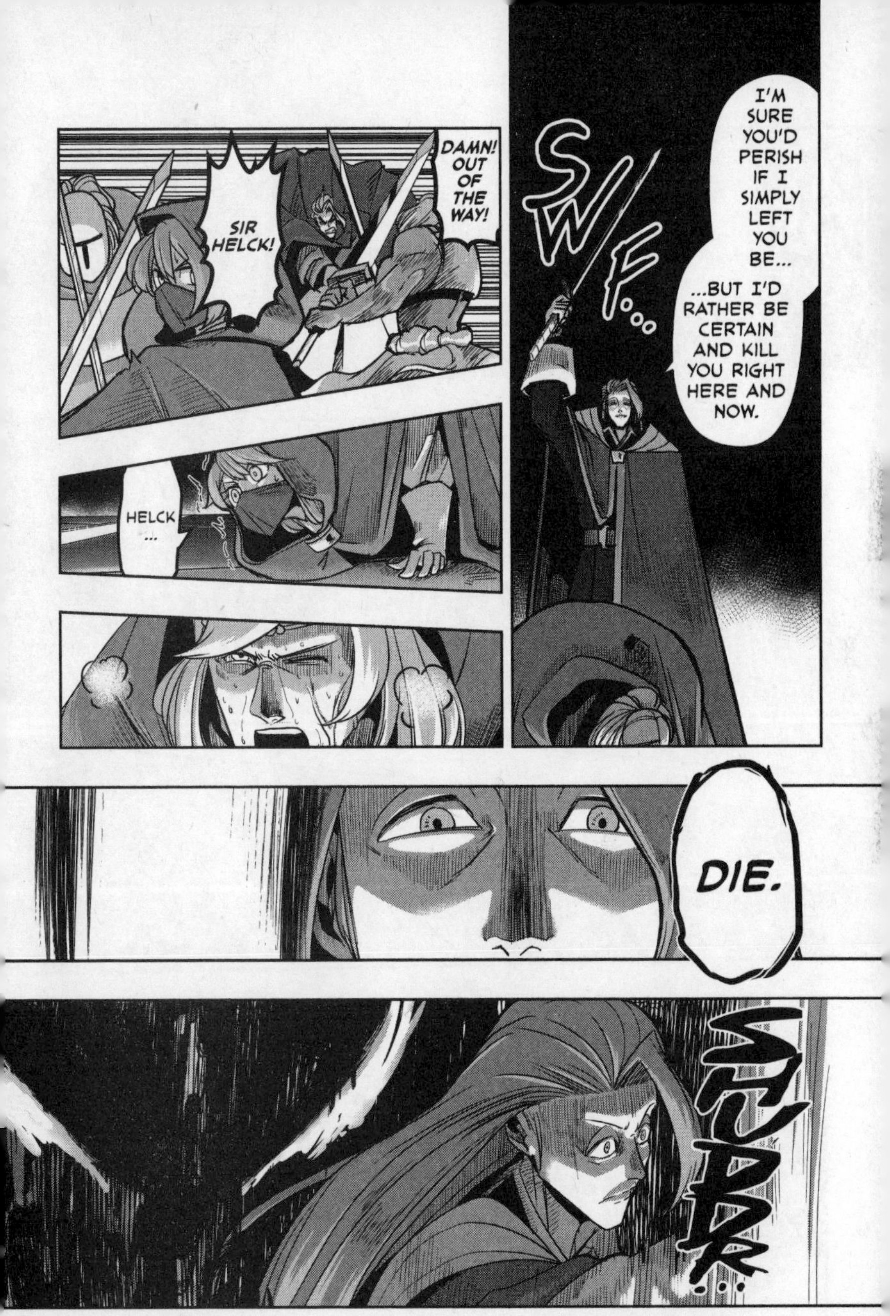
I'M SURE YOU'D PERISH IF I SIMPLY LEFT YOU BE...
...BUT I'D RATHER BE CERTAIN AND KILL YOU RIGHT HERE AND NOW.
SWF...
DAMN! OUT OF THE WAY!
SIR HELCK!
HELCK...
DIE.
SHDR...

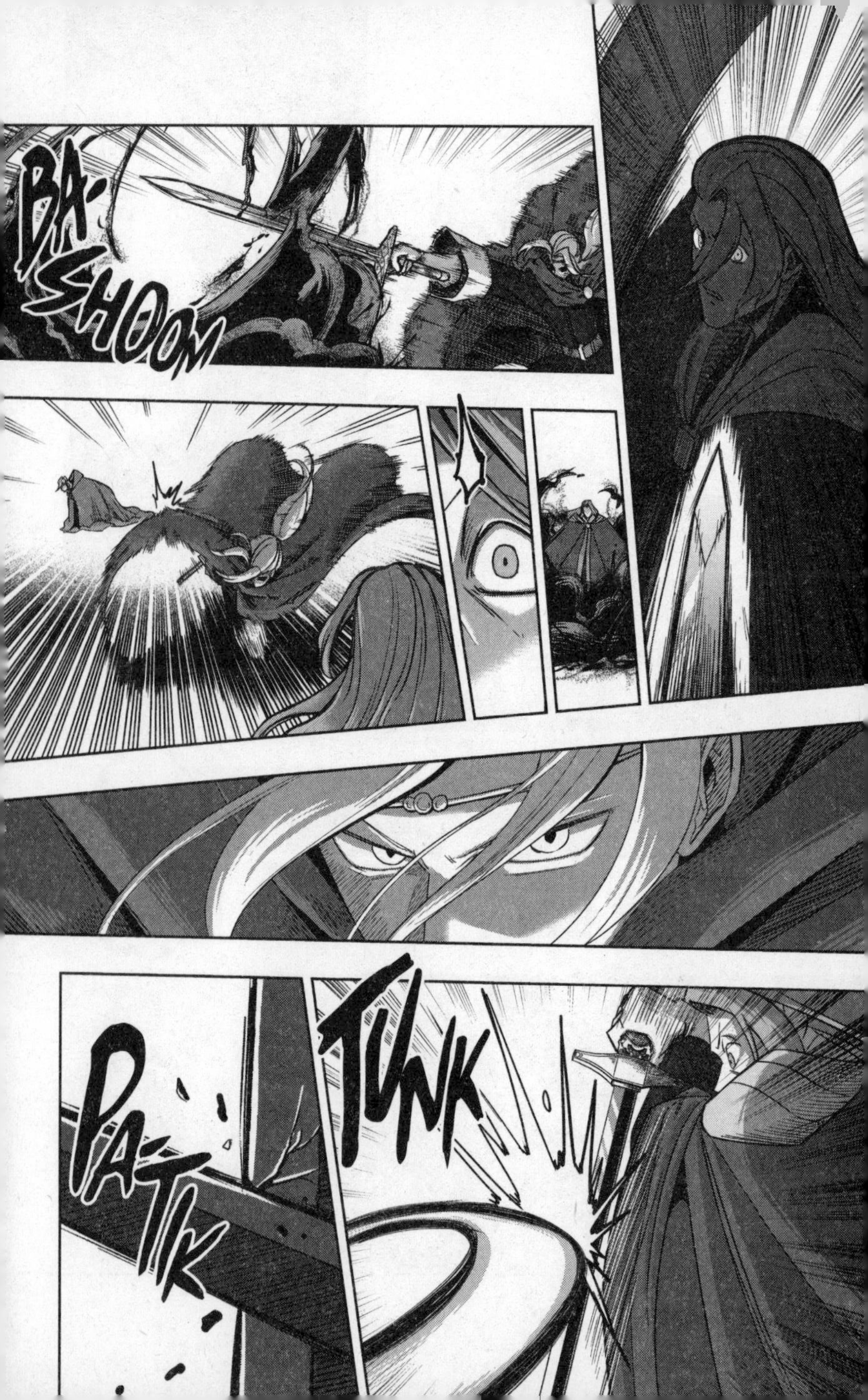
BA-SHOOM
TUNK
PA-TIK

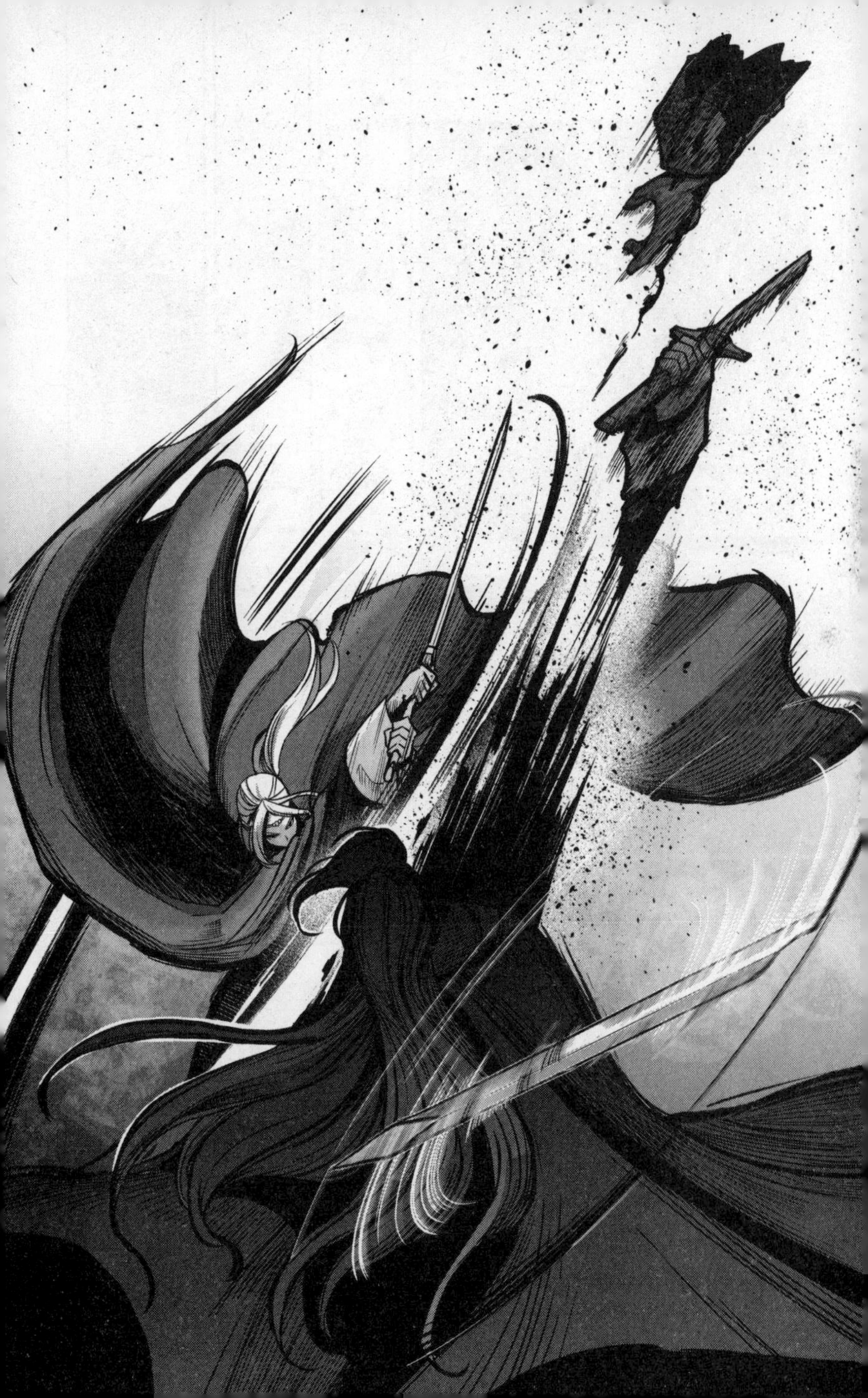

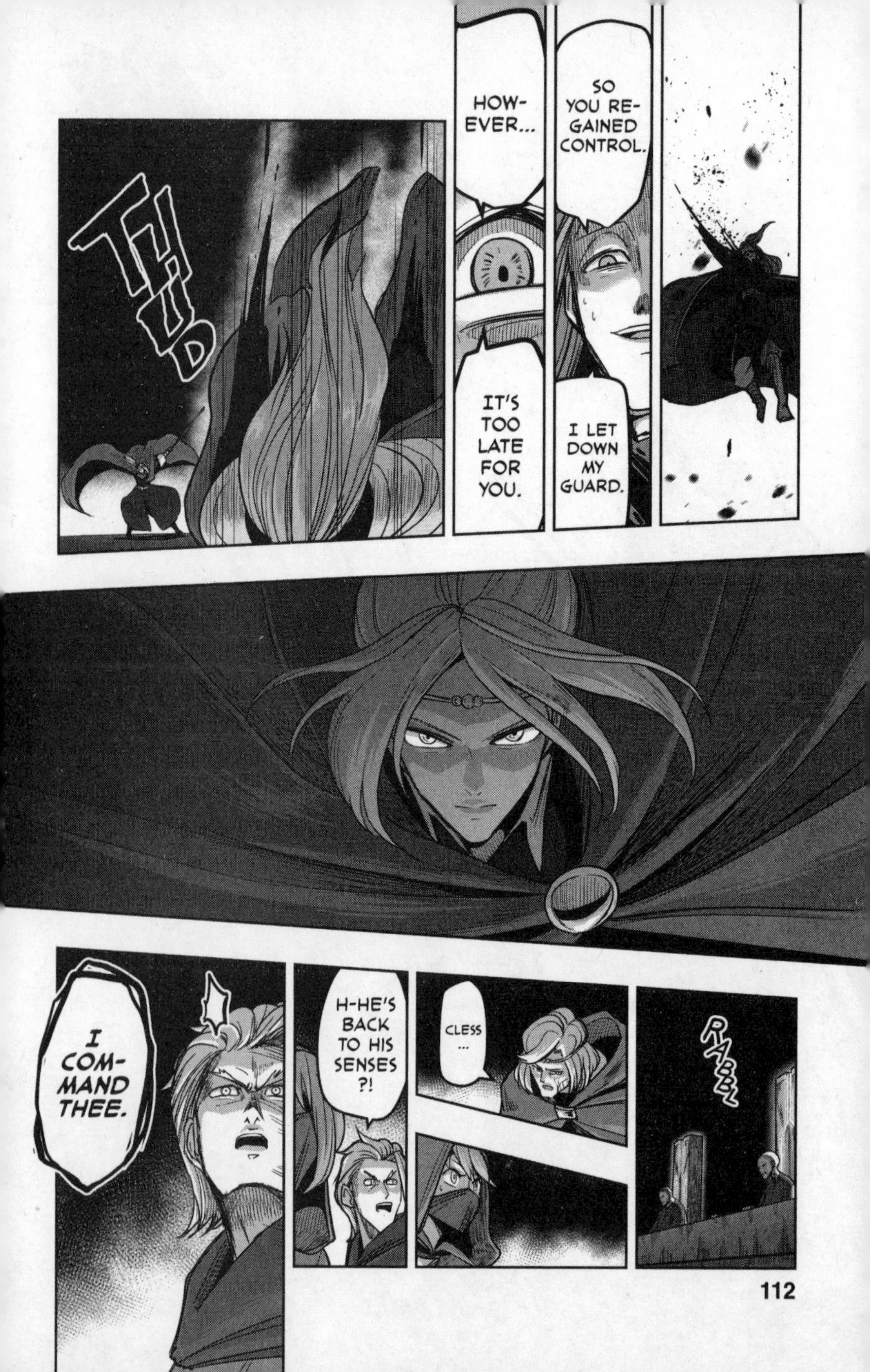
SO YOU RE-GAINED CONTROL.
I LET DOWN MY GUARD.
HOW-EVER...
IT'S TOO LATE FOR YOU.
THUD
RABBL
CLESS...
H-HE'S BACK TO HIS SENSES?!
I COM-MAND THEE.

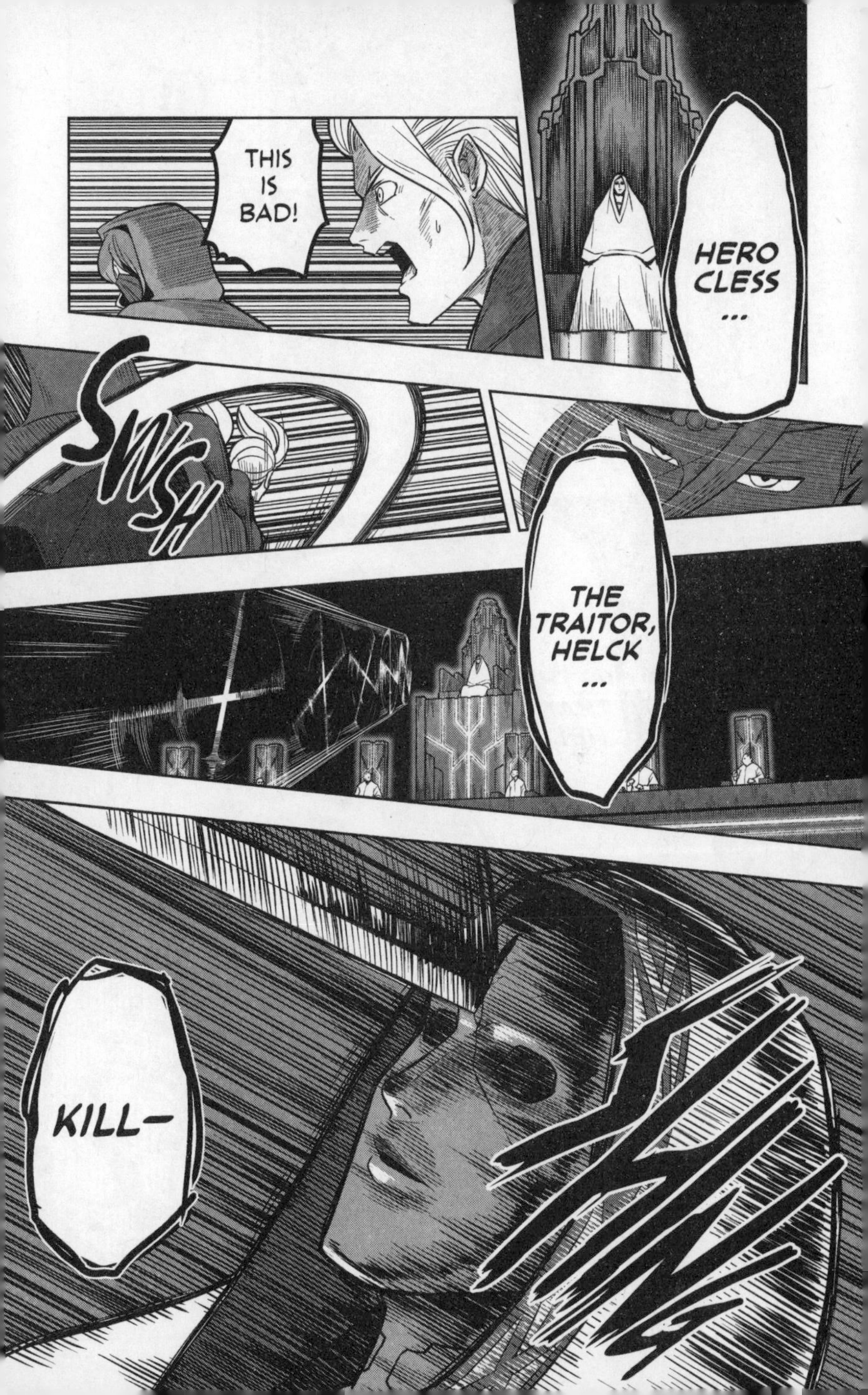
HERO CLESS ...
THIS IS BAD!
THE TRAITOR, HELCK ...
SWSH
KILL-

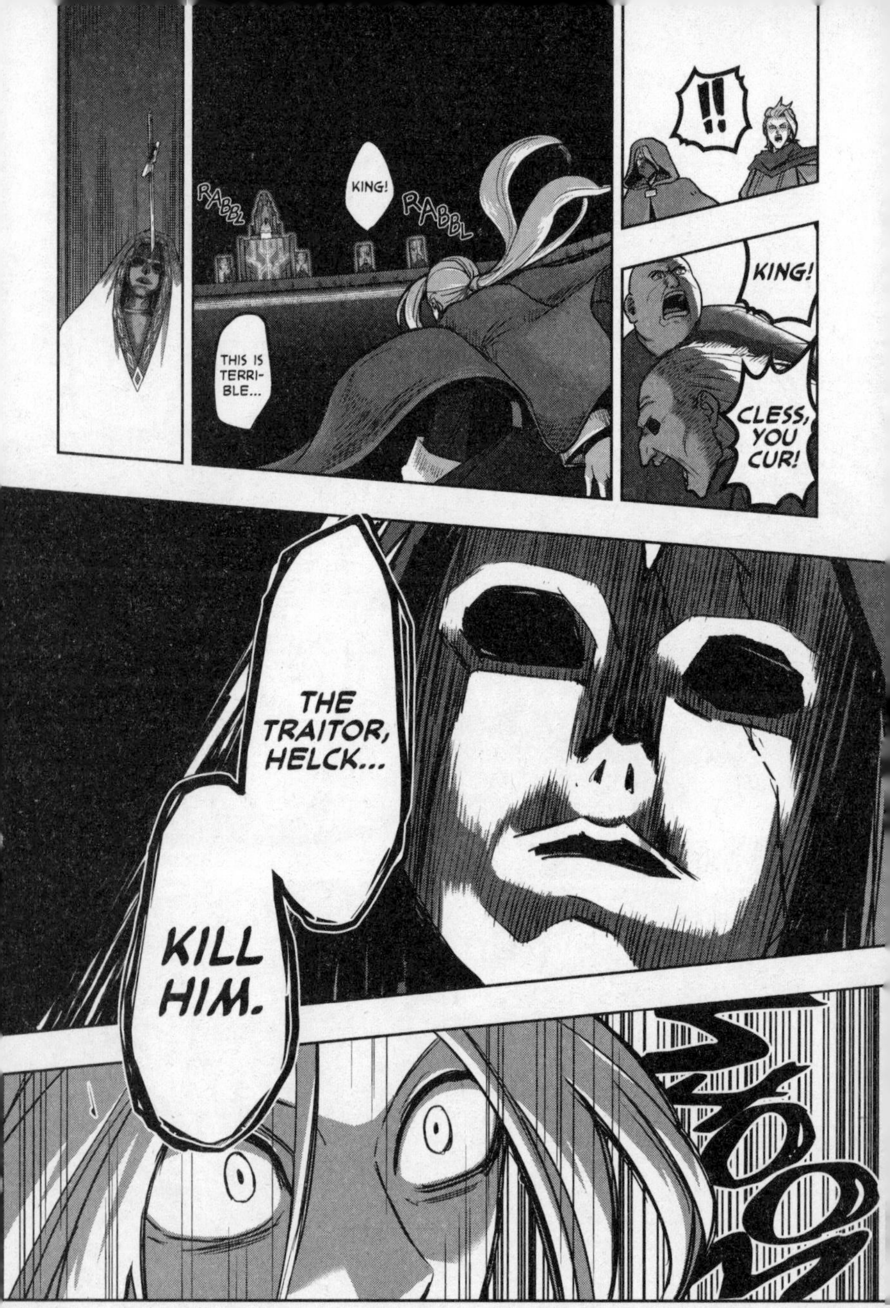
!!
KING!
CLESS, YOU CUR!
RABBL
KING!
RABBL
THIS IS TERRI-BLE...
THE TRAITOR, HELCK...
KILL HIM.
WHOOM

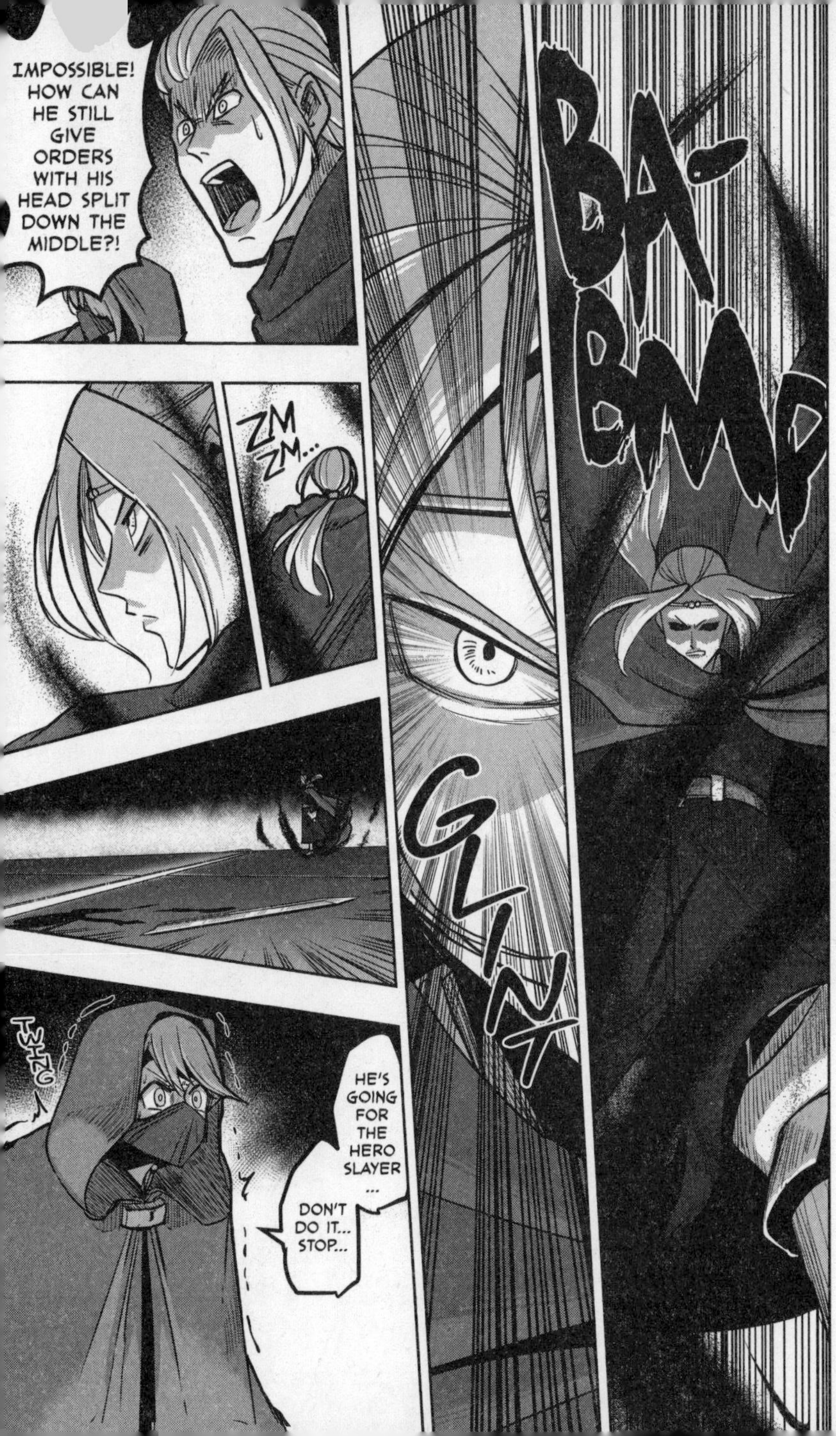
BA-BMP
GLINT
IMPOSSIBLE! HOW CAN HE STILL GIVE ORDERS WITH HIS HEAD SPLIT DOWN THE MIDDLE?!
ZM ZM...
TWING
HE'S GOING FOR THE HERO SLAYER ...
DON'T DO IT... STOP...

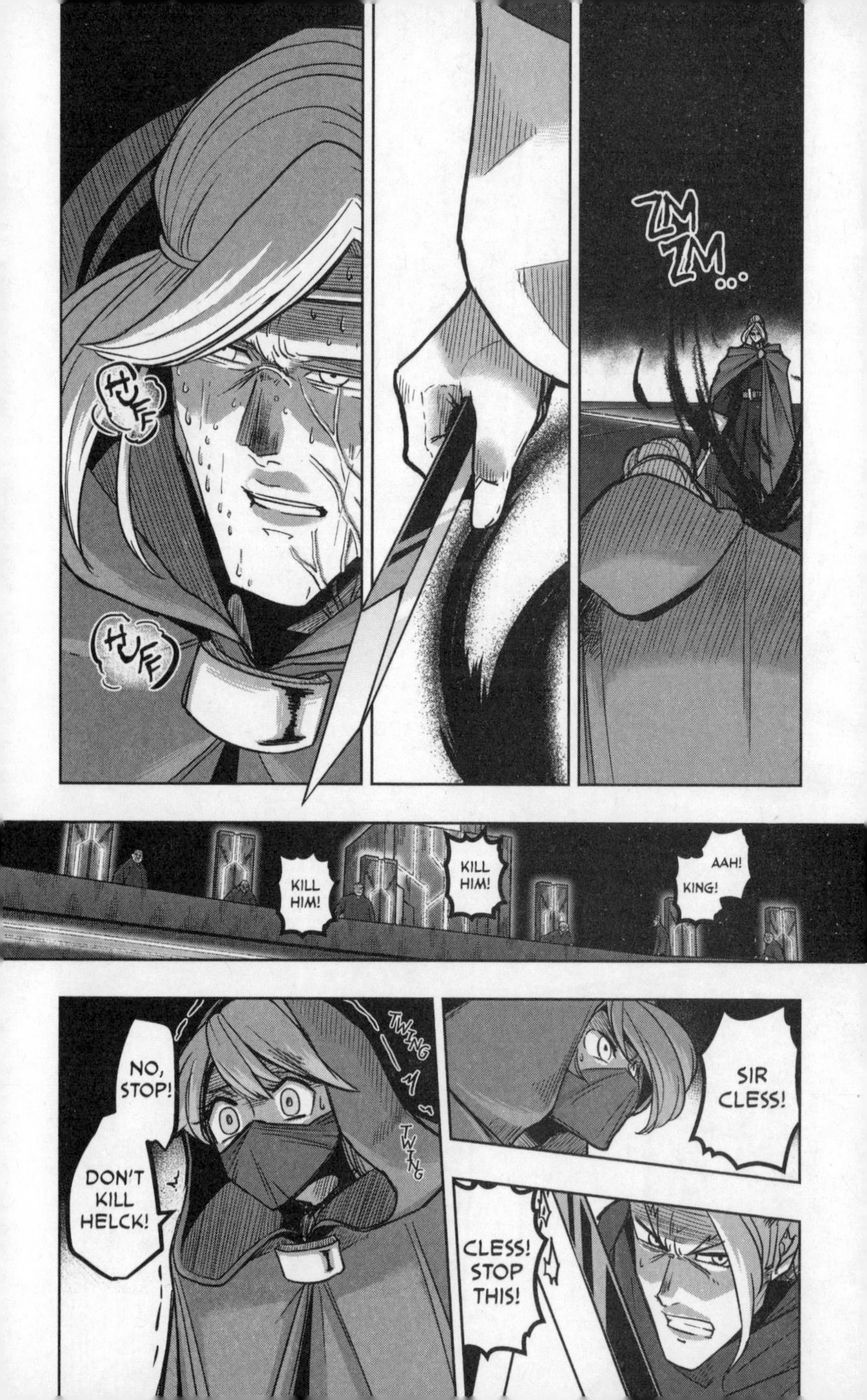
ZM ZM...
HUFF
HUFF
AAH! KING!
KILL HIM!
KILL HIM!
SIR CLESS!
CLESS! STOP THIS!
NO, STOP!
TWING
TWING
DON'T KILL HELCK!

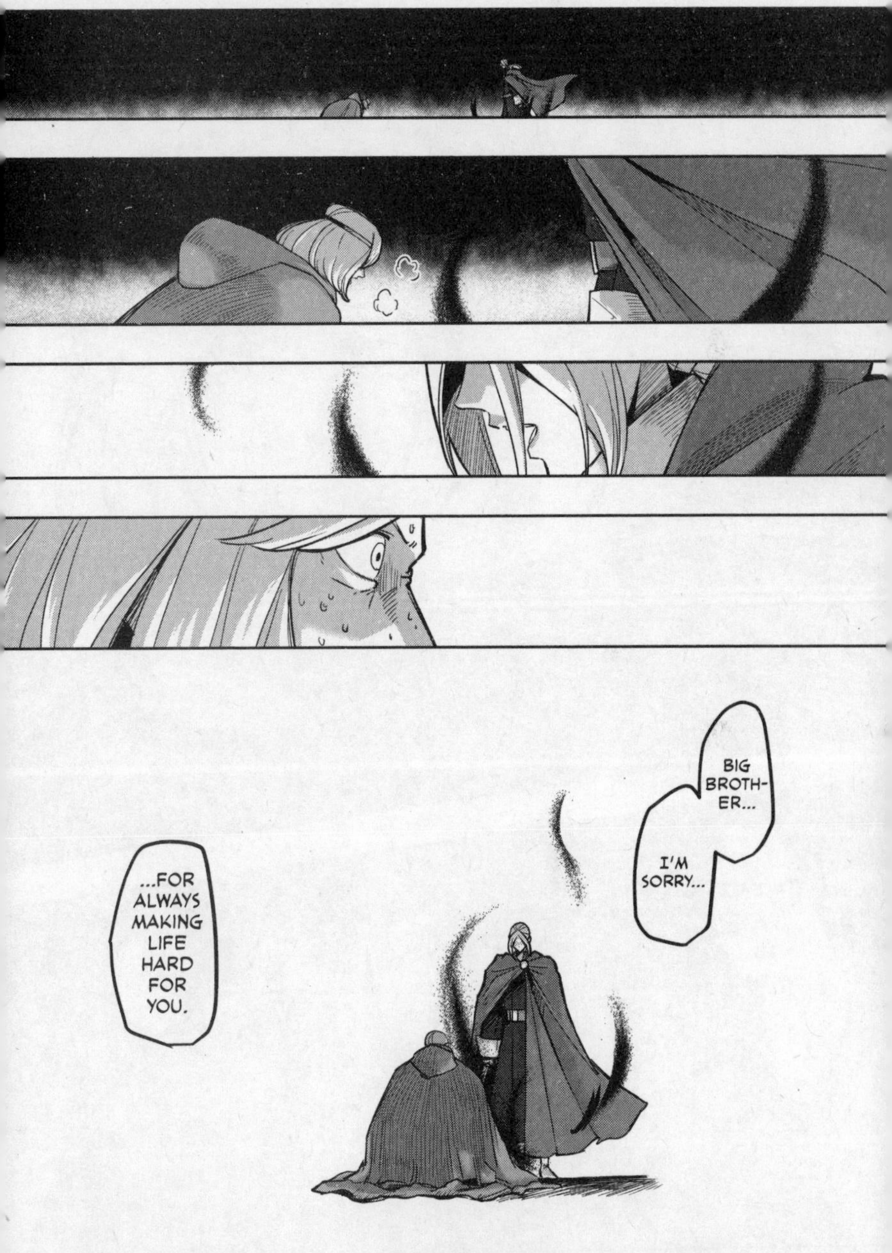
BIG BROTH-ER...
I'M SORRY...
...FOR ALWAYS MAKING LIFE HARD FOR YOU.

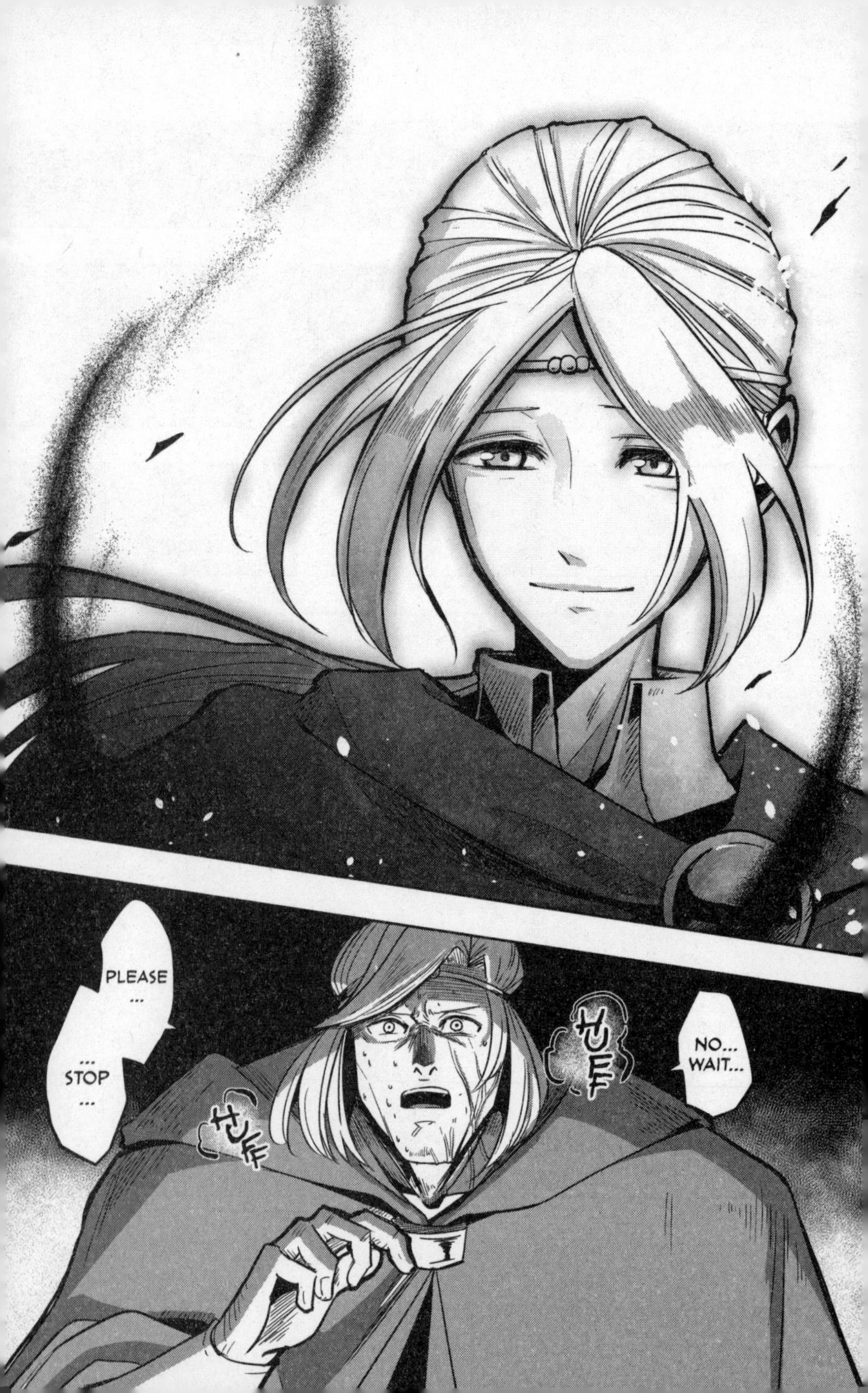
NO... WAIT...
HUFF
PLEASE ...
... STOP ...
HUFF

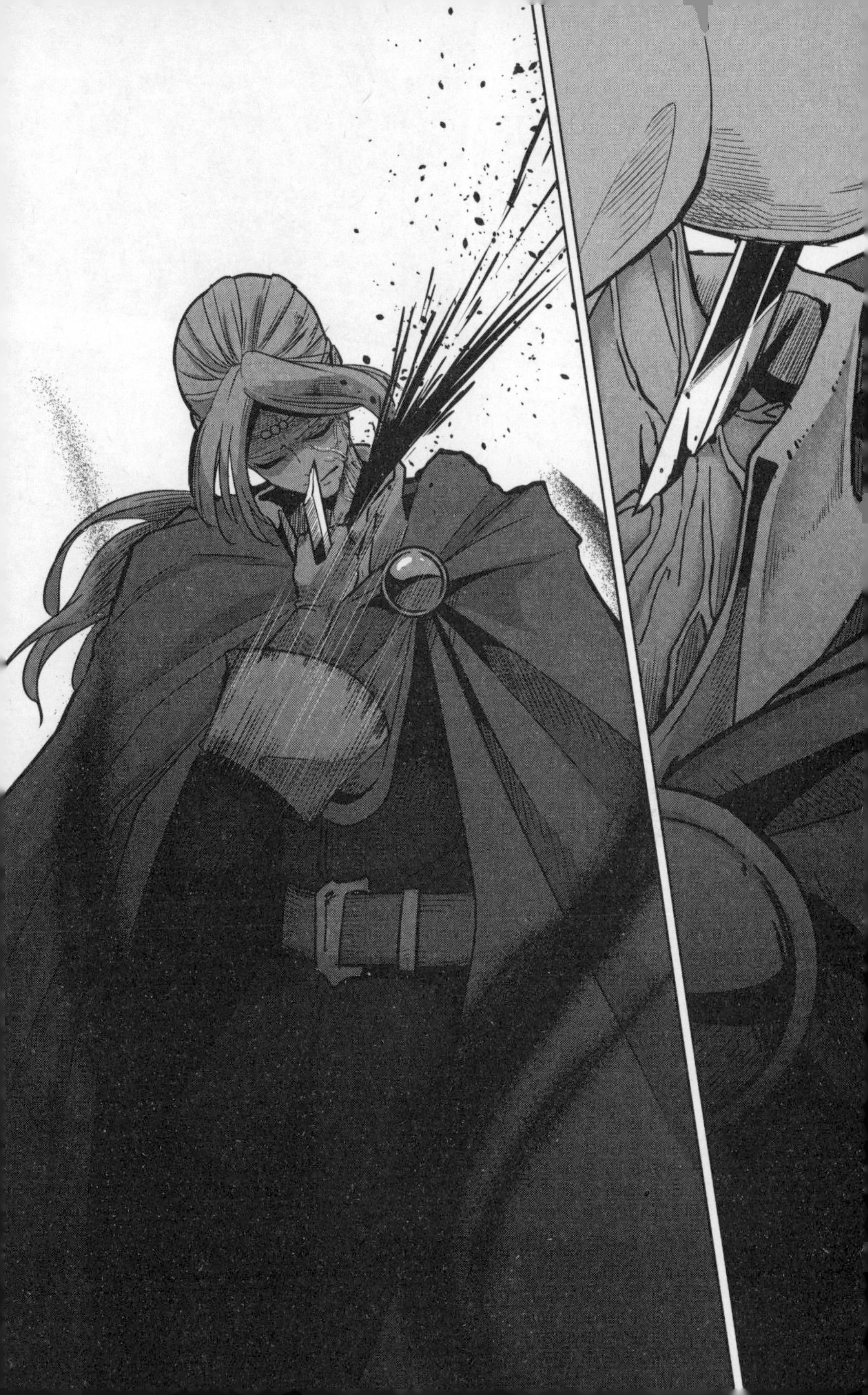

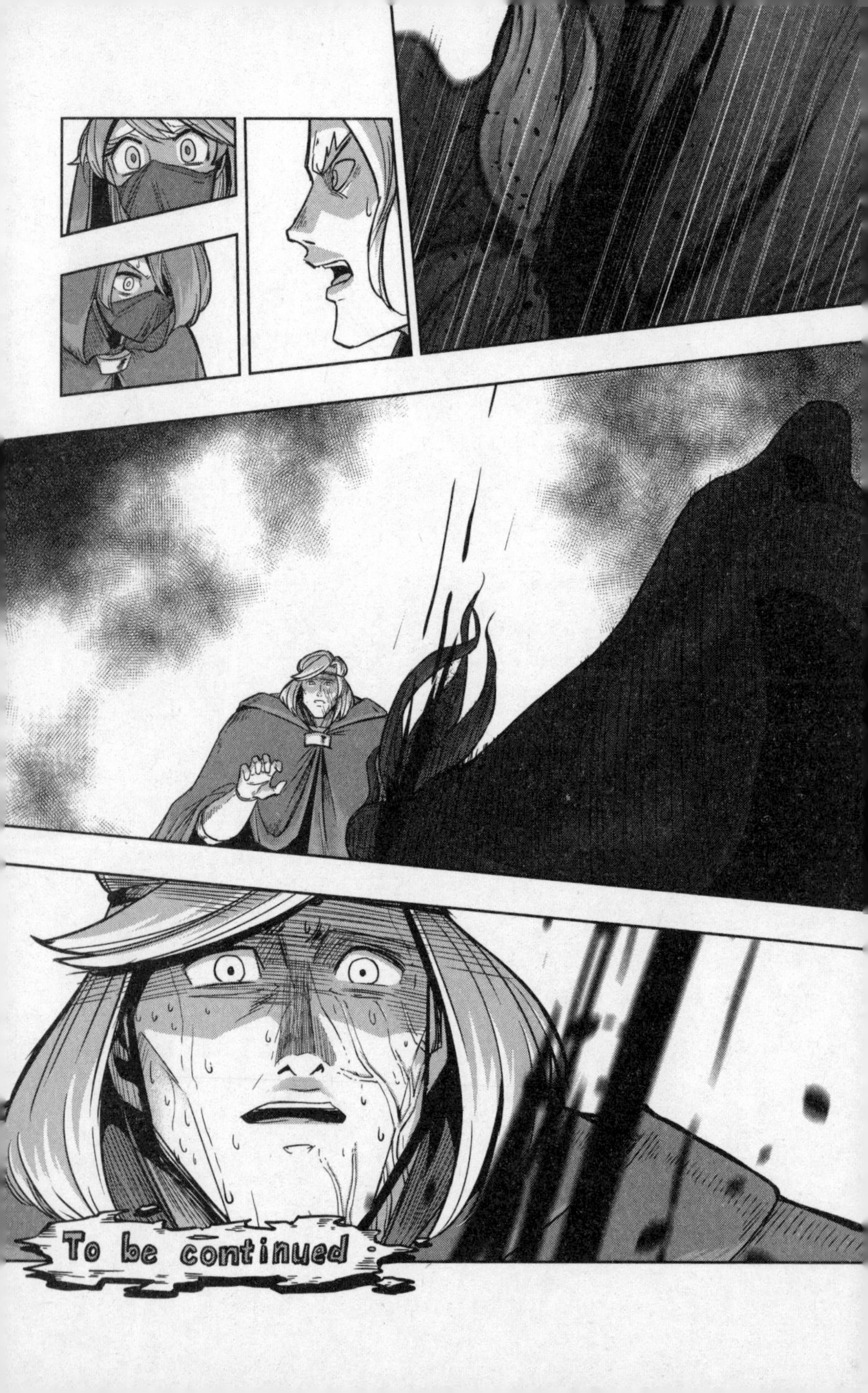
To be continued

Chapter 49: Helck's Past XIV

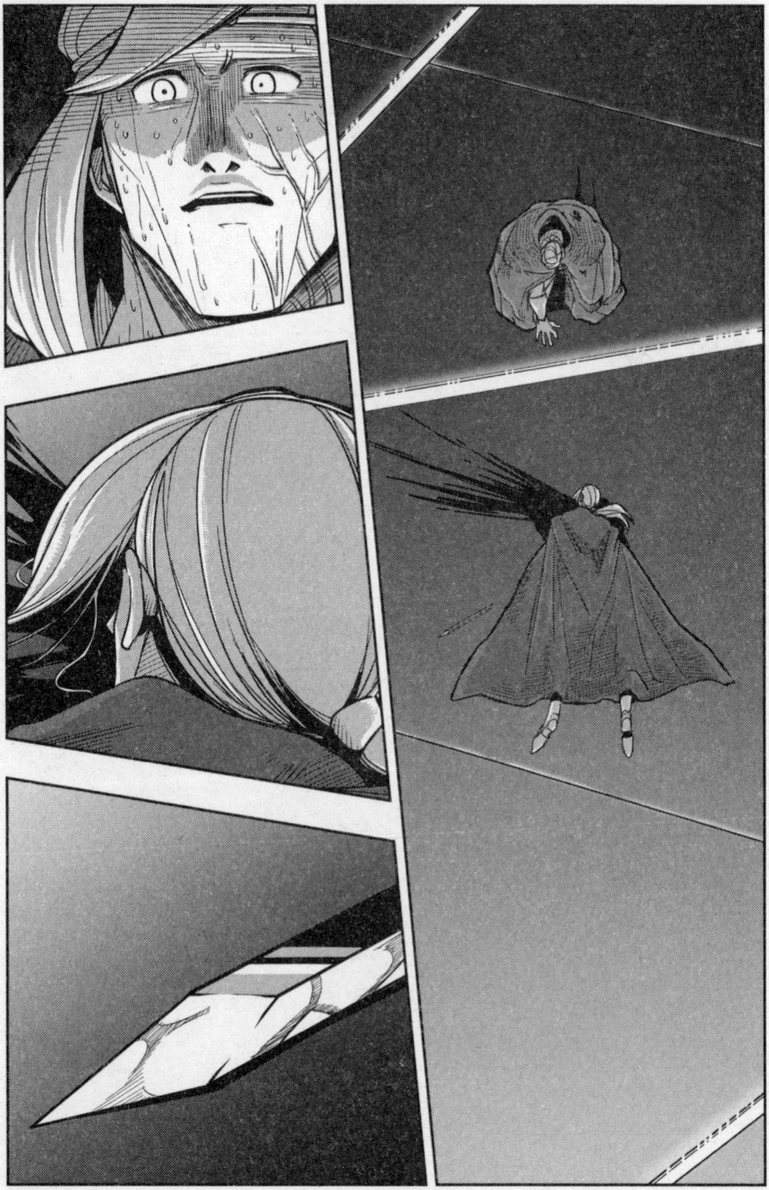

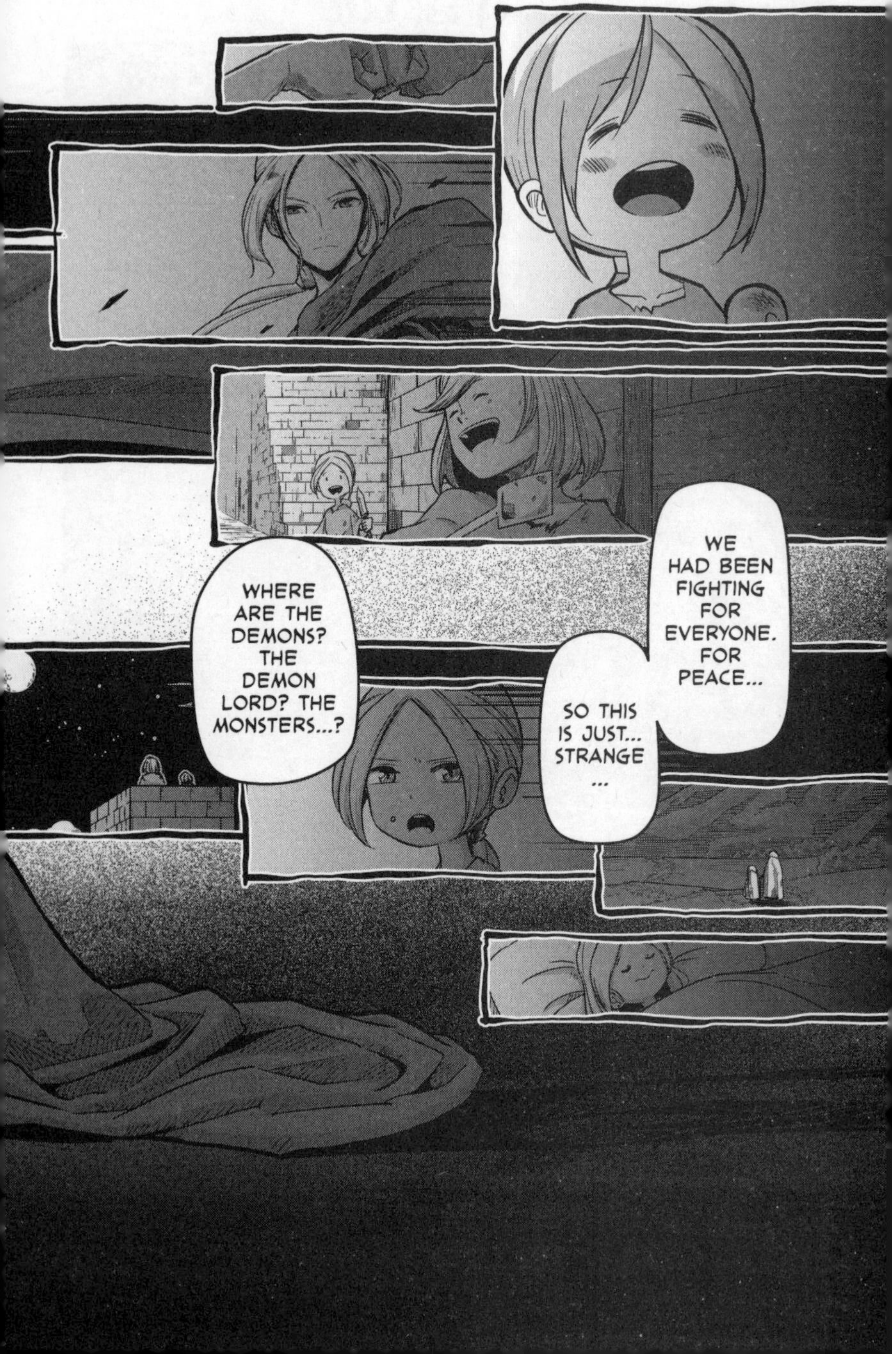
WE HAD BEEN FIGHTING FOR EVERYONE. FOR PEACE...
SO THIS IS JUST... STRANGE ...
WHERE ARE THE DEMONS? THE DEMON LORD? THE MONSTERS...?

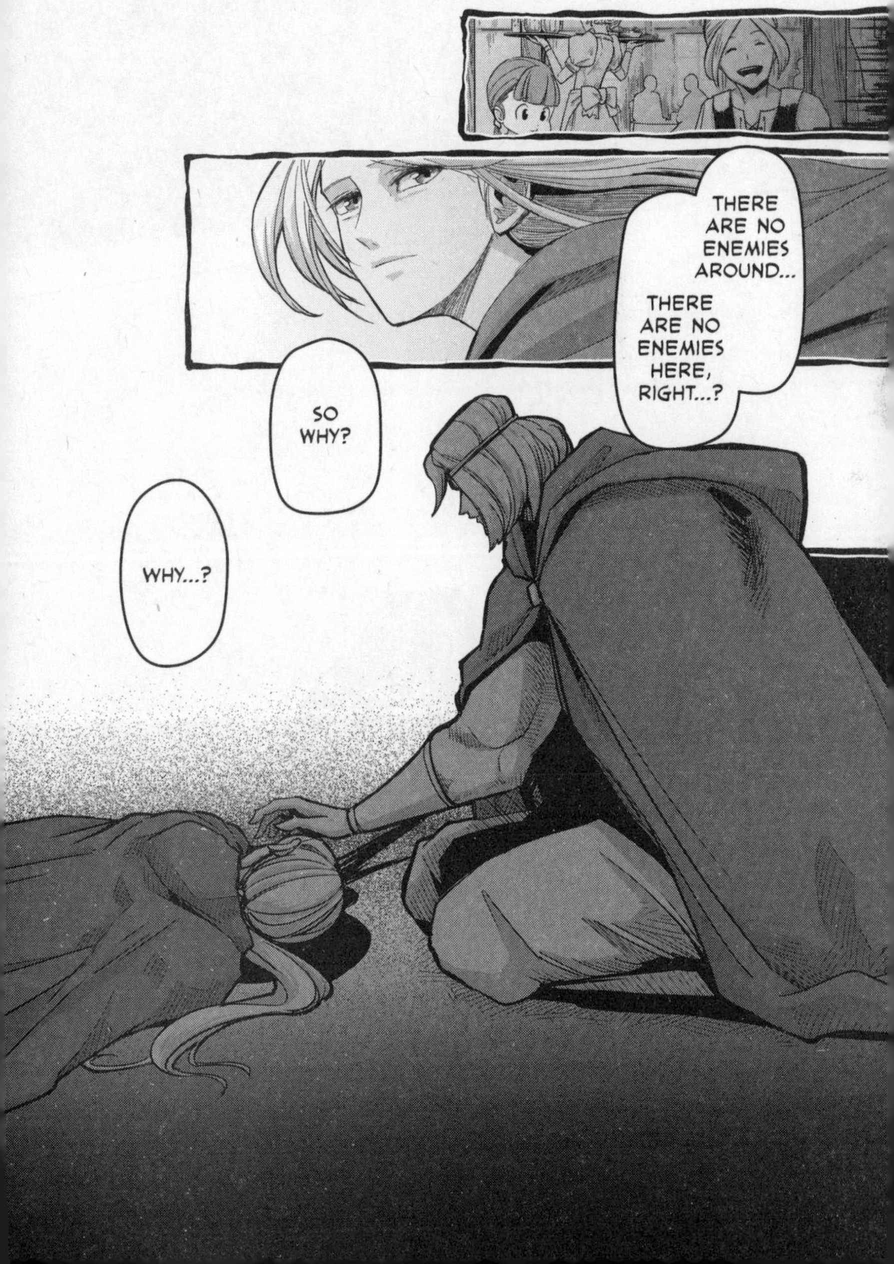
THERE ARE NO ENEMIES AROUND...
THERE ARE NO ENEMIES HERE, RIGHT...?
SO WHY?
WHY...?

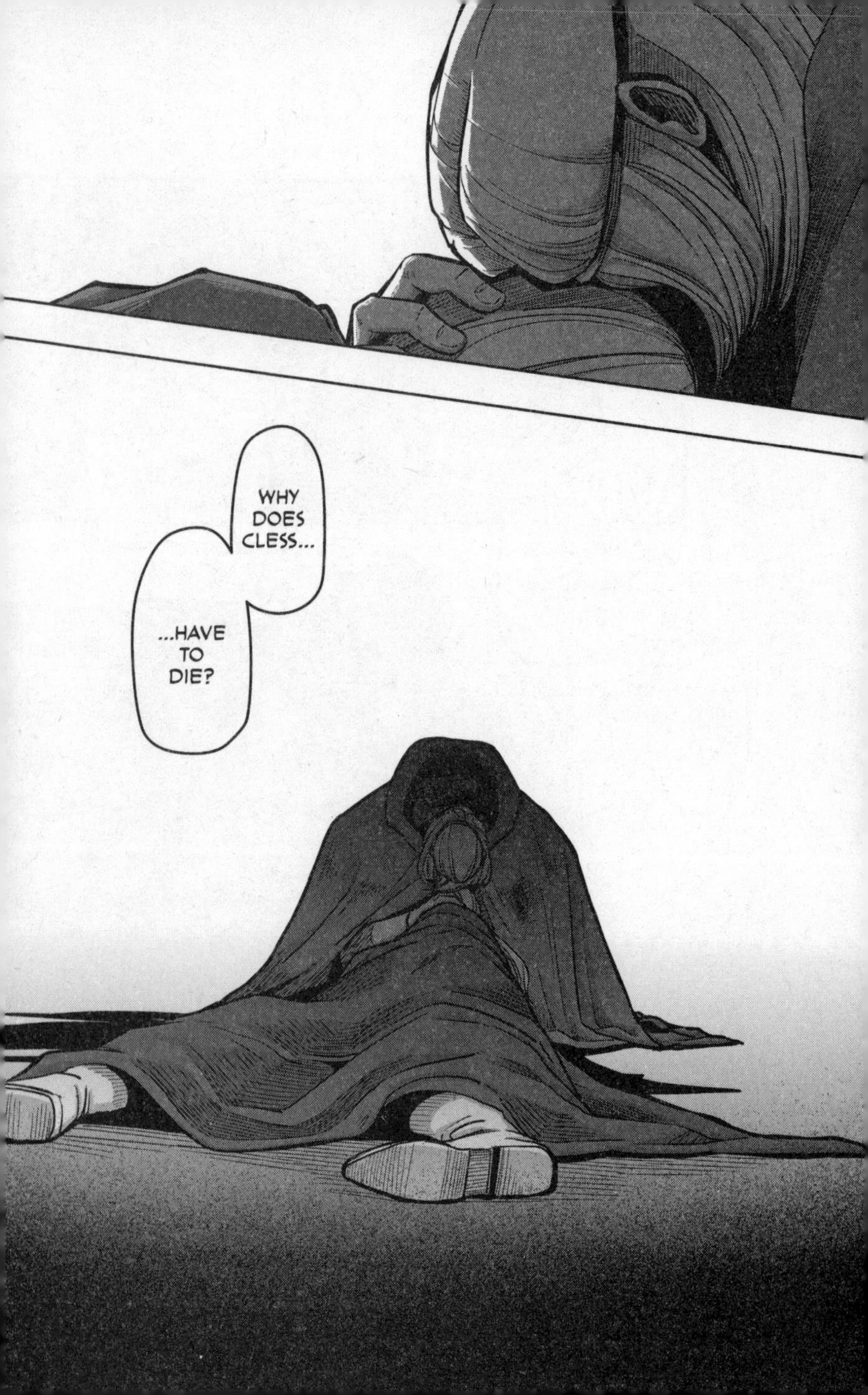
WHY DOES CLESS...
...HAVE TO DIE?

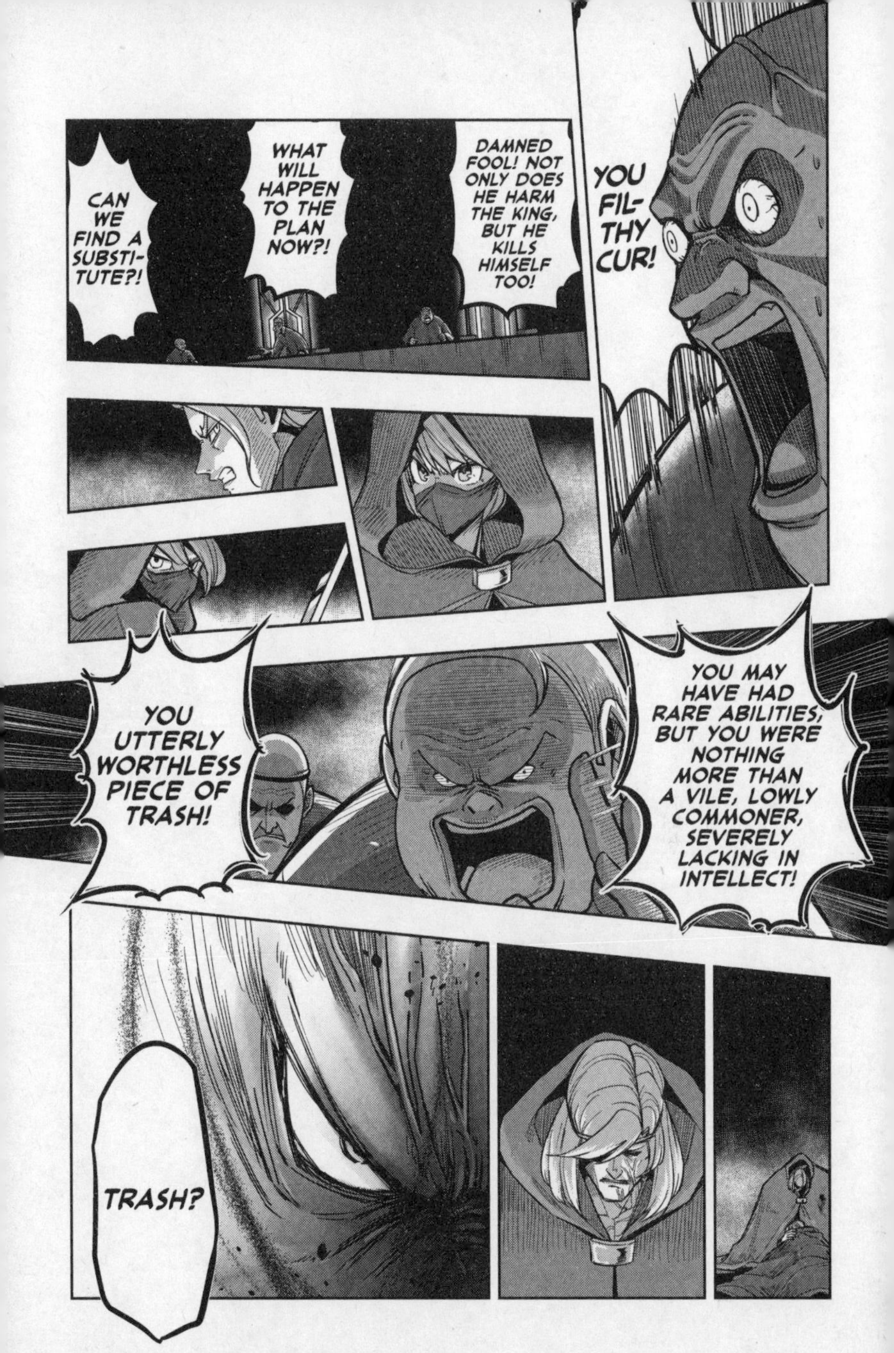
YOU FIL-THY CUR!
DAMNED FOOL! NOT ONLY DOES HE HARM THE KING, BUT HE KILLS HIMSELF TOO!
WHAT WILL HAPPEN TO THE PLAN NOW?!
CAN WE FIND A SUBSTI-TUTE?!
YOU MAY HAVE HAD RARE ABILITIES, BUT YOU WERE NOTHING MORE THAN A VILE, LOWLY COMMONER, SEVERELY LACKING IN INTELLECT!
YOU UTTERLY WORTHLESS PIECE OF TRASH!
TRASH?

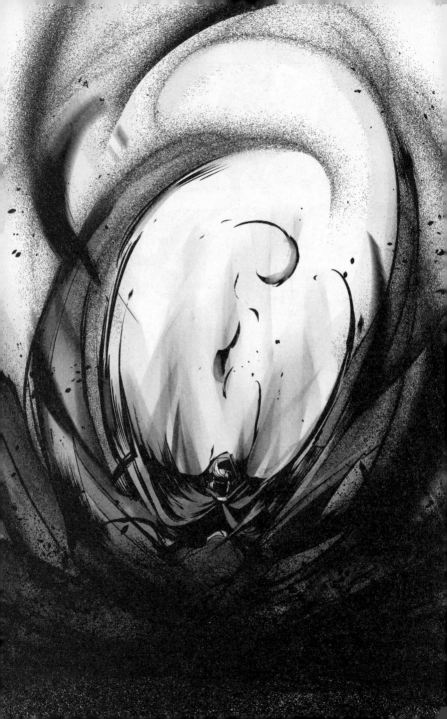

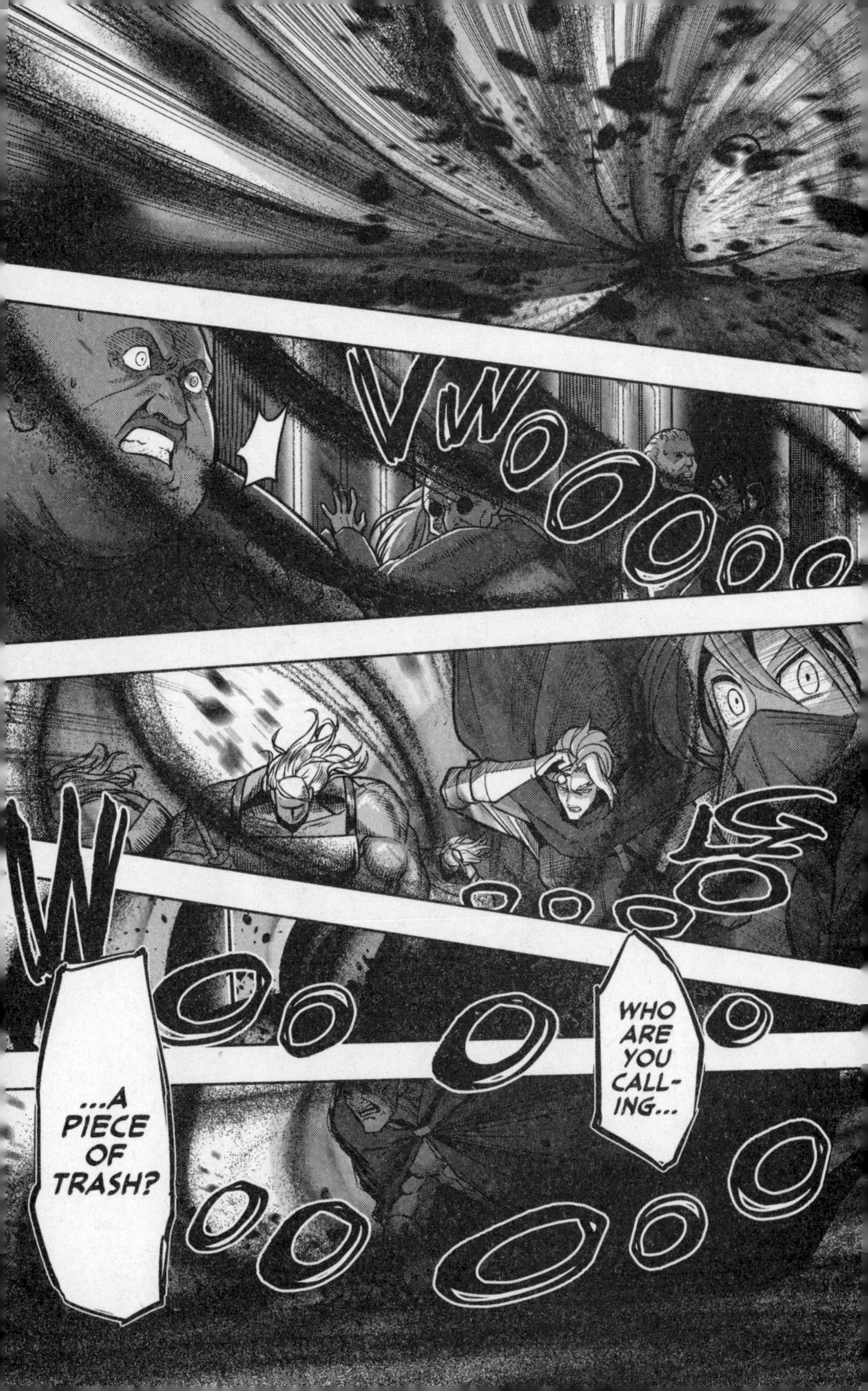
VWOOOOOOO
GOOOOOO
WHO ARE YOU CALL-ING...
WOOOOOOOOOO
...A PIECE OF TRASH?

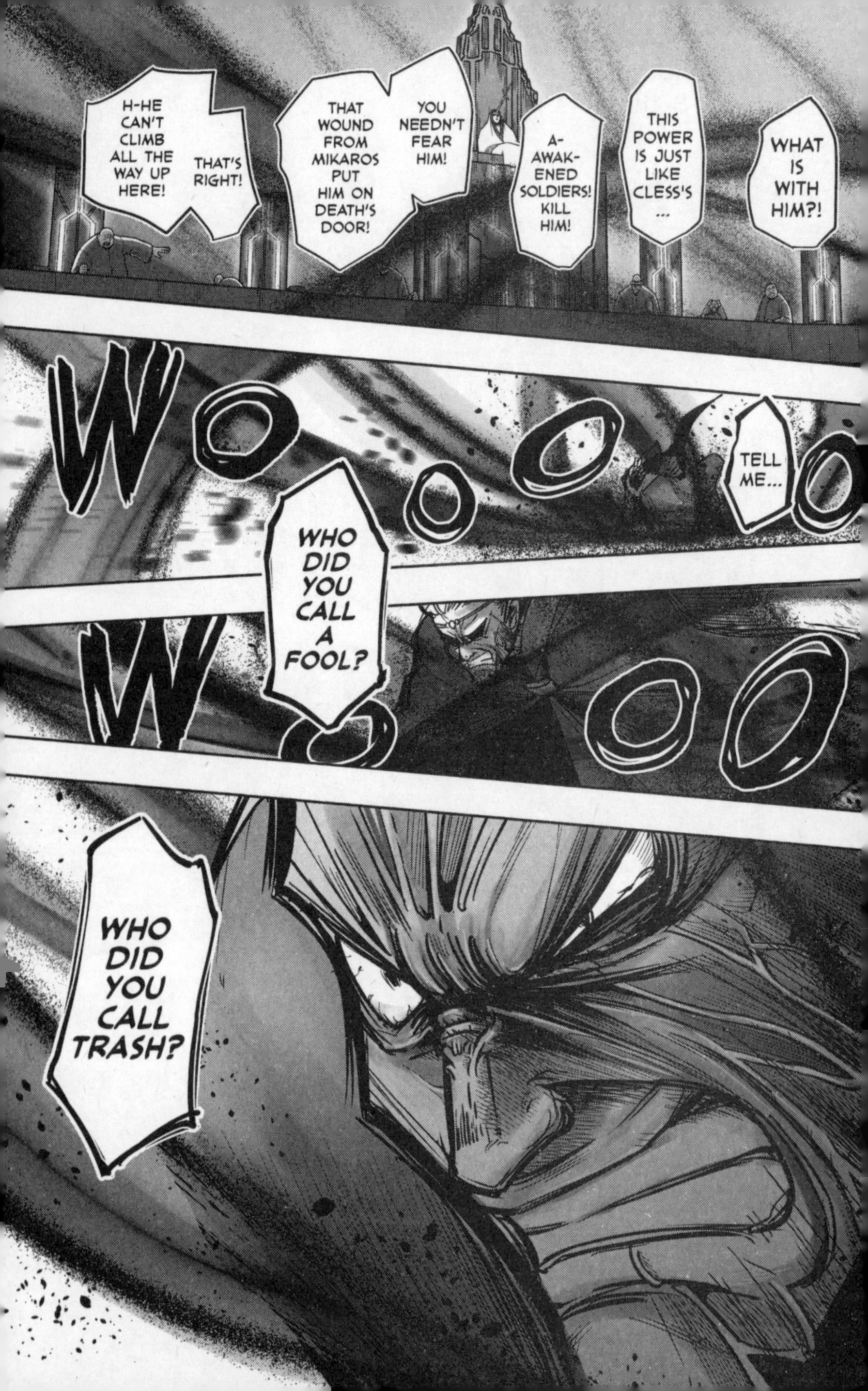
WHAT IS WITH HIM?!
THIS POWER IS JUST LIKE CLESS'S ...
A-AWAKENED SOLDIERS! KILL HIM!
YOU NEEDN'T FEAR HIM!
THAT WOUND FROM MIKAROS PUT HIM ON DEATH'S DOOR!
THAT'S RIGHT!
H-HE CAN'T CLIMB ALL THE WAY UP HERE!
WOOOOOOO
TELL ME...
WHO DID YOU CALL A FOOL?
WOOOO
WHO DID YOU CALL TRASH?

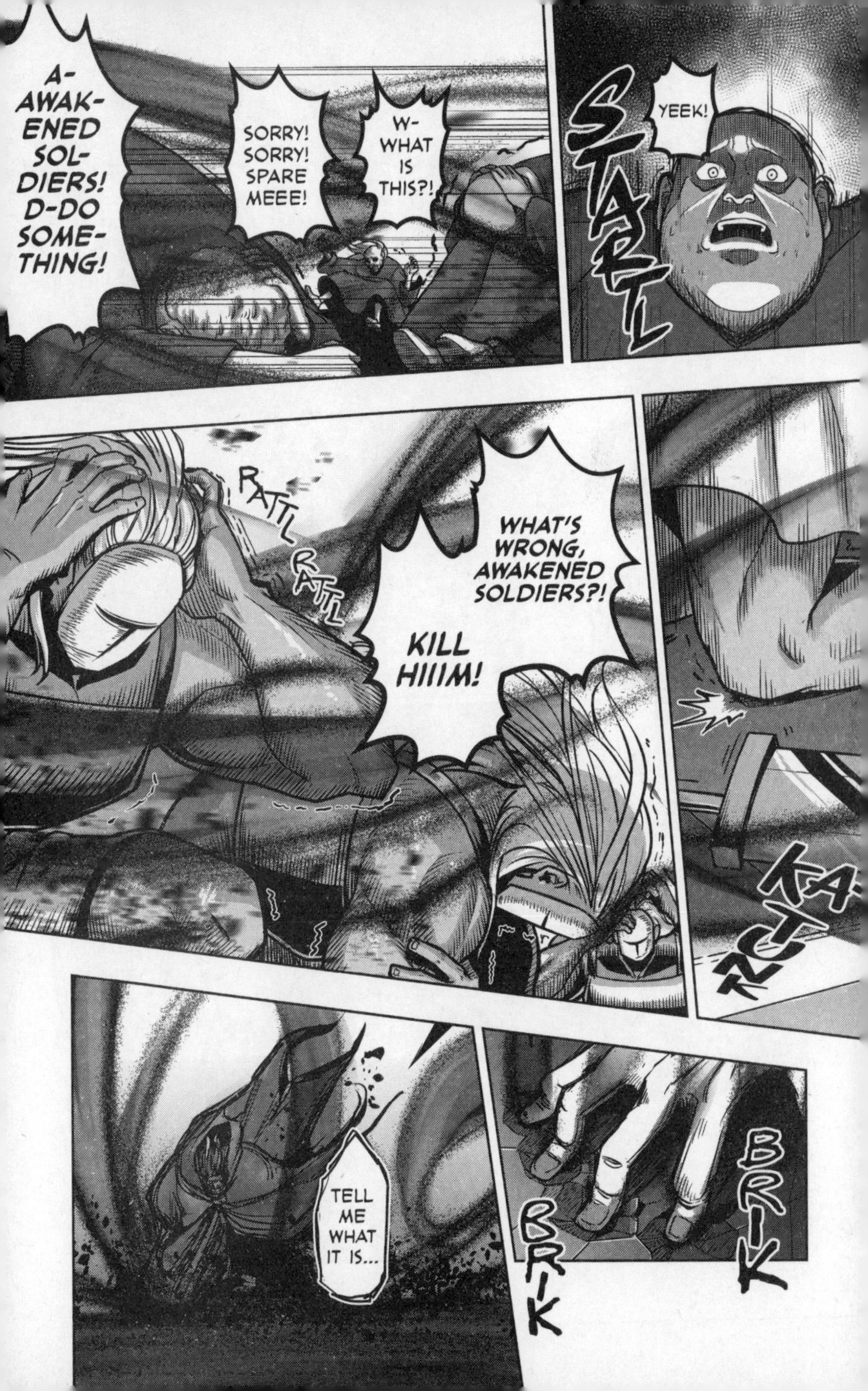
STARTL
YEEK!
W- WHAT IS THIS?!
SORRY! SORRY! SPARE MEEE!
A- AWAK- ENED SOL- DIERS! D-DO SOME- THING!
KA-JUNK
WHAT'S WRONG, AWAKENED SOLDIERS?!
KILL HIIIM!
RATTL
RATTL
BRIK
BRIK
TELL ME WHAT IT IS...

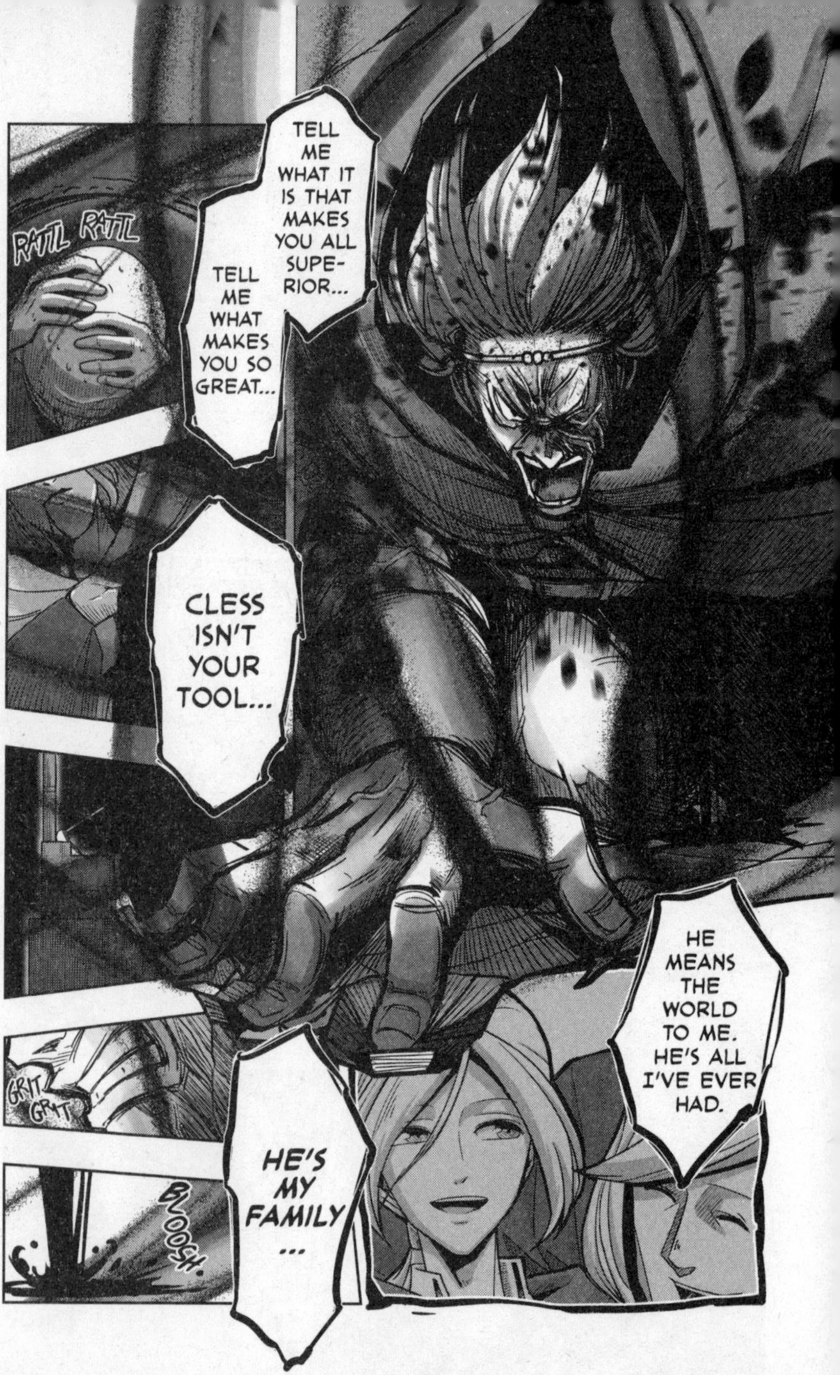

TELL ME WHAT IT IS THAT MAKES YOU ALL SUPER-RIOR...
TELL ME WHAT MAKES YOU SO GREAT...
RATTL RATTL
CLESS ISN'T YOUR TOOL...
HE MEANS THE WORLD TO ME. HE'S ALL I'VE EVER HAD.
HE'S MY FAMILY...
GRIT GRIT
BLOOSH

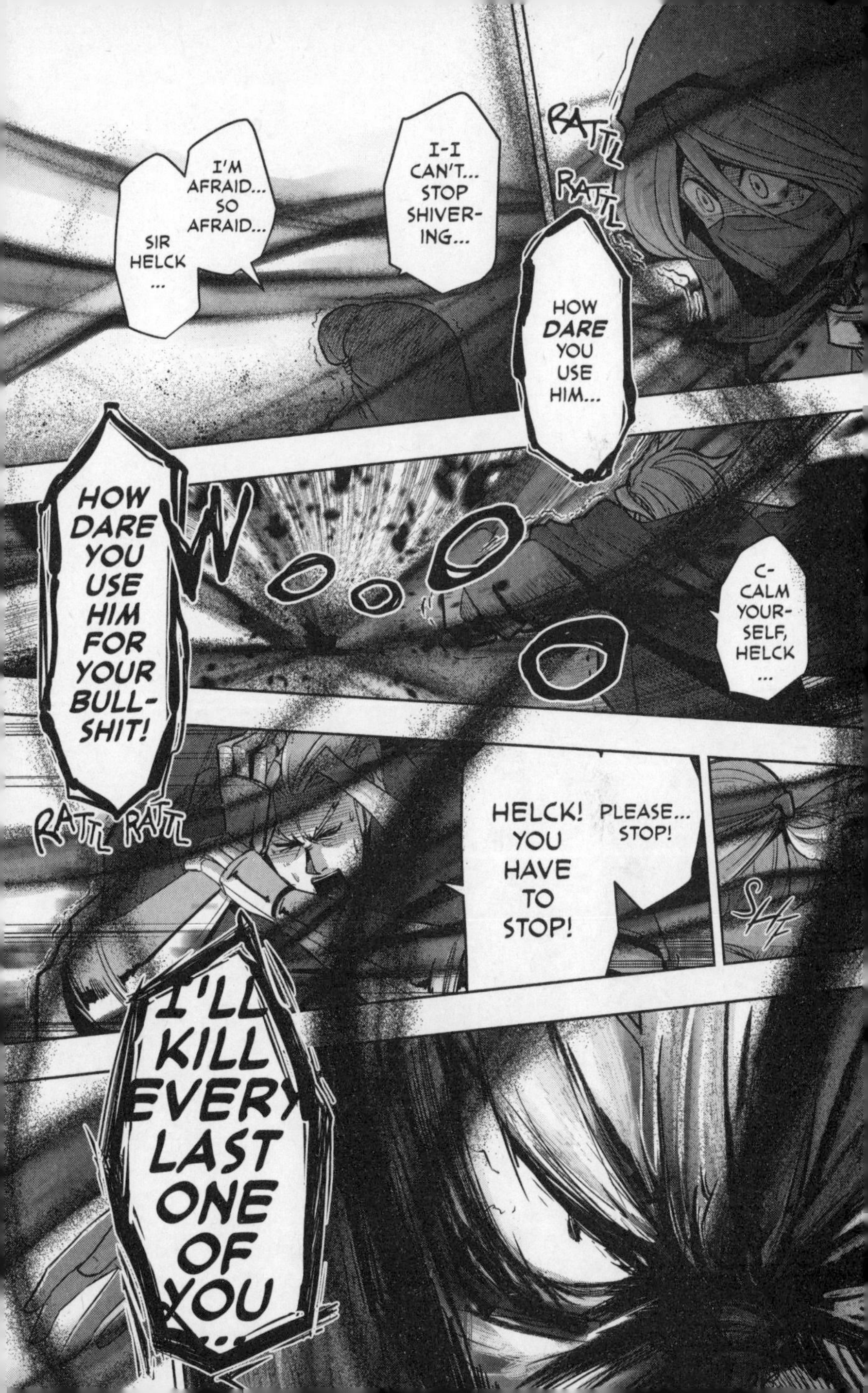
RATTL RATTL
I-I CAN'T... STOP SHIVER-ING...
I'M AFRAID... SO AFRAID... SIR HELCK...
HOW DARE YOU USE HIM...
C-CALM YOUR-SELF, HELCK...
WOOOO
HOW DARE YOU USE HIM FOR YOUR BULL-SHIT!
RATTL RATTL
SH
PLEASE... STOP!
HELCK! YOU HAVE TO STOP!
I'LL KILL EVERY LAST ONE OF YOU...

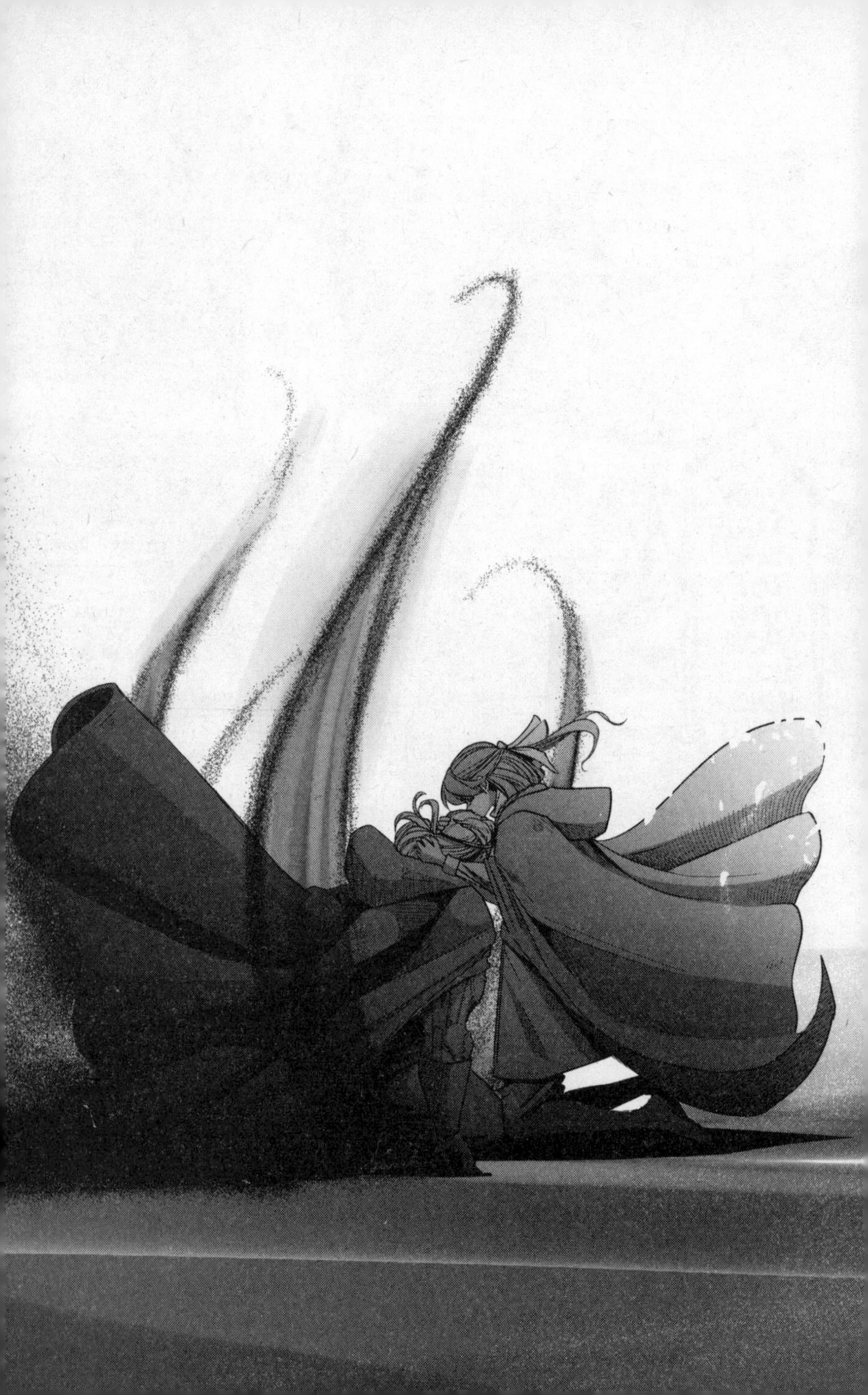

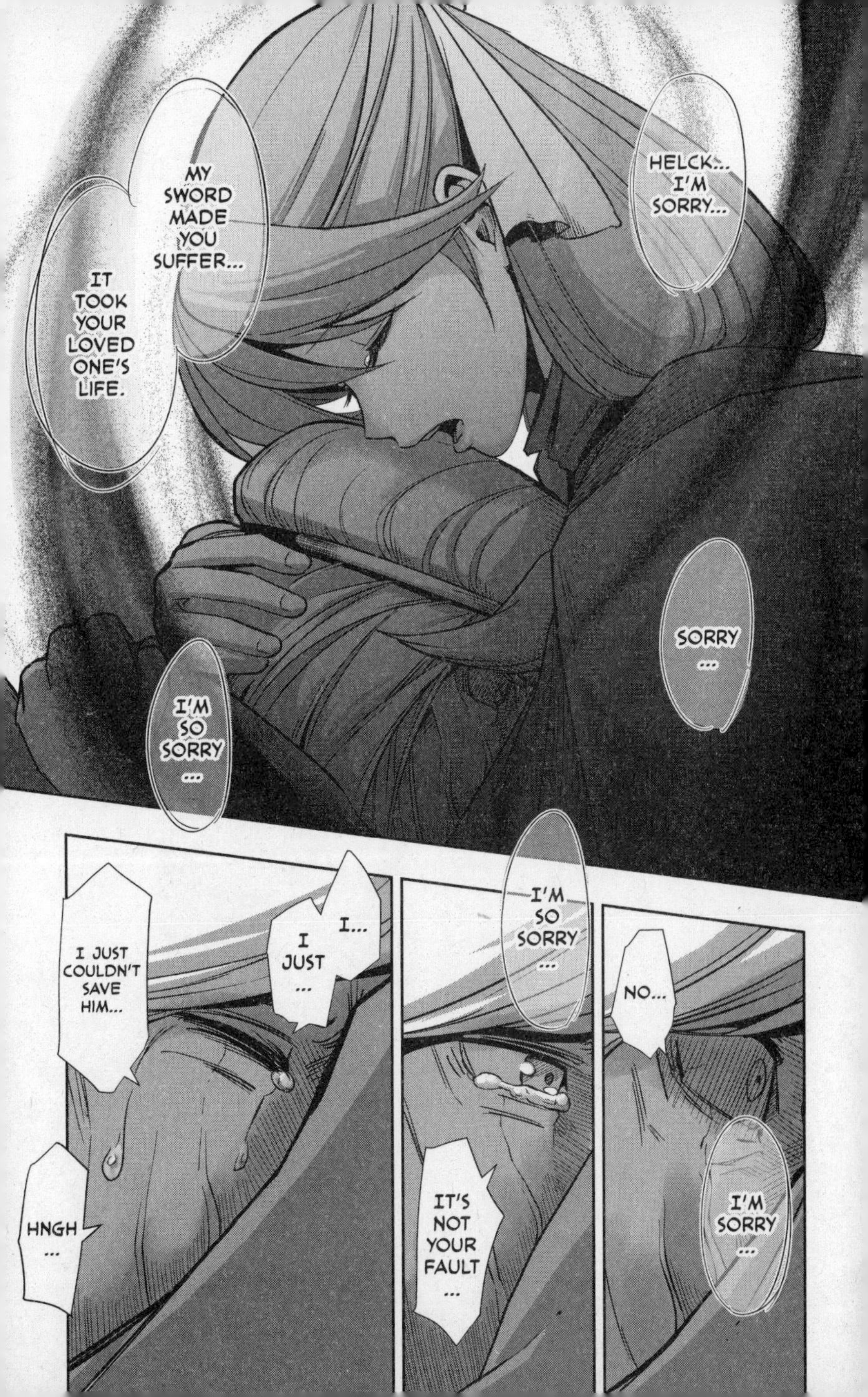
HELCK... I'M SORRY...
MY SWORD MADE YOU SUFFER...
IT TOOK YOUR LOVED ONE'S LIFE.
SORRY...
I'M SO SORRY...
NO...
I'M SORRY...
I'M SO SORRY...
IT'S NOT YOUR FAULT...
I...
I JUST...
I JUST COULDN'T SAVE HIM...
HNGH...

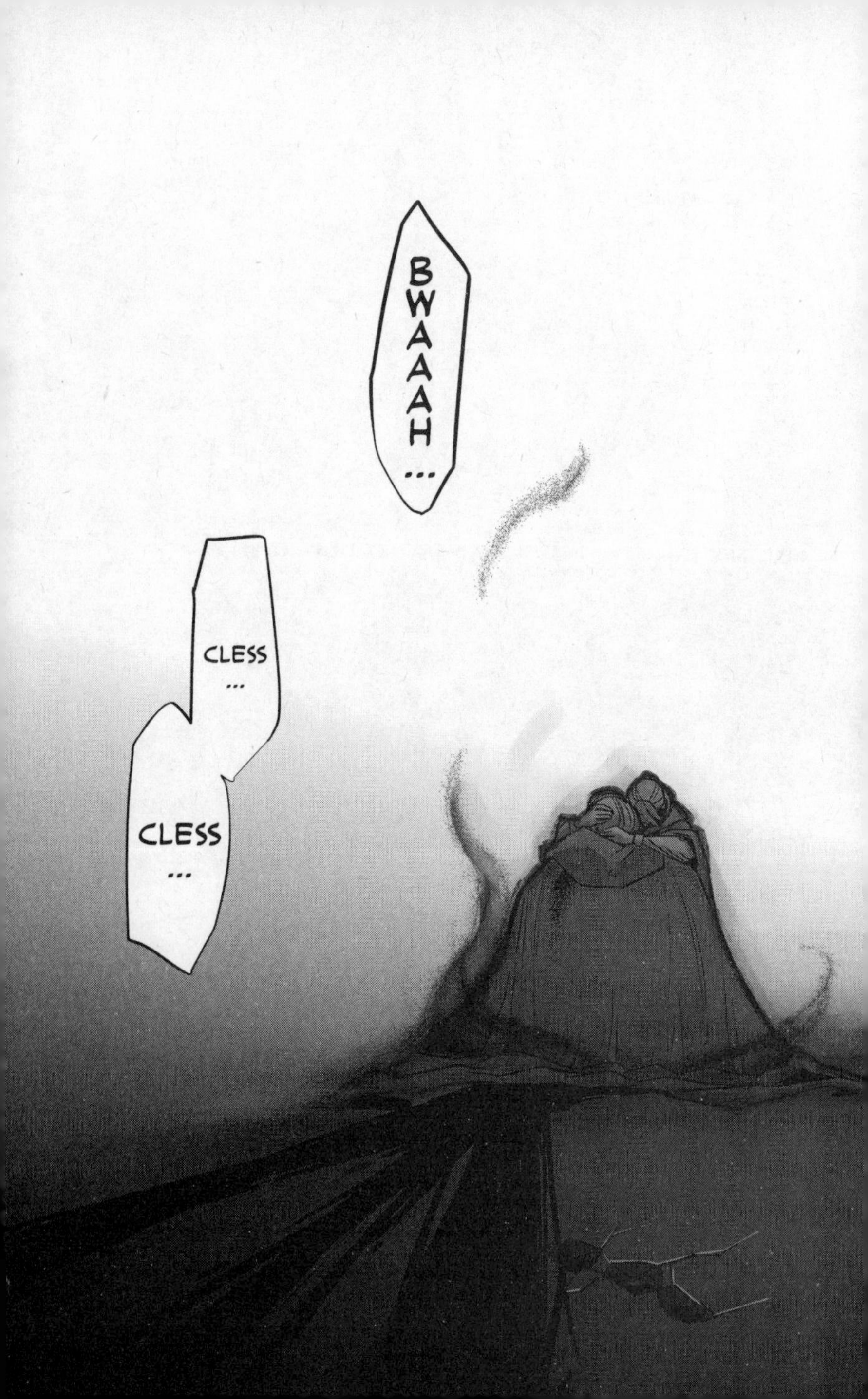
BWAAAH...
CLESS...
CLESS...

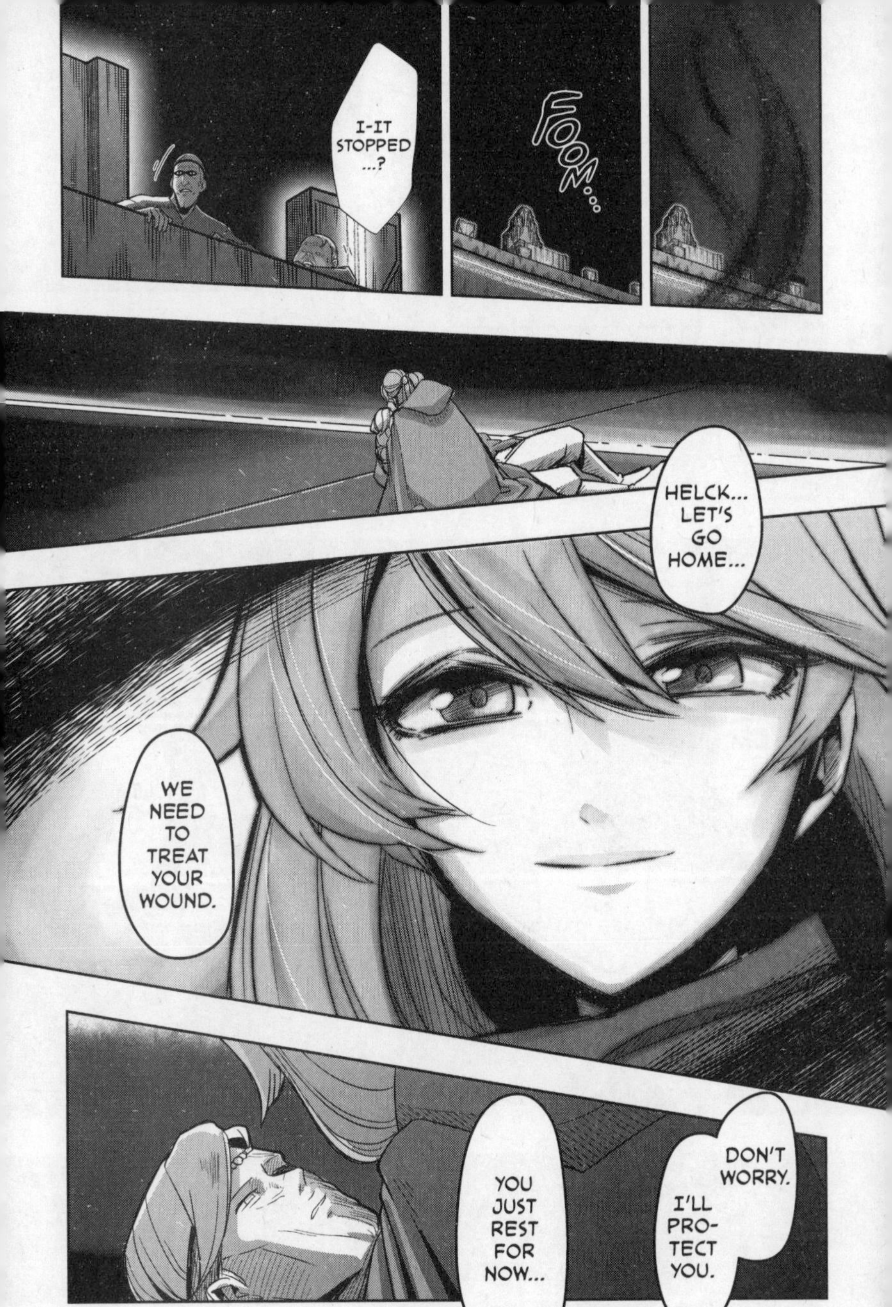
FOOM...
I-IT STOPPED ...?
HELCK... LET'S GO HOME...
WE NEED TO TREAT YOUR WOUND.
DON'T WORRY.
I'LL PRO-TECT YOU.
YOU JUST REST FOR NOW...

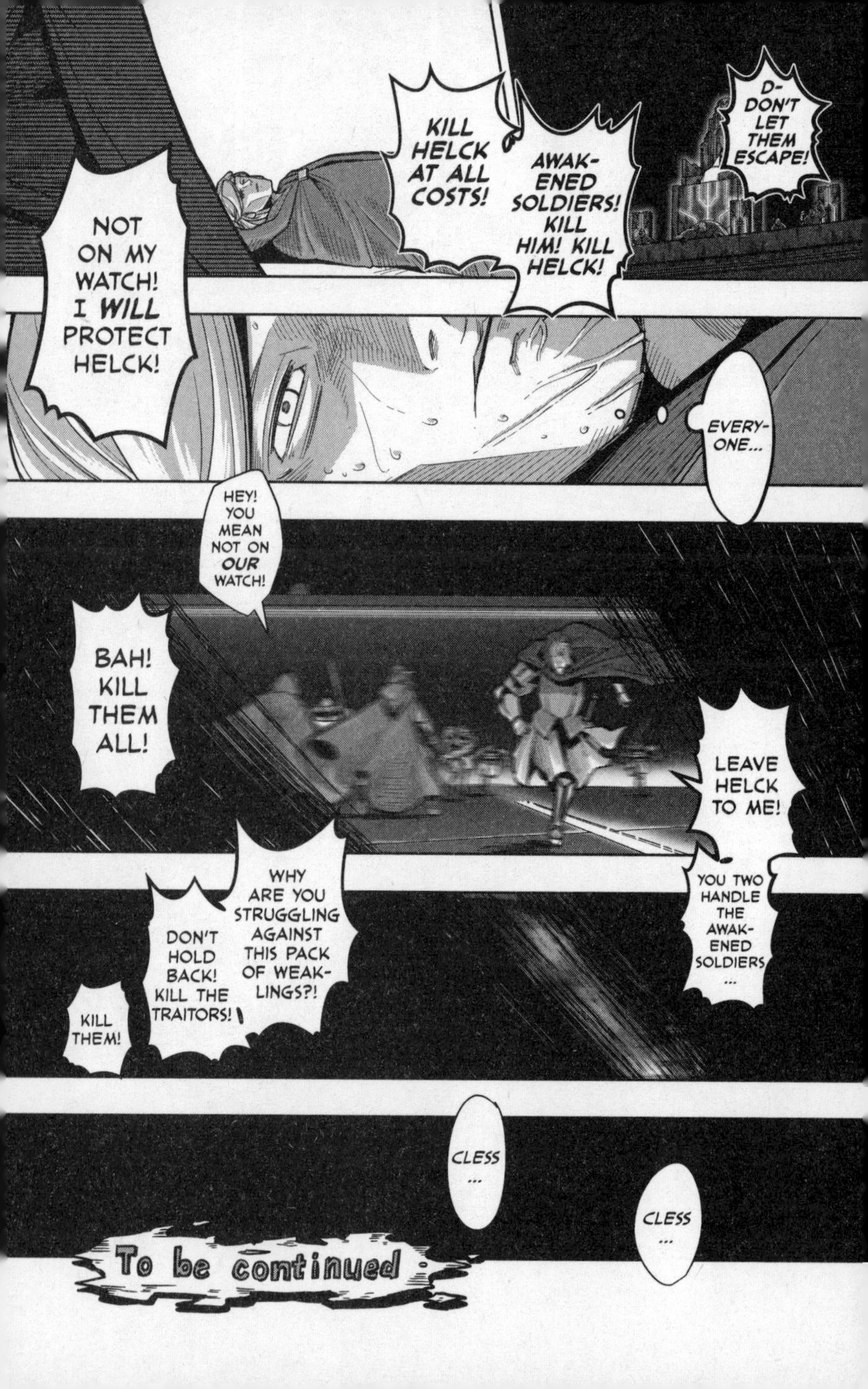
D-DON'T LET THEM ESCAPE!
AWAK-ENED SOLDIERS! KILL HIM! KILL HELCK!
KILL HELCK AT ALL COSTS!
NOT ON MY WATCH! I *WILL* PROTECT HELCK!
EVERY-ONE...
HEY! YOU MEAN NOT ON *OUR* WATCH!
LEAVE HELCK TO ME!
BAH! KILL THEM ALL!
YOU TWO HANDLE THE AWAK-ENED SOLDIERS...
WHY ARE YOU STRUGGLING AGAINST THIS PACK OF WEAK-LINGS?!
DON'T HOLD BACK! KILL THE TRAITORS!
KILL THEM!
CLESS...
CLESS...
To be continued

Chapter 50: Helck's Past XV

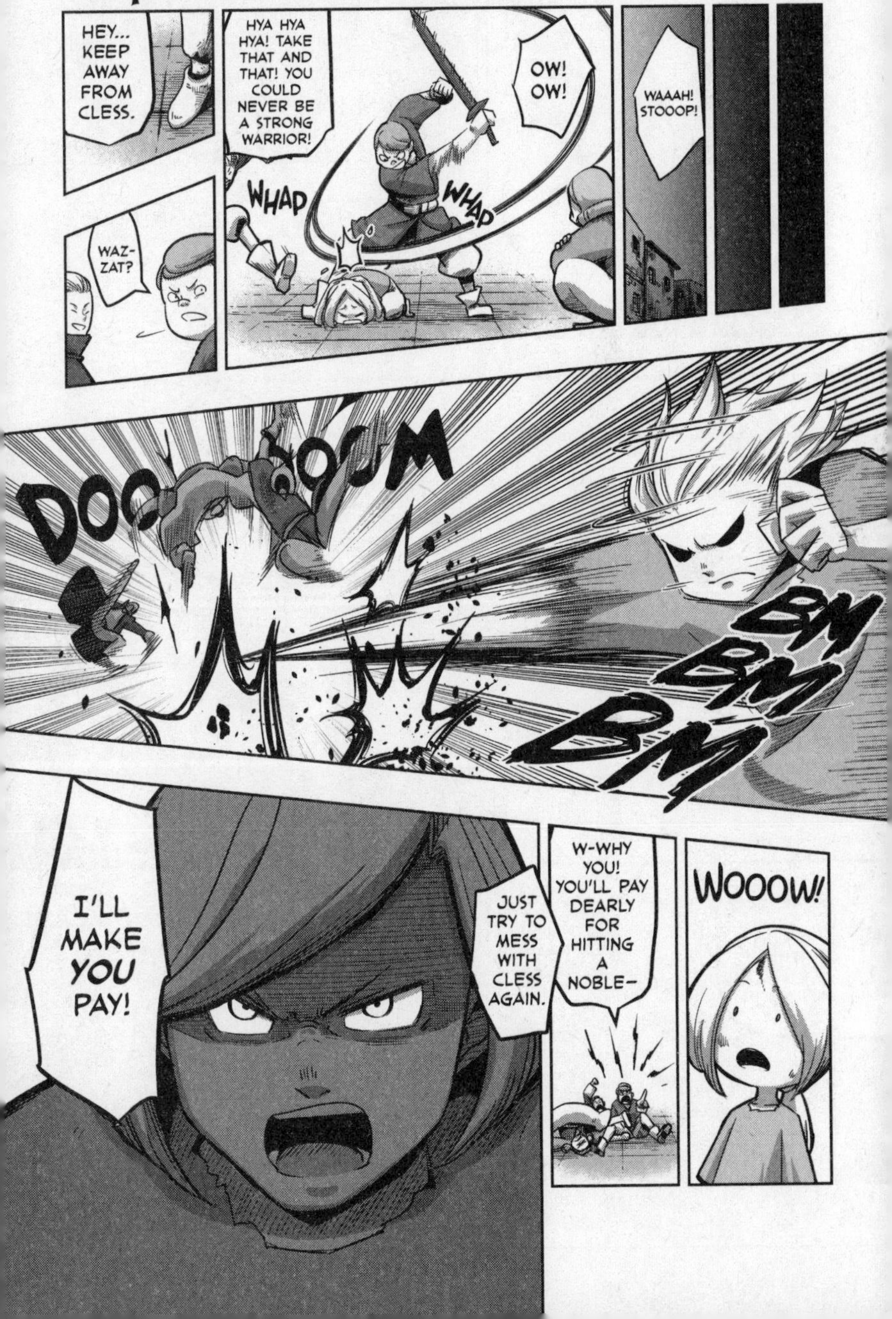
WAAAH! STOOOP!
OW! OW!
HYA HYA HYA! TAKE THAT AND THAT! YOU COULD NEVER BE A STRONG WARRIOR!
WHAP
WHAP
HEY... KEEP AWAY FROM CLESS.
WAZ-ZAT?
BM BM BM
DOOOOOM
WOOOW!
W-WHY YOU! YOU'LL PAY DEARLY FOR HITTING A NOBLE—
JUST TRY TO MESS WITH CLESS AGAIN.
I'LL MAKE YOU PAY!

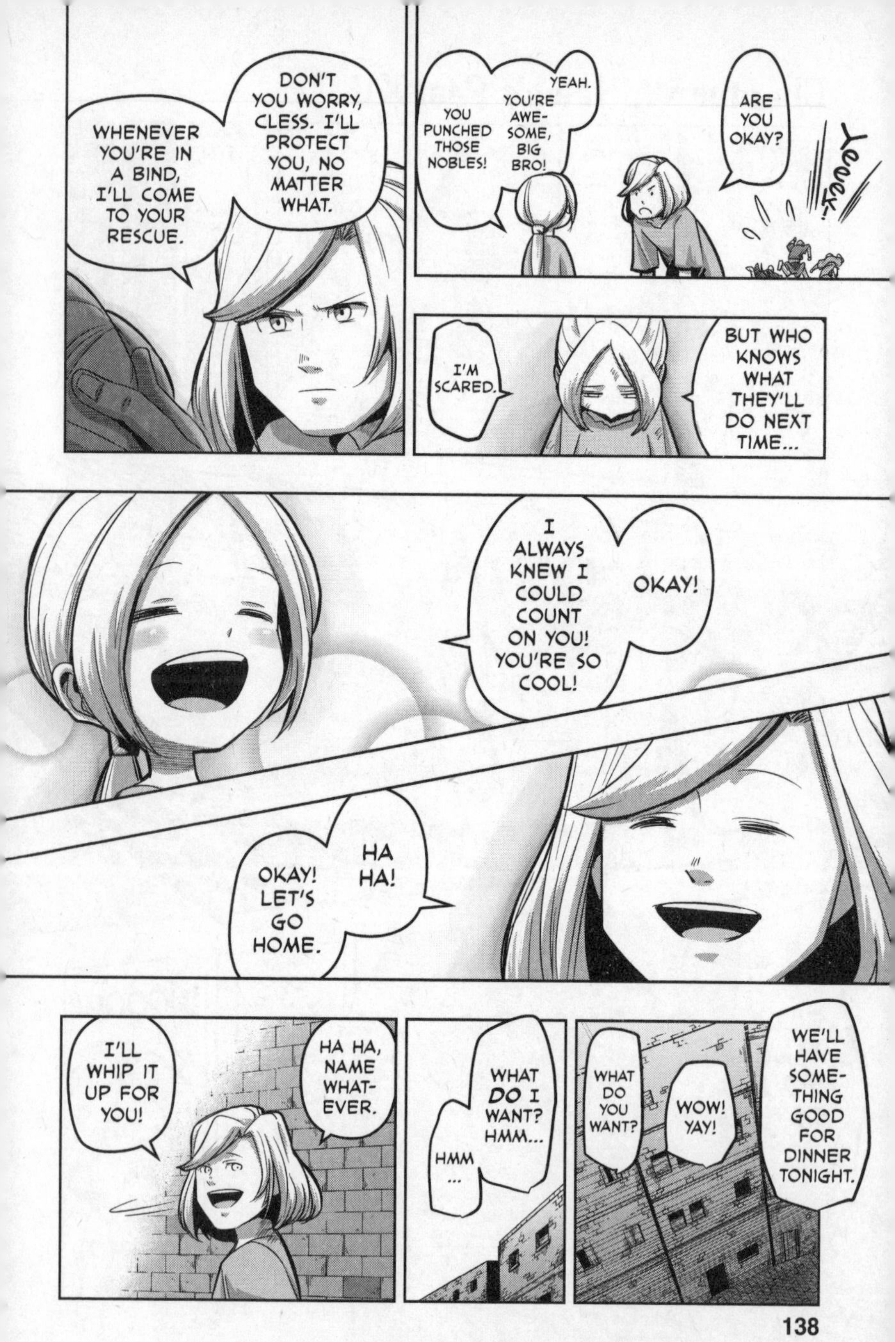
ARE YOU OKAY?
YEOWCH!
YEAH. YOU'RE AWESOME, BIG BRO!
YOU PUNCHED THOSE NOBLES!
BUT WHO KNOWS WHAT THEY'LL DO NEXT TIME...
I'M SCARED.
DON'T YOU WORRY, CLESS. I'LL PROTECT YOU, NO MATTER WHAT.
WHENEVER YOU'RE IN A BIND, I'LL COME TO YOUR RESCUE.
OKAY!
I ALWAYS KNEW I COULD COUNT ON YOU! YOU'RE SO COOL!
HA HA!
OKAY! LET'S GO HOME.
WE'LL HAVE SOMETHING GOOD FOR DINNER TONIGHT.
WOW! YAY!
WHAT DO YOU WANT?
WHAT *DO* I WANT? HMM...
HMM...
HA HA, NAME WHATEVER.
I'LL WHIP IT UP FOR YOU!

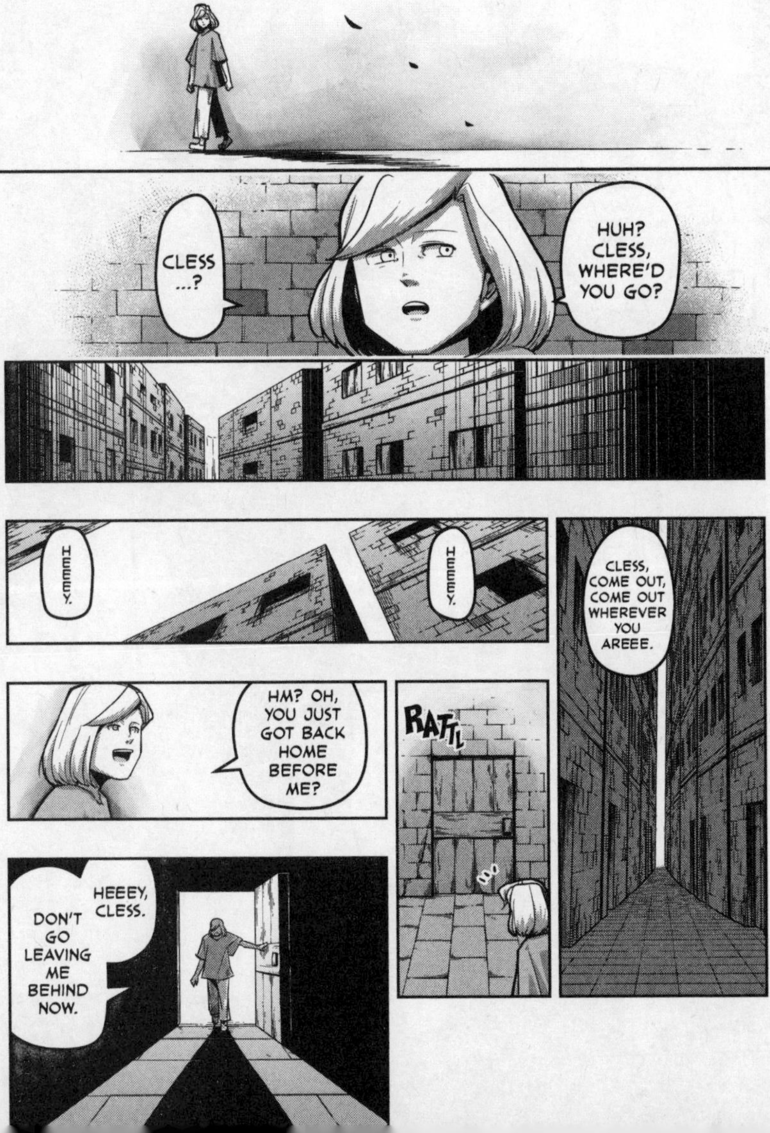
HUH? CLESS, WHERE'D YOU GO?
CLESS ...?
CLESS, COME OUT, COME OUT WHEREVER YOU AREEE.
HEEEY.
HEEEY.
RATTL
HM? OH, YOU JUST GOT BACK HOME BEFORE ME?
HEEEY, CLESS.
DON'T GO LEAVING ME BEHIND NOW.

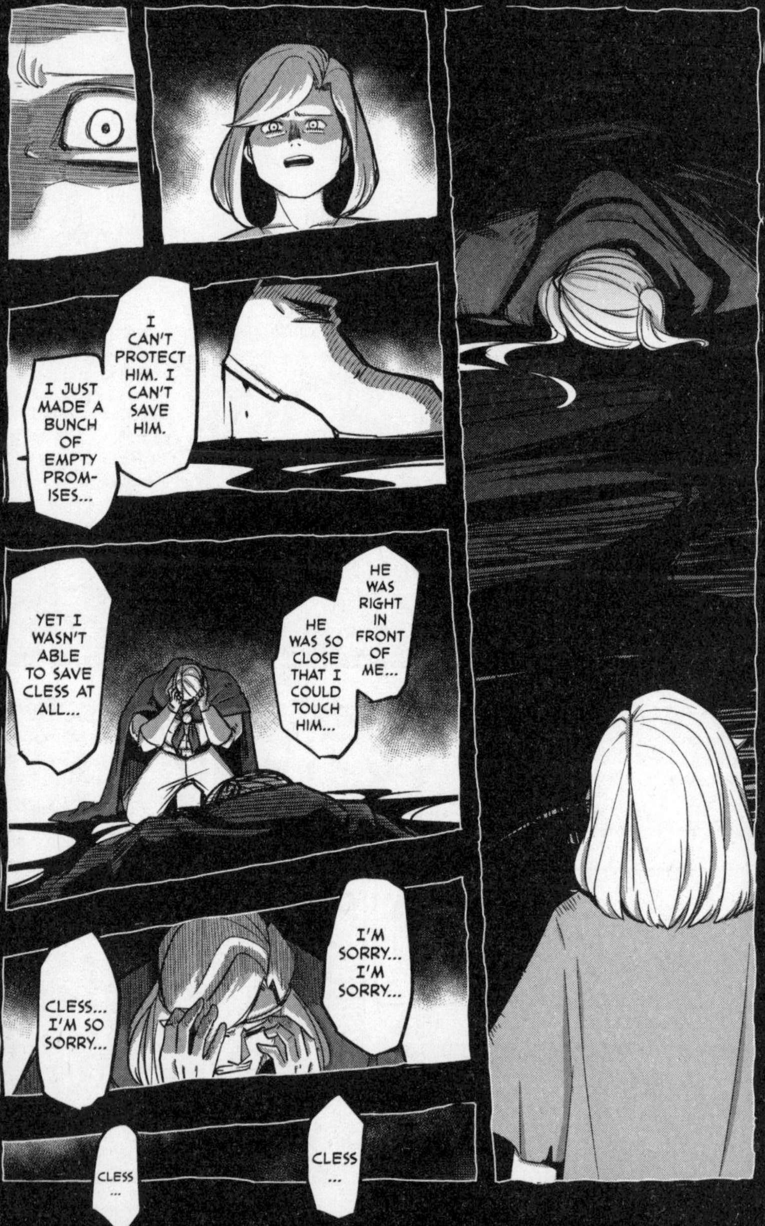
I CAN'T PROTECT HIM. I CAN'T SAVE HIM.
I JUST MADE A BUNCH OF EMPTY PROM-ISES...
HE WAS RIGHT IN FRONT OF ME...
HE WAS SO CLOSE THAT I COULD TOUCH HIM...
YET I WASN'T ABLE TO SAVE CLESS AT ALL...
I'M SORRY... I'M SORRY...
CLESS... I'M SO SORRY...
CLESS ...
CLESS ...

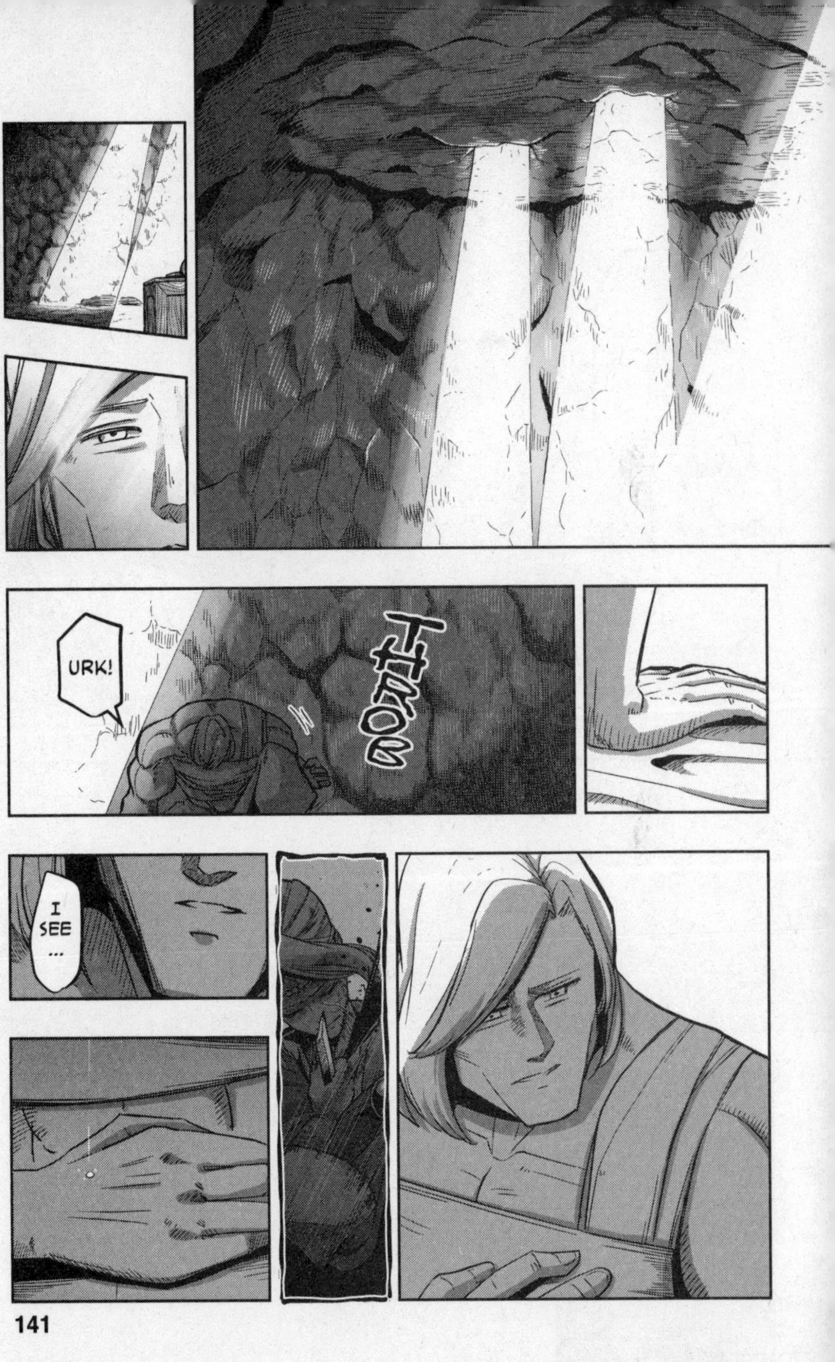
THROB
URK!
I SEE ...

IT...

...WASN'T A DREAM.

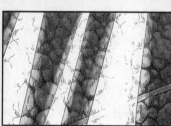

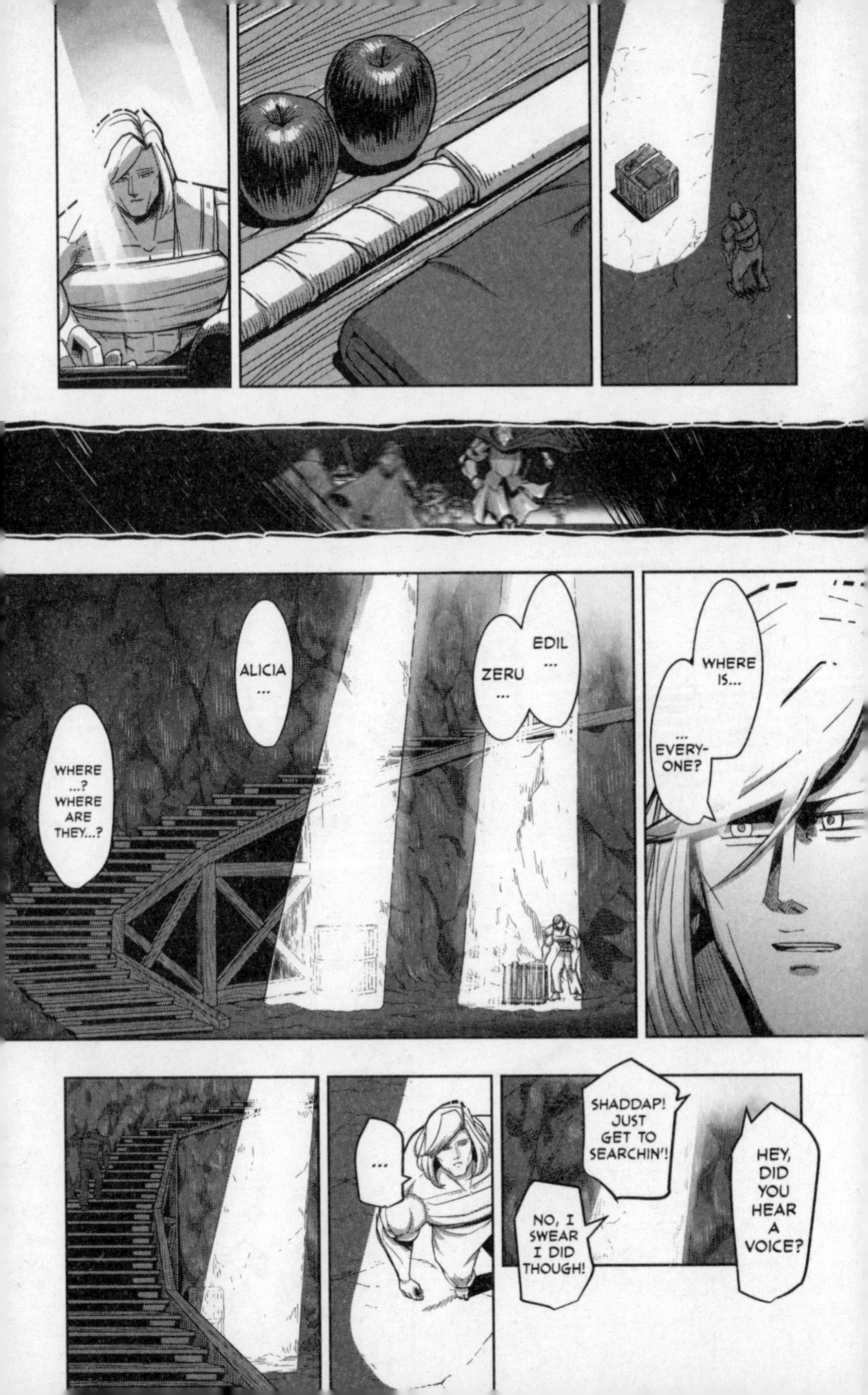
WHERE IS... ...EVERYONE?
EDIL ...
ZERU ...
ALICIA ...
WHERE ...? WHERE ARE THEY...?
HEY, DID YOU HEAR A VOICE?
SHADDAP! JUST GET TO SEARCHIN'!
NO, I SWEAR I DID THOUGH!
...

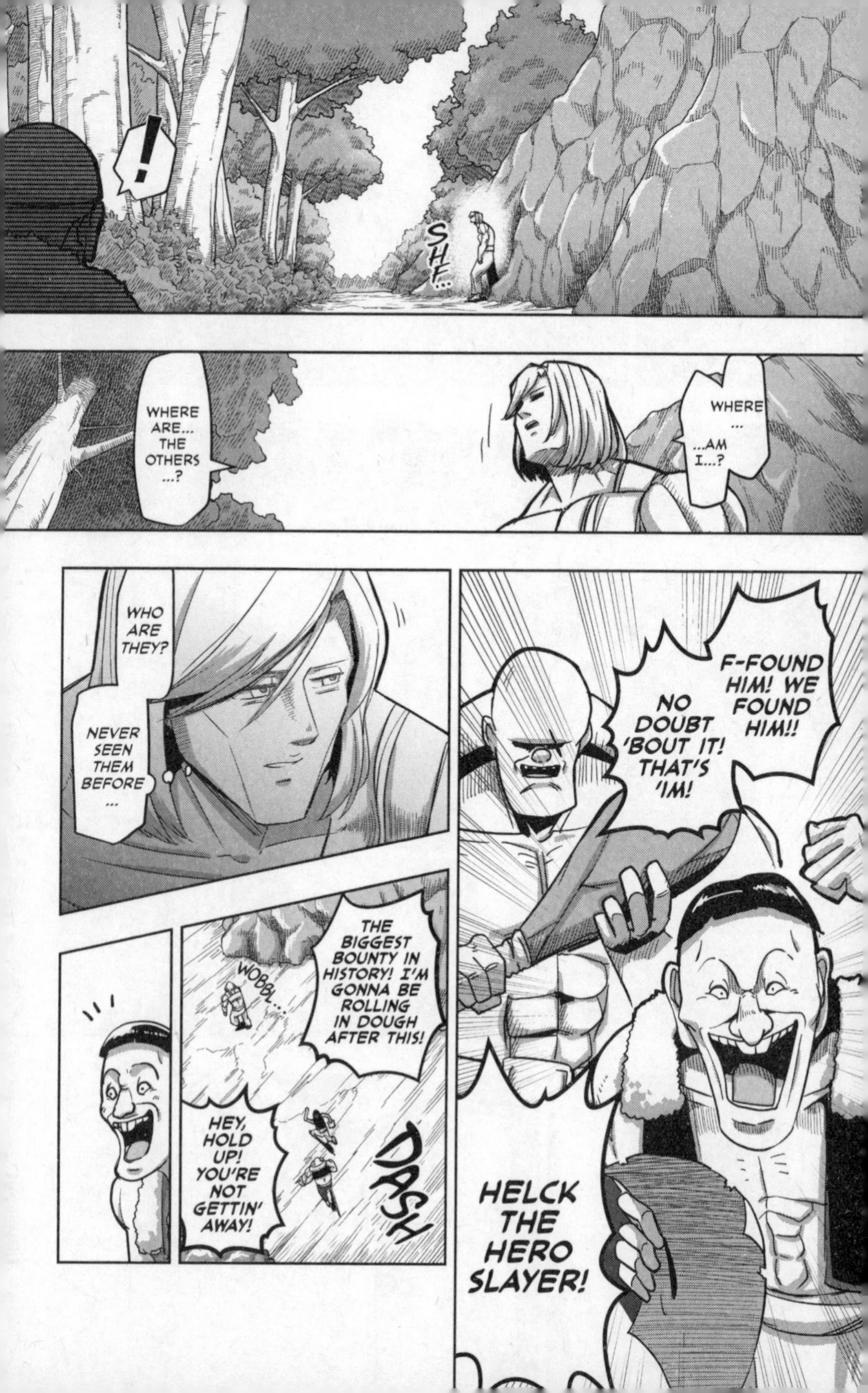
!
SHF...
WHERE ... ...AM I...?
WHERE ARE... THE OTHERS ...?
F-FOUND HIM! WE FOUND HIM!!
NO DOUBT 'BOUT IT! THAT'S 'IM!
HELCK THE HERO SLAYER!
WHO ARE THEY?
NEVER SEEN THEM BEFORE ...
THE BIGGEST BOUNTY IN HISTORY! I'M GONNA BE ROLLING IN DOUGH AFTER THIS!
WOBBL...
HEY, HOLD UP! YOU'RE NOT GETTIN' AWAY!
DASH

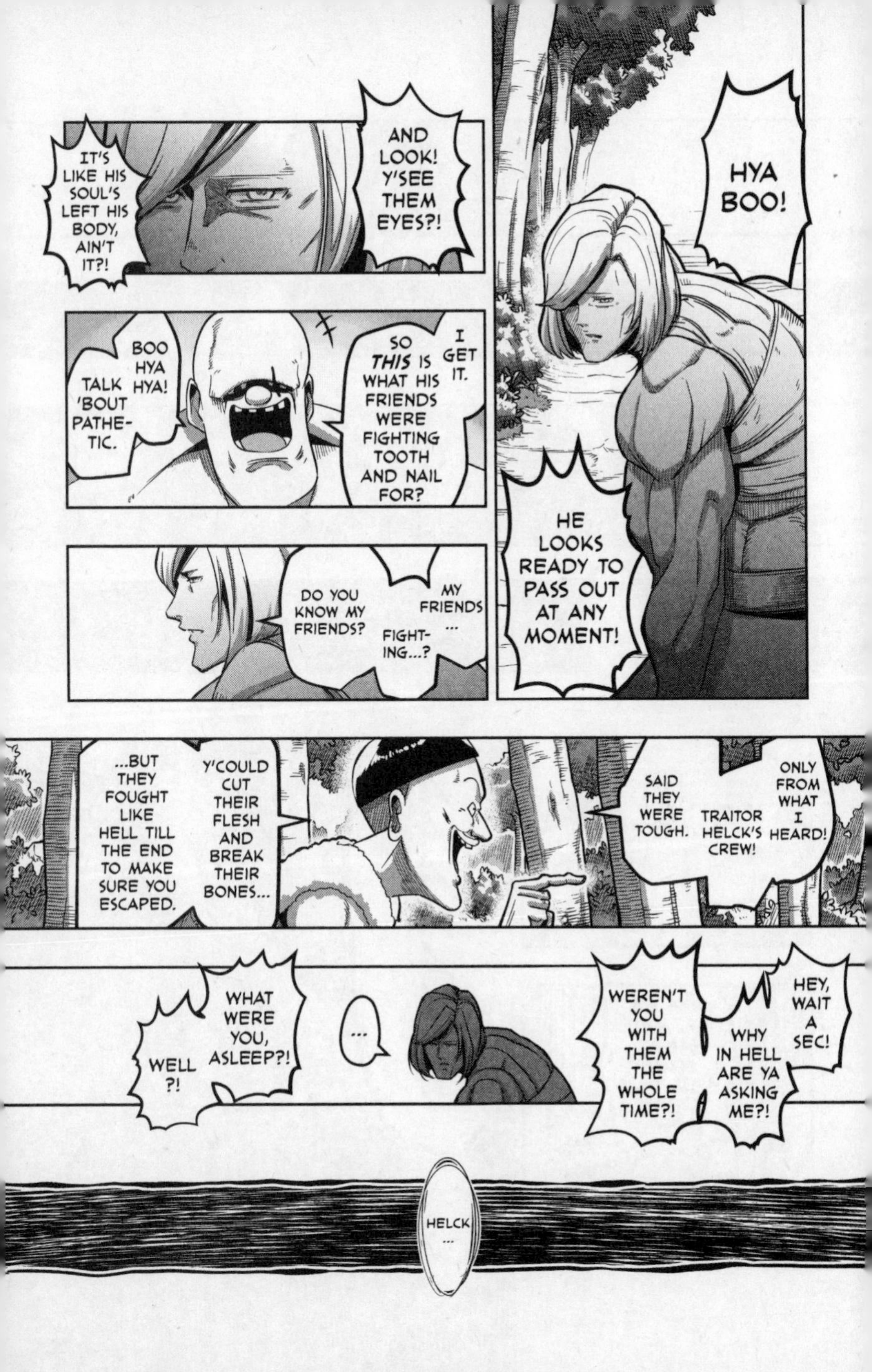
HYA BOO!
HE LOOKS READY TO PASS OUT AT ANY MOMENT!
AND LOOK! Y'SEE THEM EYES?!
IT'S LIKE HIS SOUL'S LEFT HIS BODY, AIN'T IT?!
I GET IT.
SO *THIS* IS WHAT HIS FRIENDS WERE FIGHTING TOOTH AND NAIL FOR?
BOO HYA HYA!
TALK 'BOUT PATHETIC.
MY FRIENDS ...
FIGHTING...?
DO YOU KNOW MY FRIENDS?
ONLY FROM WHAT I HEARD!
TRAITOR HELCK'S CREW!
SAID THEY WERE TOUGH.
Y'COULD CUT THEIR FLESH AND BREAK THEIR BONES...
...BUT THEY FOUGHT LIKE HELL TILL THE END TO MAKE SURE YOU ESCAPED.
HEY, WAIT A SEC!
WHY IN HELL ARE YA ASKING ME?!
WEREN'T YOU WITH THEM THE WHOLE TIME?!
...
WHAT WERE YOU, ASLEEP?!
WELL?!
HELCK ...

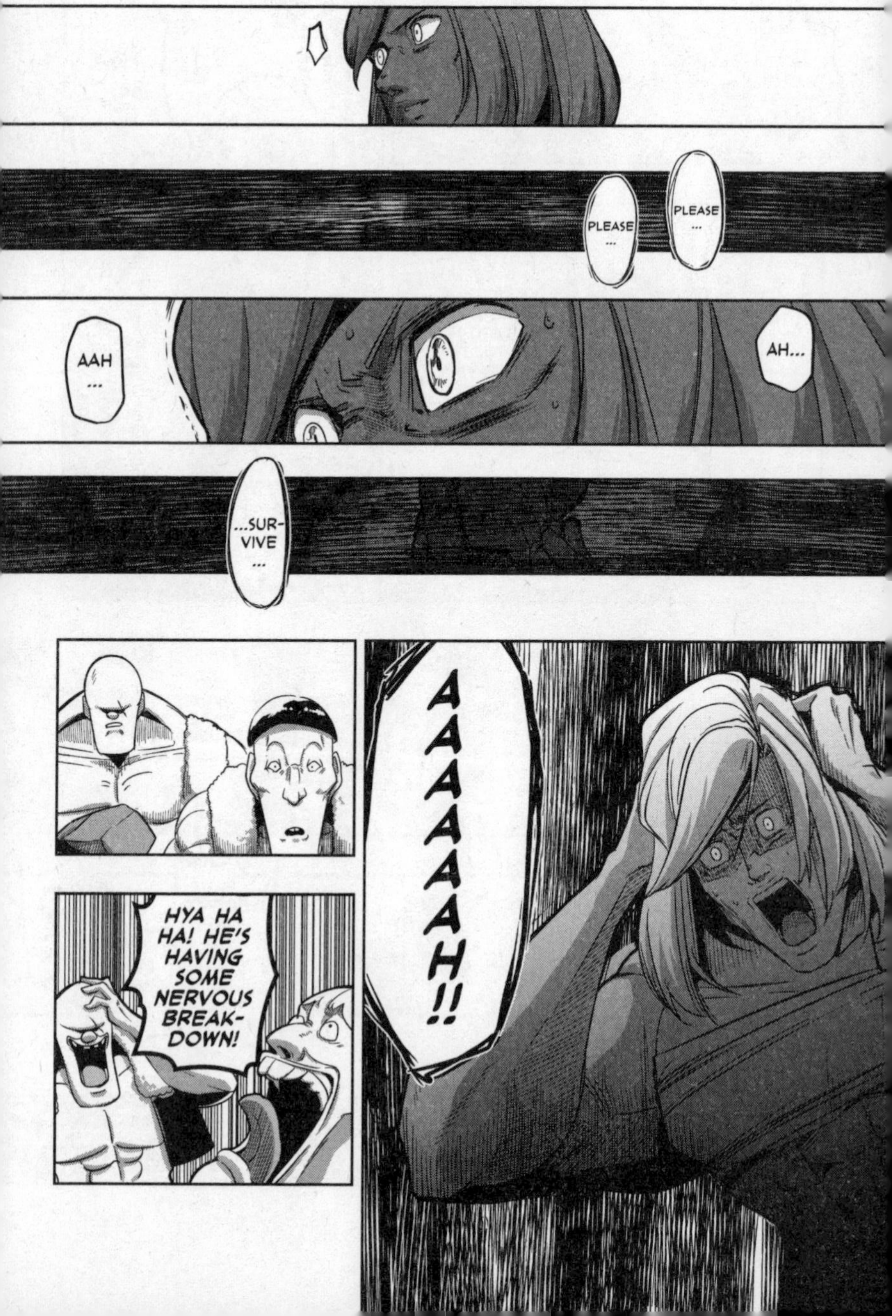
PLEASE...
PLEASE...
AH...
AAH...
...SURVIVE...
AAAAAAH!!
HYA HA HA! HE'S HAVING SOME NERVOUS BREAKDOWN!

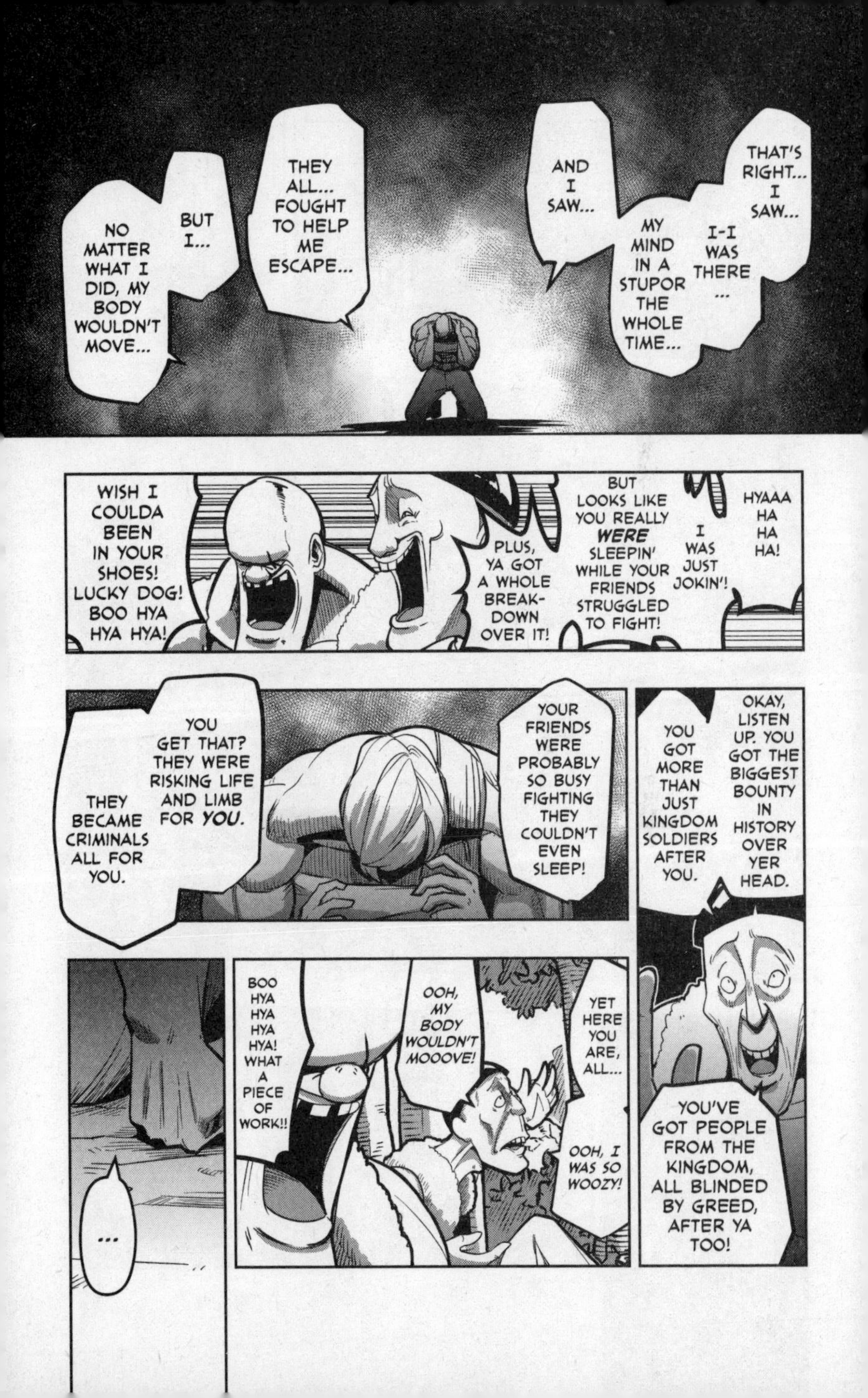
THAT'S RIGHT... I SAW...
I-I WAS THERE...
MY MIND IN A STUPOR THE WHOLE TIME...
AND I SAW...
THEY ALL... FOUGHT TO HELP ME ESCAPE...
BUT I...
NO MATTER WHAT I DID, MY BODY WOULDN'T MOVE...
HYAAA HA HA HA!
I WAS JUST JOKIN'!
BUT LOOKS LIKE YOU REALLY *WERE* SLEEPIN' WHILE YOUR FRIENDS STRUGGLED TO FIGHT!
PLUS, YA GOT A WHOLE BREAK-DOWN OVER IT!
WISH I COULDA BEEN IN YOUR SHOES! LUCKY DOG! BOO HYA HYA HYA!
OKAY, LISTEN UP. YOU GOT THE BIGGEST BOUNTY IN HISTORY OVER YER HEAD.
YOU GOT MORE THAN JUST KINGDOM SOLDIERS AFTER YOU.
YOU'VE GOT PEOPLE FROM THE KINGDOM, ALL BLINDED BY GREED, AFTER YA TOO!
YOUR FRIENDS WERE PROBABLY SO BUSY FIGHTING THEY COULDN'T EVEN SLEEP!
YOU GET THAT? THEY WERE RISKING LIFE AND LIMB FOR *YOU*.
THEY BECAME CRIMINALS ALL FOR YOU.
YET HERE YOU ARE, ALL...
OOH, MY BODY WOULDN'T MOOOVE!
OOH, I WAS SO WOOZY!
BOO HYA HYA HYA HYA! WHAT A PIECE OF WORK!!
...

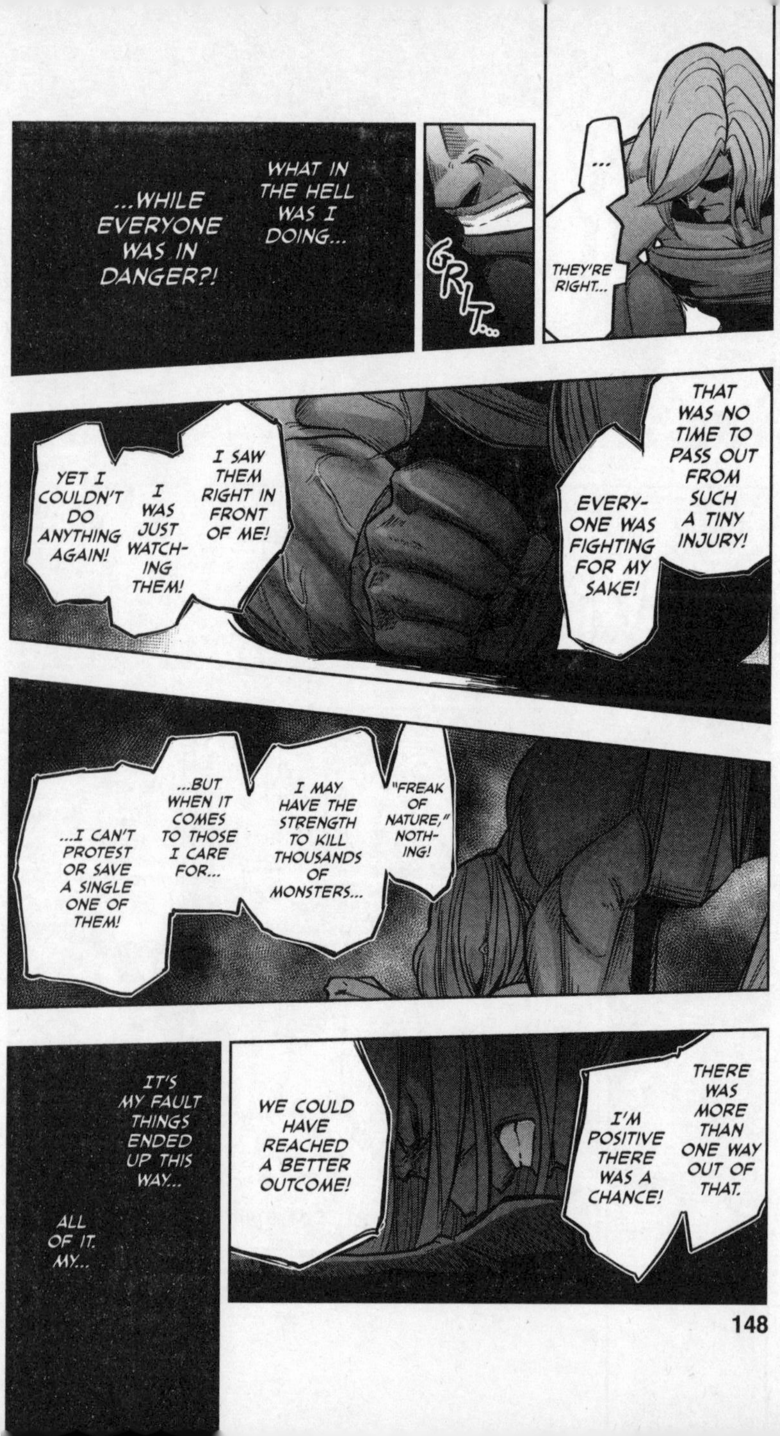
...
THEY'RE RIGHT...
GRIT...
WHAT IN THE HELL WAS I DOING...
...WHILE EVERYONE WAS IN DANGER?!
THAT WAS NO TIME TO PASS OUT FROM SUCH A TINY INJURY!
EVERY-ONE WAS FIGHTING FOR MY SAKE!
I SAW THEM RIGHT IN FRONT OF ME!
I WAS JUST WATCH-ING THEM!
YET I COULDN'T DO ANYTHING AGAIN!
"FREAK OF NATURE," NOTH-ING!
I MAY HAVE THE STRENGTH TO KILL THOUSANDS OF MONSTERS...
...BUT WHEN IT COMES TO THOSE I CARE FOR...
...I CAN'T PROTEST OR SAVE A SINGLE ONE OF THEM!
THERE WAS MORE THAN ONE WAY OUT OF THAT.
I'M POSITIVE THERE WAS A CHANCE!
WE COULD HAVE REACHED A BETTER OUTCOME!
IT'S MY FAULT THINGS ENDED UP THIS WAY...
ALL OF IT. MY...

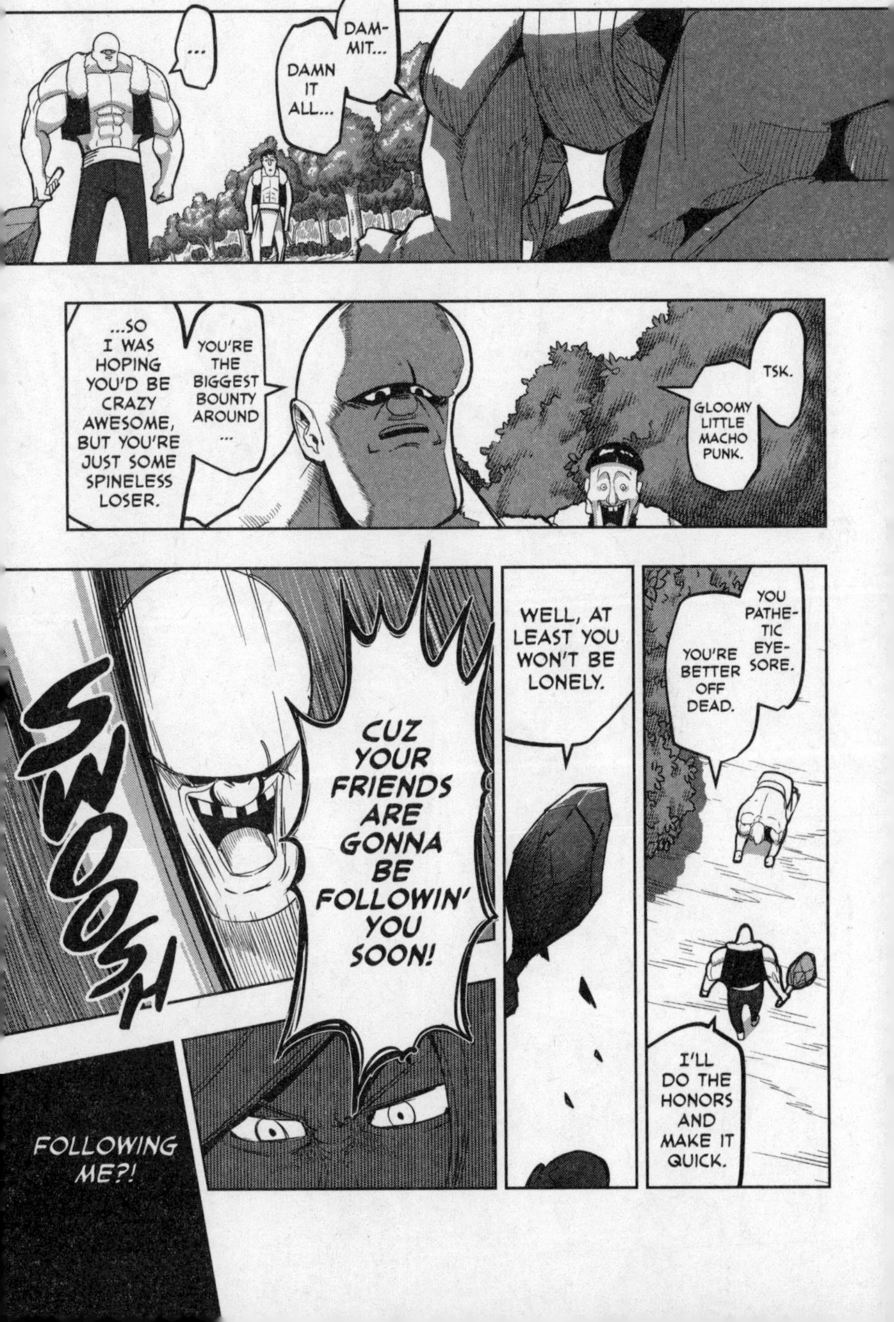
DAM-MIT...
DAMN IT ALL...
...
TSK.
GLOOMY LITTLE MACHO PUNK.
YOU'RE THE BIGGEST BOUNTY AROUND...
...SO I WAS HOPING YOU'D BE CRAZY AWESOME, BUT YOU'RE JUST SOME SPINELESS LOSER.
YOU PATHETIC EYESORE.
YOU'RE BETTER OFF DEAD.
I'LL DO THE HONORS AND MAKE IT QUICK.
WELL, AT LEAST YOU WON'T BE LONELY.
CUZ YOUR FRIENDS ARE GONNA BE FOLLOWIN' YOU SOON!
SWOOSH
FOLLOWING ME?!

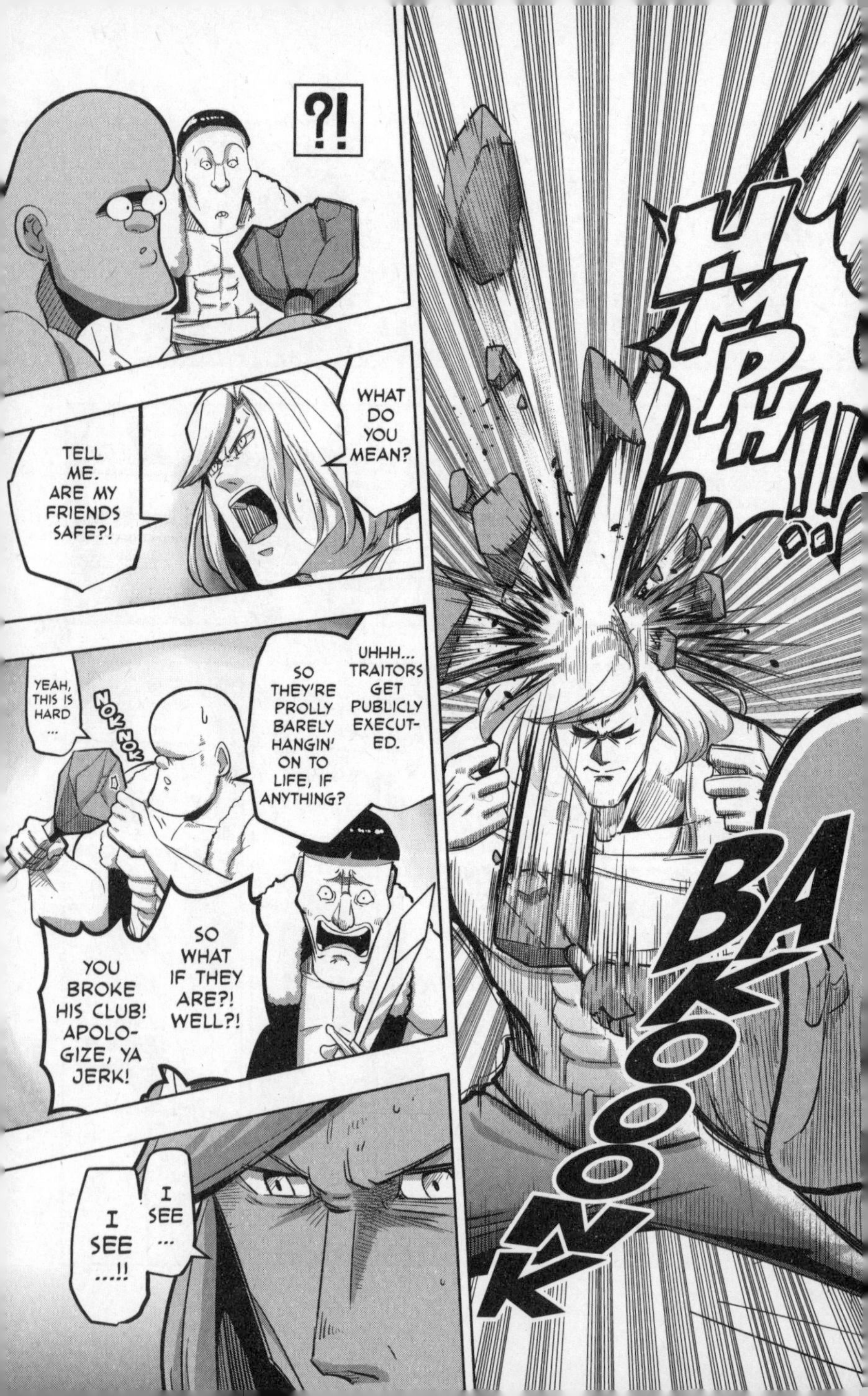
HMPH!!..
BAKOOOONK
?!
WHAT DO YOU MEAN?
TELL ME. ARE MY FRIENDS SAFE?!
UHHH... TRAITORS GET PUBLICLY EXECUT-ED.
SO THEY'RE PROLLY BARELY HANGIN' ON TO LIFE, IF ANYTHING?
YEAH, THIS IS HARD ...
NOW NOW
SO WHAT IF THEY ARE?! WELL?!
YOU BROKE HIS CLUB! APOLO-GIZE, YA JERK!
I SEE ...
I SEE ...!!

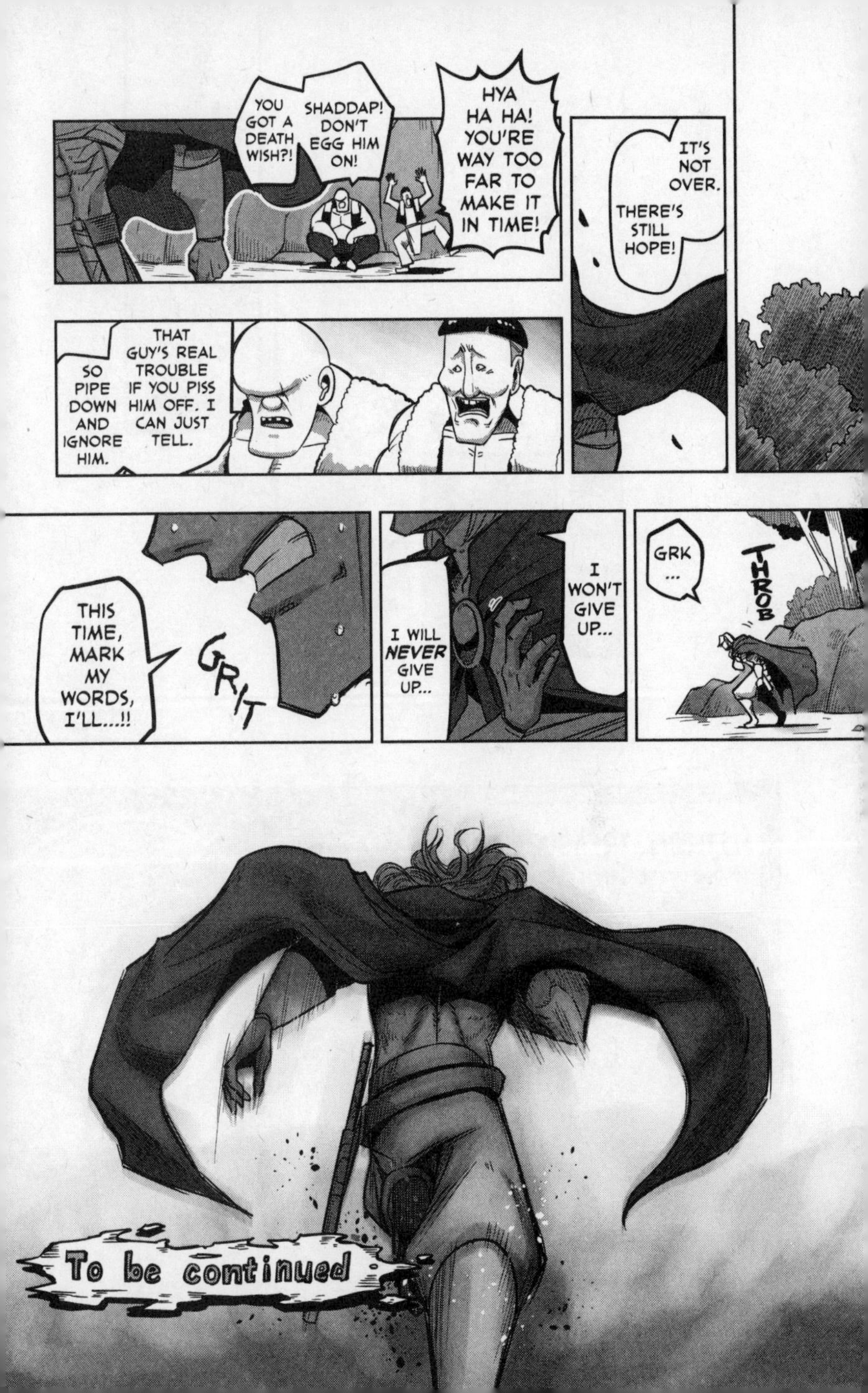
IT'S NOT OVER.
THERE'S STILL HOPE!
HYA HA HA! YOU'RE WAY TOO FAR TO MAKE IT IN TIME!
SHADDAP! DON'T EGG HIM ON!
YOU GOT A DEATH WISH?!
THAT GUY'S REAL TROUBLE IF YOU PISS HIM OFF. I CAN JUST TELL.
SO PIPE DOWN AND IGNORE HIM.
GRK ...
THROB
I WON'T GIVE UP...
I WILL NEVER GIVE UP...
GRIT
THIS TIME, MARK MY WORDS, I'LL...!!
To be continued

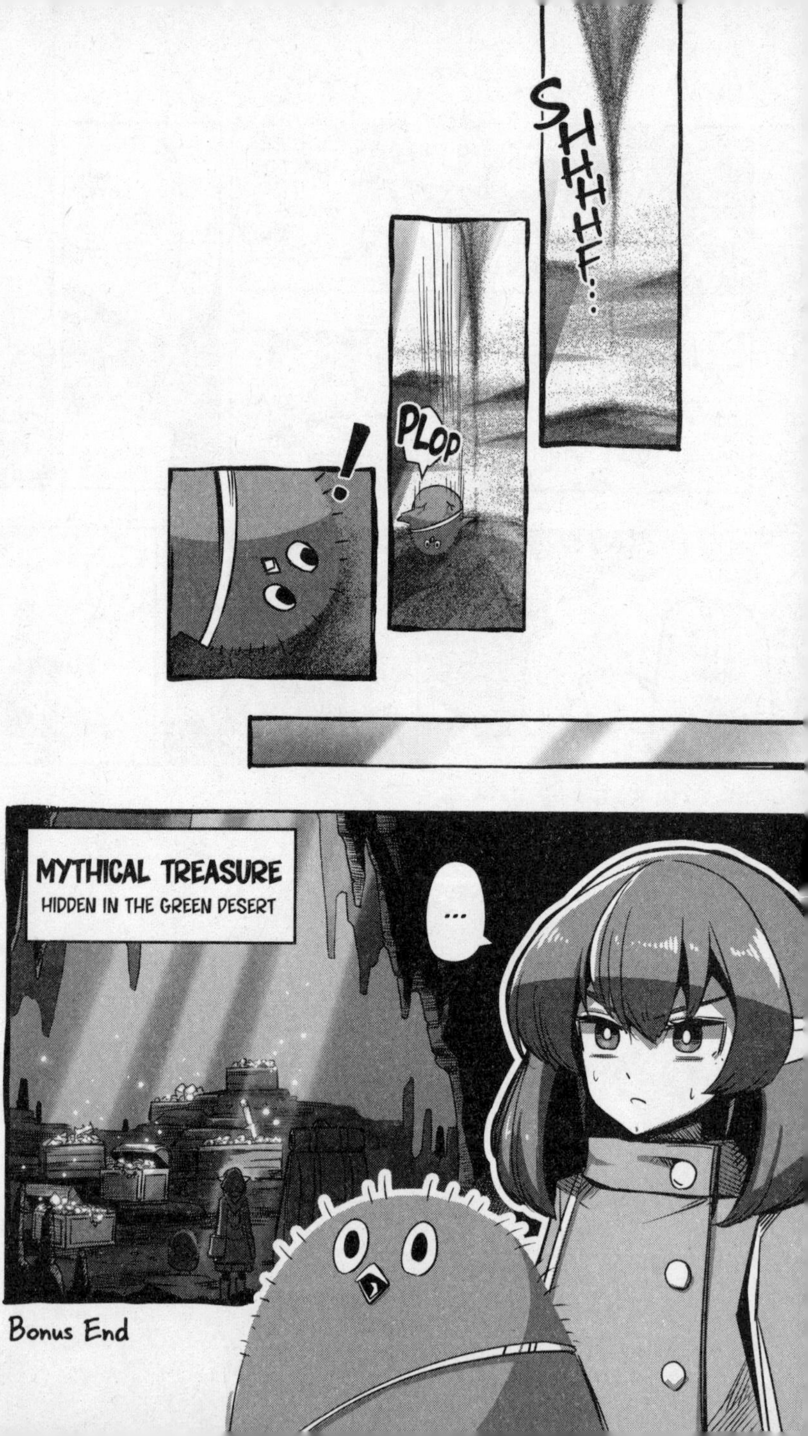
SHHHHF...
PLOP
!
MYTHICAL TREASURE
HIDDEN IN THE GREEN DESERT
...
Bonus End

Chapter 51: Helck's Past XVI

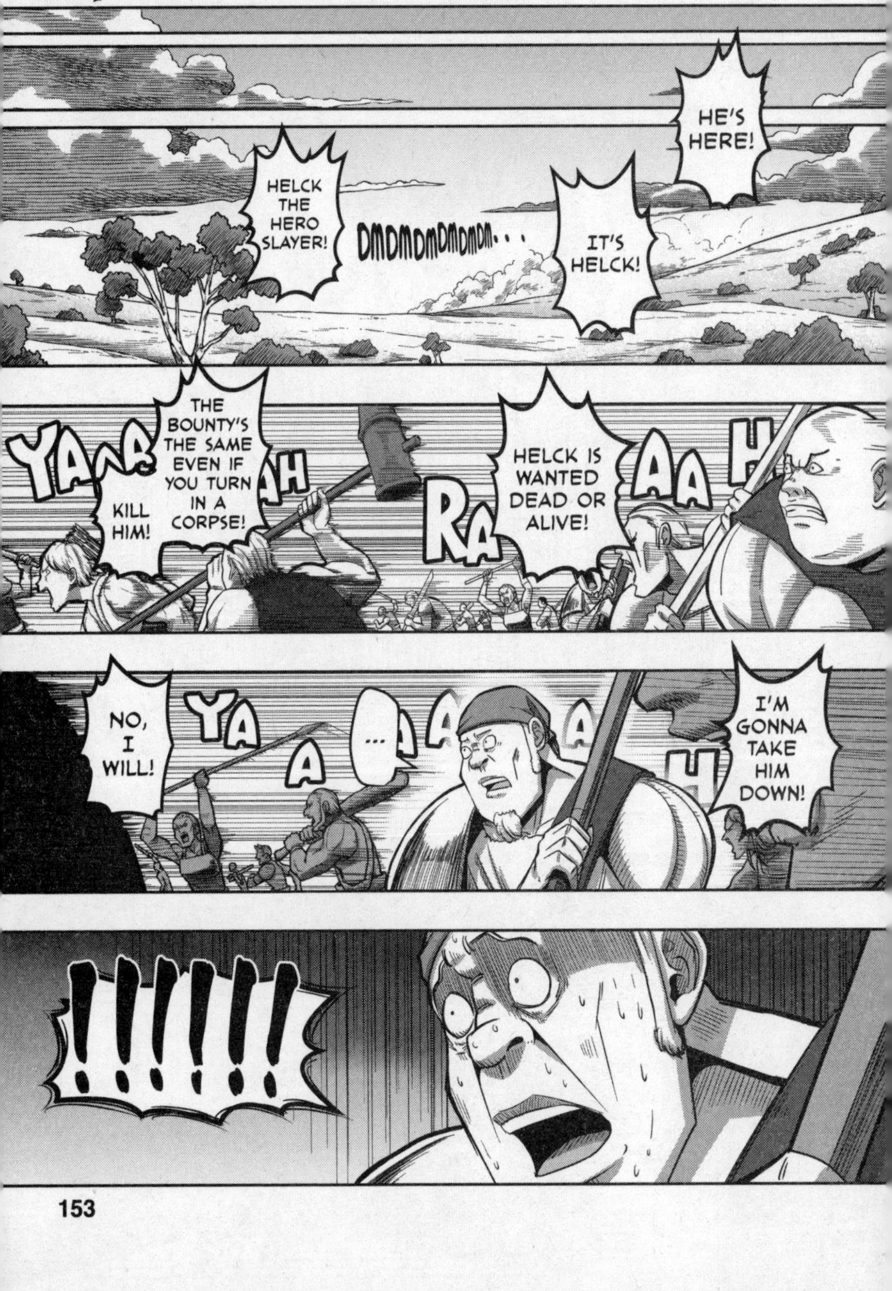
HE'S HERE!
IT'S HELCK!
DMDMDMDMDMDM...
HELCK THE HERO SLAYER!
HELCK IS WANTED DEAD OR ALIVE!
AA H
RA
YA~R AH
THE BOUNTY'S THE SAME EVEN IF YOU TURN IN A CORPSE!
KILL HIM!
I'M GONNA TAKE HIM DOWN!
...
NO, I WILL!
YA A A A A H
!!!!!!

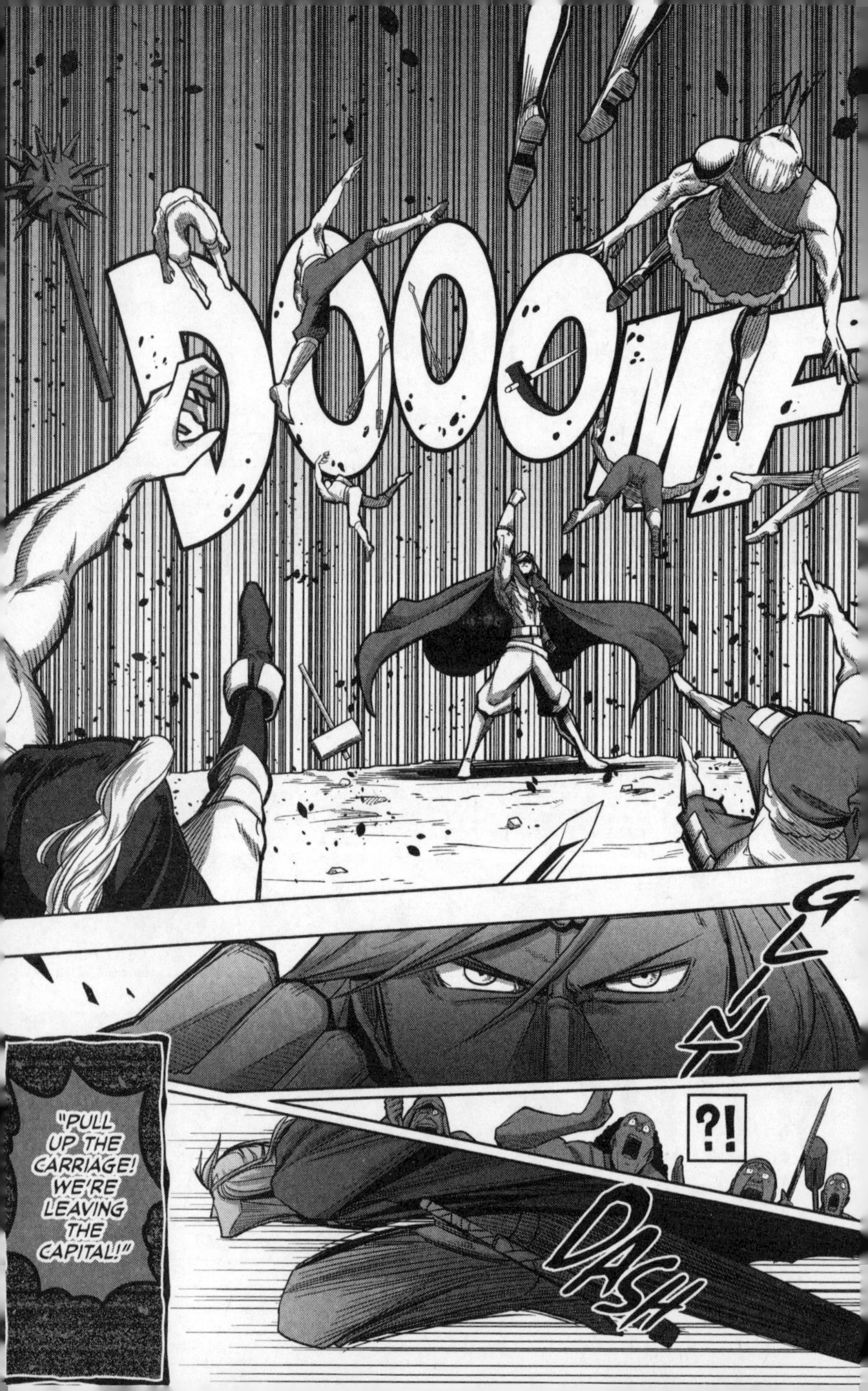
DOOOMF
GLINT
?!
DASH
"PULL UP THE CARRIAGE! WE'RE LEAVING THE CAPITAL!"

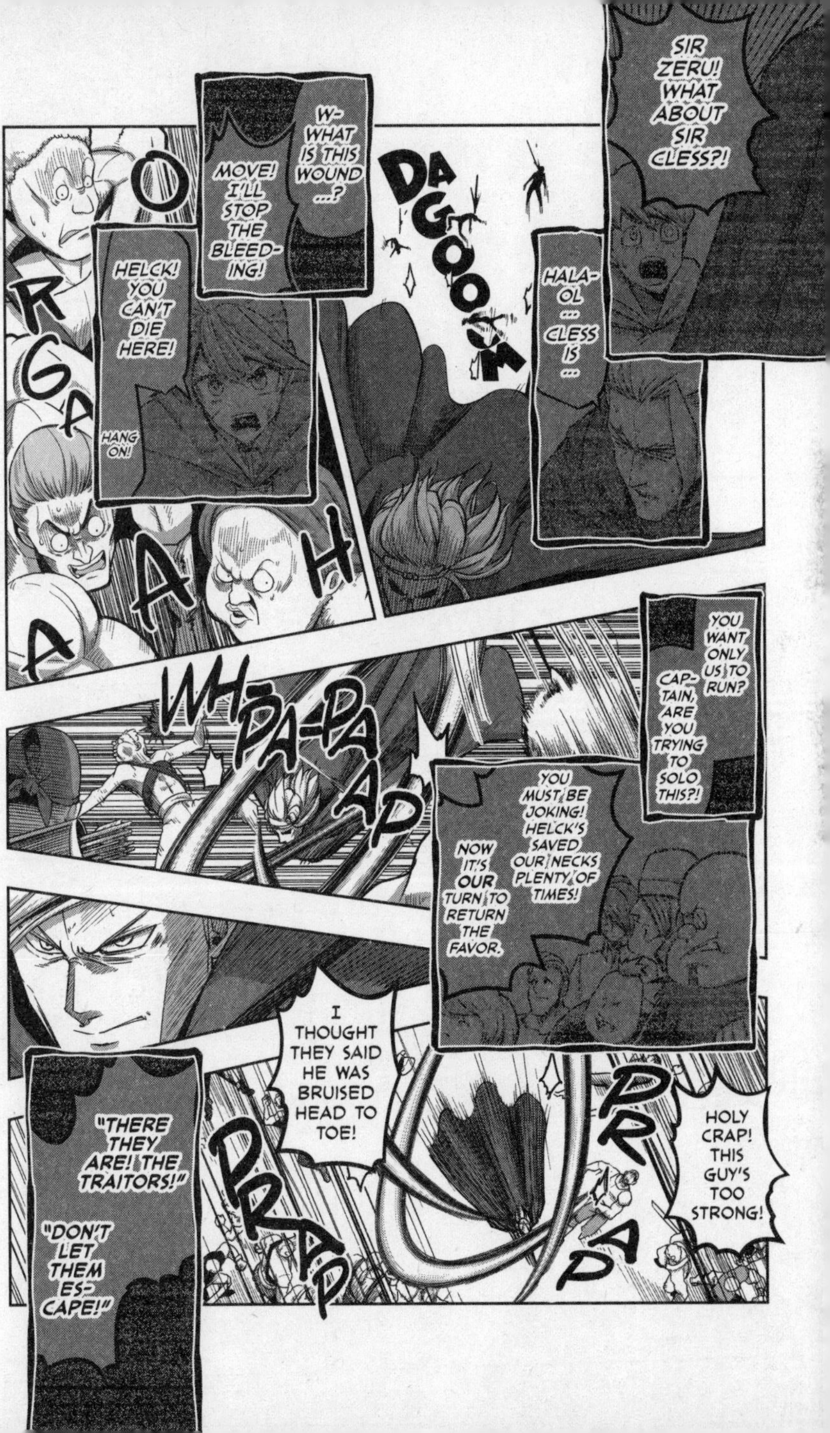
SIR ZERU! WHAT ABOUT SIR CLESS?!
HALAL-OL ... CLESS IS ...
DAGOOOM
W-WHAT IS THIS WOUND ...?
MOVE! I'LL STOP THE BLEED-ING!
HELCK! YOU CAN'T DIE HERE!
HANG ON!
ORGAAAH
YOU WANT ONLY US TO RUN?
CAP-TAIN, ARE YOU TRYING TO SOLO THIS?!
WH-DA-DAP
YOU MUST BE JOKING! HELCK'S SAVED OUR NECKS PLENTY OF TIMES!
NOW IT'S OUR TURN TO RETURN THE FAVOR.
HOLY CRAP! THIS GUY'S TOO STRONG!
PRAP
I THOUGHT THEY SAID HE WAS BRUISED HEAD TO TOE!
PRRAP
"THERE THEY ARE! THE TRAITORS!"
"DON'T LET THEM ES-CAPE!"

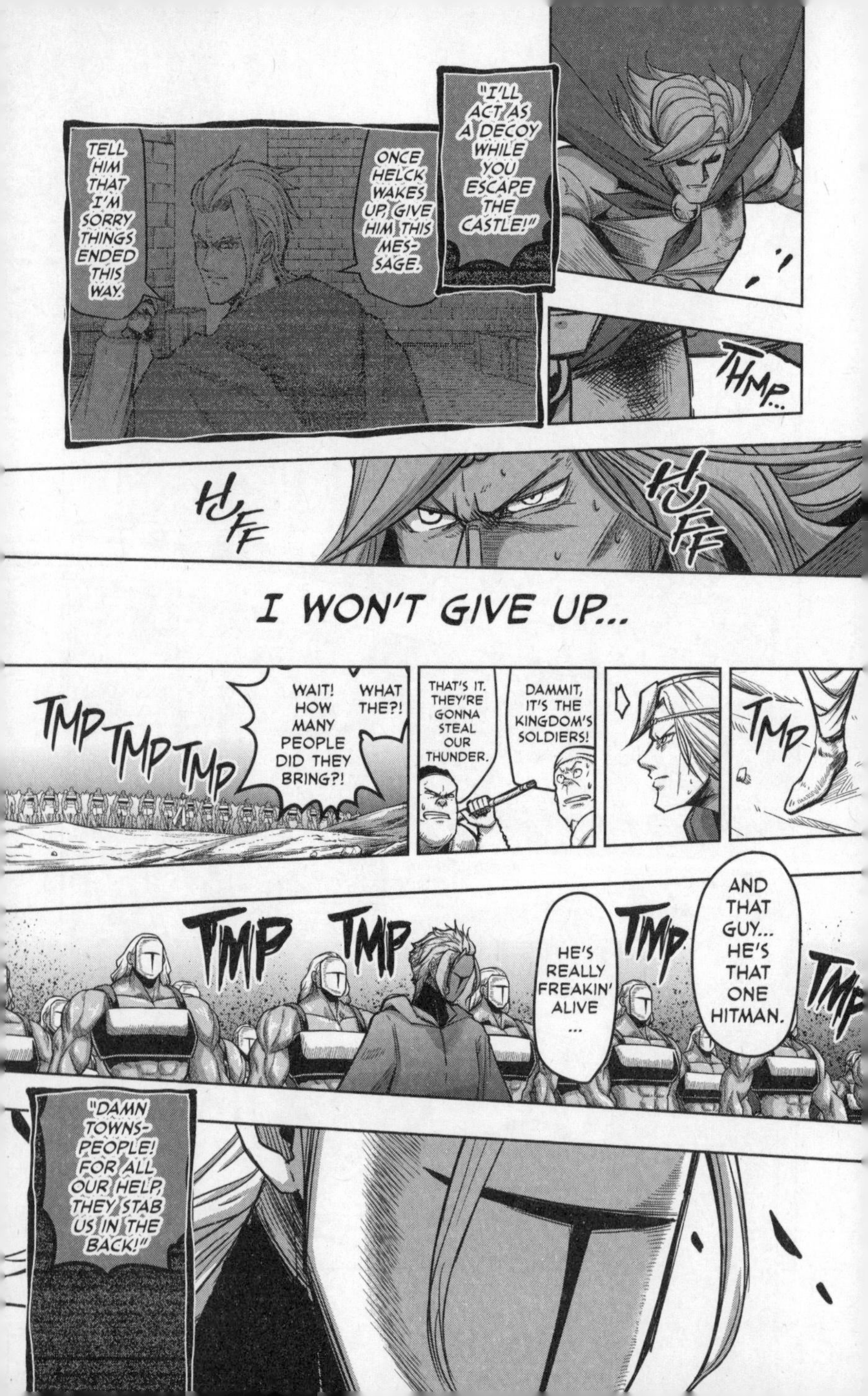
"I'LL ACT AS A DECOY WHILE YOU ESCAPE THE CASTLE!"
THMP...
ONCE HELCK WAKES UP, GIVE HIM THIS MES-SAGE.
TELL HIM THAT I'M SORRY THINGS ENDED THIS WAY.
HUFF
HUFF
I WON'T GIVE UP...
TMP
DAMMIT, IT'S THE KINGDOM'S SOLDIERS!
THAT'S IT. THEY'RE GONNA STEAL OUR THUNDER.
WHAT THE?!
WAIT! HOW MANY PEOPLE DID THEY BRING?!
TMP TMP TMP
TMP
AND THAT GUY... HE'S THAT ONE HITMAN.
TMP
HE'S REALLY FREAKIN' ALIVE ...
TMP TMP
"DAMN TOWNS-PEOPLE! FOR ALL OUR HELP, THEY STAB US IN THE BACK!"

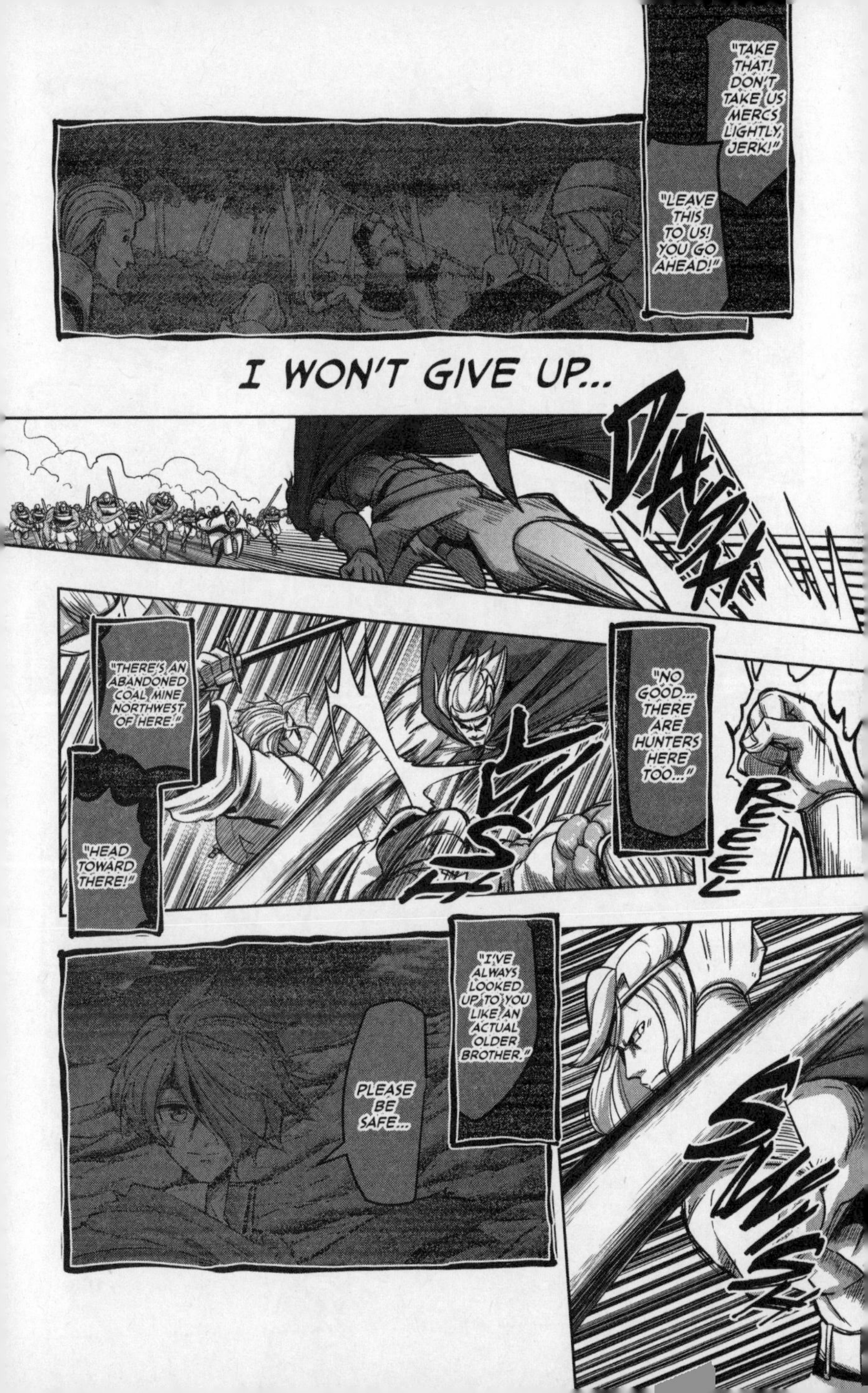
"TAKE THAT! DON'T TAKE US MERCS LIGHTLY, JERK!"
"LEAVE THIS TO US! YOU GO AHEAD!"
I WON'T GIVE UP...
"NO GOOD... THERE ARE HUNTERS HERE TOO..."
"THERE'S AN ABANDONED COAL MINE NORTHWEST OF HERE."
"HEAD TOWARD THERE!"
"I'VE ALWAYS LOOKED UP TO YOU LIKE AN ACTUAL OLDER BROTHER."
PLEASE BE SAFE...

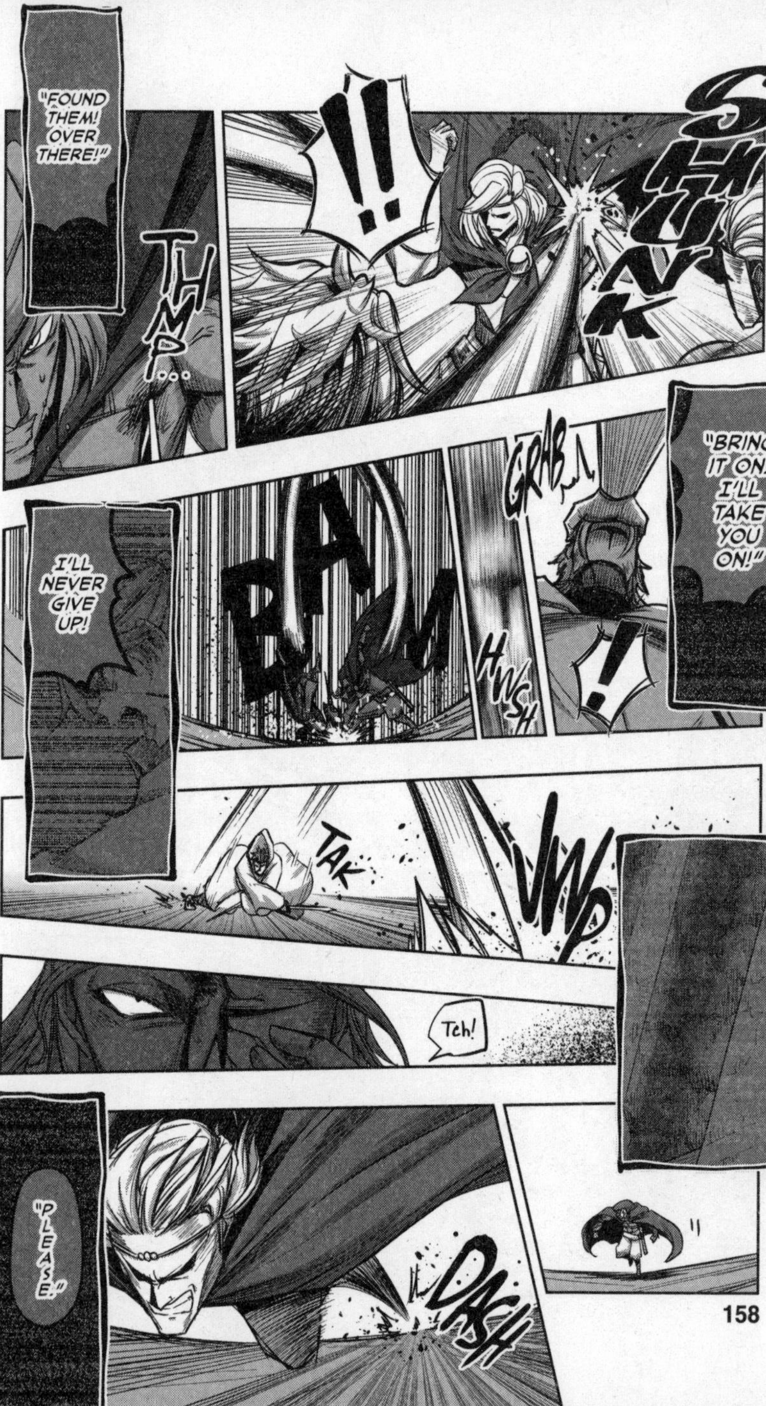
SHUNK
!!
"FOUND THEM! OVER THERE!"
THMP...
"BRING IT ON! I'LL TAKE YOU ON!"
GRAB
!
HWSH
BAM
I'LL NEVER GIVE UP!
VWWP
TAK
Tch!
DASH
"PLEASE."

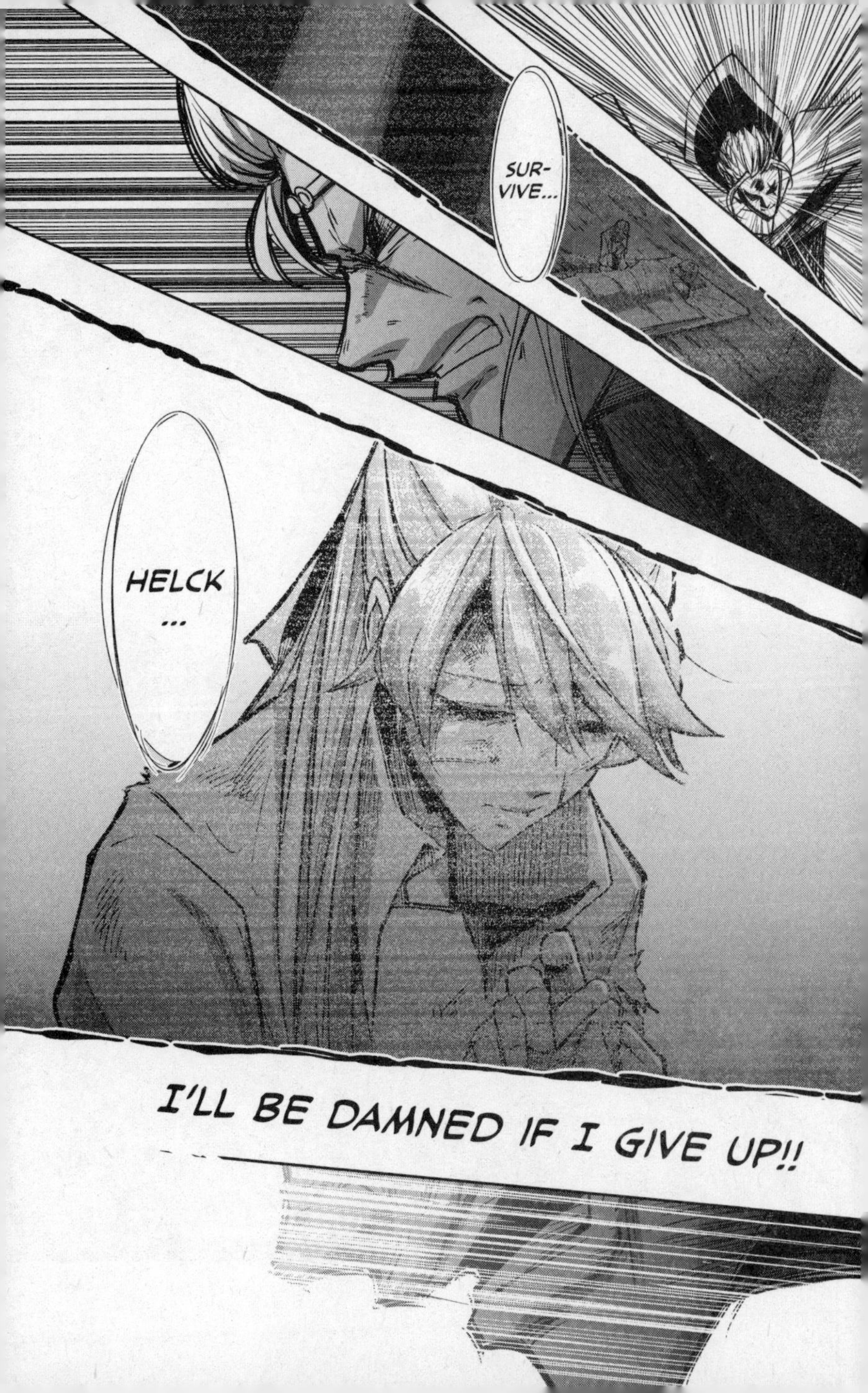
SUR-VIVE...
HELCK ...
I'LL BE DAMNED IF I GIVE UP!!

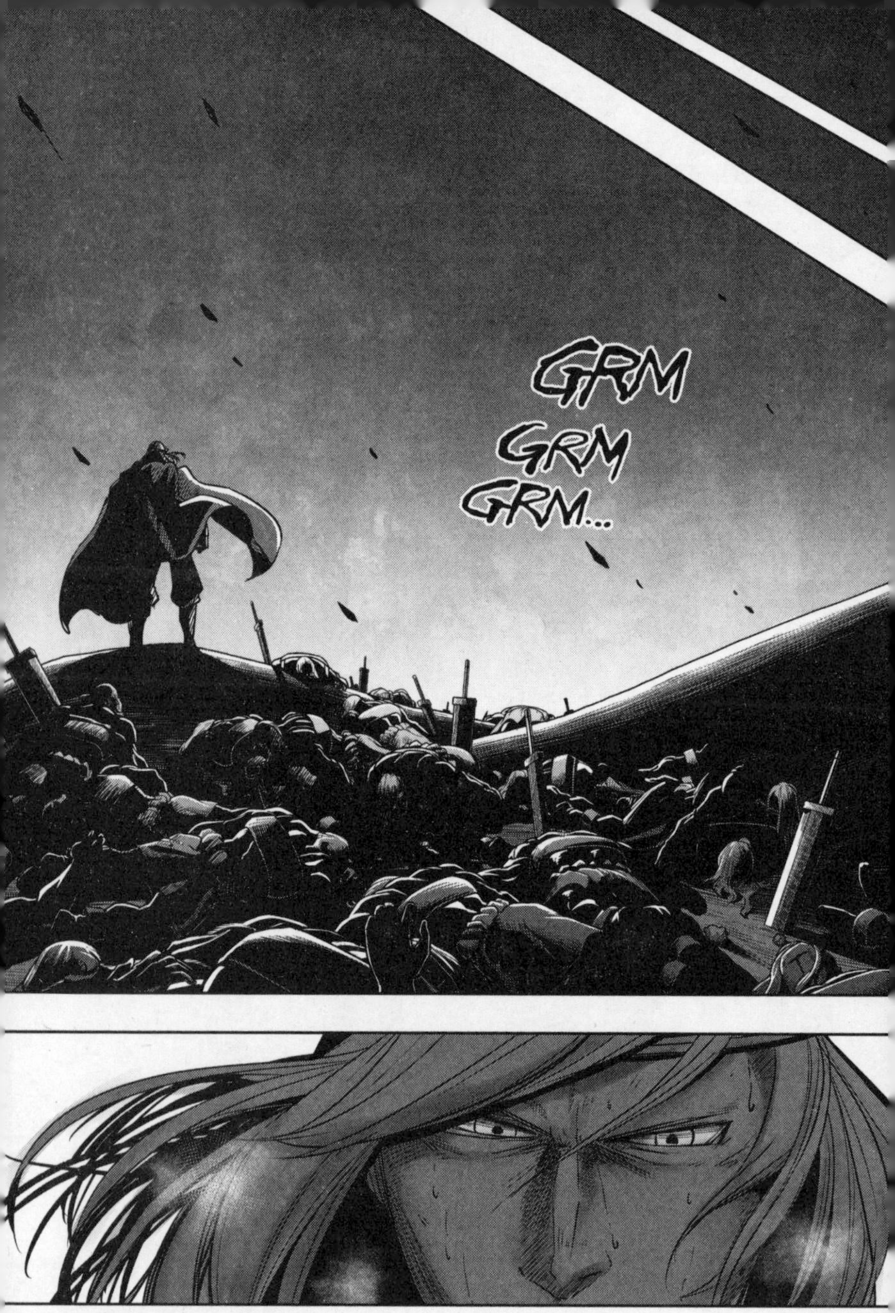
GRM GRM GRM...

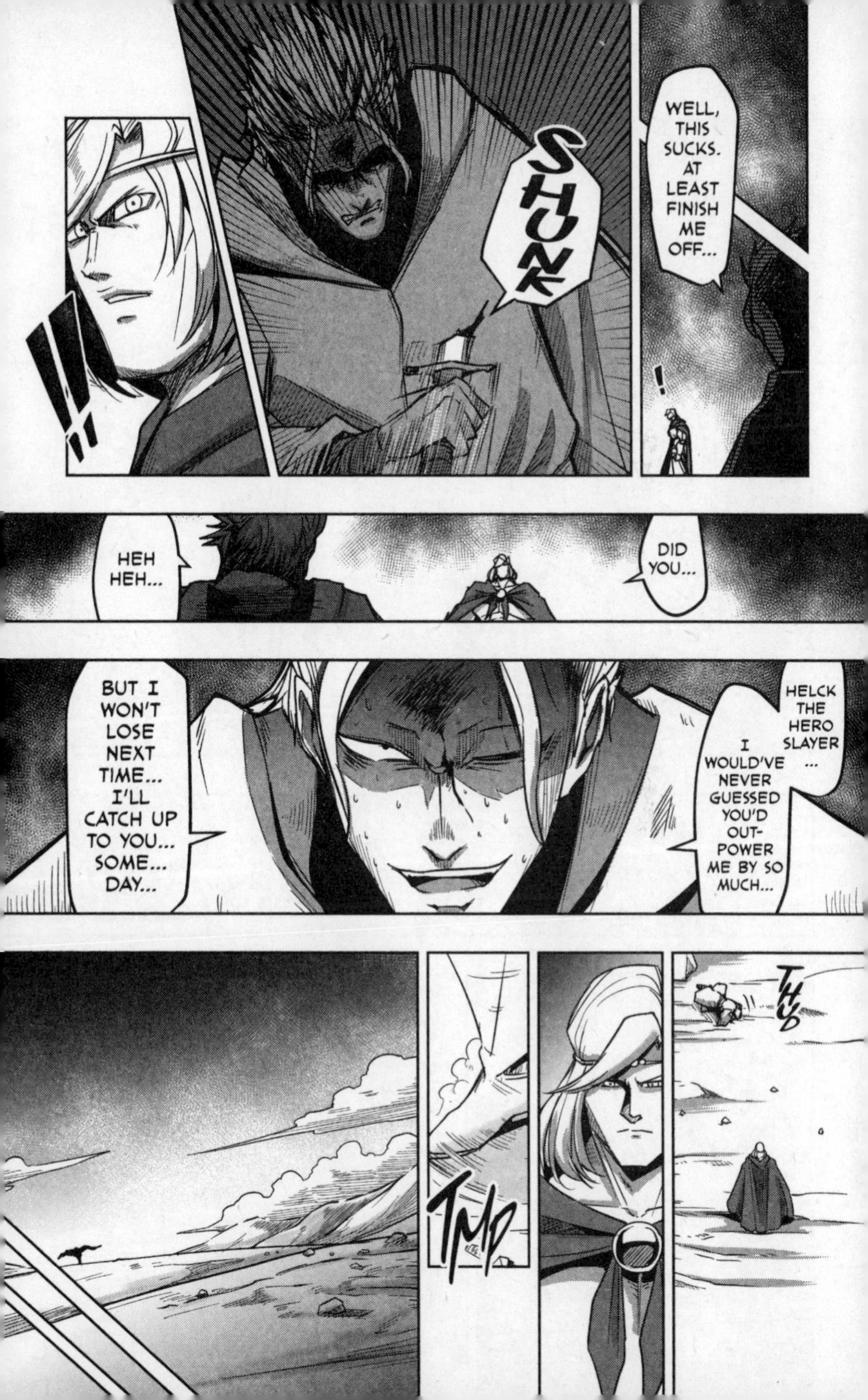
WELL, THIS SUCKS. AT LEAST FINISH ME OFF...
!
SHUNK
!!
DID YOU...
HEH HEH...
HELCK THE HERO SLAYER...
I WOULD'VE NEVER GUESSED YOU'D OUT-POWER ME BY SO MUCH...
BUT I WON'T LOSE NEXT TIME... I'LL CATCH UP TO YOU... SOME... DAY...
THUD
TMP

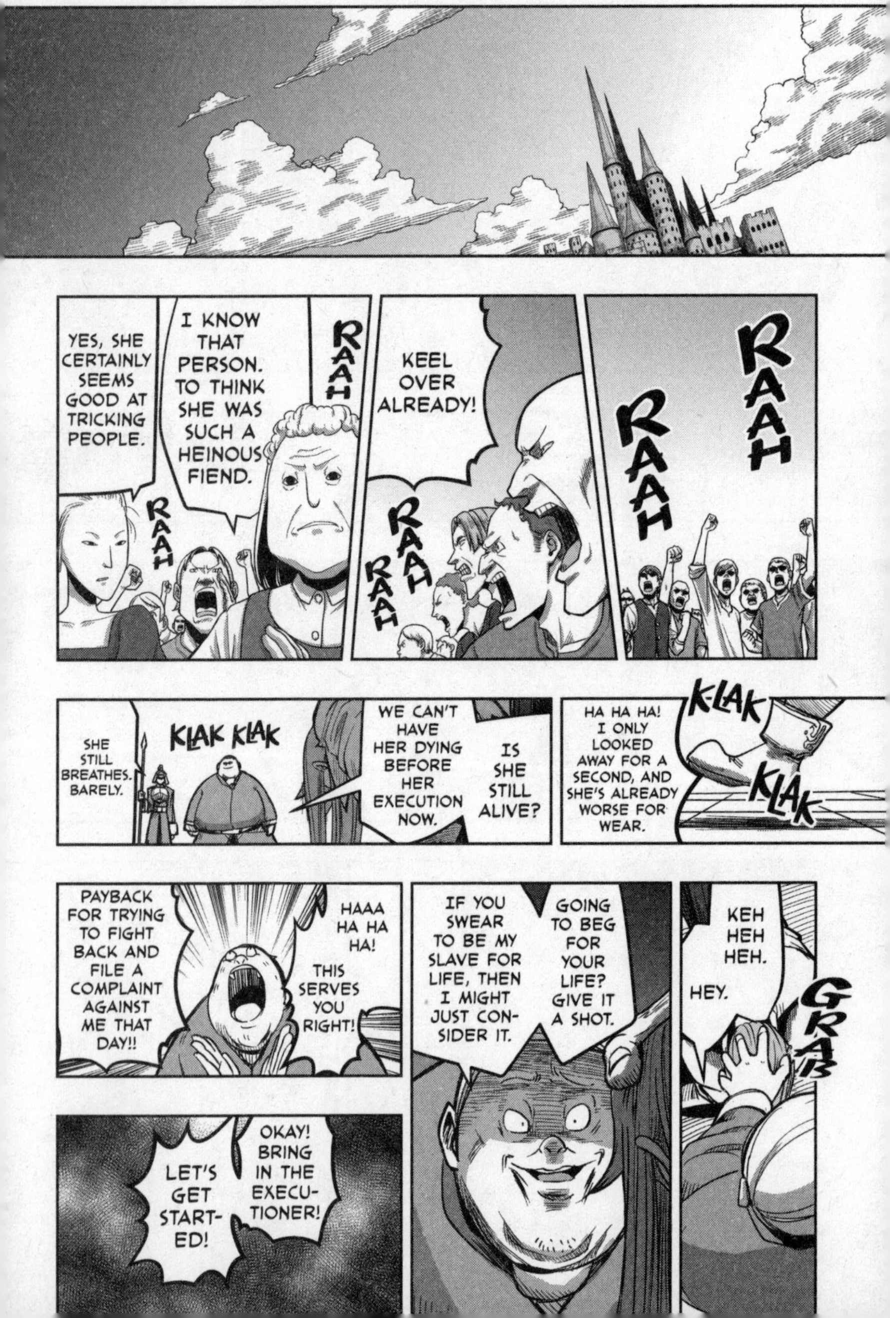
RAAH
RAAH
KEEL OVER ALREADY!
RAAH
RAAH
RAAH
I KNOW THAT PERSON. TO THINK SHE WAS SUCH A HEINOUS FIEND.
YES, SHE CERTAINLY SEEMS GOOD AT TRICKING PEOPLE.
RAAH
K-LAK
KLAK
HA HA HA! I ONLY LOOKED AWAY FOR A SECOND, AND SHE'S ALREADY WORSE FOR WEAR.
IS SHE STILL ALIVE?
WE CAN'T HAVE HER DYING BEFORE HER EXECUTION NOW.
KLAK KLAK
SHE STILL BREATHES. BARELY.
KEH HEH HEH.
HEY.
GRAB
GOING TO BEG FOR YOUR LIFE? GIVE IT A SHOT.
IF YOU SWEAR TO BE MY SLAVE FOR LIFE, THEN I MIGHT JUST CON-SIDER IT.
HAAA HA HA HA!
THIS SERVES YOU RIGHT!
PAYBACK FOR TRYING TO FIGHT BACK AND FILE A COMPLAINT AGAINST ME THAT DAY!!
OKAY! BRING IN THE EXECU-TIONER!
LET'S GET START-ED!

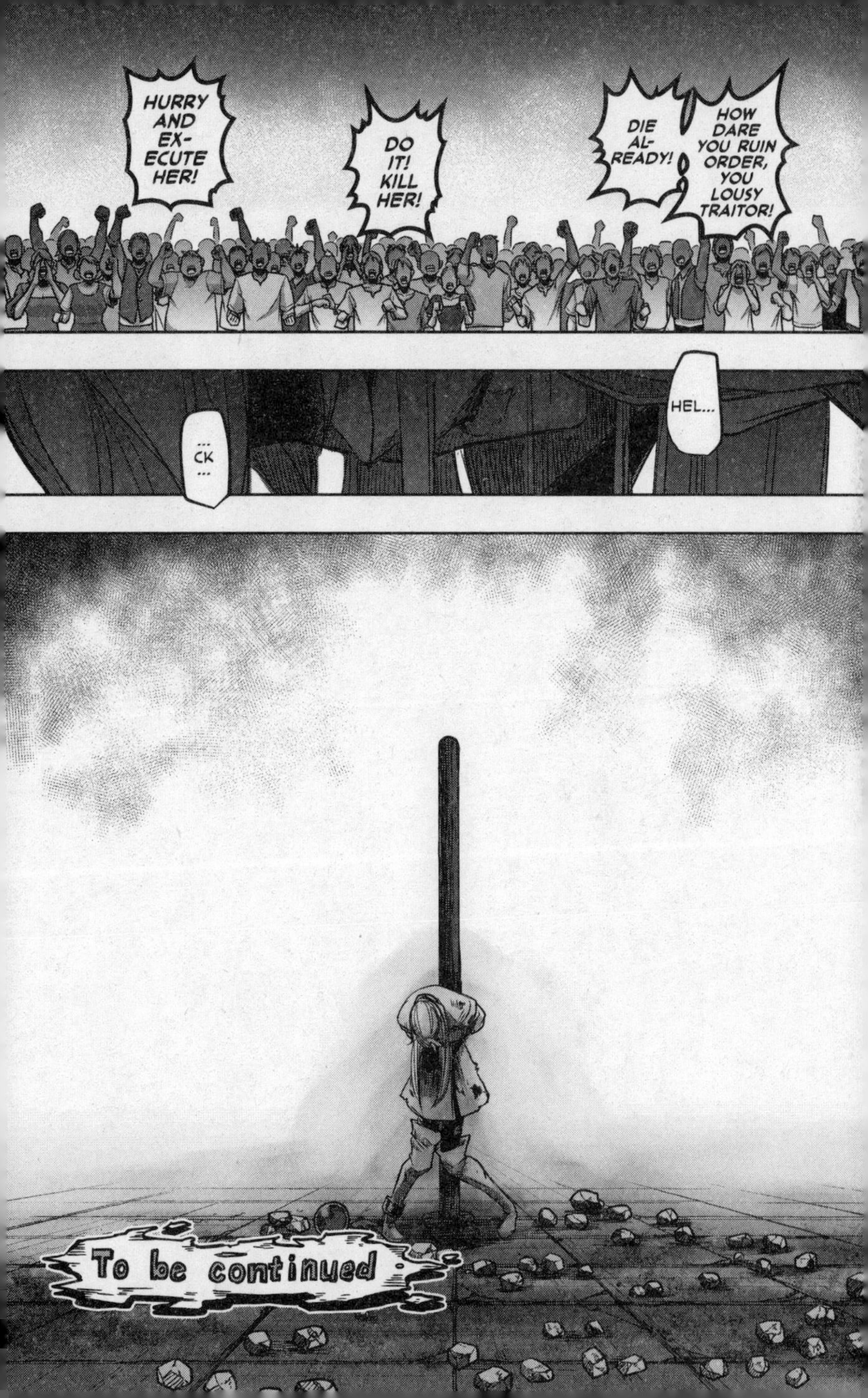
HOW DARE YOU RUIN ORDER, YOU LOUSY TRAITOR!
DIE AL-READY!
DO IT! KILL HER!
HURRY AND EX-ECUTE HER!
HEL...
...CK...
To be continued

Helck

Chapter 52: Helck's Past XVII

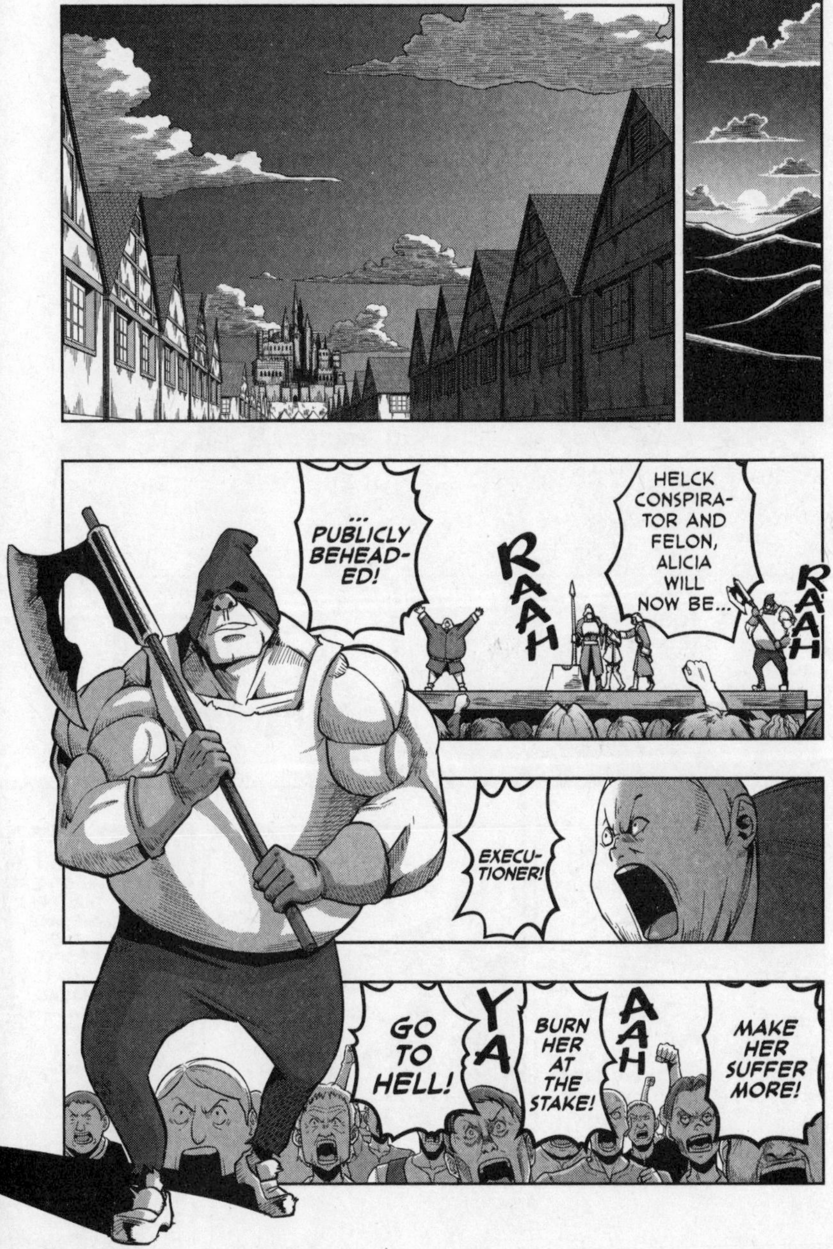
HELCK CONSPIRATOR AND FELON, ALICIA WILL NOW BE...
RAAH
RAAH
...PUBLICLY BEHEADED!
EXECUTIONER!
MAKE HER SUFFER MORE!
AAH
BURN HER AT THE STAKE!
YA
GO TO HELL!

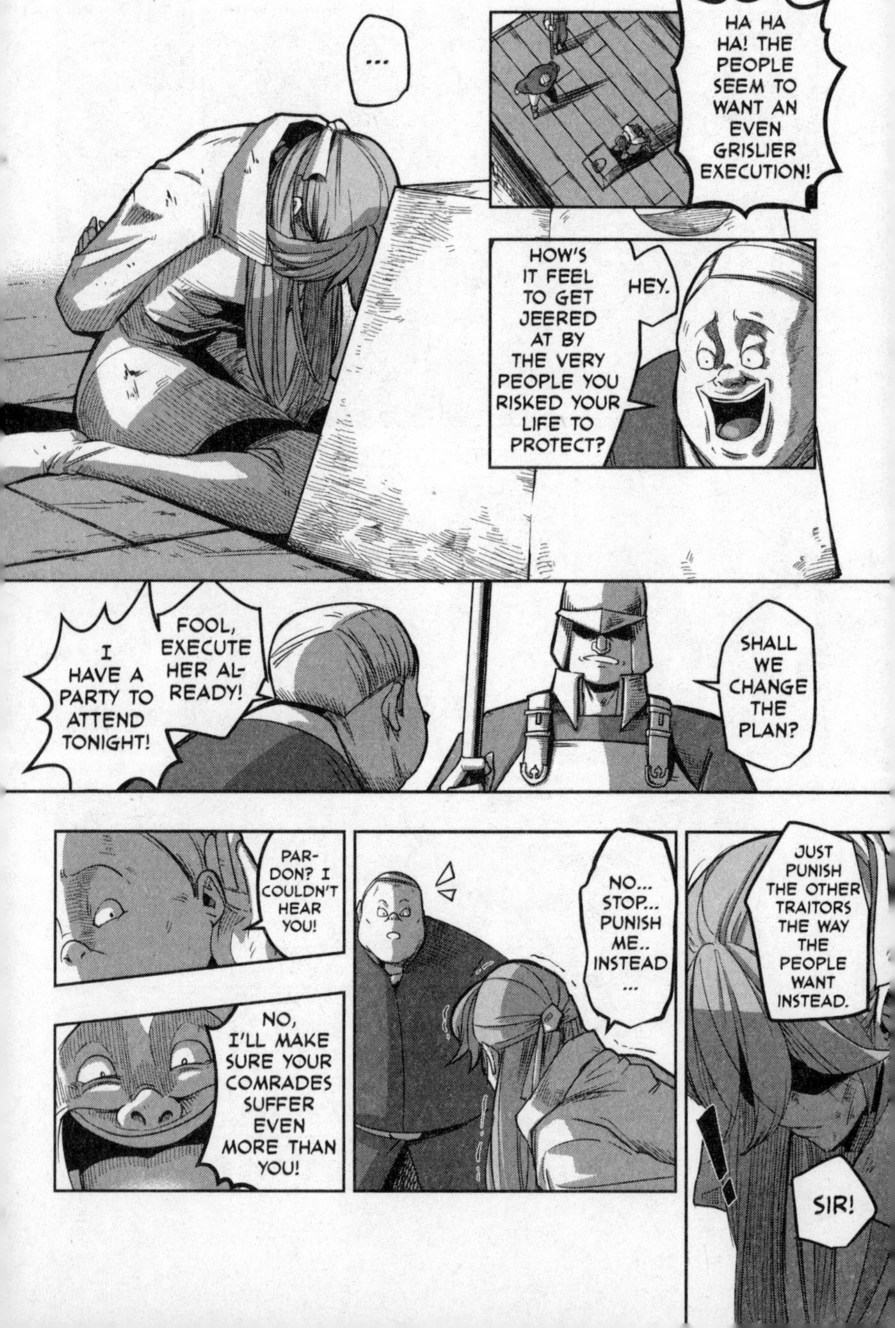
HA HA HA! THE PEOPLE SEEM TO WANT AN EVEN GRISLIER EXECUTION!
HEY.
HOW'S IT FEEL TO GET JEERED AT BY THE VERY PEOPLE YOU RISKED YOUR LIFE TO PROTECT?
...
SHALL WE CHANGE THE PLAN?
FOOL, EXECUTE HER AL-READY!
I HAVE A PARTY TO ATTEND TONIGHT!
JUST PUNISH THE OTHER TRAITORS THE WAY THE PEOPLE WANT INSTEAD.
SIR!
NO... STOP... PUNISH ME.. INSTEAD ...
PAR-DON? I COULDN'T HEAR YOU!
NO, I'LL MAKE SURE YOUR COMRADES SUFFER EVEN MORE THAN YOU!

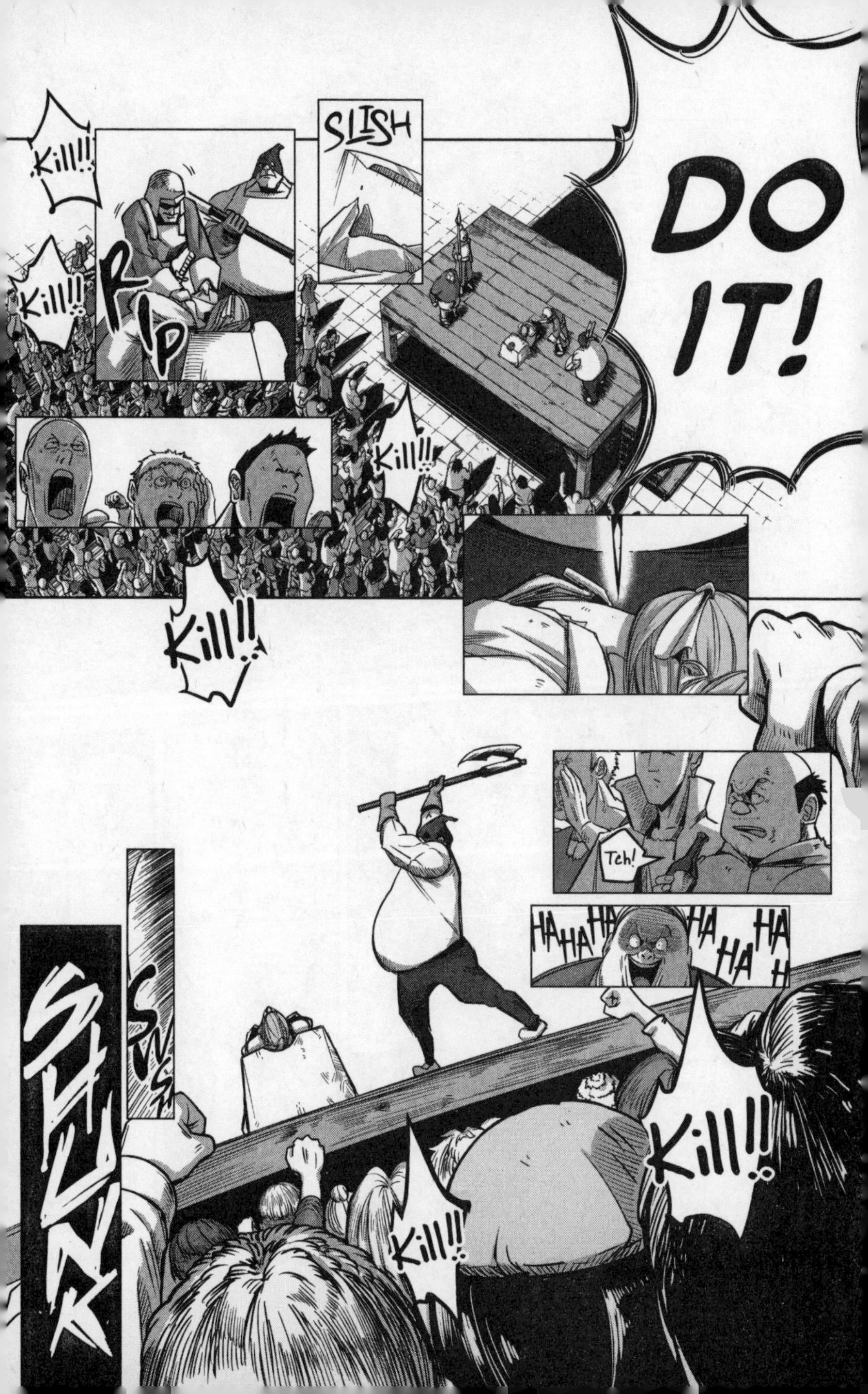
DO IT!
SLISH
RIP
Kill!!
Kill!!
Kill!!
Kill!!
Tch!
HA HA HA HA HA HA HA H
SHUNK
SNSK
Kill!!
Kill!!

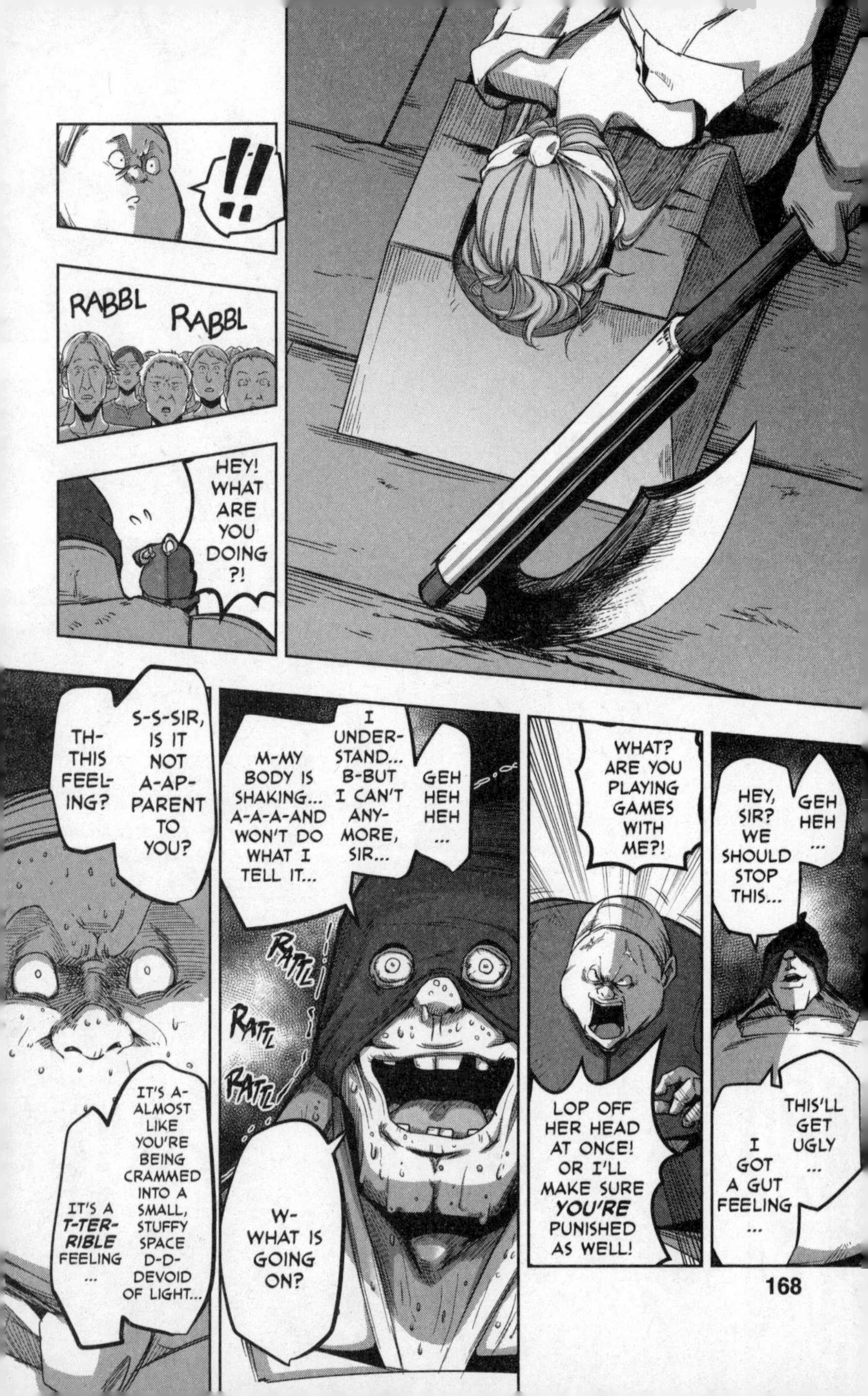
!!
RABBL
RABBL
HEY! WHAT ARE YOU DOING?!
GEH HEH ...
HEY, SIR? WE SHOULD STOP THIS...
THIS'LL GET UGLY ...
I GOT A GUT FEELING ...
WHAT? ARE YOU PLAYING GAMES WITH ME?!
LOP OFF HER HEAD AT ONCE! OR I'LL MAKE SURE *YOU'RE* PUNISHED AS WELL!
GEH HEH HEH ...
I UNDERSTAND... B-BUT I CAN'T ANYMORE, SIR...
M-MY BODY IS SHAKING... A-A-A-AND WON'T DO WHAT I TELL IT...
RATTL
RATTL
RATTL
W-WHAT IS GOING ON?
S-S-SIR, IS IT NOT A-APPARENT TO YOU?
TH-THIS FEEL-ING?
IT'S A-ALMOST LIKE YOU'RE BEING CRAMMED INTO A SMALL, STUFFY SPACE D-D-DEVOID OF LIGHT...
IT'S A *T-TERRIBLE* FEELING ...

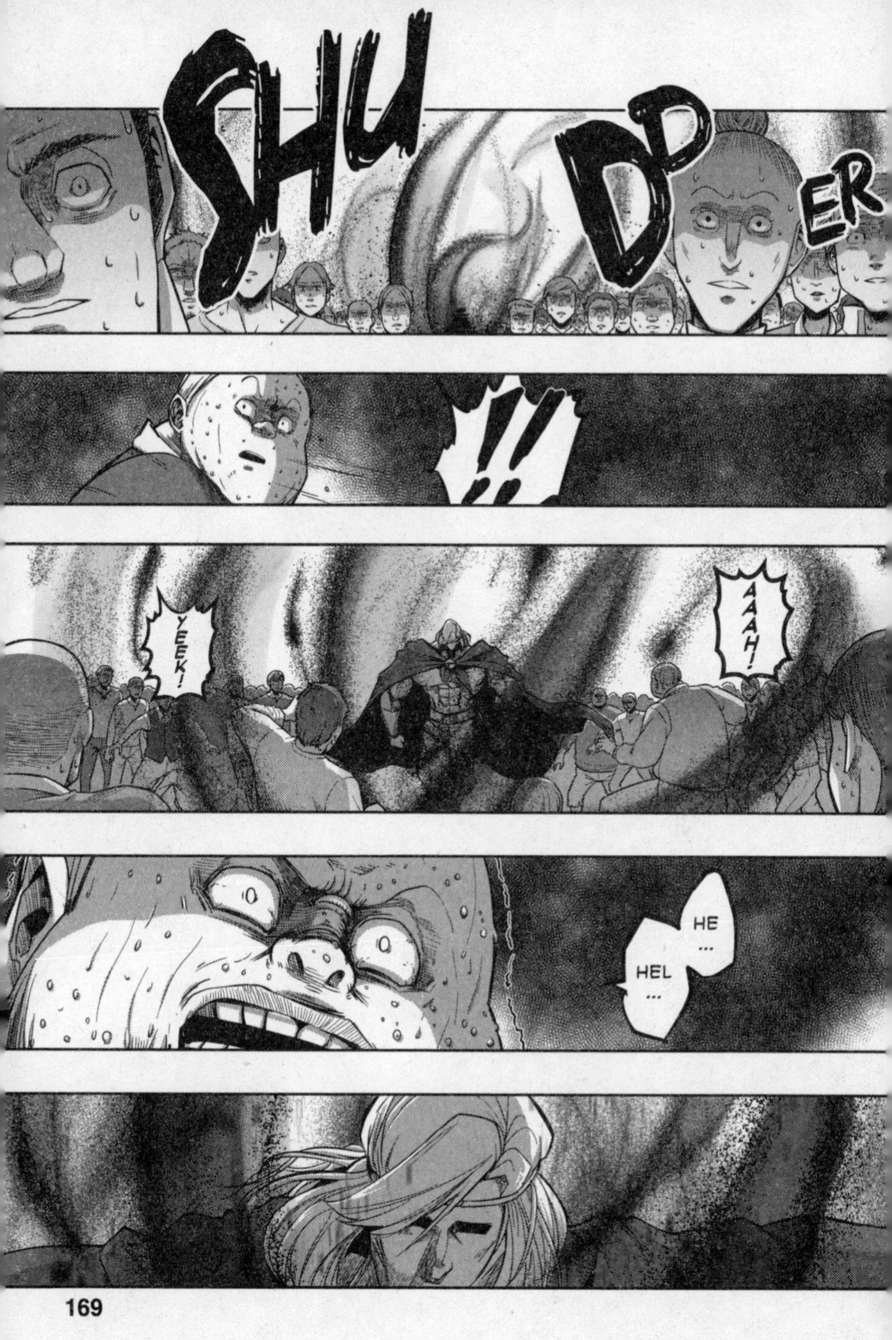
SHUDDER
!!
AAAAH!
YEEEK!
HE...
HEL...

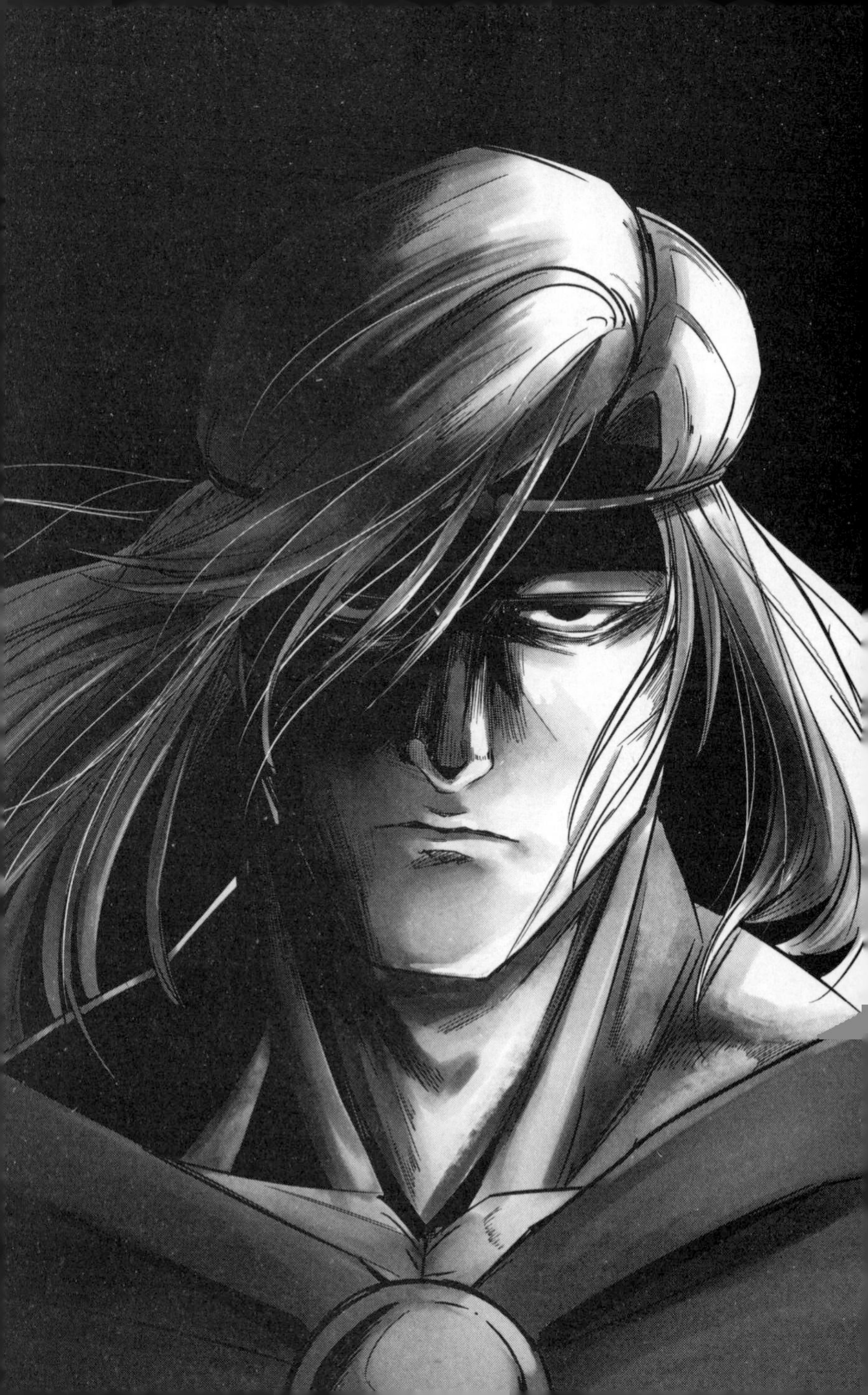

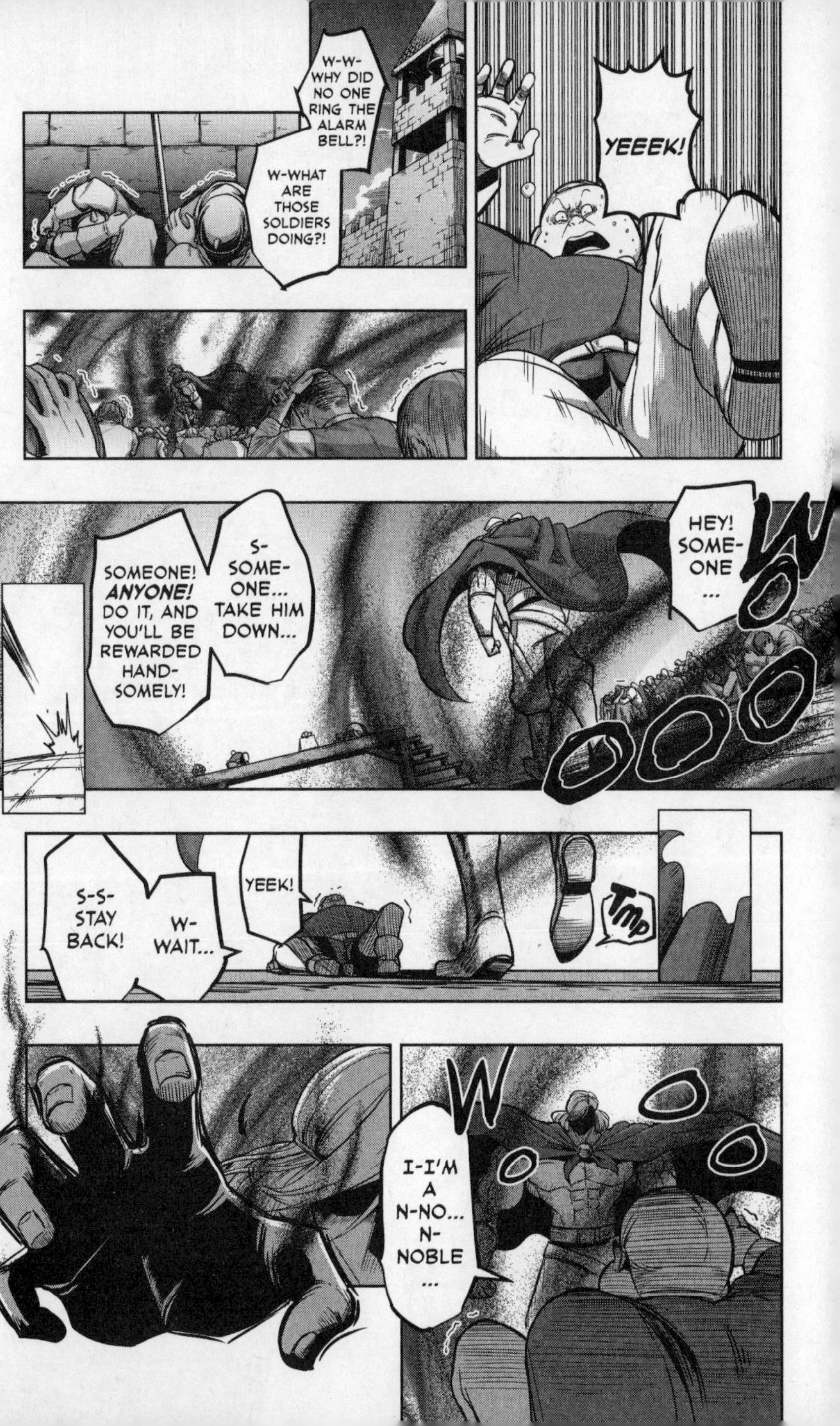

YEEEK!
W-W-WHY DID NO ONE RING THE ALARM BELL?!
W-WHAT ARE THOSE SOLDIERS DOING?!
WOOOOOO
HEY! SOMEONE...
S-SOMEONE... TAKE HIM DOWN...
SOMEONE! ANYONE! DO IT, AND YOU'LL BE REWARDED HANDSOMELY!
TMP
YEEK!
W-WAIT...
S-S-STAY BACK!
WOOOO
I-I'M A N-NO... N-NOBLE...

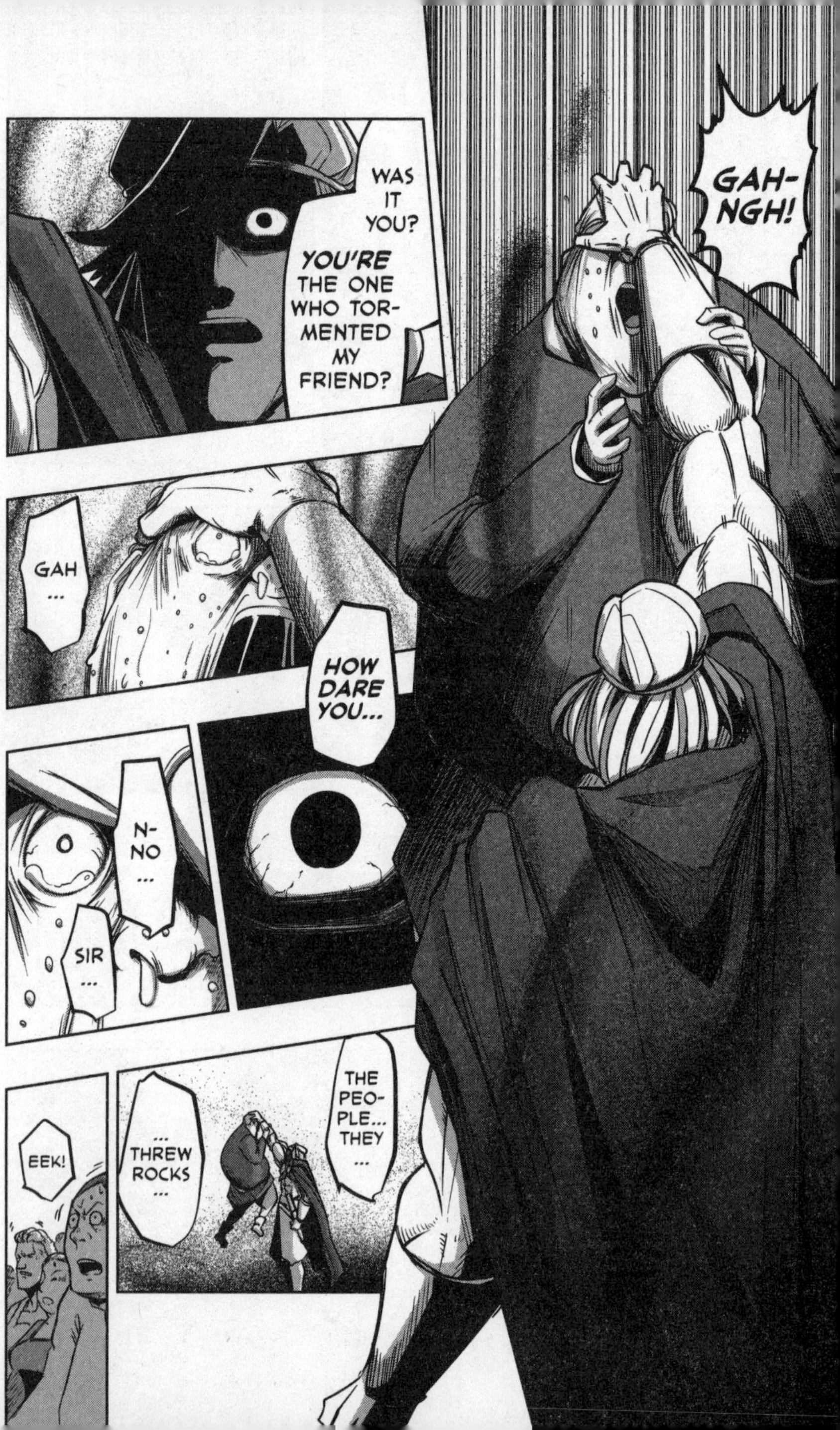
GAH-NGH!
WAS IT YOU?
YOU'RE THE ONE WHO TORMENTED MY FRIEND?
GAH...
HOW DARE YOU...
N-NO...
SIR...
THE PEOPLE... THEY...
...THREW ROCKS...
EEK!

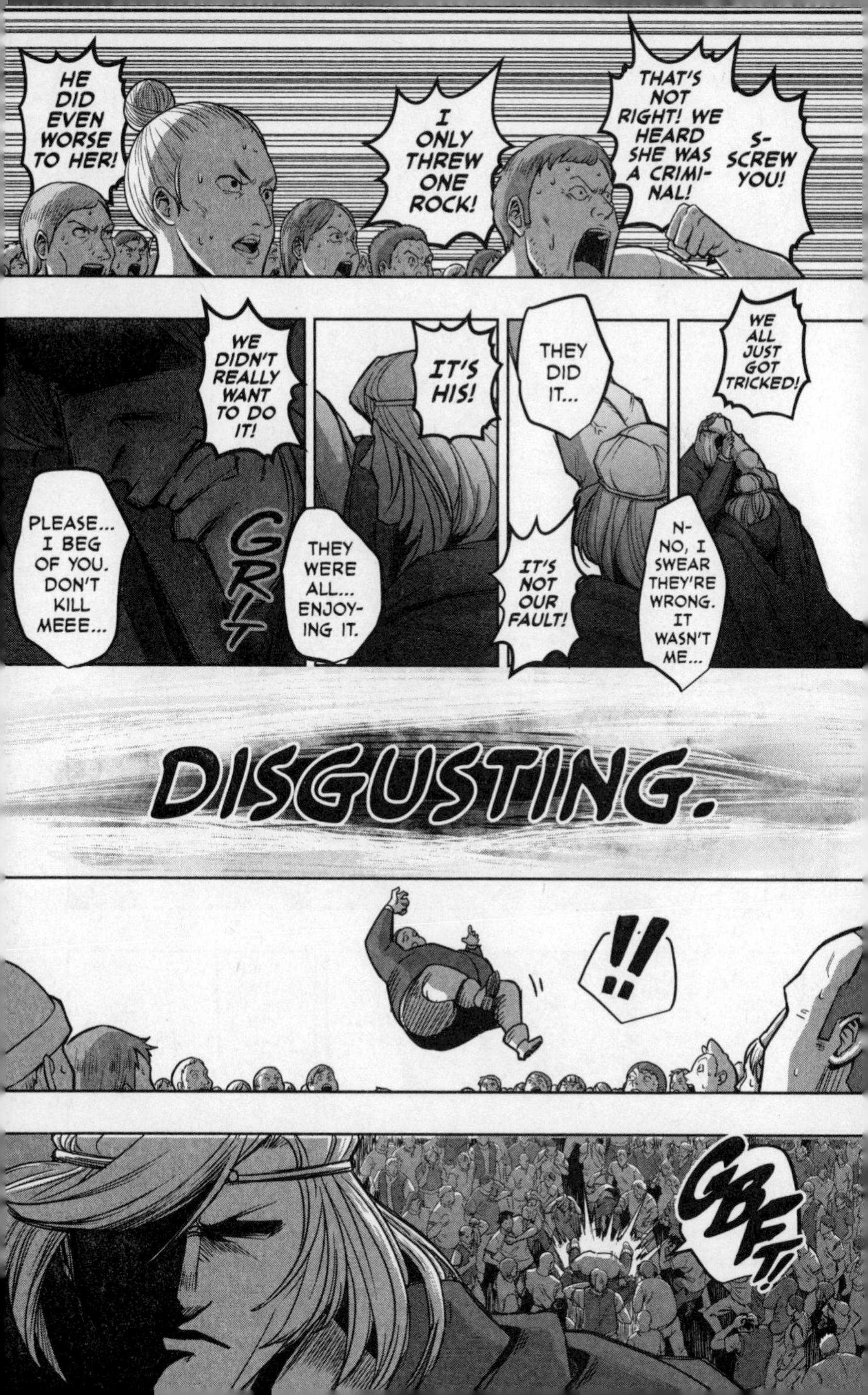
S-SCREW YOU!
THAT'S NOT RIGHT! WE HEARD SHE WAS A CRIMINAL!
I ONLY THREW ONE ROCK!
HE DID EVEN WORSE TO HER!
WE ALL JUST GOT TRICKED!
N-NO, I SWEAR THEY'RE WRONG. IT WASN'T ME...
THEY DID IT...
IT'S NOT OUR FAULT!
IT'S HIS!
THEY WERE ALL... ENJOYING IT.
WE DIDN'T REALLY WANT TO DO IT!
GRIT
PLEASE... I BEG OF YOU. DON'T KILL MEEE...
DISGUSTING.
!!

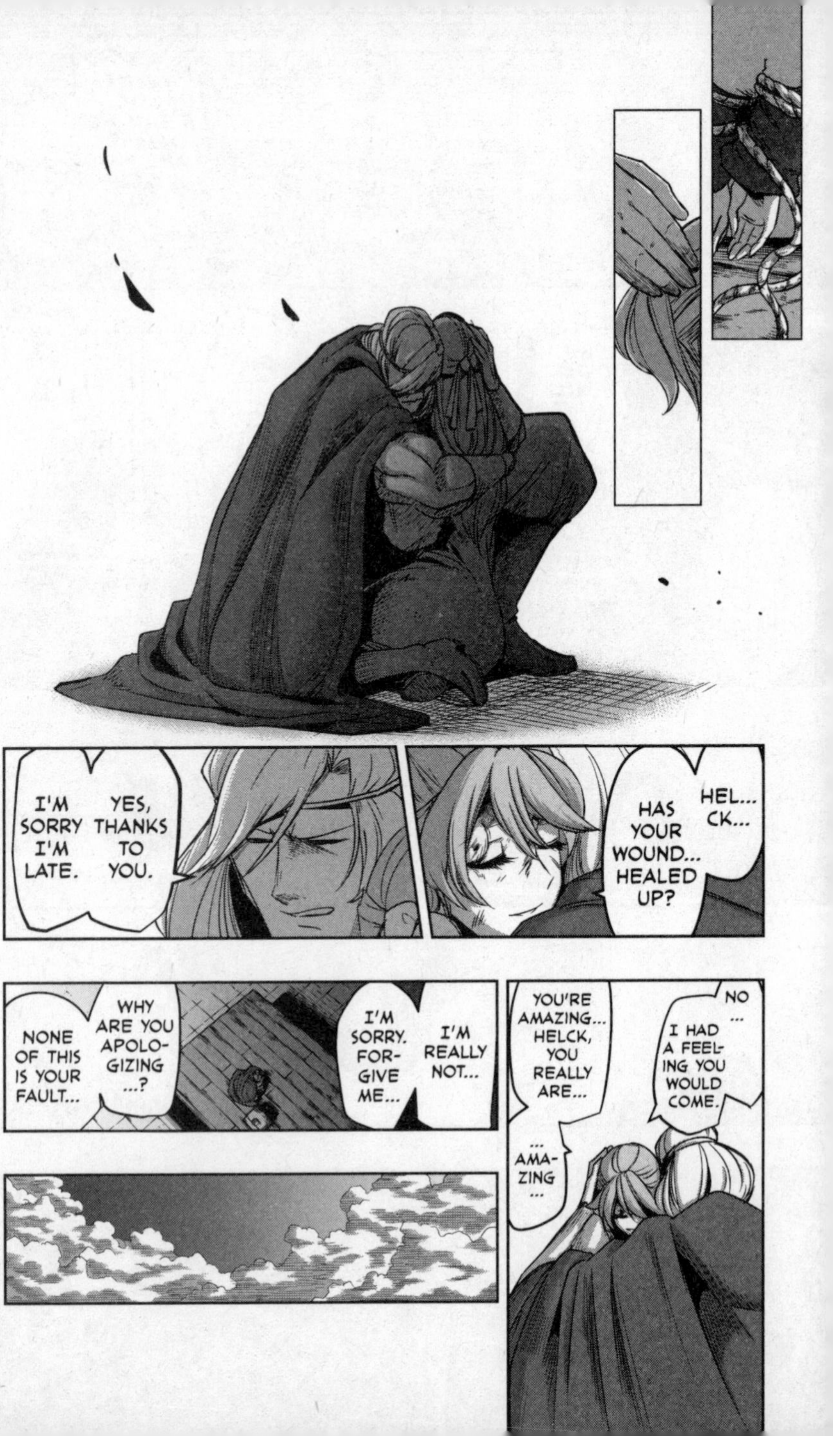
HEL... CK...
HAS YOUR WOUND... HEALED UP?
YES, THANKS TO YOU.
I'M SORRY I'M LATE.
NO ...
I HAD A FEEL-ING YOU WOULD COME.
YOU'RE AMAZING... HELCK, YOU REALLY ARE...
... AMA-ZING ...
I'M REALLY NOT...
I'M SORRY. FOR-GIVE ME...
WHY ARE YOU APOLO-GIZING ...?
NONE OF THIS IS YOUR FAULT...

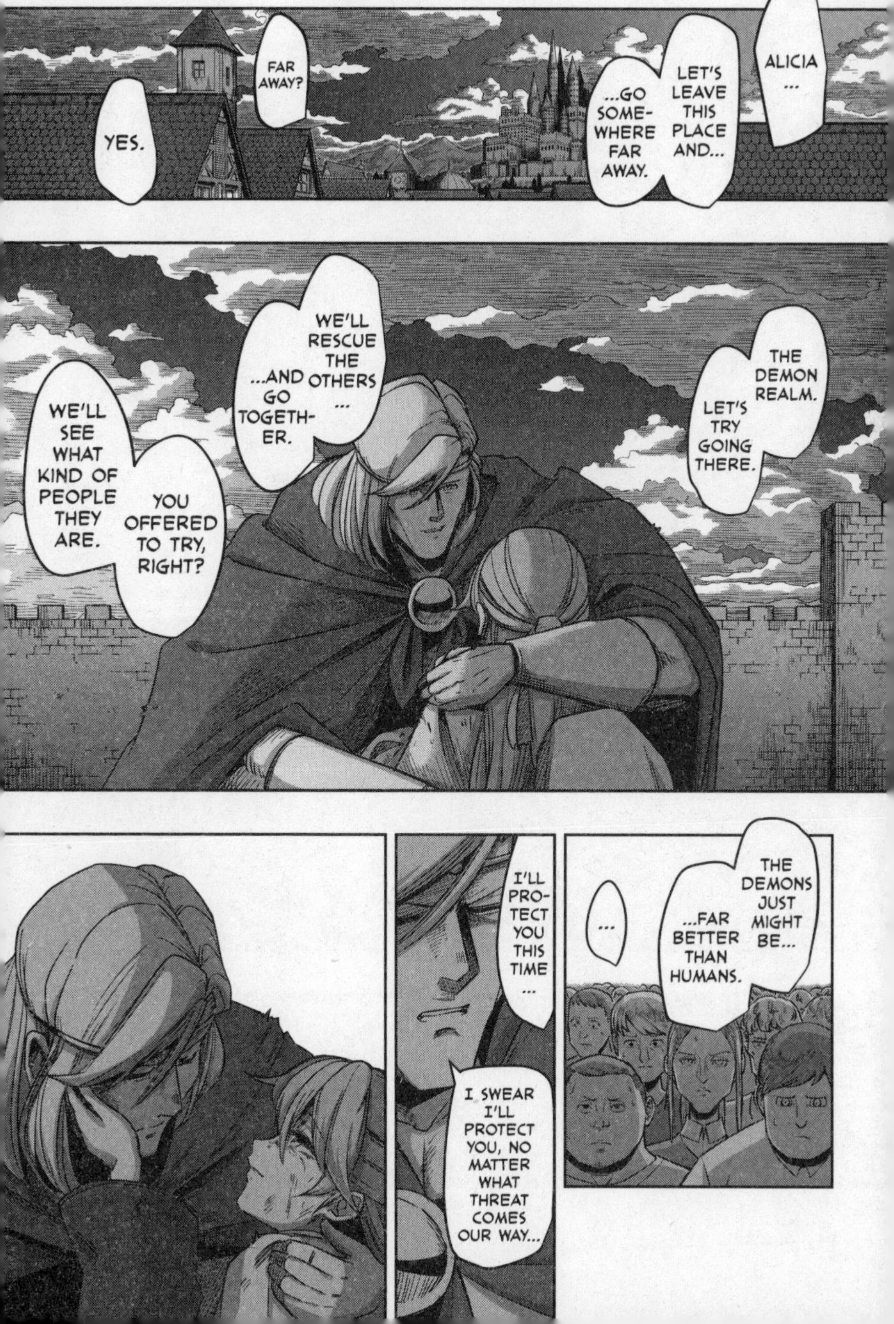

ALICIA...
LET'S LEAVE THIS PLACE AND...
...GO SOMEWHERE FAR AWAY.
FAR AWAY?
YES.
THE DEMON REALM.
LET'S TRY GOING THERE.
WE'LL RESCUE THE OTHERS...
...AND GO TOGETHER.
YOU OFFERED TO TRY, RIGHT?
WE'LL SEE WHAT KIND OF PEOPLE THEY ARE.
THE DEMONS JUST MIGHT BE...
...FAR BETTER THAN HUMANS.
...
I'LL PROTECT YOU THIS TIME...
I SWEAR I'LL PROTECT YOU, NO MATTER WHAT THREAT COMES OUR WAY...

YES... I'LL COME WITH YOU...

I'LL GO WHEREVER YOU GO, HELCK...

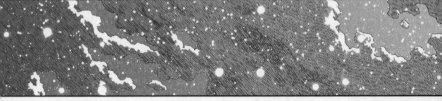

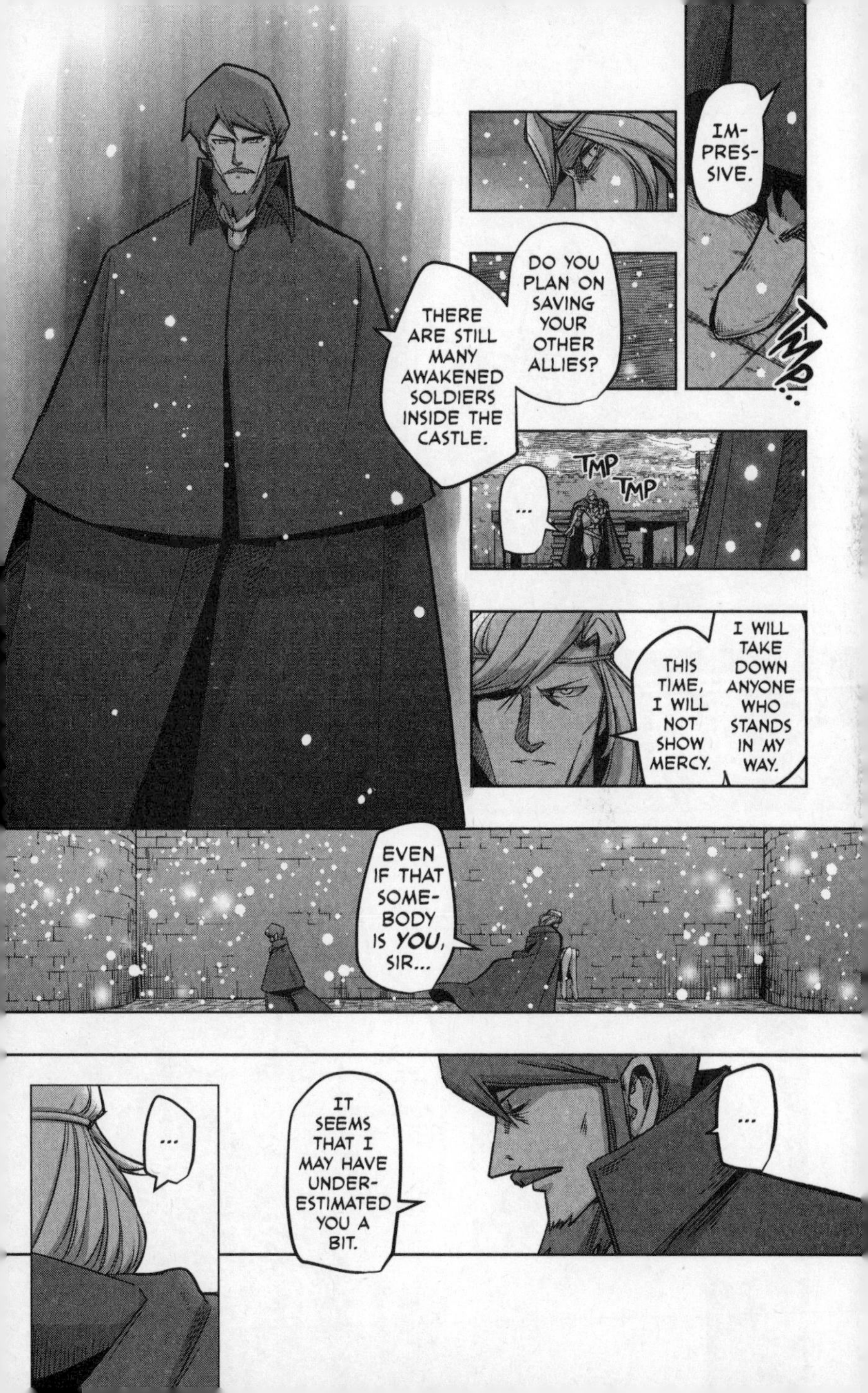
IM-PRES-SIVE.
TMP...
DO YOU PLAN ON SAVING YOUR OTHER ALLIES?
THERE ARE STILL MANY AWAKENED SOLDIERS INSIDE THE CASTLE.
TMP TMP
...
I WILL TAKE DOWN ANYONE WHO STANDS IN MY WAY.
THIS TIME, I WILL NOT SHOW MERCY.
EVEN IF THAT SOMEBODY IS *YOU*, SIR...
...
IT SEEMS THAT I MAY HAVE UNDER-ESTIMATED YOU A BIT.
...

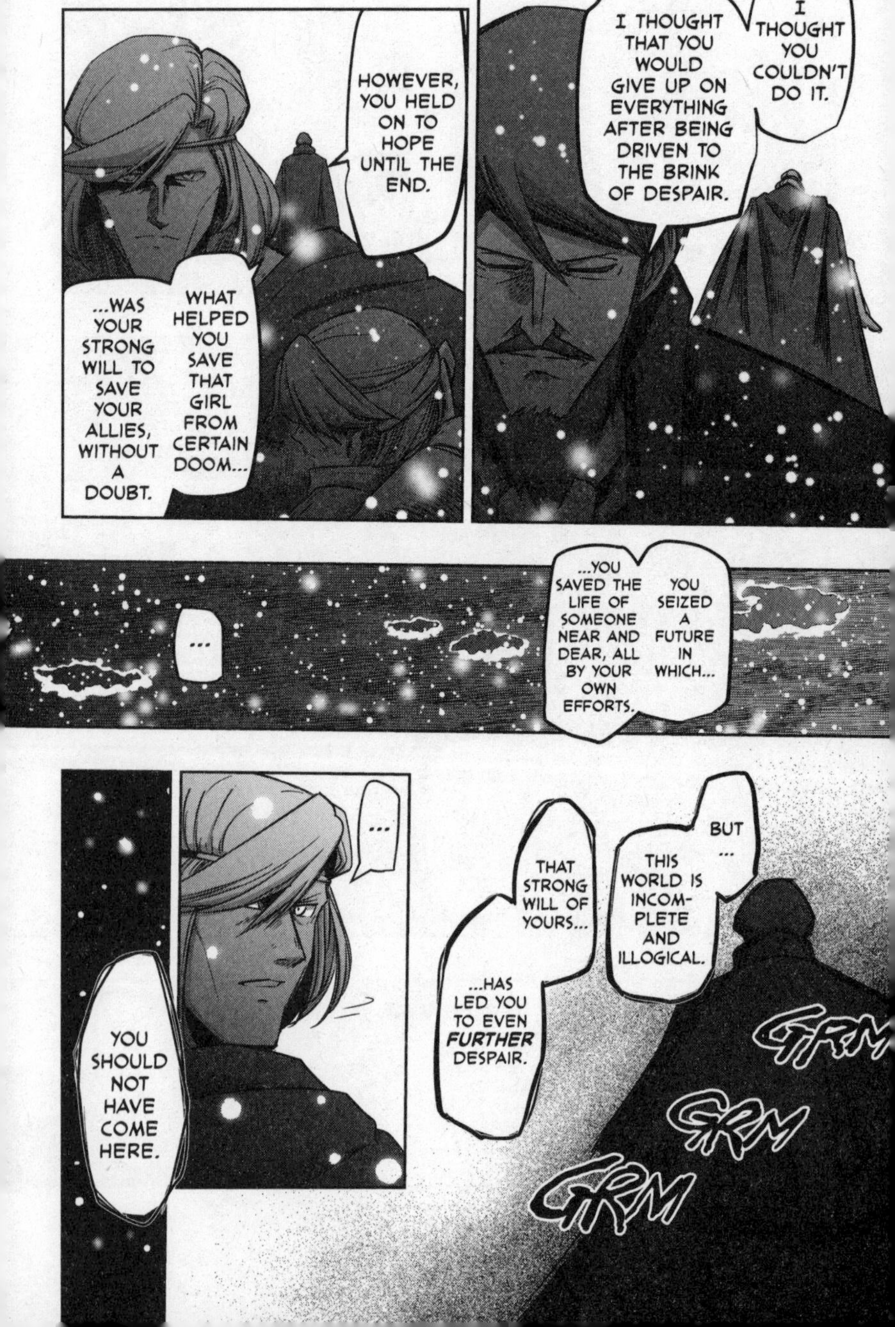
I THOUGHT YOU COULDN'T DO IT.
I THOUGHT THAT YOU WOULD GIVE UP ON EVERYTHING AFTER BEING DRIVEN TO THE BRINK OF DESPAIR.
HOWEVER, YOU HELD ON TO HOPE UNTIL THE END.
WHAT HELPED YOU SAVE THAT GIRL FROM CERTAIN DOOM...
...WAS YOUR STRONG WILL TO SAVE YOUR ALLIES, WITHOUT A DOUBT.
YOU SEIZED A FUTURE IN WHICH...
...YOU SAVED THE LIFE OF SOMEONE NEAR AND DEAR, ALL BY YOUR OWN EFFORTS.
...
BUT ...
THIS WORLD IS INCOMPLETE AND ILLOGICAL.
THAT STRONG WILL OF YOURS...
...HAS LED YOU TO EVEN *FURTHER* DESPAIR.
GRM
GRM
GRM
...
YOU SHOULD NOT HAVE COME HERE.

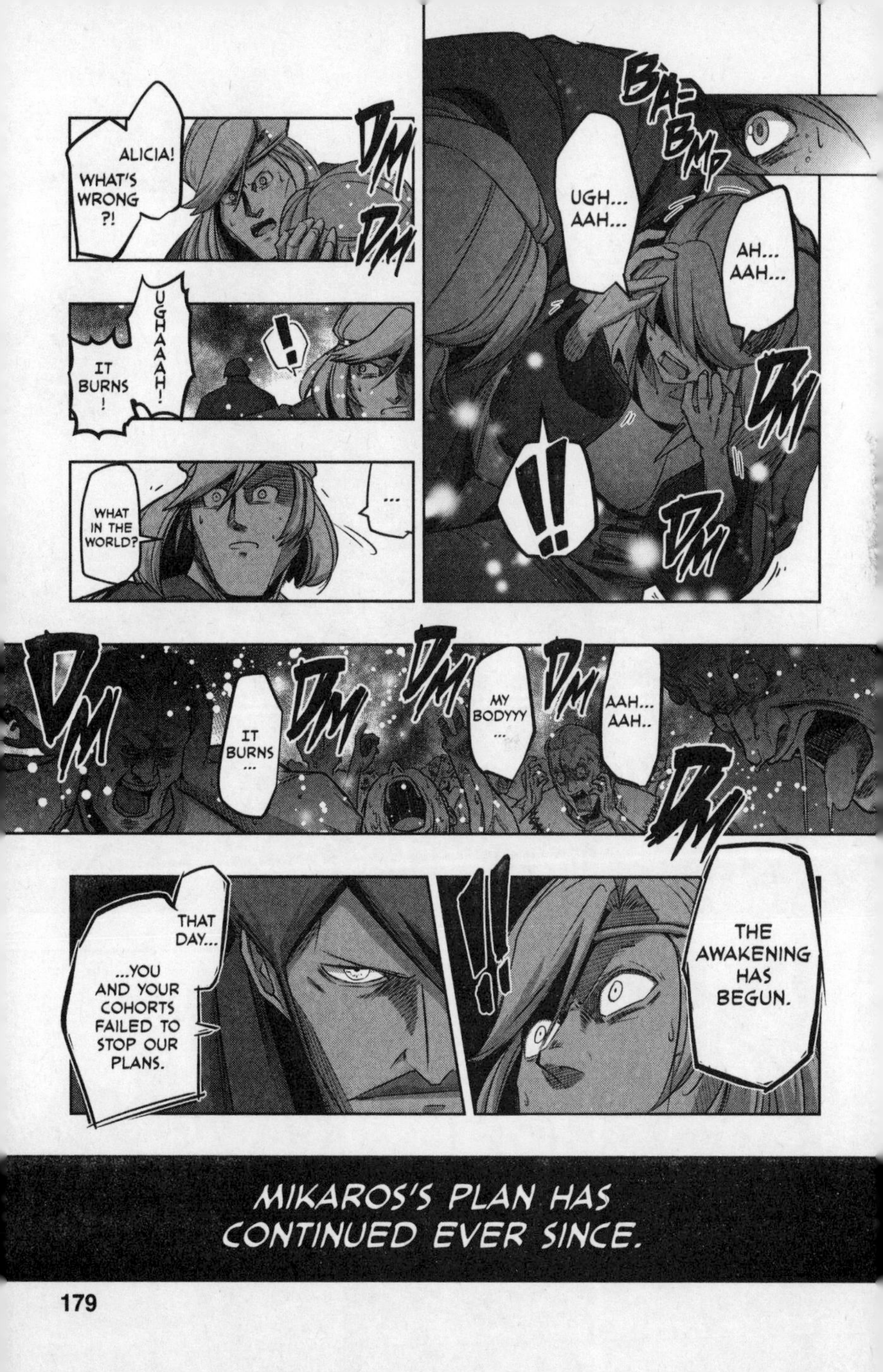
BA-BMP
AH... AAH...
UGH... AAH...
DM
!!
DM
DM
DM
ALICIA! WHAT'S WRONG?!
!
UGHAAAH!
IT BURNS!
...
WHAT IN THE WORLD?
DM
AAH... AAH..
DM
MY BODYYY...
DM
DM
IT BURNS...
DM
THE AWAKENING HAS BEGUN.
!!
THAT DAY...
...YOU AND YOUR COHORTS FAILED TO STOP OUR PLANS.
MIKAROS'S PLAN HAS CONTINUED EVER SINCE.

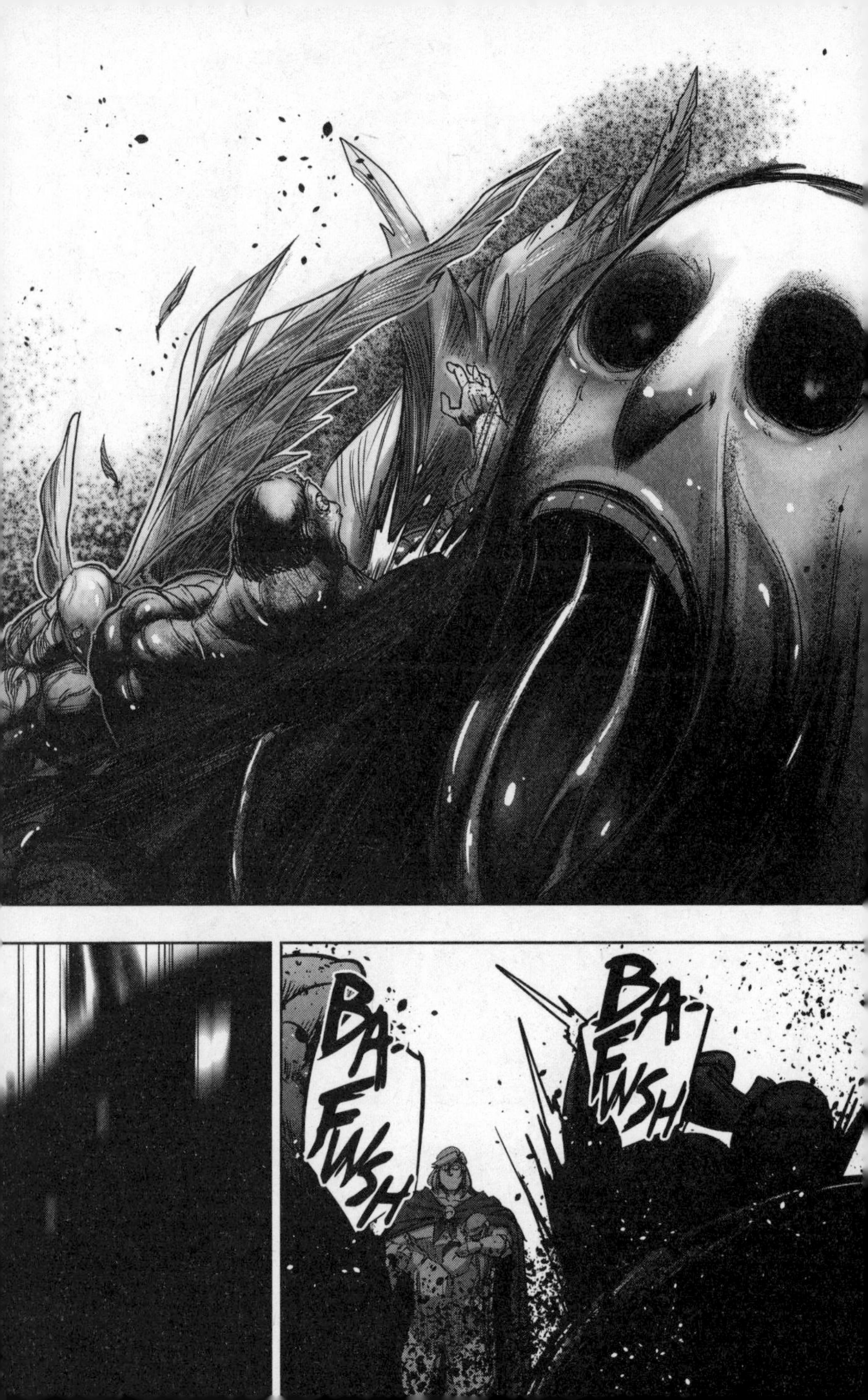
BA-FWSH
BA-FWSH

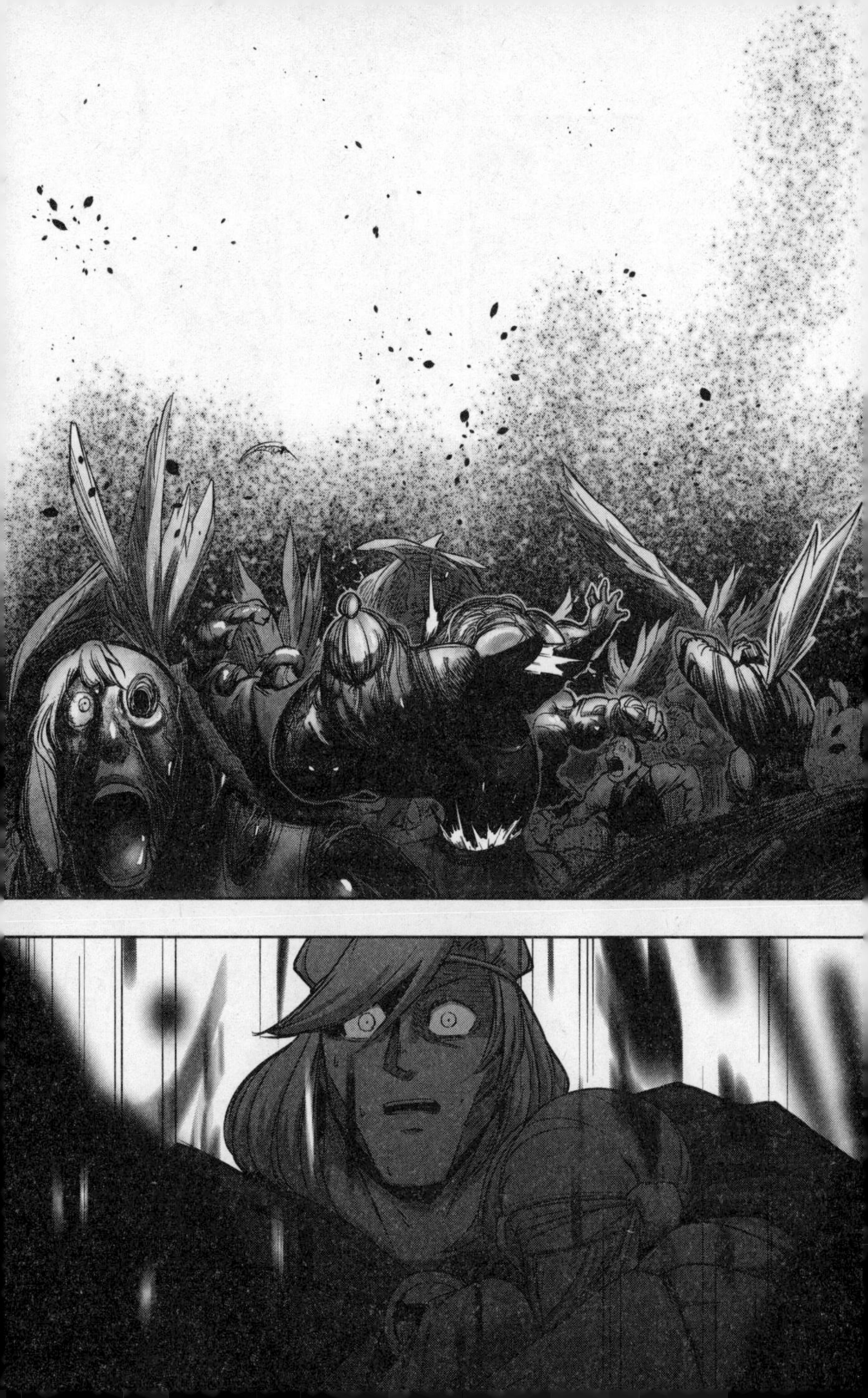

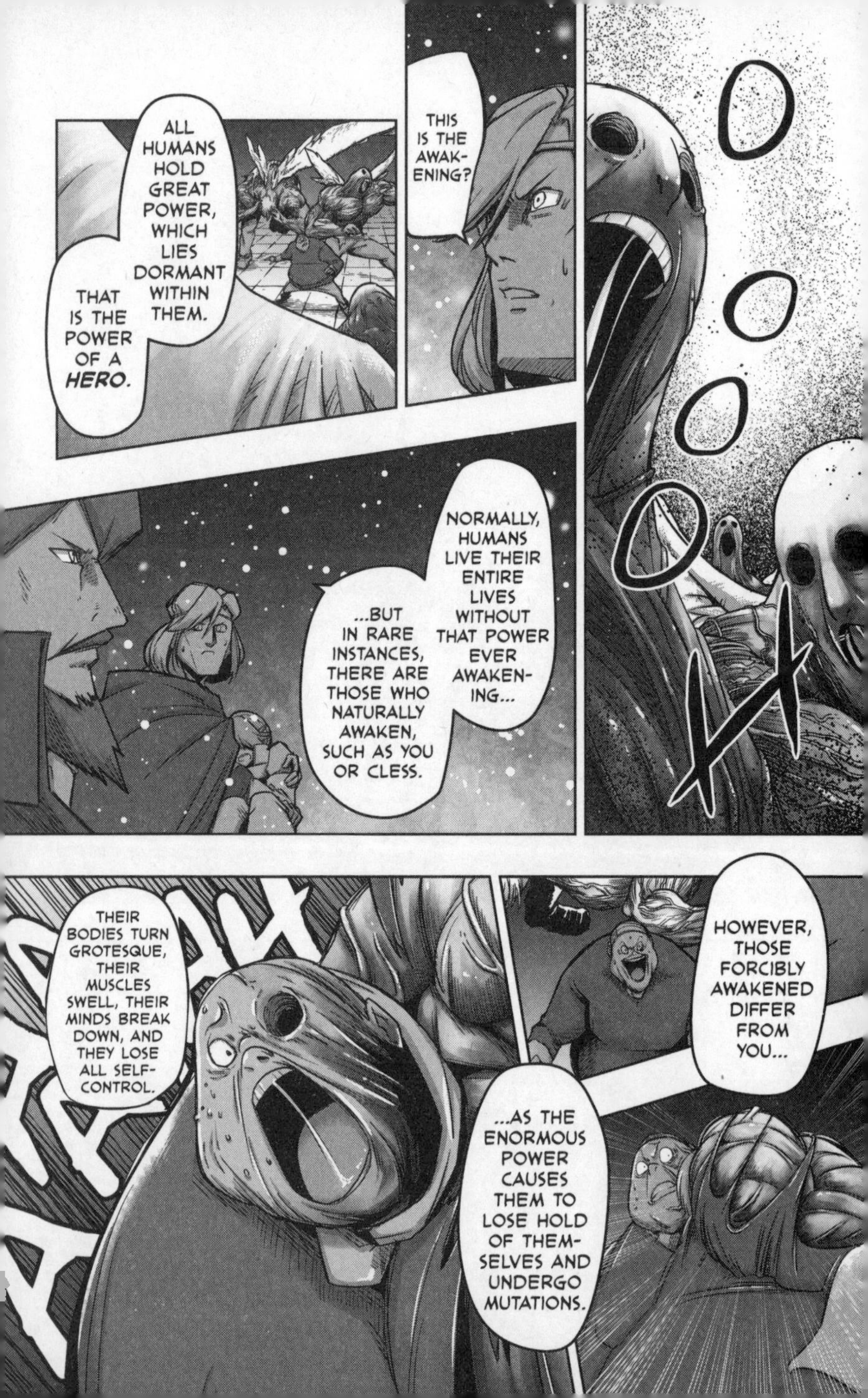
THIS IS THE AWAKENING?
ALL HUMANS HOLD GREAT POWER, WHICH LIES DORMANT WITHIN THEM.
THAT IS THE POWER OF A *HERO*.
NORMALLY, HUMANS LIVE THEIR ENTIRE LIVES WITHOUT THAT POWER EVER AWAKENING...
...BUT IN RARE INSTANCES, THERE ARE THOSE WHO NATURALLY AWAKEN, SUCH AS YOU OR CLESS.
HOWEVER, THOSE FORCIBLY AWAKENED DIFFER FROM YOU...
...AS THE ENORMOUS POWER CAUSES THEM TO LOSE HOLD OF THEMSELVES AND UNDERGO MUTATIONS.
THEIR BODIES TURN GROTESQUE, THEIR MUSCLES SWELL, THEIR MINDS BREAK DOWN, AND THEY LOSE ALL SELF-CONTROL.

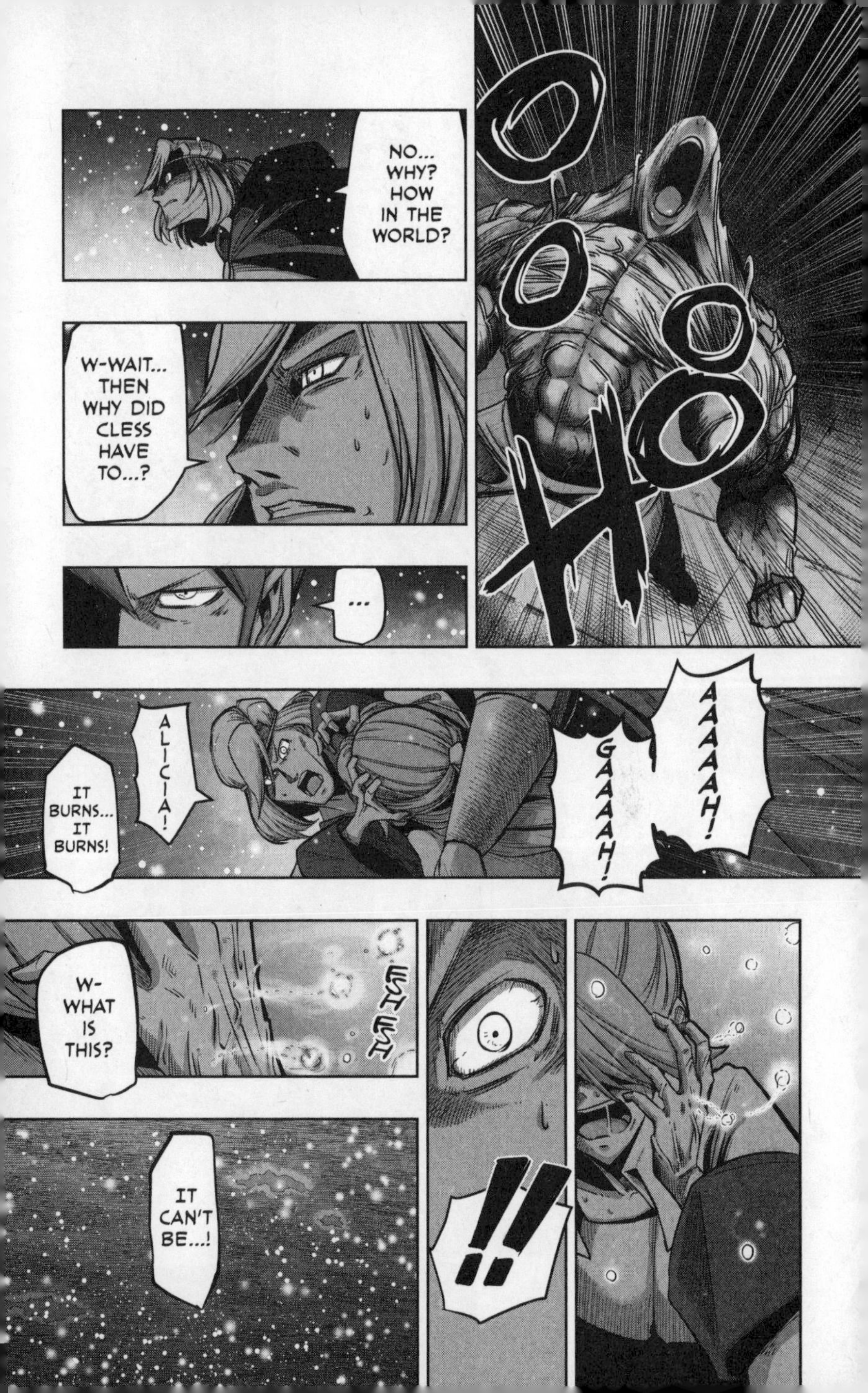
OOOOX
NO... WHY? HOW IN THE WORLD?
W-WAIT... THEN WHY DID CLESS HAVE TO...?
...
AAAAAH!
GAAAAH!
ALICIA!
IT BURNS... IT BURNS!
!!
SHESH
W- WHAT IS THIS?
IT CAN'T BE...!

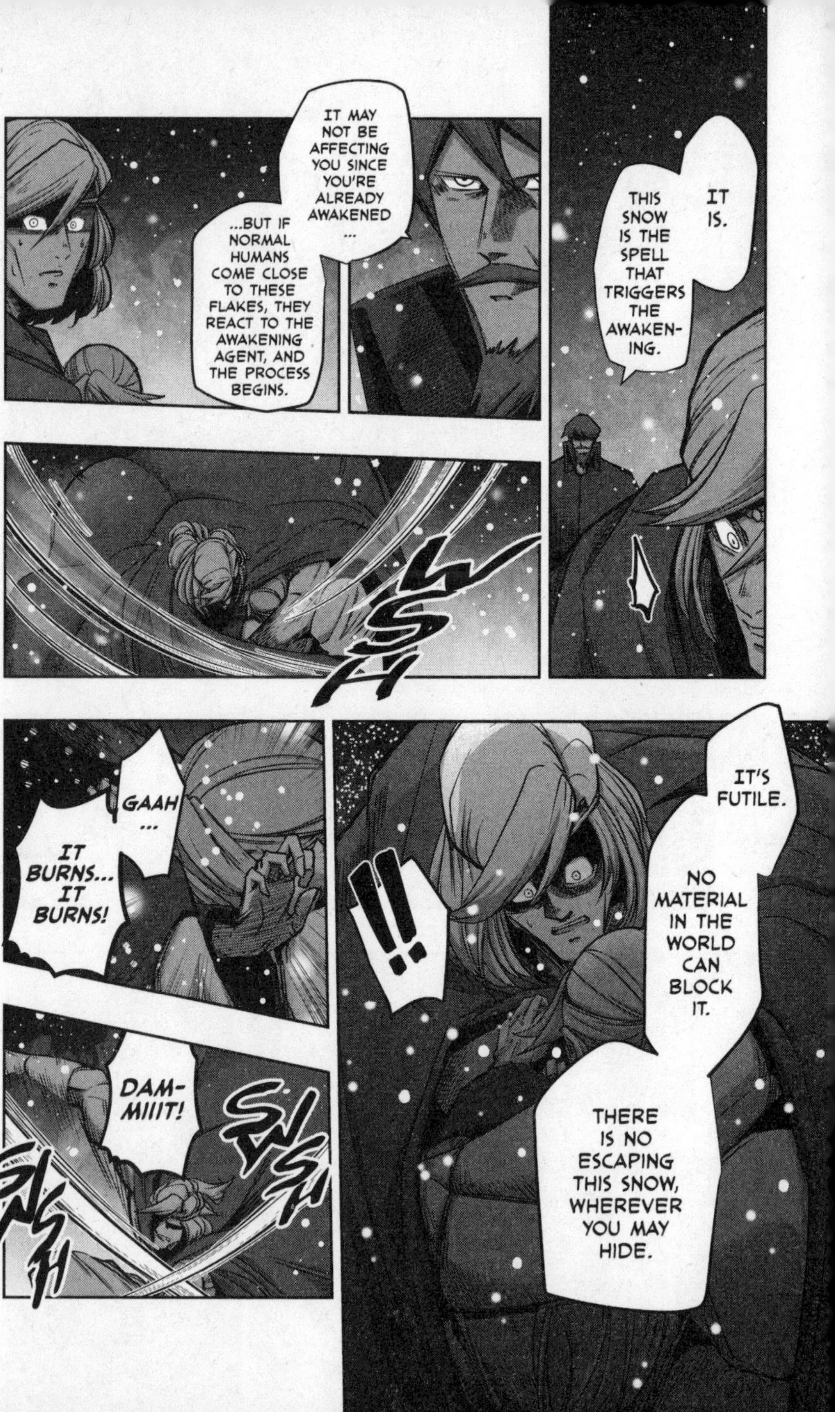
IT IS.
THIS SNOW IS THE SPELL THAT TRIGGERS THE AWAKENING.
IT MAY NOT BE AFFECTING YOU SINCE YOU'RE ALREADY AWAKENED ...
...BUT IF NORMAL HUMANS COME CLOSE TO THESE FLAKES, THEY REACT TO THE AWAKENING AGENT, AND THE PROCESS BEGINS.
SWSH
IT'S FUTILE.
!!
NO MATERIAL IN THE WORLD CAN BLOCK IT.
THERE IS NO ESCAPING THIS SNOW, WHEREVER YOU MAY HIDE.
GAAH ...
IT BURNS... IT BURNS!
DAM-MIIIT!
SWSH
SWSH

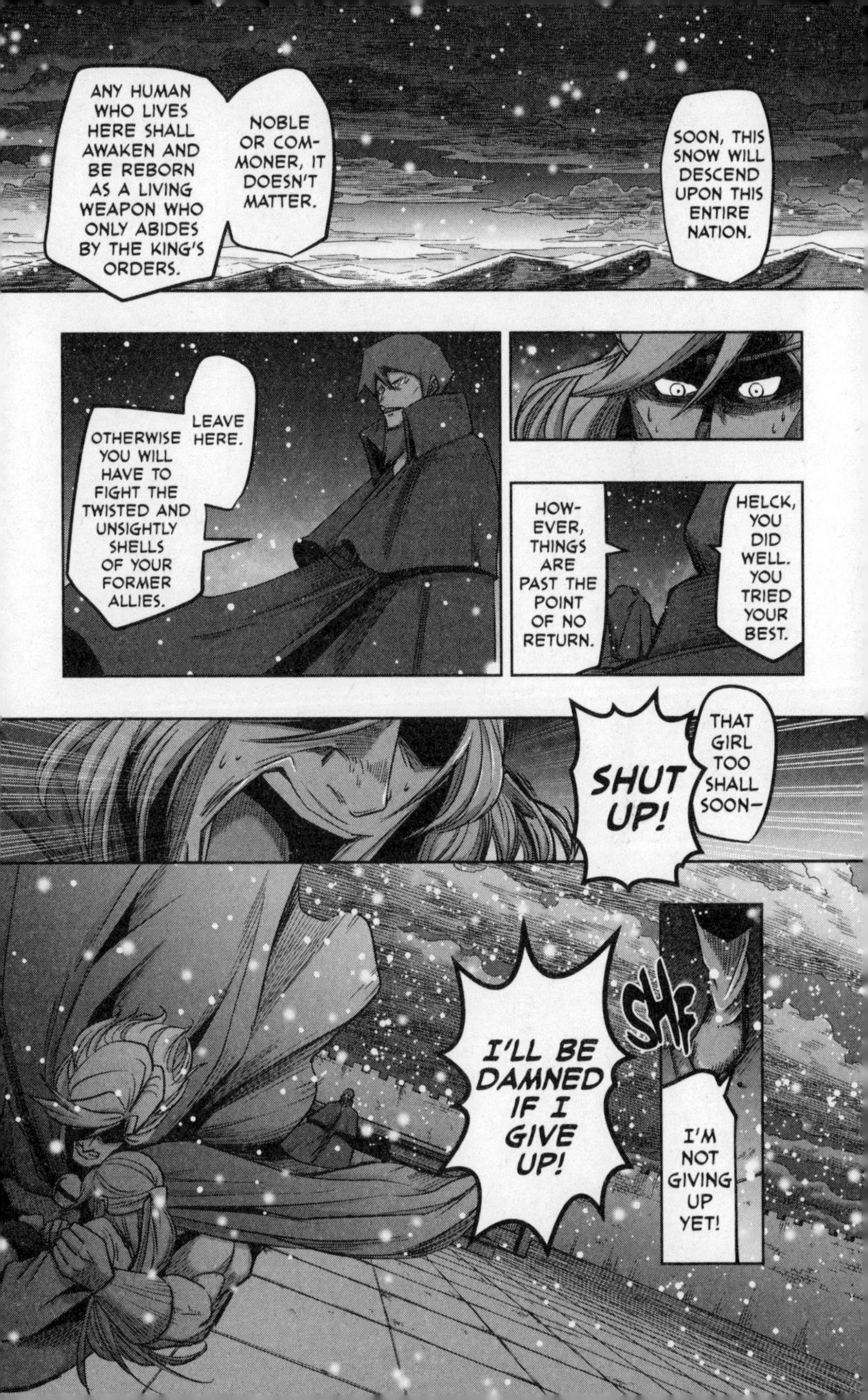
SOON, THIS SNOW WILL DESCEND UPON THIS ENTIRE NATION.
NOBLE OR COMMONER, IT DOESN'T MATTER.
ANY HUMAN WHO LIVES HERE SHALL AWAKEN AND BE REBORN AS A LIVING WEAPON WHO ONLY ABIDES BY THE KING'S ORDERS.
HELCK, YOU DID WELL. YOU TRIED YOUR BEST.
HOWEVER, THINGS ARE PAST THE POINT OF NO RETURN.
LEAVE HERE.
OTHERWISE YOU WILL HAVE TO FIGHT THE TWISTED AND UNSIGHTLY SHELLS OF YOUR FORMER ALLIES.
THAT GIRL TOO SHALL SOON—
SHUT UP!
SHF
I'M NOT GIVING UP YET!
I'LL BE DAMNED IF I GIVE UP!

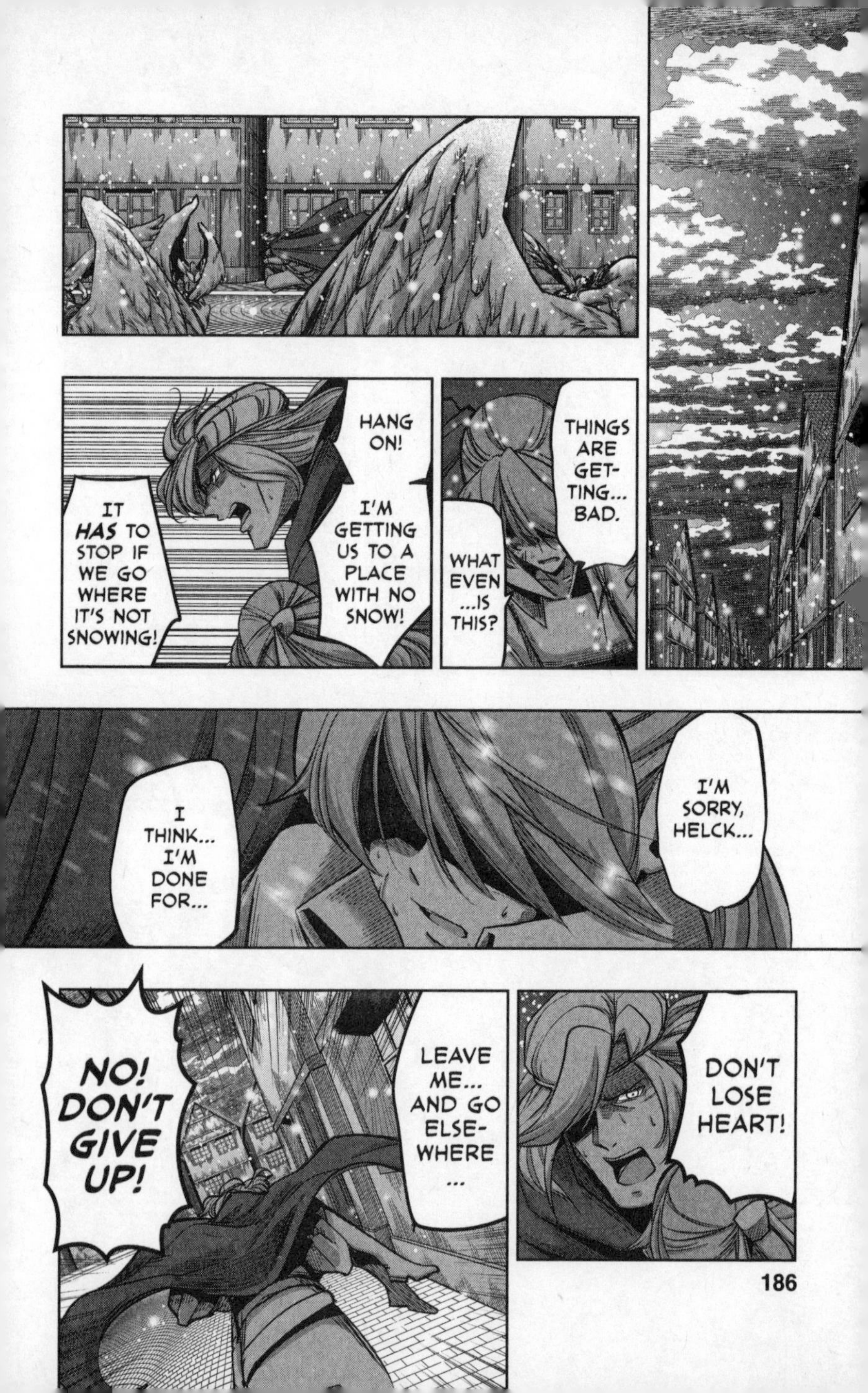
THINGS ARE GET-TING... BAD.
WHAT EVEN ...IS THIS?
HANG ON!
I'M GETTING US TO A PLACE WITH NO SNOW!
IT ***HAS*** TO STOP IF WE GO WHERE IT'S NOT SNOWING!
I'M SORRY, HELCK...
I THINK... I'M DONE FOR...
DON'T LOSE HEART!
LEAVE ME... AND GO ELSE-WHERE ...
NO! DON'T GIVE UP!

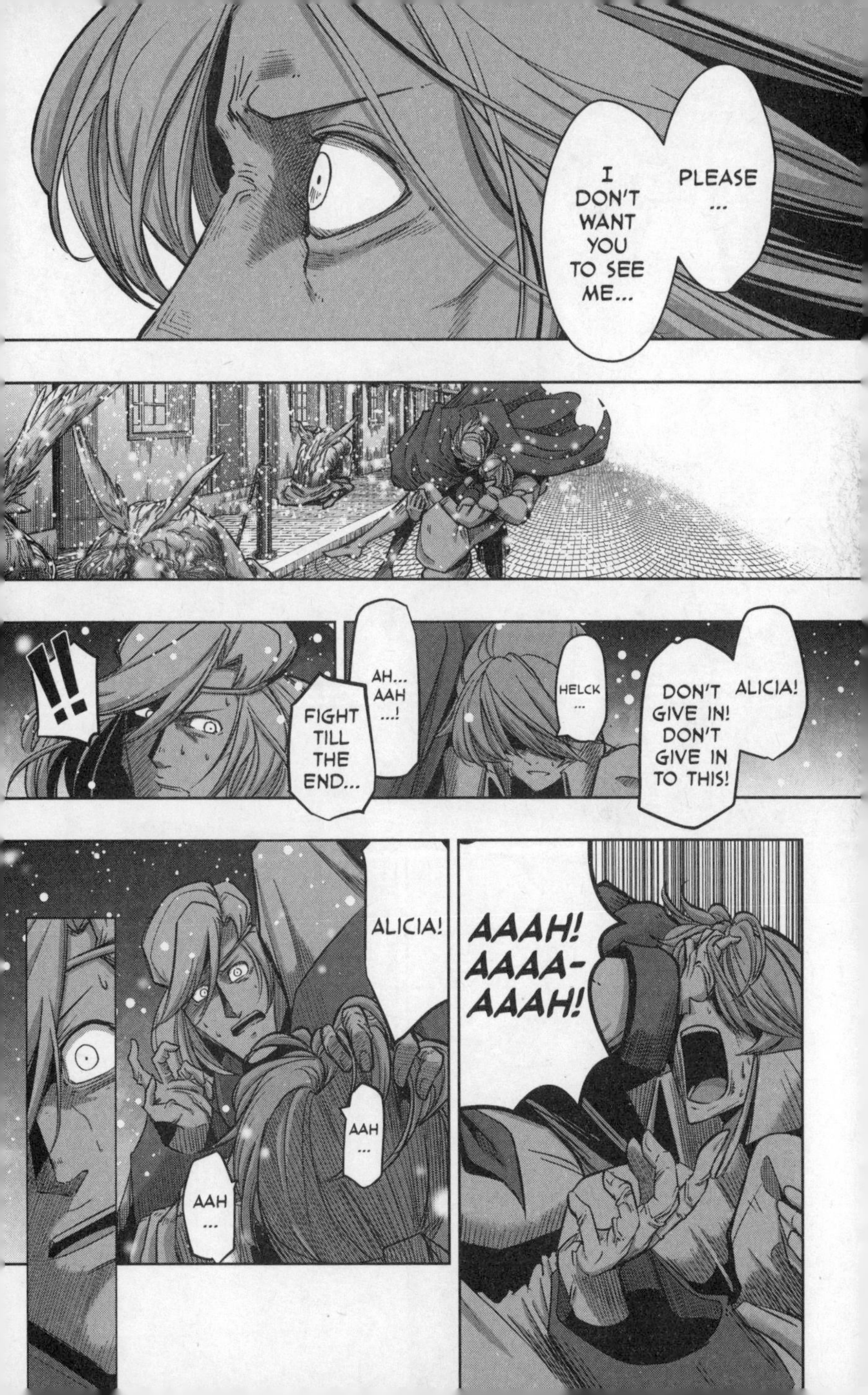
PLEASE ...
I DON'T WANT YOU TO SEE ME...
ALICIA!
DON'T GIVE IN! DON'T GIVE IN TO THIS!
HELCK ...
AH... AAH ...!
FIGHT TILL THE END...
!!
AAAH! AAAA-AAAH!
ALICIA!
AAH ...
AAH ...

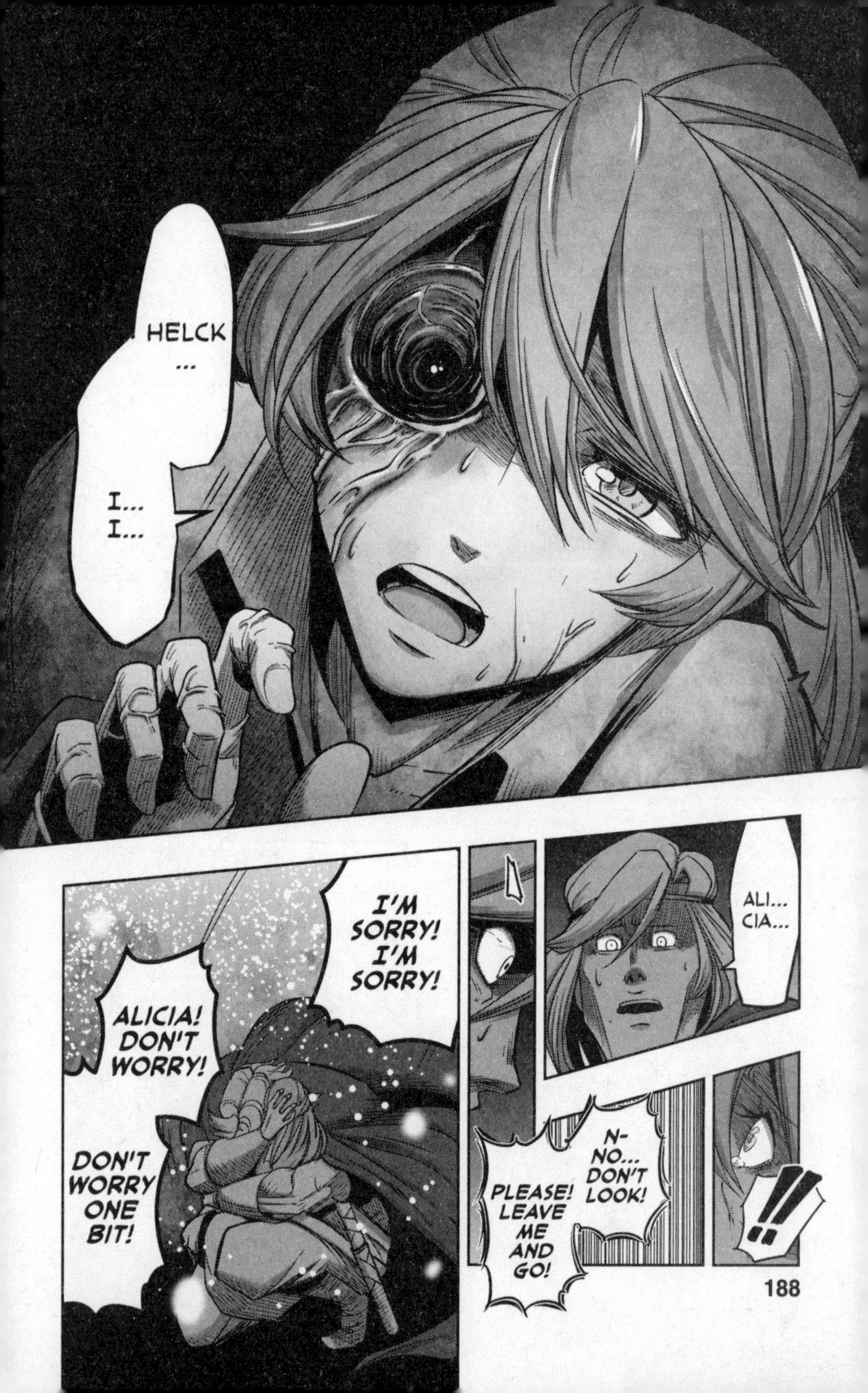
HELCK ...
I... I...
ALI... CIA...
!
!!
N-NO... DON'T LOOK!
PLEASE! LEAVE ME AND GO!
I'M SORRY! I'M SORRY!
ALICIA! DON'T WORRY!
DON'T WORRY ONE BIT!

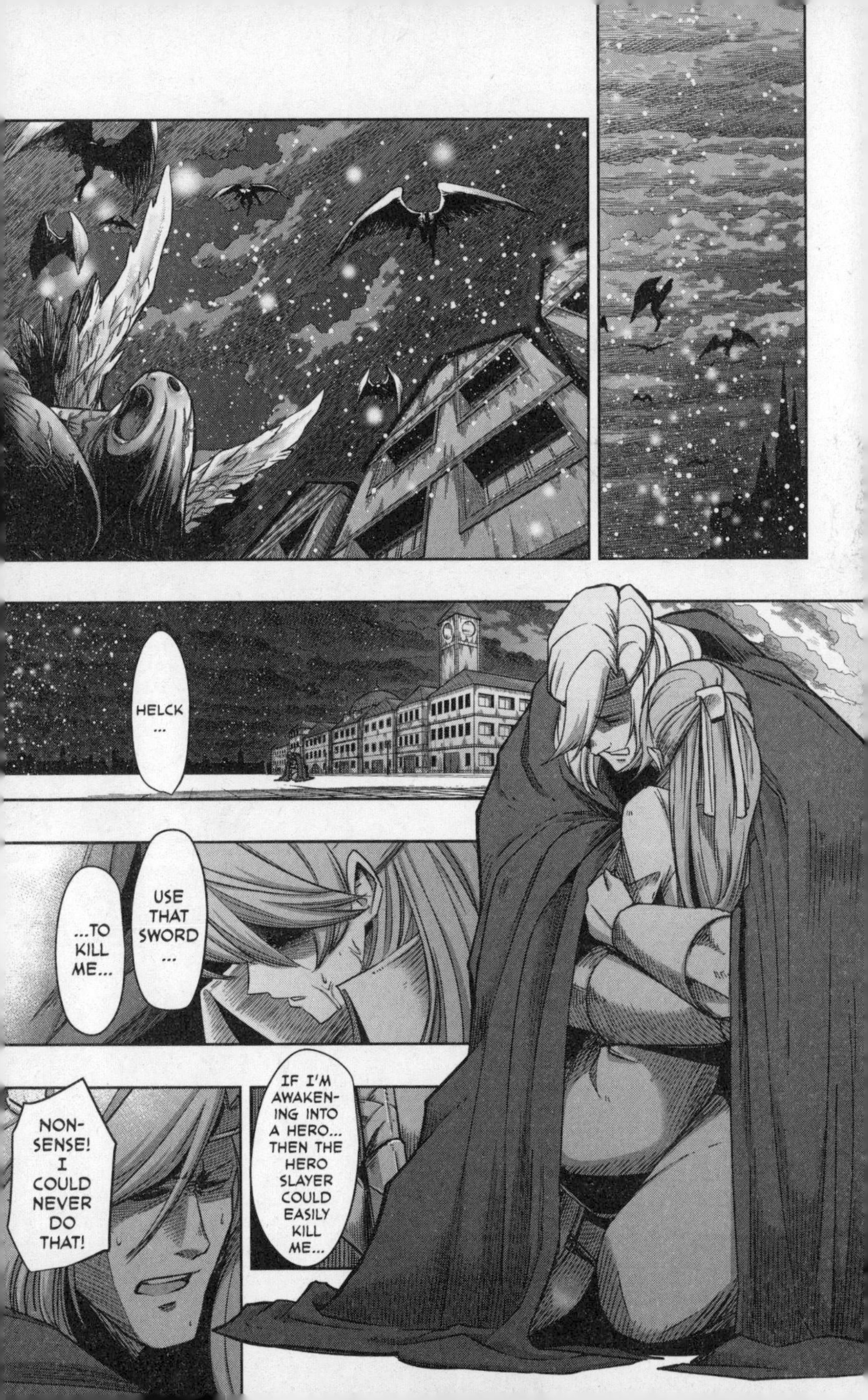
HELCK ...
USE THAT SWORD ...
...TO KILL ME...
IF I'M AWAKEN-ING INTO A HERO... THEN THE HERO SLAYER COULD EASILY KILL ME...
NON-SENSE! I COULD NEVER DO THAT!

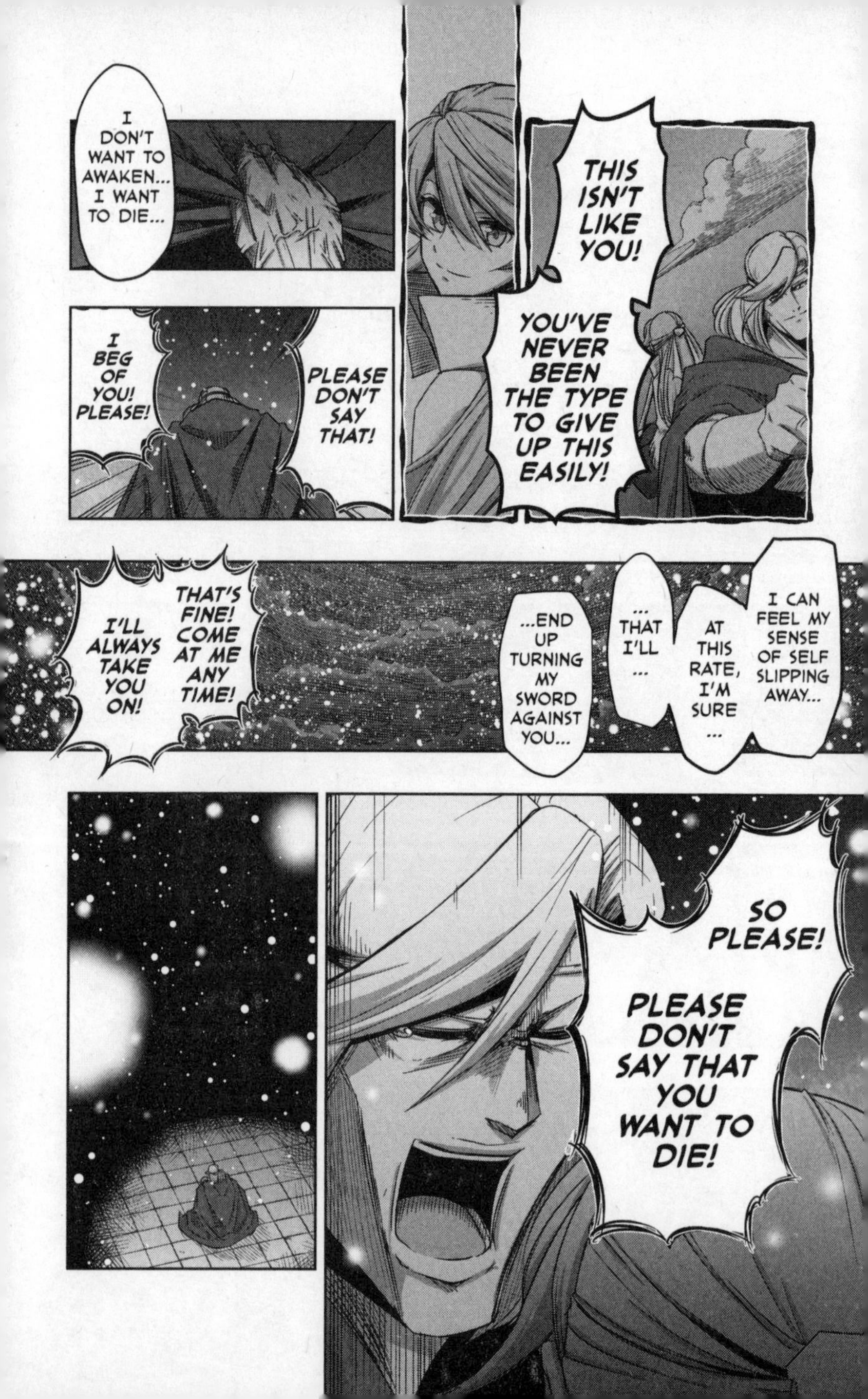
THIS ISN'T LIKE YOU!
YOU'VE NEVER BEEN THE TYPE TO GIVE UP THIS EASILY!
I DON'T WANT TO AWAKEN... I WANT TO DIE...
PLEASE DON'T SAY THAT!
I BEG OF YOU! PLEASE!
I CAN FEEL MY SENSE OF SELF SLIPPING AWAY...
AT THIS RATE, I'M SURE ...
... THAT I'LL ...
...END UP TURNING MY SWORD AGAINST YOU...
THAT'S FINE! COME AT ME ANY TIME!
I'LL ALWAYS TAKE YOU ON!
SO PLEASE!
PLEASE DON'T SAY THAT YOU WANT TO DIE!

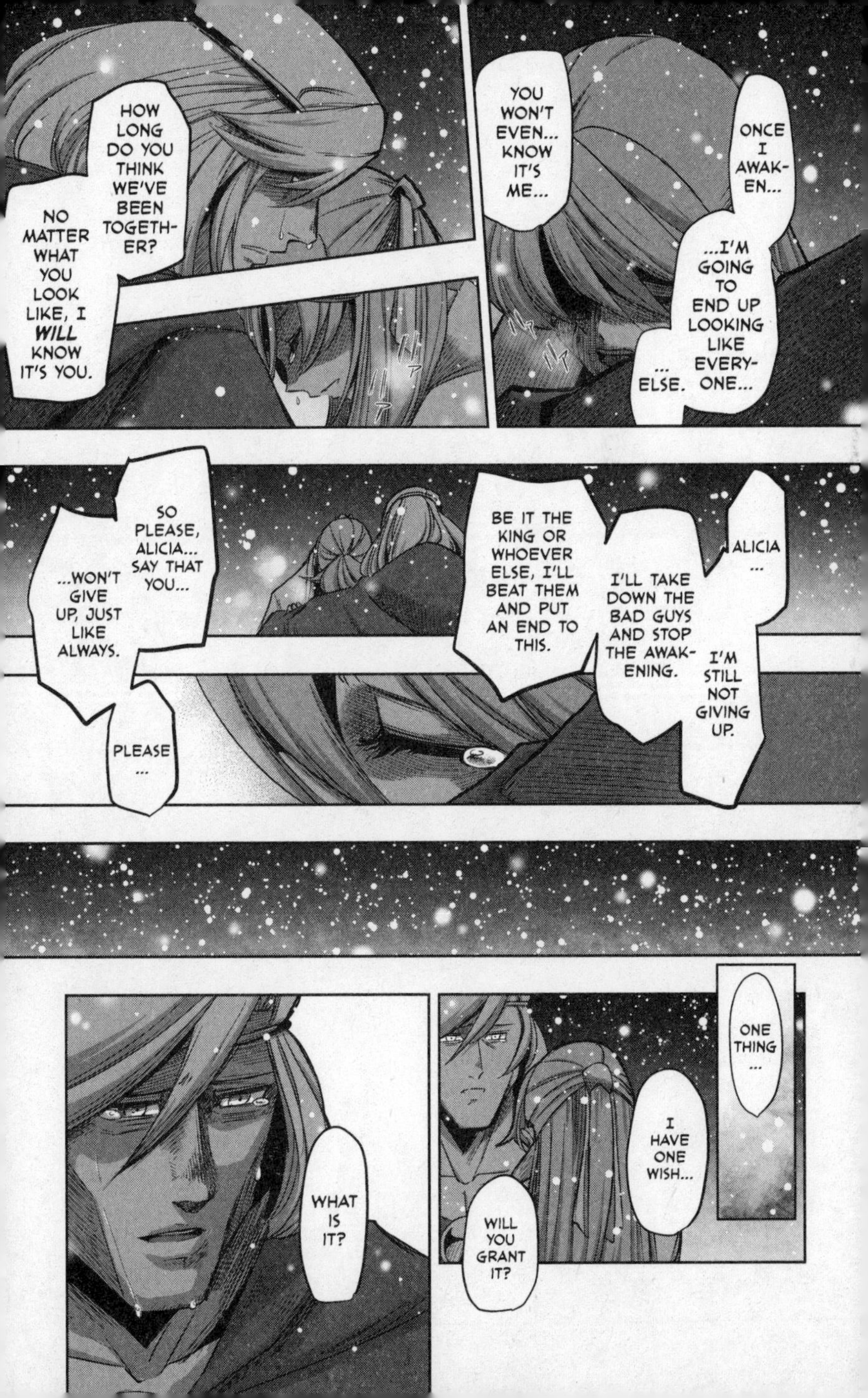

ONCE I AWAKEN...
...I'M GOING TO END UP LOOKING LIKE EVERYONE...
...ELSE.
YOU WON'T EVEN... KNOW IT'S ME...
HOW LONG DO YOU THINK WE'VE BEEN TOGETHER?
NO MATTER WHAT YOU LOOK LIKE, I *WILL* KNOW IT'S YOU.
ALICIA...
I'M STILL NOT GIVING UP.
I'LL TAKE DOWN THE BAD GUYS AND STOP THE AWAKENING.
BE IT THE KING OR WHOEVER ELSE, I'LL BEAT THEM AND PUT AN END TO THIS.
SO PLEASE, ALICIA... SAY THAT YOU...
...WON'T GIVE UP, JUST LIKE ALWAYS.
PLEASE...
ONE THING...
I HAVE ONE WISH...
WILL YOU GRANT IT?
WHAT IS IT?

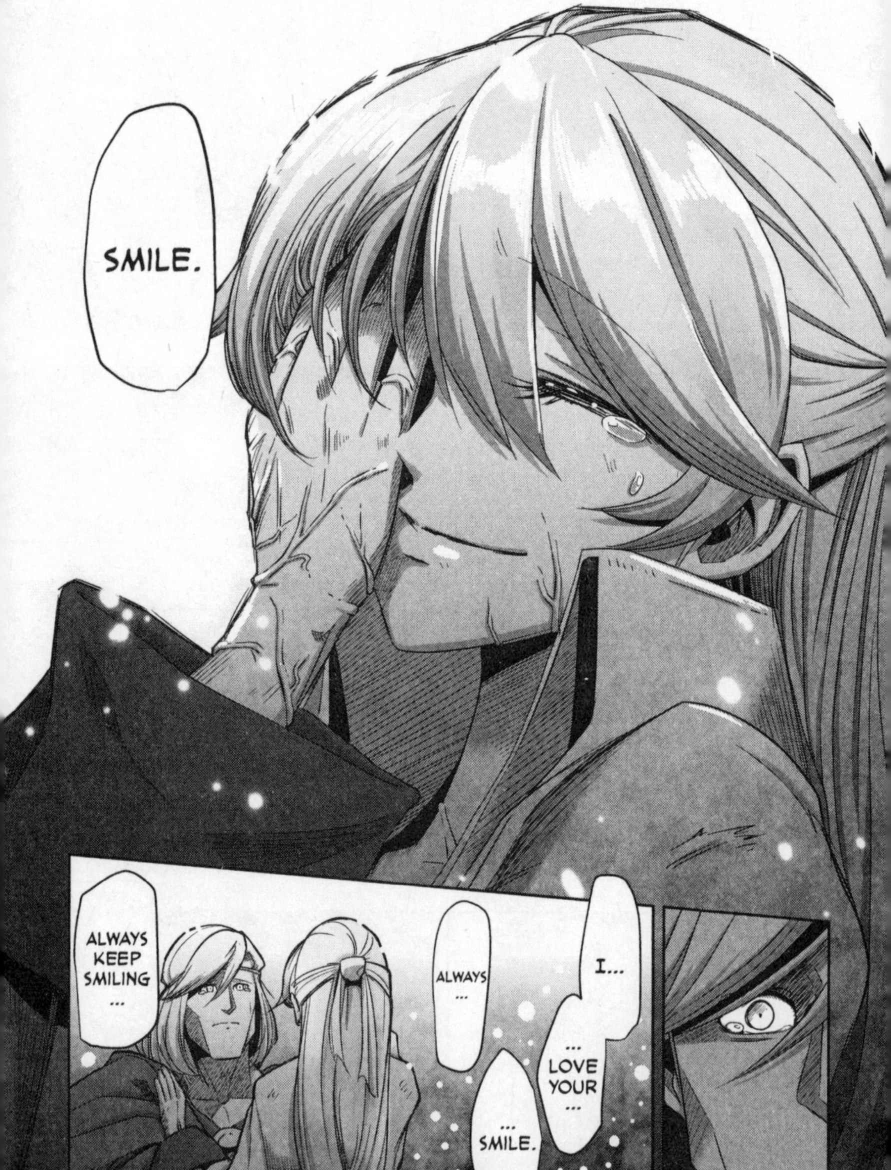
SMILE.
I...
ALWAYS ...
... LOVE YOUR ...
... SMILE.
ALWAYS KEEP SMILING ...

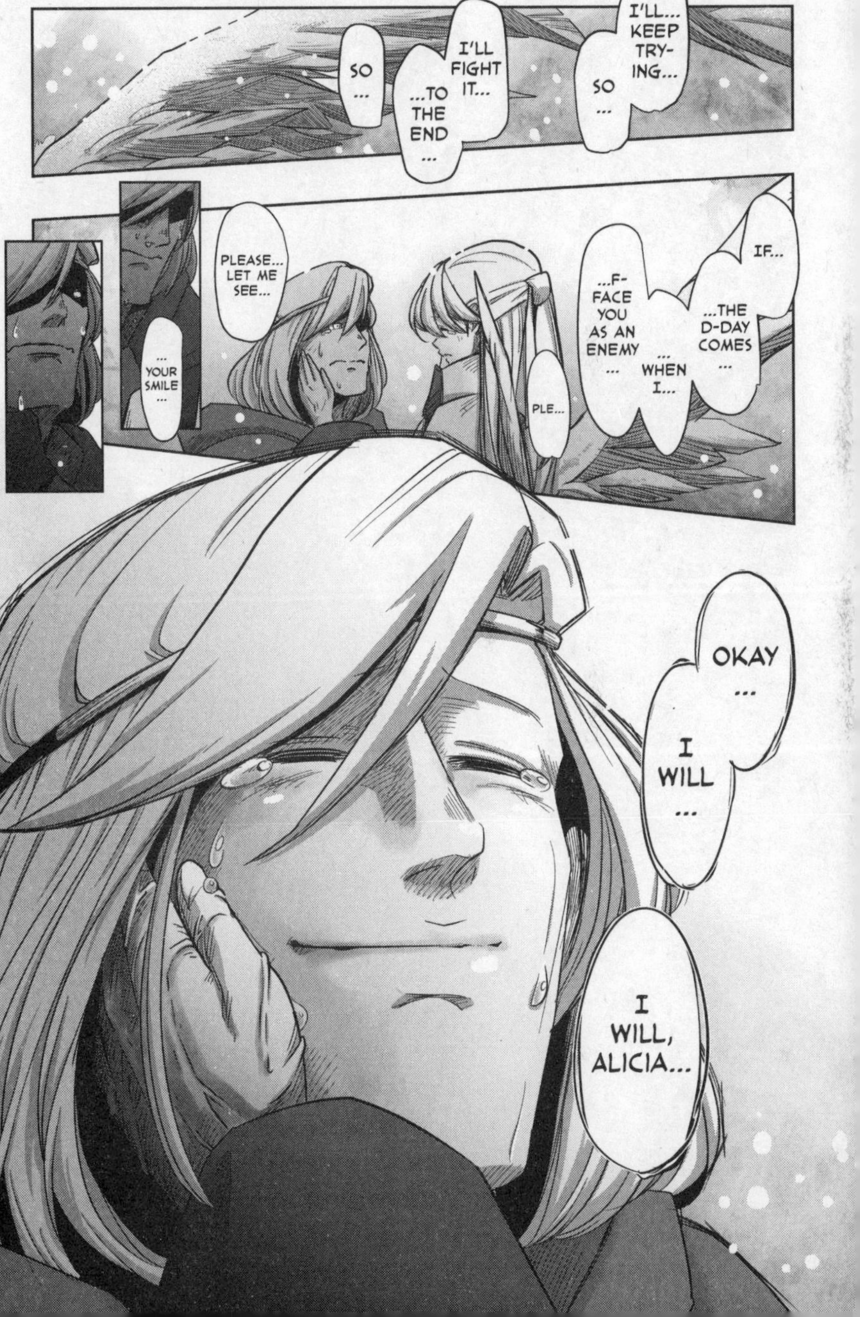
I'LL... KEEP TRY- ING...
SO ...
I'LL FIGHT IT...
...TO THE END ...
SO ...
IF...
...THE D-DAY COMES ...
... WHEN I...
...F- FACE YOU AS AN ENEMY ...
PLE...
PLEASE... LET ME SEE...
... YOUR SMILE ...
OKAY ...
I WILL ...
I WILL, ALICIA...

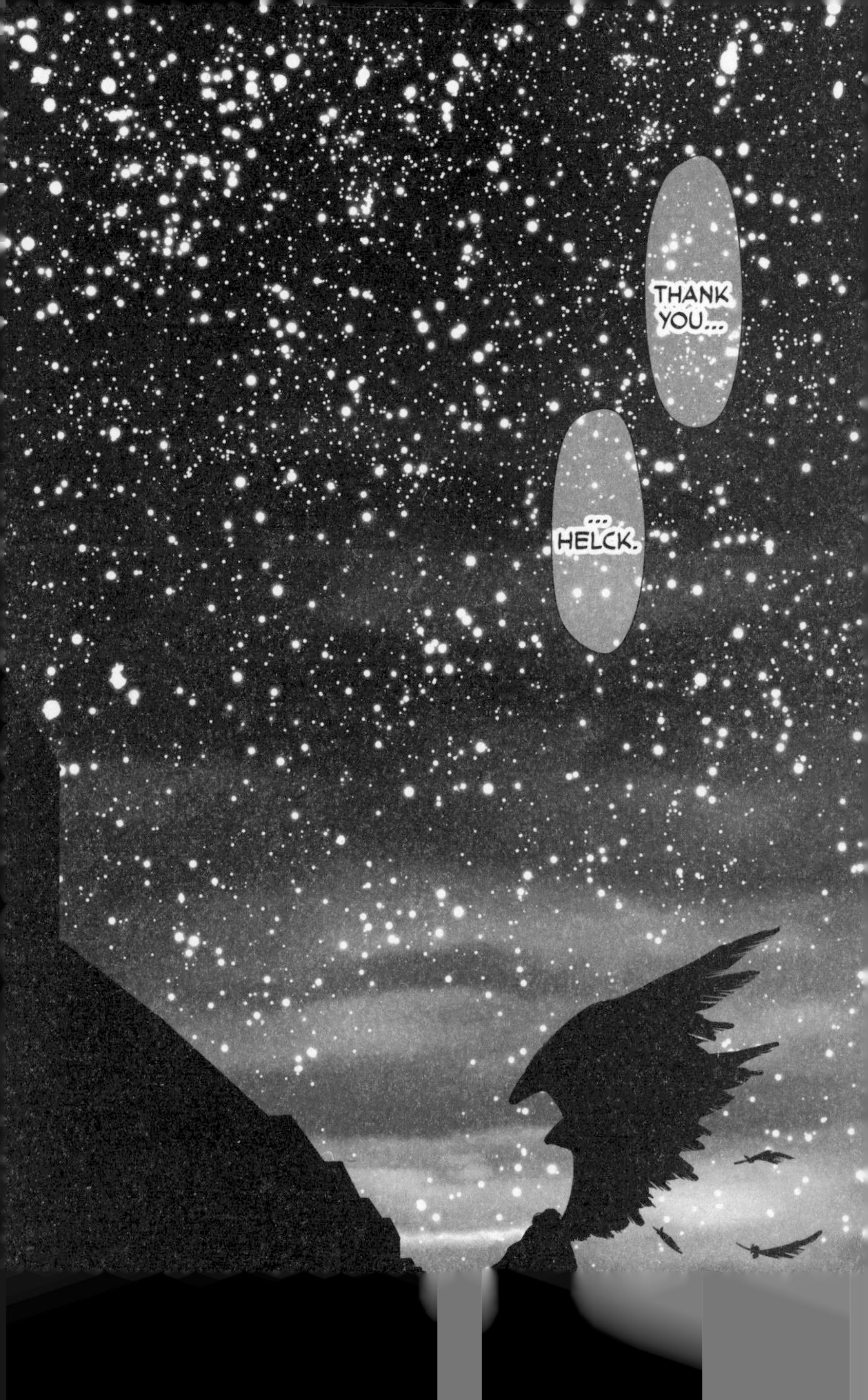
THANK YOU...
... HELCK.

BONUS COMIC

HALF-NUDE WARRIOR HELCK

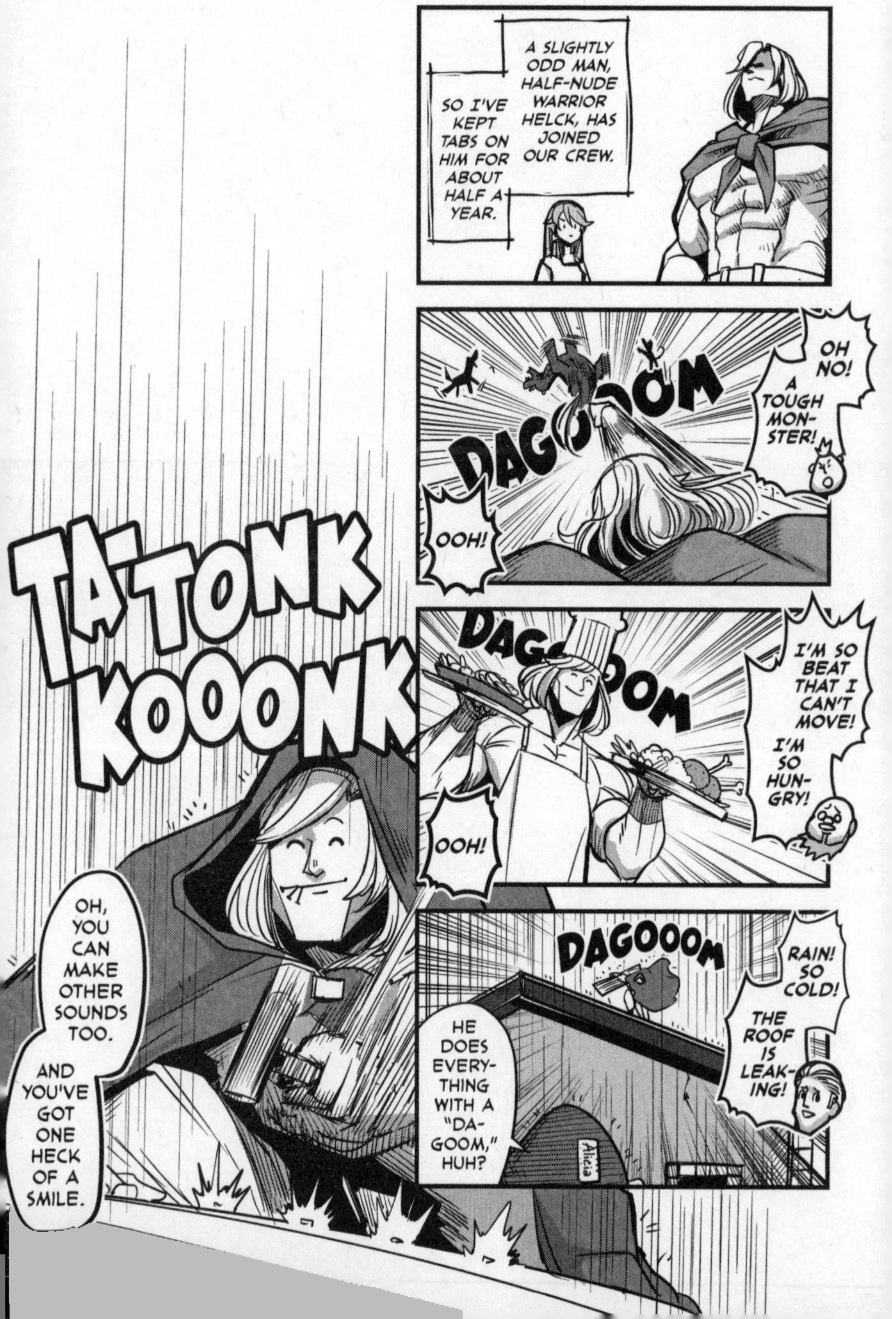
A SLIGHTLY ODD MAN, HALF-NUDE WARRIOR HELCK, HAS JOINED OUR CREW.
SO I'VE KEPT TABS ON HIM FOR ABOUT HALF A YEAR.
OH NO! A TOUGH MONSTER!
OOH!
I'M SO BEAT THAT I CAN'T MOVE!
I'M SO HUNGRY!
OOH!
RAIN! SO COLD!
THE ROOF IS LEAKING!
DAGOOOM
HE DOES EVERYTHING WITH A "DAGOOM," HUH?
Alicia
TA-TONK KOOOONK
OH, YOU CAN MAKE OTHER SOUNDS TOO.
AND YOU'VE GOT ONE HECK OF A SMILE.

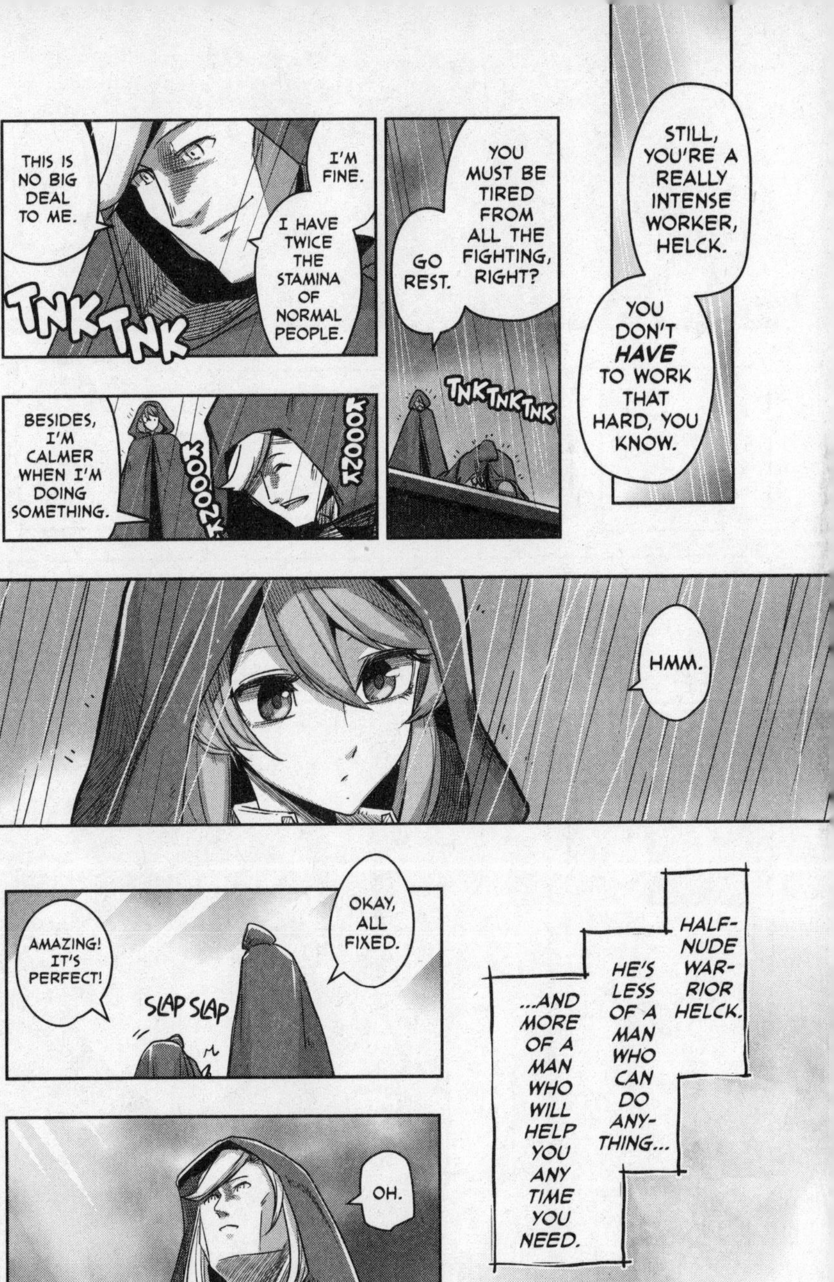
STILL, YOU'RE A REALLY INTENSE WORKER, HELCK.
YOU DON'T *HAVE* TO WORK THAT HARD, YOU KNOW.
YOU MUST BE TIRED FROM ALL THE FIGHTING, RIGHT?
GO REST.
TNKTNKTNK
I'M FINE.
I HAVE TWICE THE STAMINA OF NORMAL PEOPLE.
THIS IS NO BIG DEAL TO ME.
TNK TNK
KOOONK
KOOONK
BESIDES, I'M CALMER WHEN I'M DOING SOMETHING.
HMM.
HALF-NUDE WAR-RIOR HELCK.
HE'S LESS OF A MAN WHO CAN DO ANY-THING...
...AND MORE OF A MAN WHO WILL HELP YOU ANY TIME YOU NEED.
OKAY, ALL FIXED.
AMAZING! IT'S PERFECT!
SLAP SLAP
OH.

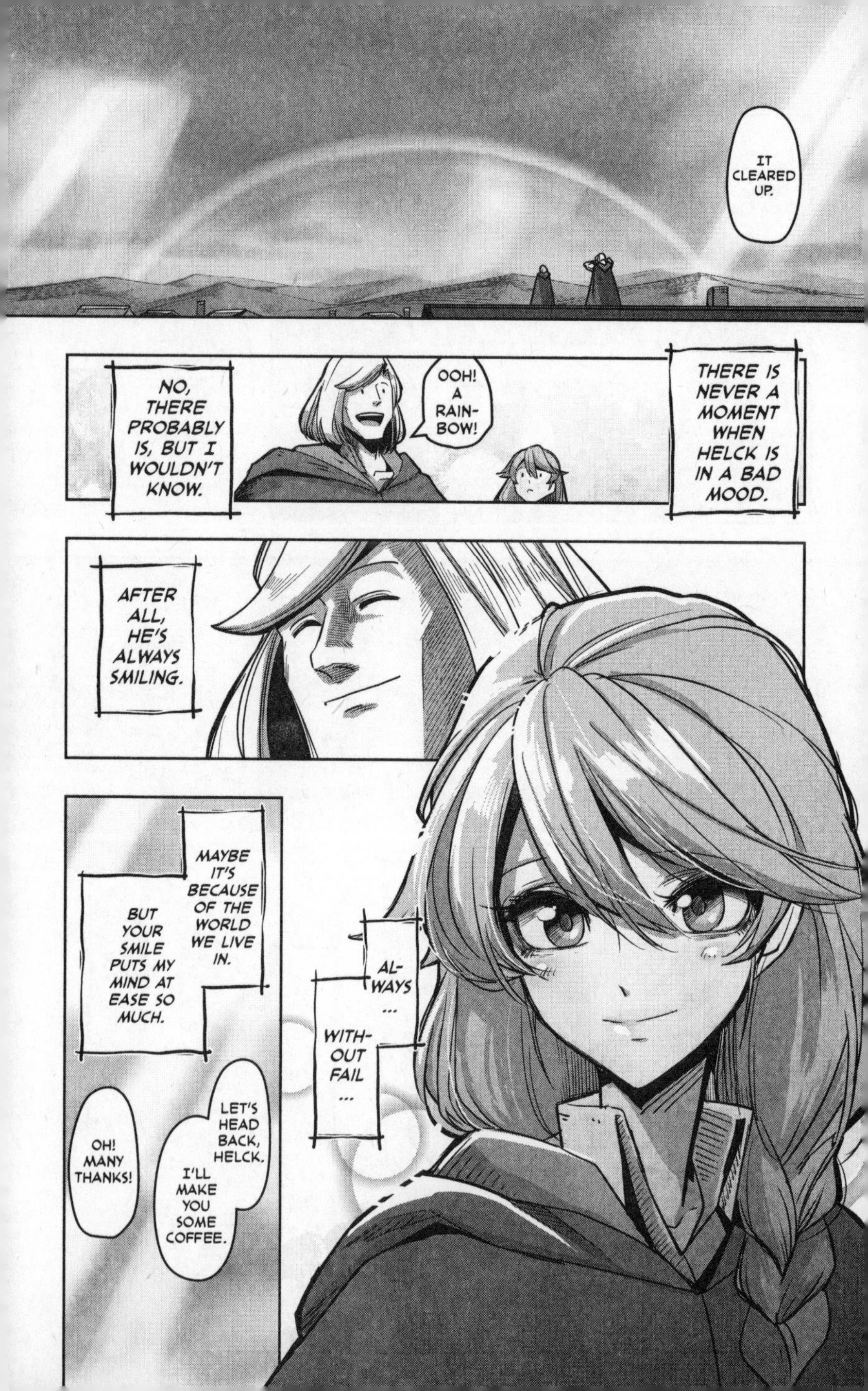
IT CLEARED UP.
THERE IS NEVER A MOMENT WHEN HELCK IS IN A BAD MOOD.
OOH! A RAIN-BOW!
NO, THERE PROBABLY IS, BUT I WOULDN'T KNOW.
AFTER ALL, HE'S ALWAYS SMILING.
AL-WAYS ... WITH-OUT FAIL ...
MAYBE IT'S BECAUSE OF THE WORLD WE LIVE IN.
BUT YOUR SMILE PUTS MY MIND AT EASE SO MUCH.
LET'S HEAD BACK, HELCK. I'LL MAKE YOU SOME COFFEE.
OH! MANY THANKS!

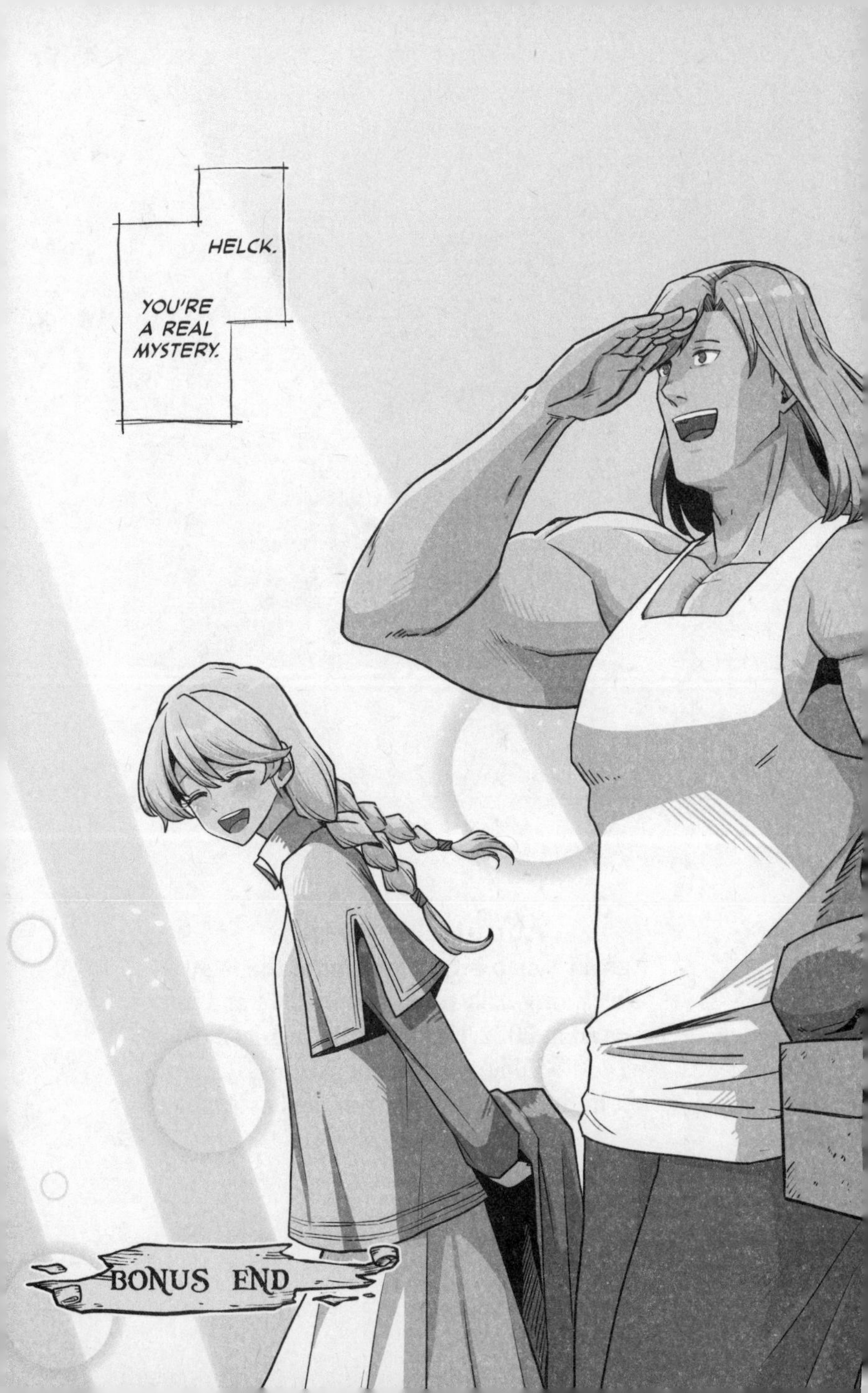
HELCK.
YOU'RE A REAL MYSTERY.
BONUS END

About the Author

Nanaki Nanao is best known for the manga *Helck*, originally published in 2014 and re-released in 2022. Nanao's other works include *Piwi* and *Völundo: Divergent Sword Saga*, both set in the world of *Helck*, as well as *Acaria*.

Helck

5

Story and Art by NANAKI NANAO

Translation: **DAVID EVELYN**
Touch-Up Art & Lettering: **ANNALIESE "ACE" CHRISTMAN**
Design: **KAM LI**
Editor: **JACK CARRILLO CONCORDIA**

HELCK SHINSOBAN Vol. 5
by Nanaki NANAO
© 2022 Nanaki NANAO
All rights reserved.
Original Japanese edition published by SHOGAKUKAN.
English translation rights in the United States of America, Canada, the
United Kingdom, Ireland, Australia and New Zealand arranged with
SHOGAKUKAN.

Original Cover Design: Masato ISHIZAWA + Bay Bridge Studio

The stories, characters, and incidents mentioned in this publication are
entirely fictional.

Published by VIZ Media, LLC
P.O. Box 77010
San Francisco, CA 94107

10 9 8 7 6 5 4 3 2 1
First printing, September 2023

viz.com

shonensunday.com

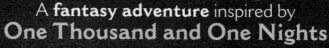

A new feudal fairytale begins!

YASHAHIME

—PRINCESS HALF-DEMON—

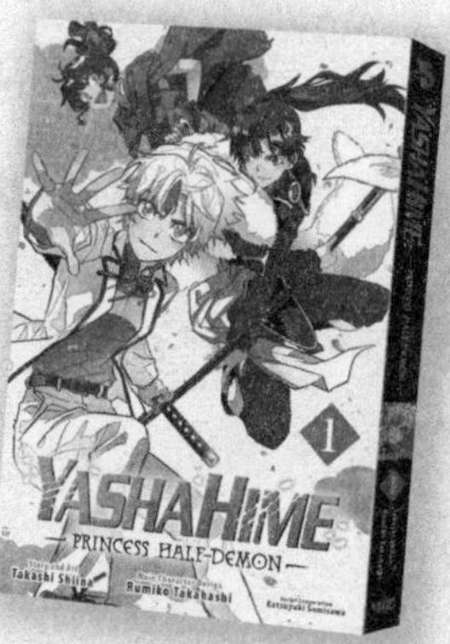
1
YASHAHIME
PRINCESS HALF-DEMON
Takashi Shiina
Rumiko Takahashi

Story and Art
Takashi Shiina

Main Character Design
Rumiko Takahashi

Script Cooperation Katsuyuki Sumisawa

Can the three teenage daughters of demon dog half-brothers Inuyasha and Sesshomaru save their parents, themselves, and both realms from the menace of the seven mystical Rainbow Pearls?

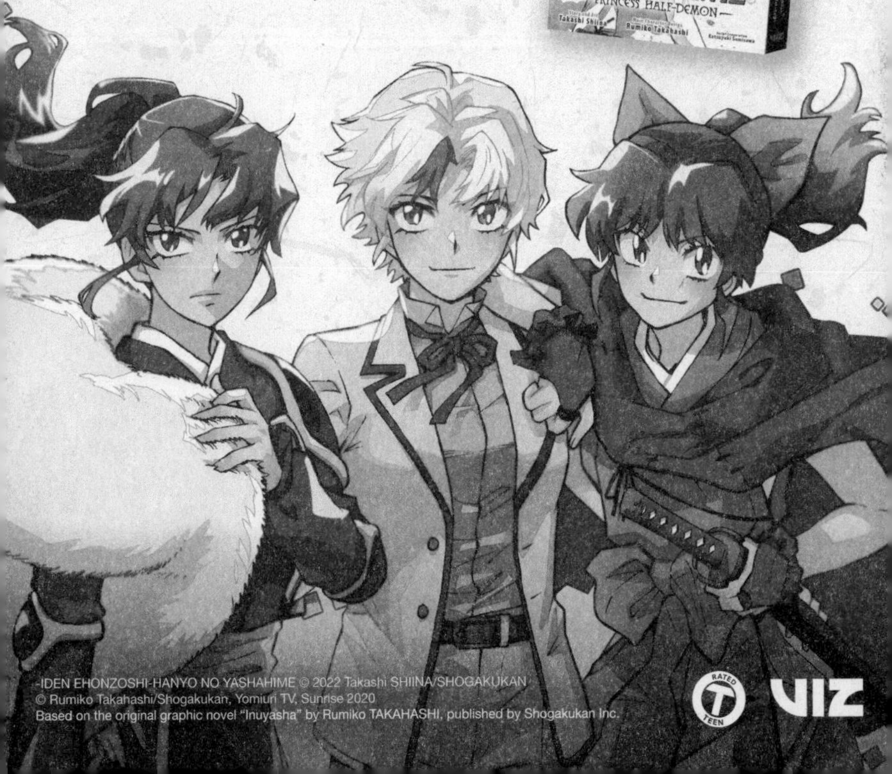

Kidnapped by the Demon King and imprisoned in his castle, Princess Syalis is...bored.

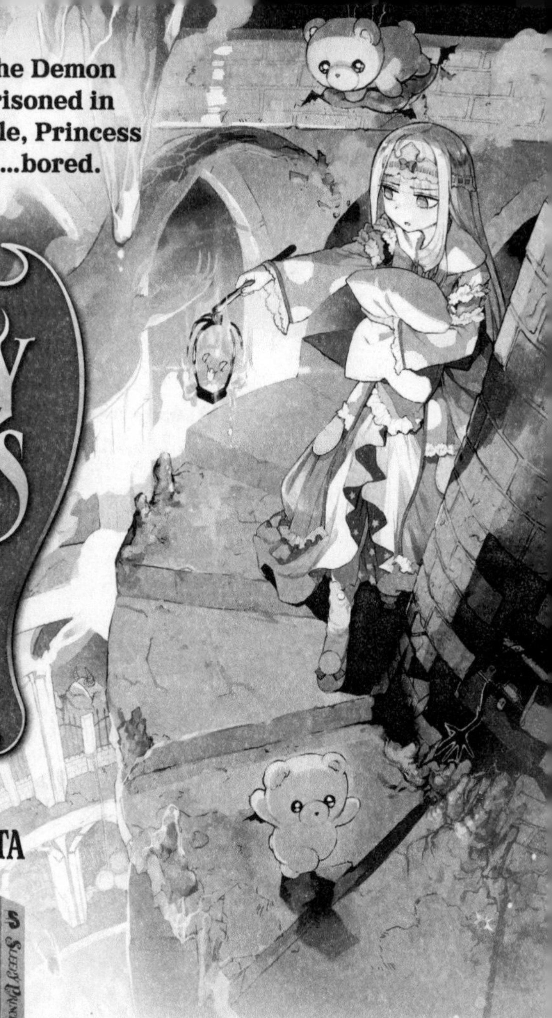

SLEEPY PRINCESS IN THE DEMON CASTLE

Story & Art by
KAGIJI KUMANOMATA

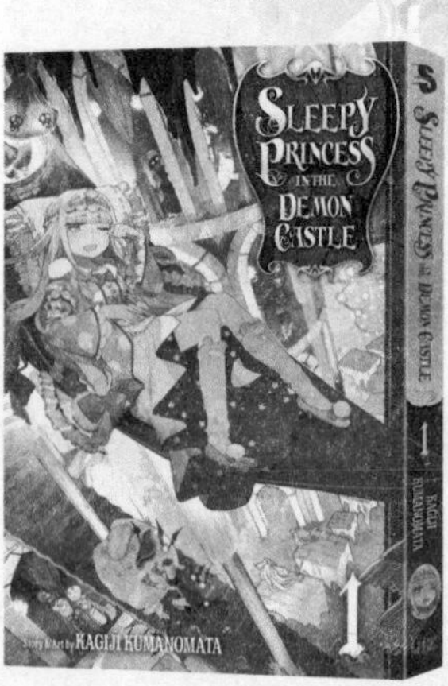
SLEEPY PRINCESS IN THE DEMON CASTLE
Story & Art by KAGIJI KUMANOMATA
1
SLEEPY PRINCESS IN THE DEMON CASTLE
1
KAGIJI KUMANOMATA

Captured princess Syalis decides to while away her hours in the Demon Castle by sleeping, but getting a good night's rest turns out to be a lot of work! She begins by fashioning a DIY pillow out of the fur of her Teddy Demon guards and an "air mattress" from the magical Shield of the Wind. Things go from bad to worse—for her captors—when some of Princess Syalis's schemes end in her untimely—if temporary—demise and she chooses the Forbidden Grimoire for her bedtime reading...

RATED T TEEN

VIZ

Komi Can't Communicate

Story & Art by Tomohito Oda

The journey to a hundred friends begins with a single conversation.

Socially anxious high school student Shoko Komi's greatest dream is to make some friends, but everyone at school mistakes her crippling social anxiety for cool reserve. With the whole student body keeping its distance and Komi unable to utter a single word, friendship might be forever beyond her reach.

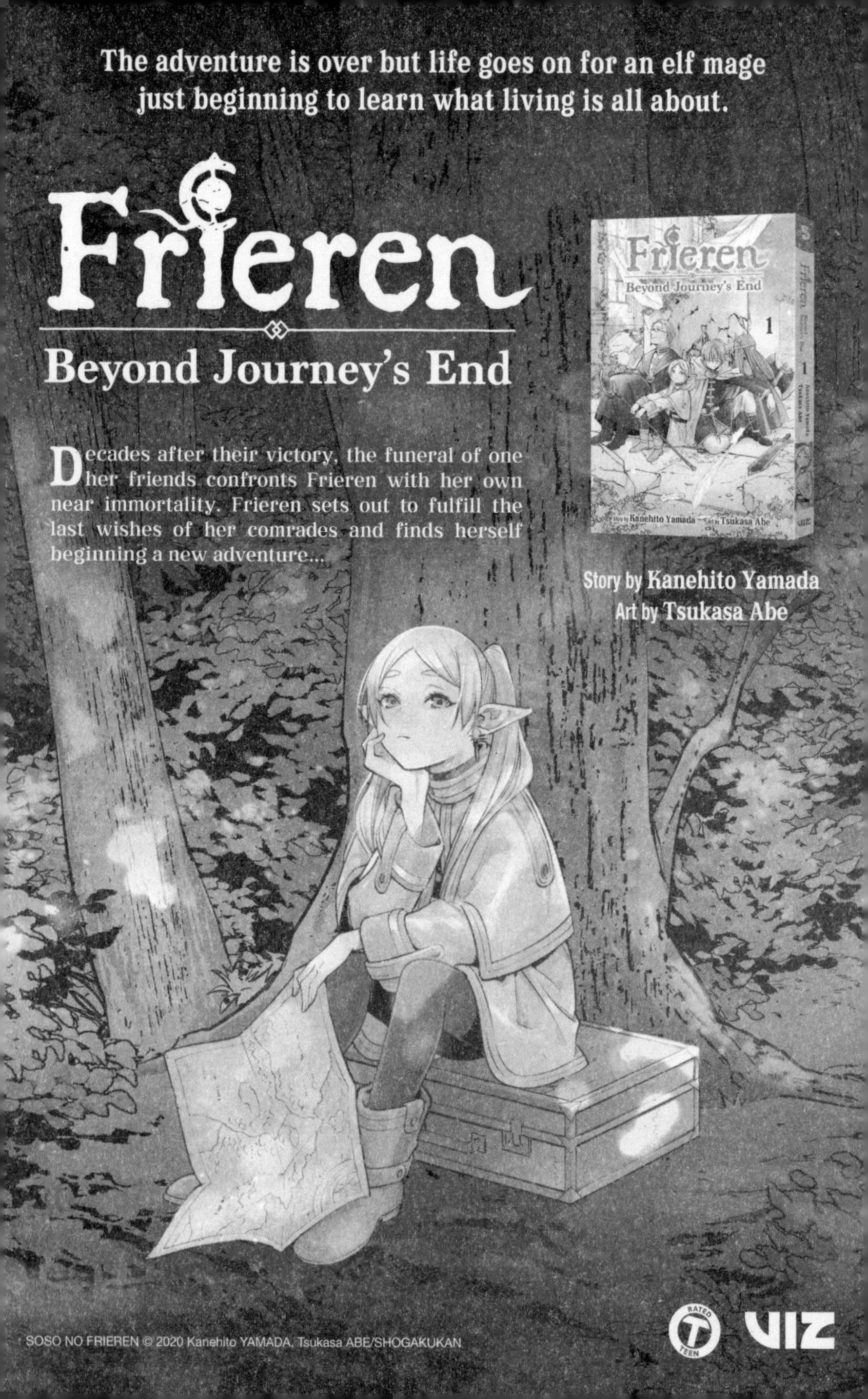
The adventure is over but life goes on for an elf mage just beginning to learn what living is all about.
Frieren
Beyond Journey's End
Decades after their victory, the funeral of one her friends confronts Frieren with her own near immortality. Frieren sets out to fulfill the last wishes of her comrades and finds herself beginning a new adventure...
Frieren Beyond Journey's End 1
Story by Kanehito Yamada Art by Tsukasa Abe
Story by Kanehito Yamada
Art by Tsukasa Abe
RATED T TEEN
VIZ
SOSO NO FRIEREN © 2020 Kanehito YAMADA, Tsukasa ABE/SHOGAKUKAN

Queen's Quality

Story & Art by
Kyousuke Motomi

Fumi Nishioka lives with Kyutaro Horikita
and his family of "Sweepers," people who
specialize in cleaning the minds of those
overcome by negative energy and harmful
spirits. Fumi has always displayed mysterious
abilities, but will those powers be used for
evil when she begins to truly awaken
as a Queen?

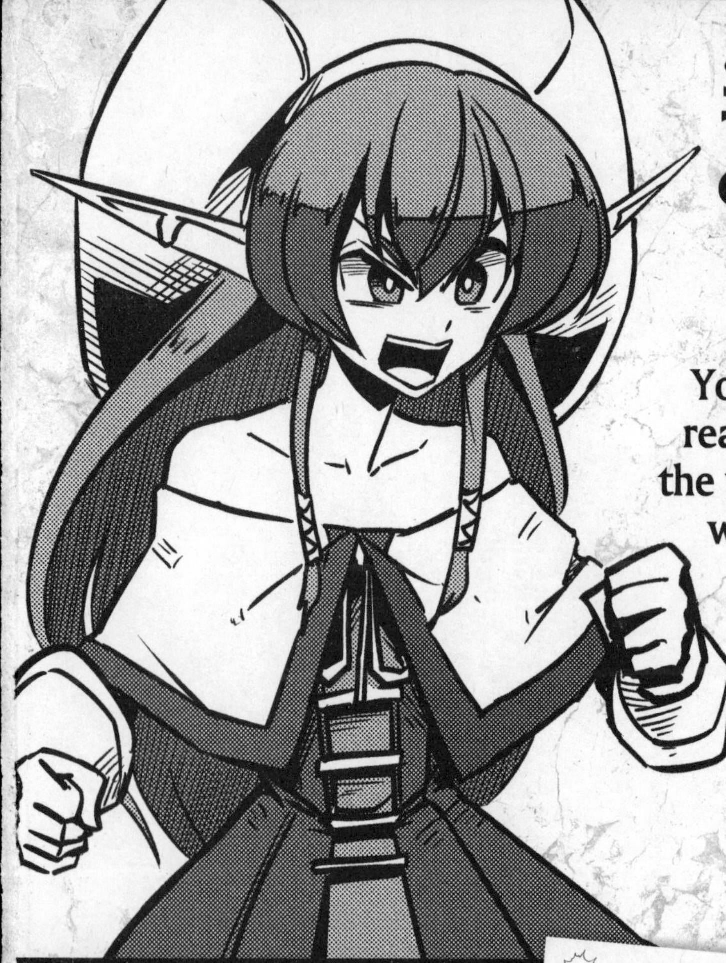

STOP!

You're reading the wrong way!

In keeping with the original Japanese comic format, this book reads from right to left—so action, sound effects, and word balloons are completely reversed to preserve the orientation of the original artwork.

Check out the diagram shown here to get the hang of things, and then turn to the other side of the book to get started!

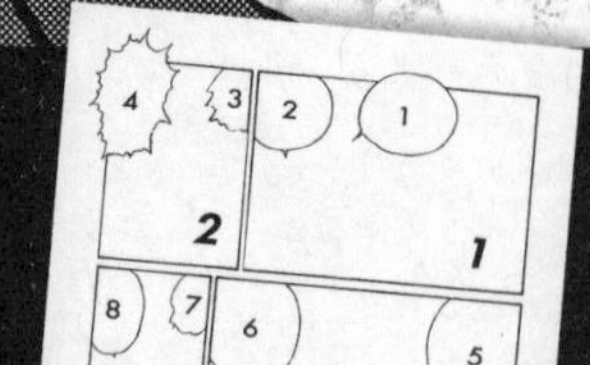

1
2
1
3
4
2
5
6
3
7
8
4
9
5
142

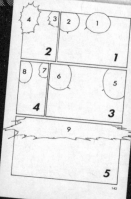